Current work on the transition from communism in Eastern Europe and the former Soviet Union has emphasized the political and economic transition. *The Social Legacy of Communism* analyzes the social transformation and helps fill an important gap in the literature. It summarizes developments and imposes coherence on the subject by treating four basic areas: ethnic issues, deviance and health, social cleavages, and labor and elitism.

As Joseph S. Berliner states in his concluding chapter, "In the normal course of scholarship the social fabric is examined one strand at a time: politics, the family, ethnicity, and so on. This volume of essays, however, invites the reader to contemplate the fabric on a grand scale. The entire social legacy of Soviet-type communism is spread out for examination."

WOODROW WILSON CENTER SERIES

The social legacy of communism

Other books in the series

The social legacy
of communism

Edited by
JAMES R. MILLAR and SHARON L. WOLCHIK

WOODROW WILSON CENTER PRESS

AND

 CAMBRIDGE
UNIVERSITY PRESS

PUBLISHED BY THE WOODROW WILSON CENTER PRESS AND
THE PRESS SYNDICATE OF THE UNIVERSITY OF CAMBRIDGE
The Pitt Building, Trumpington Street, Cambridge CB2 1RP, United Kingdom

CAMBRIDGE UNIVERSITY PRESS
The Edinburgh Building, Cambridge CB2 2RU, United Kingdom
40 West 20th Street, New York, NY 10011-4211, USA
10 Stamford Road, Oakleigh, Melbourne 3166, Australia

© 1994 by the Woodrow Wilson International Center for Scholars

First published 1994
Reprinted 1997

Printed in the United States of America

Typeset in Sabon

Library of Congress Cataloging-in-Publication Data
The Social legacy of communism / edited by James R. Millar and Sharon
L. Wolchik.
p.   cm.—(Woodrow Wilson Center series)
Papers presented at a symposium sponsored by the Institute for
European, Russian, and Eurasian Studies and the Russian and East
European Studies Program of the Elliott School of International
Affairs of George Washington University, and the Kennan Institute
for Advanced Russian Studies and the East European Studies Program
of the Woodrow Wilson Center, held at the Woodrow Wilson
International Center for Scholars on Feb. 20–22, 1992.
Includes index.
ISBN 0-521-46182-0 (hc).—ISBN 0-521-46748-9 (pbk.)
1. Soviet Union—Social conditions—1970–1991—Congresses.
2. Former Soviet republics—Social conditions—Congresses.
3. Europe, Eastern—Social conditions—Congresses. 4. Post-
communism—Former Soviet republics—Congresses. I. Millar, James
R., 1936–   . II. Wolchik, Sharon L. III. Series.
HN523.5.S573   1994
306'.0947—dc20   94-2
                                  CIP

A catalog record for this book is available from the British Library.

ISBN 0-521-46182-0 hardback
ISBN 0-521-46748-9 paperback

WOODROW WILSON INTERNATIONAL CENTER FOR SCHOLARS

The Center is the "living memorial" of the United States of America to the nation's twenty-eighth president, Woodrow Wilson. The U.S. Congress established the Woodrow Wilson Center in 1968 as an international institute for advanced study, "symbolizing and strengthening the fruitful relationship between the world of learning and the world of public affairs." The Center opened in 1970 under its own board of trustees, which includes citizens appointed by the president of the United States, federal government officials who serve ex officio, and an additional representative named by the president from within the federal government.

In all its activities the Woodrow Wilson Center is a nonprofit, nonpartisan organization, supported financially by annual appropriations from the U.S. Congress, and by the contributions of foundations, corporations, and individuals.

WOODROW WILSON CENTER PRESS

The Woodrow Wilson Center Press publishes the best work emanating from the Center's programs and from fellows and guest scholars, and assists in publication, in-house or outside, of research works produced at the Center and judged worthy of dissemination. Conclusions or opinions expressed in Center publications and programs are those of the authors and speakers and do not necessarily reflect the views of the Center staff, fellows, trustees, advisory groups, or any individuals or organizations that provide financial support to the Center.

Woodrow Wilson Center Press
Editorial Offices
370 L'Enfant Promenade, S.W., Suite 704
Washington, D.C. 20024-2518
telephone: (202) 287-3000, ext. 218

Contents

Figures and tables

FIGURES

TABLES

ix

Acknowledgments

The essays collected in this volume were presented originally at a symposium held at the Woodrow Wilson International Center for Scholars on 20–22 February 1992. The event was jointly sponsored by the Institute for European, Russian, and Eurasian Studies and the Russian and East European Studies Program of the Elliott School of International Affairs of the George Washington University, and by the Kennan Institute for Advanced Russian Studies and the East European Studies Program of the Woodrow Wilson Center. The symposium was held in celebration of the twenty-fifth anniversary of the founding of the Elliott School of International Affairs.

We thank Suzanne Stephenson for her help in arranging the conference and Xiaohui Zhao, Waldemar Wajszczuk, and Kevin Jernegan for their assistance in preparing the volume for publication.

1

Introduction: The social legacies and the aftermath of communism

JAMES R. MILLAR and SHARON L. WOLCHIK

In contrast to most earlier studies, which have examined the economic and political aspects of the transition from communist rule, the essays in this volume focus on the social dimension. This aspect of transition, which is less immediately evident than the high politics of free elections and government changes or the drama of large-scale economic reform, has not yet received a great deal of attention, but it is nonetheless critical. As the chapters herein demonstrate, the patterns of political organization, economic development, and social transformation associated with communist systems have had a major impact on the social structure and on social relations in the former Soviet Union and the formerly communist countries of Central and Eastern Europe. One-party rule, a command economy, and the effort to control information and culture also resulted in a situation in which a variety of social problems common to developed countries have manifested themselves in distinct ways in the erstwhile communist world. The repluralization of political life, efforts to re-create market economies, and the opening of borders have had a similarly great impact on social structures and relations. At the same time, the social legacies of communist rule continue to condition the transition to postcommunist political systems and economies, as do the social changes that have accompanied the transition.

At this early stage in postcommunist history it is difficult to sort legacies of communism from pure aftermath. The essays collected in this volume deal with both phenomena, though to differing degrees. Technically, the term "aftermath" refers to the condition of a field after the harvest. For grain, for example, it would consist of stubble, chaff, weeds, and gleanings; conceptually, these leftovers are usually thought

1

of as transient and possibly negative features. Thus, in Russia, the poor quality of medical care, for example, may be regarded as part of the social aftermath of Soviet communism. A legacy, on the other hand, is usually conceived of as an enduring intergenerational transfer from the past to the present. Expectations of free, universal education and medical care exemplify legacies of communism.

This volume represents an early attempt to sort through some of the social legacies and aftermath of communism in the former Soviet Union and Central and Eastern Europe. No attempt has been made to achieve a comprehensive account—that would doubtless require a multivolume effort. We hope and expect that our effort will be followed by others, as scholars in the various disciplines attempt to come to a better understanding of the transition processes in formerly communist states.

THE POLITICAL AND ECONOMIC FRAMEWORK

Although this volume focuses on the social legacies of communist rule, it is important to view that legacy within the framework of the economic and political organization and choices that shaped the social transformation that took place. In the political realm, these factors included the fact of one-party rule which, however modified in certain countries such as former Yugoslavia, Poland, and Hungary during the last two decades of communist rule, nevertheless restricted the access of most individuals and groups to the political process and shaped the kinds of alternatives that could be considered as well as other aspects of the policy-making process. Although dissident groups were tolerated in several of these countries during the later years of communism, in all the party remained the locus of effective decision making and in most those citizens who disagreed with official policies had limited room to make their views known. Similarly, even in those countries in which specialists and professionals were invited into the decision-making process on occasion or routinely, the alternatives to existing policies that could be considered to deal with social ills were limited in most cases. As a later section of this chapter discusses in greater detail, the lack of any meaningful way to participate in the political process and reliance on the part of most communist leaders on material rewards or coercion to keep the population in line also led to high levels of alienation from politics and to the adoption of the view that politics was not really the business of ordinary or honest people. The alienation from and disgust with the corruption, privilege, and lack of rationality that came to characterize these political systems led many citizens to retreat to the private sphere and some to engage in social deviance. All of these features of communist politics meant that it was difficult to correct social problems or address social ills effectively during the communist period. As several of the chapters to follow demonstrate, unwilling populations often resisted the imposition of social change by political leaders from above, if only passively. Policies adopted to achieve high priority goals, including industrialization and the maintenance of the system, often had unintended and negative social consequences.

The economic organization of these societies and the economic priorities adopted by their leaders also had important implications for the social structure and social issues considered in this book. Centralized control of economic planning and production, ambitious plans for rapid industrialization and the neglect of the consumer sector and agriculture, isolation from the world market, lack of consideration of the social, environmental, and medical impact of economic policies—these together shaped the social legacies of communist rule in the region.

SOCIAL CHANGE DURING THE COMMUNIST ERA: THE POSITIVE SIDE

The focus of this volume is primarily on the negative legacies of communist rule in the former Soviet Union and the formerly communist countries of Central and Eastern Europe. It is important to acknowledge, however, that there were also positive social changes that occurred during the communist period. These include the fact that all of these countries became more developed economically, and in most, the social structure became more differentiated. Although communist social structures displayed peculiarities that are well known, the level of urbanization and educational attainment increased dramatically in most countries, particularly among those groups that were previously least advantaged, such as women and ethnic minorities. Ironically, these changes, which many termed the "successes" of communist regimes, did far more to destabilize these systems than to support them. Increased social complexity and differentiation, as well as the conflict that developed between the technical imperatives of more developed economies and the command economic and political systems, were often identified in fact as potential sources of crisis in communist states prior to the collapse.[1] Similar arguments may be made concerning the impact of economic development on ethnic relations during the communist period.

As the essays in this volume illustrate, many of the positive changes one can identify had negative counterparts. Thus modernization was achieved at the cost of environmental degradation and a serious decline in the health of the population. Educational levels increased, but the content of education was distorted in many areas. Women found new opportunities, but also many additional burdens. And there is no doubt that the negative features eventually greatly outnumbered the positive. At the same time, it is important not to lose sight of the fact that certain aspects of the social transformation brought about during the communist era, such as increased urbanization and higher educational attainment, remain and will continue to shape the options of political elites and the responses of the population in the postcommunist period.

SOCIAL LEGACIES: SOME BENCHMARKS

We propose to consider the social consequences of communism under three broad headings: (1) legacies that flow from the tacit social contract between the population and the state, (2) legacies that represent values, attitudes, and behavior that the state attempted to either instill or extirpate in the subject population, and (3) the aftermath—that is, the unintended consequences of communist rule.

It is essential to this kind of effort to establish benchmarks against which contemporary developments may be measured. The "social contract" between communist states and their citizens offers an important starting point for identifying the social legacies of communism and understanding the social problems and pathologies that have come into the open during the transition to postcommunist rule. The Soviet Interview Project (SIP), by means of which thousands of former Soviet citizens were interviewed about their lives at the close of the Brezhnev era, offers one source of data on the terms and conditions of the social contract in the former Soviet Union.[2] Interviews conducted in the Soviet

[1]See Chalmers Johnson, ed., *Change in Communist Systems* (Stanford: Stanford University Press, 1970), for a collection of some of the earliest of these analyses. See Karen Dawisha, *Eastern Europe, Gorbachev, and Reform: The Great Challenge*, 2d ed. (Cambridge: Cambridge University Press, 1990), for a more recent discussion.
[2]For a description of the Soviet Interview Project, see James R. Millar, "History, Method and the Problem of Bias" (chap. 1), and Michael Swafford et al., "Response Effects in SIP's General Survey of Soviet Emigrants" (appendix B), both in James R. Millar, ed., *Politics, Work, and Daily Life in the USSR: A Survey of Former Soviet Citizens* (Cambridge: Cambridge University Press, 1987).

Table 1.1. *Average satisfaction scores among Soviet emigrants, by age in LNP (quartiles)*

	Standard of living	Housing	Goods	Job	Medical care
Very satisfied					
N	310	645	139	711	518
%	11.1	23.1	5.0	25.5	18.5
Somewhat satisfied					
N	1,343	1,213	488	1,054	1,142
%	48.1	43.4	17.5	37.7	40.9
Somewhat dissatisfied					
N	694	379	634	303	570
%	24.8	13.6	22.7	10.8	20.4
Very dissatisfied					
N	403	533	1,477	170	450
%	14.4	19.1	52.9	6.1	16.1
Missing values					
N	43	23	55	555	113
%	1.5	0.9	1.9	19.9	4.0
Total N	2,793	2,793	2,793	2,793	2,793

Source: James R. Millar, ed., *Politics, Work and Daily Life in the USSR: A Survey of Former Soviet Citizens* (Cambridge: Cambridge University Press, 1987), Table 2.1, 33. LNP = last normal period of life in the USSR.

Union during the Gorbachev period offer additional and supplementary information on attitudes, behavior, and values during the last days of communism that may be used along with SIP data to construct a framework for analyzing the social legacies of communism.

The SIP and subsequent surveys may be used to identify the main components of the communist social contract as devised in the Soviet Union and adopted in other European communist states with local variations. The communist social system offered a wide range of social entitlements to citizens, and it is clear that many citizens of postcommunist societies still attach positive evaluations to most of these entitlements. SIP respondents were asked, for example, to report on the degree to which they had been satisfied or dissatisfied with their standard of living, housing, goods availability, jobs, and health care during their "last normal period of life" (LNP) in the Soviet Union (that is, before they decided to leave), which for most respondents referred to 1978–83. More than 60 percent reported that they had been either "very satisfied" or "somewhat satisfied" with their housing, jobs, medical care, and general standard of living (Table 1.1). As expected, the exception was with respect to the availability of goods, about which respondents indi-

Table 1.2. *What to keep from the Soviet system*

Question: Think for a moment about the Soviet system with its good and bad points. Suppose you could create a system of government in the Soviet Union that is different from the one which currently exists. What things in the present Soviet system would you want to keep in the new one?

	1st answer (%)	2d answer (%)	3d answer (%)	Total (%)
Health care	26.5	24.7	17.7	68.9
Free public education	12.2	29.5	5.4	47.1
Crime control	6.3	4.0	10.5	20.8
Job security	3.1	3.1	11.2	17.4
Inexpensive housing	1.1	1.5	10.2	12.8
Keep nothing	19.4	0.2	—	19.6

Source: James R. Millar, "*Perestroika* and *Glasnost*': Gorbachev's Gamble on Youth and Truth," in Susan J. Linz, ed., *The Soviet Economic Experiment* (Urbana: University of Illinois Press, 1990), Table 4, 281.

cated here and elsewhere in the survey their unhappiness about the need to queue and the unpleasant side effects of shortages, such as nepotism, corruption, and black markets.

When asked what they would keep if they "could create a system of government in the Soviet Union that is different from the one which currently exists," the characteristics most frequently mentioned by the emigrants were free comprehensive health care, free public education, control of crime (in the streets), job security, and inexpensive housing (Table 1.2). Another completely open-ended question asked SIP respondents what they thought the United States could learn from the Soviet Union. Although about 17 percent replied that the United States could "learn nothing," significant numbers reported that the United States could learn something about controlling crime, access to education, health care, the upkeep of cities, and public transportation from Soviet practices.[3] It is worth stressing that these responses were from former Soviet citizens who had been living in the United States for from several months to several years.

A little reflection on the categories that received approval from significant numbers of SIP respondents reveals that almost all of them fall

[3]James R. Millar, "*Perestroika* and *Glasnost*': Gorbachev's Gamble on Youth and Truth," in Susan J. Linz, ed., *The Soviet Economic Experiment* (Urbana: University of Illinois Press, 1990), Table 3, 280.

under the generic heading of welfare entitlements. Moreover, although there was great dissatisfaction with the availability of goods and services in the public sector, it was matched by dissatisfaction with the prices of these same commodities on the legal private and secondhand markets. Subsidized food prices obviously represent another kind of entitlement former Soviet citizens expected as part of their social contract.

More recent surveys in the former Soviet Union show the durability of these preferences. When asked in a United States Information Agency (USIA)–sponsored survey (conducted by Russian Public Opinion and Market Research [ROMIR]) in December 1991 their opinion on what the state's role should be in the economy, 79 percent of respondents reported that "guaranteed work for all citizens" should be "a main feature of our social-economic system in the future," and 77 percent voted for "guaranteed free health care for all."[4] A survey conducted in June 1992 found that 68 percent of Russians believed that the government should provide for the "basic material needs of citizens" (Table 1.3).

The belief in and desire for an extensive system of welfare entitlements, therefore, represents a significant legacy of Soviet-style communism. Certainly the Soviet system was not overthrown as a result of dissatisfaction with the standard of living or its determinants. The system unraveled from the top down. The post-Brezhnev population is perhaps best described as having been self-indulgent about reform, for it wanted all of the old entitlements, plus more and better goods at low prices. The Communist party itself had become by this time mainly a super entitlement program which allowed members in good standing to jump queues and gave them access to rare perquisites such as chauffeured cars, special medical clinics, travel abroad, and state dachas.

There is ample evidence that many of these attitudes were also held in formerly communist Central and Eastern Europe. As Table 1.4 illustrates, a large proportion of citizens surveyed in the Czech Lands and Slovakia looked to the state to guarantee a minimum standard of living to all citizens. Significant numbers, particularly in Slovakia, also wanted the government to ensure employment for all citizens, as well as health care and housing. These expectations, which were much more wide-

---

[4]Office of Research, United States Information Agency (USIA), "Russians Support Limited Privatization in Context of a Mixed Economy," *USIA Research Memorandum*, 26 February 1992, 10. The research firm ROMIR interviewed a representative sample of 1,804 adults in the Russian Federation between 11 December 1991 and 2 January 1992.

Table 1.3. *Aspects of democracy considered "essential," grouped by age and education (Russia, June 1992; N = 1,800)*

Question: People have various ideas about what makes a state a "democracy." For each of the characteristics on this card please tell me whether you think it is essential, important but not essential, not very important, or not at all important for determining whether a state is a democracy.

	Total population (N = 1,800) (%)	Age				
		18–29 (N = 441) (%)	30–39 (N = 413) (%)	40–49 (N = 263) (%)	50–59 (N = 303) (%)	60+ (N = 380) (%)
Judicial system that treats everyone equally	74	81	78	74	73	61
Economic prosperity in the country	68	67	72	71	68	63
Government that provides for basic material needs of citizens	68	65	68	70	72	66
Protection of rights of minorities	52	57	55	48	52	45
Free market economy	44	55	51	50	37	27
Freedom to criticize the government	42	48	41	44	44	34
At least two strong political parties competing in elections	39	46	39	39	39	27

Source: Office of Research, USIA, "Russians Link Democracy to Prosperity and Equal Justice," *USIA Opinion Research Memorandum,* 16 October 1992, 8.

spread in Slovakia than in the Czech Lands, were one of the factors that led to the eventual dissolution of the Czechoslovak federation.

Surveys conducted for USIA in the early postcommunist period document similar differences in several other Central and Eastern European countries. A majority of respondents in Romania and 44 percent of those in Hungary surveyed in 1992, for example, indicated that they preferred a "state guarantees" society rather than a society that stresses individual opportunities or one that combines features of both (Table 1.5). Support for a society that puts most responsibility on the individual was greater in the Czech Republic and in Poland, but even in those countries a majority of respondents wanted the state to play a relatively large role or favored "middle-of-the-road" societies.

A large share of Romanians surveyed between October 1991 (65

Table 1.4. *Comparison of political and economic views of inhabitants of the Czech and Slovak republics, 1990*

	Czech Republic (%)	Slovak Republic (%)
Satisfied with the current political situation	70	58
Agree that unemployment should be avoided even at the cost of hindering or even suspending economic reform	19	34
Would select a harsher and more accelerated version of economic reform	61	51
Would accede to 50 percent price increases in essential goods	53	39
Willing to accept the loss of current employment	48	37
Fears about a decline in the standard of living	60	70
Would strike following a considerable increase in the cost of essential goods	37	50
Would strike if major cut in social security	62	61
Think that the state should bear complete responsibility for finding employment for every citizen	32	47
Think that the state should bear complete responsibility for ensuring a decent standard of living for each citizen	34	46
Willing to achieve a top level in job or occupation	39	44
Prefer being self-employed, intend to start a private enterprise	7	7
Plan to set up private enterprise	14	13

Source: Marek Boguszak, Ivan Gabal, and Vladimír Rak, *Československo-leden 1990* (Prague: Skupina pro nezávislou socialni´analyzu, 1990).

percent) and May 1993 (73 percent) also felt that the government should minimize unemployment because of its negative impact on the population. The proportion of those who felt that unemployment was an "inevitable condition of economic improvement," despite the hardships it caused, decreased from 31 percent in October 1991 to 23 percent in May 1993. Approximately three-quarters (70 percent in October 1991 and 76 percent in May 1993) of respondents believed that the government should not allow uncontrolled price increases because of the hardships inflation creates.[5] These results are similar to those obtained in parallel surveys in Hungary in June 1991 and January 1992, when

[5]USIA, "Support for Market Economy Edges Up in Romania," *USIA Opinion Research Memorandum,* 23 July 1993, 15. A representative national probability sample of 1,015 adults 18 years of age were interviewed between 15 and 29 May 1993 by SOCIOBIT of Bucharest.

Table 1.5. *Preferred society*

	Preferred society					
	Czechs 12/92 (%)	Poles 5/92 (%)	Bulgarians 4/92 (%)	Slovaks 12/92 (%)	Hungarians 11/92 (%)	Romanians 9/92 (%)
"Individual opportunities" society	43	34	28	28	17	16
Middle-of-the- roaders	34	36	44	37	39	32
"State guar- antees" society	24	30	29	35	44	53

Source: USIA, "Transition to What? Publics Confront Change in Central and Eastern Europe," *USIA Opinion Research Memorandum, 29* January 1993. Surveys were based on national clustered probability samples of adults (18 years and older). Conducted by AISA (*N* = 1,033) in the Czech Republic and (1,075) in Slovakia; Demoskop (901) in Poland; Center for the Study of Democracy (1,472) in Bulgaria; MEDIAN (1,001) in Hungary; and SOCIOBIT (1,050) in Romania. See Mary McIntosh and Martha Abele Mac Iver, "Transition to What? Publics Confront Change in Central and Eastern Europe," Woodrow Wilson Center Occasional Paper (Washington, D.C.: Woodrow Wilson International Center for Scholars, 1993), for further information on questions and methodology.

72 percent and 64 percent of respondents, respectively, felt that the government should prevent unemployment.[6]

Let us turn now to the second category of social legacies—the values, attitudes, and behavior of the population. Some of these were inculcated during the years of communist rule, whereas others were not explicitly promulgated or even approved by the regime but developed as the result of living under a communist system. SIP respondents, who left the Soviet Union in the late 1970s, were asked a six-panel question designed to assess popular support for or rejection of norms that were fundamental to the Soviet regime, including state ownership of heavy industry, state provision of health care, state dominance of agricultural production and distribution, and the legal precedence of society's rights over those of an individual accused of crime. Respondents were asked to place themselves on a seven-point scale ranging from one extreme position to the other. Each question was couched in terms comparable to the following: "Some people in the Soviet Union say that the state should own all heavy industry. Others say that all heavy industry should be owned

[6]USIA, "Hungarians Voice Mixed Reviews of Free Market Economy," *USIA Research Memorandum,* 19 June 1992, Table 10, 12. MEDIAN conducted face-to-face interviews with representative samples of 1,000 and 999 adults 18 years and older in June 1991 and January 1992, respectively.

privately. Where would you have placed yourself on this issue at the end of your last normal period of life in the USSR?" More than 65 percent placed themselves in support of state ownership of heavy industry and the provision of health care by the state; 75 percent supported privatization of agricultural production and distribution; and a small plurality voted for the rights of the individual over those of society.[7]

A survey conducted by ROMIR for USIA in June 1992 asked a similar question about ten spheres of the economy and obtained more detailed but comparable results. About 80 percent of respondents replied that heavy industry, health care, railroads, and airlines should be owned "exclusively by the state" or "mainly by the state." From 58 to 66 percent supported public ownership of enterprises that manufactured consumer goods, banking sources, radio, television, and newspapers. Only in the case of farming (62 percent), shops and food stores (48 percent), and restaurants and cafés (62 percent) did support for private ownership and operation predominate. Many other studies have confirmed these general contours with respect to private and public ownership of economic activities.[8]

In the December 1991 survey conducted by ROMIR respondents were also asked about their preferred type of economic system. Some 25 percent responded that they preferred that most businesses and farms be private; 40 percent wanted some private, some owned by the state; 19 percent wanted most owned by the state; and about 15 percent either did not know or gave no answer. Interestingly, 77 percent believed that guaranteed work for all citizens "should be a main feature of our social-economic system in the future." But 77 percent also agreed that people "should have opportunity to earn as much as they can," as opposed to 15 percent who felt the state should actively reduce income differences.[9]

Survey research conducted in Central and Eastern Europe amply documents similar popular reservations concerning the shift to the market. As a recent discussion notes, attitudes toward the market in Central and Eastern Europe reflect the recent experiences of each country with the market as well as with its "economic culture."[10] As Table 1.6

[7]Brian D. Silver, "Political Beliefs of the Soviet Citizen: Sources of Support for Regime Norms," in Millar, *Politics, Work, and Daily Life in the USSR,* 110.
[8]Office of Research, USIA, "Russians Express No Consensus on Privatization or Foreign Investment," *USIA Opinion Research Memorandum,* 12 August 1992, 10–11. ROMIR interviewed 1,800 adults between 1 and 21 January 1992 in Russia.
[9]Office of Research, USIA, "Russians Support Limited Privatization in Context of a Mixed Economy," *USIA Research Memorandum,* 26 February 1992, 11.
[10]USIA, "Transition to What? Publics Confront Change in Central and Eastern Europe," *USIA Opinion Research Memorandum,* 29 January 1993, 1.

Table 1.6. *Support for market economy in selected Central and Eastern European countries*

	Czechs 12/92 (%)	Poles 5/92 (%)	Bulgarians 4/92 (%)	Slovaks 12/92 (%)	Hungarians 11/92 (%)	Romanians 9/92 (%)
Free market	38	16	18	25	17	20
Middle-of-the-roaders	44	50	48	47	59	45
Regulated market	18	34	24	28	24	35

Source: USIA, "Transition to What? Publics Confront Change in Central and Eastern Europe," *USIA Opinion Research Memorandum,* 29 January 1993. See Table 1.5 for further information on surveys and polling techniques.

illustrates, in 1992 support for a market economy was greatest among respondents in the Czech Republic. In the other countries for which comparable data are available, the largest number of respondents preferred a mixed economy (see also Table 1.4).

As in the former Soviet Union attitudes differed on private ownership of various kinds of enterprises. In Hungary, for example, 81 percent of those surveyed by MEDIAN in Budapest in June 1992 for USIA favored continued state ownership of large- and medium-scale enterprises, and more than 70 percent favored state ownership of television and radio. Support for private ownership of enterprises that manufacture consumer goods was greater (approximately 48 percent), and 67 percent of respondents favored private ownership of shops and food stores. Support for state ownership of large-scale industry increased slightly to 85 percent in Hungary by October 1992, as did the number of those who supported state ownership of agriculture (from 50 to 57 percent).[11] Most Hungarians surveyed by MEDIAN in June 1991 indicated a preference for gradual rather than radical economic reform.[12]

The results of a number of surveys conducted in Romania between December 1991 and May 1993 also document significant reservations concerning private ownership. Thus, although an increasing proportion of Romanians (from 37 percent in April 1990 to 65 percent in May

[11]USIA, "Hungarians Favor Market Economy, Yet Want Continued State Guarantees," *USIA Opinion Research Memorandum,* 7 January 1993. MEDIAN conducted face-to-face interviews with a representative nationwide sample of 1,001 adults 18 years of age and older from October to 15 November 1992.

[12]USIA, "Hungarians Voice Mixed Reviews," *USIA Research Memorandum,* 19 June 1992, 11.

1993) opposed state ownership of all enterprises, a majority (from 54 to 59 percent) of respondents in each of four surveys believed that, while some businesses should be privately owned, the majority should be state-run.[13]

As in the case of the results of the December 1991 ROMIR survey mentioned earlier, many citizens in Central and Eastern Europe hold inconsistent views regarding the market. Although many support the right of individuals to engage in private enterprise, significant numbers also fear that the shift to the market will allow certain individuals to enrich themselves at the expense of others rather than lead to a better standard of living for the majority of the population. Many also do not want to see income differentials increase substantially.[14] The Albanian case is instructive here. A survey conducted in 1991 by the Albanian Sociological Association with Gallup Budapest for USIA found that almost all (90 percent of urban and 91 percent of rural) respondents believed that a free market was necessary. At the same time, 55 percent of urban and 60 percent of rural respondents wanted the state, rather than individuals, to take responsibility for providing for citizens.[15]

The experience of living under communism also had an important impact on the political values and attitudes of citizens in the region. This influence is evident in views regarding the party system, perspectives on democracy, and the role of the individual in politics. As illustrated by the large-scale demonstrations that brought about the end of communist rule in Central and Eastern Europe and also occurred in the waning days of communist rule in the Soviet Union, large numbers of citizens were thoroughly alienated from the communist political system. Many also were eager to see an end to the monopoly of power by a single party. In the SIP general survey of the early 1980s, 17 percent of respondents (N = 2,973) indicated that the one-party system in the Soviet Union was a feature they would be "sure to change" if they had the opportunity.[16] Fifty-seven percent of respondents in an all-union survey (N = 2,504)

[13]USIA, "Support for Market Economy Edges Up in Romania," *USIA Opinion Research Memorandum,* 23 July 1993, 12.

[14]AISA, "Výzkum politckých postojů, 15–24 dubna 1992" (Prague: AISA, May 1992). See the studies in Archie Brown and Jack Gray, eds., *Political Culture and Political Change in Communist States,* 2d ed. (New York: Holmes and Meier, 1979), for references to studies that illustrate these trends during the communist period.

[15]USIA, "Albanians Speak Out on Economic Issues," *USIA Research Memorandum,* 15 July 1991, 9–14. Results are based on face-to-face interviews with a representative nationwide sample of 1,181 adults 18 years of age or older conducted by the Albanian Sociological Association between 30 April and 14 May 1991.

[16]Millar, *"Perestroika and Glasnost',"* 285.

Table 1.7. *Most important features of a democracy*

	Proportion of respondents emphasizing:	
	Economic features (%)	Political features (%)
Hungarians	70	26
Poles	70	25
Slovaks	67	29
Czechs	61	38
East Germans	46	53
Bulgarians	41	49

Source: Mary E. McIntosh, Martha Abele Mac Iver, Richard B. Dobson, and Steven A. Grant, "The Meaning of Democracy in a Redefined Europe," paper prepared for presentation at the annual meeting of the American Association for Public Opinion Research, St. Charles, Illinois, 20–23 May 1993, Figure 1. See Table 1.8 for information on the survey question and samples.

conducted by Boris Grushin in the summer of 1990 indicated that they either "strongly agreed" or "somewhat agreed" that the Soviet Union should have a multiparty system.[17] A subsequent survey conducted in Russia in December 1991 found a total of 50 percent who either "completely agree" or "partly agree" with the proposition that "Russia needs a real multiparty system."[18]

Rejection of one-party rule, however, is not necessarily tied to a well-developed understanding of the characteristics of democracy. A June 1992 survey conducted in Russia by ROMIR for USIA attempted to ascertain what characteristics respondents thought were "essential" in a democracy. As Table 1.3 illustrates, only 39 percent agreed that "at least two strong political parties competing in elections" was essential. Seventy-four percent thought that a "judicial system that treats everyone equally" was essential, but only 52 percent of all respondents thought that "protection of the rights of minorities" and 42 percent thought "freedom to criticize the government" were essential. Sixty-eight percent believed that a democracy had to assure "economic prosperity in the country" and provide "for basic material needs of citizens."

Similar concepts of democracy prevail in most of the Central and

[17]Boris A. Grushin, ed., *MIR menenii i MNENIIA o mire*, no. 1 (February 1992): 2.
[18]Office of Research, USIA, "Russians' Support for Democracy Tested by Tough Times," *USIA Opinion Research Memorandum*, 16 March 1992, 5.

Table 1.8. *Most important feature of a democracy*

Question: Which of the things on this card would you say is the most important in a democracy?

	Poles 5/92 (N=901) (%)	Czechs 11/91 (N=1,200) (%)	Slovaks 11/91 (N=812) (%)	Hungarians 11/92 (N=990) (%)	Bulgarians 3/93 (N=1,508) (%)
Economic prosperity in the country	41	22	17	35	19
A government that guarantees economic equality among its citizens	11	17	24	10	12
A government that guarantees that basic economic needs of its people will be met	18	22	26	26	16
A system of justice that treats everyone equally	12	24	15	20	32
At least two strong political parties competing in elections	7	12	12	4	11
Freedom to criticize the government	2	2	2	2	3
Minority rights/tolerance	NA	NA	NA	NA	NA
Social order	NA	NA	NA	NA	NA
Free market economy	NA	NA	NA	NA	NA

Source: Adapted from Table 1 in Mary E. McIntosh, Martha Abele Mac Iver, Richard B. Dobson, and Steven A. Grant, "The Meaning of Democracy in a Redefined Europe," paper presented at the annual meeting of the American Association for Public Opinion Research, St. Charles, Illinois, 20–23 May 1993. Surveys were based on national clustered probability samples of adults (18 and over) conducted for USIA by Demoskop in Poland; AISA in the Czech Republic; MEDIAN in Hungary; and Center for the Study of Democracy in Bulgaria. NA = no answer.

Eastern European countries. The results of surveys conducted in these countries for USIA between 1991 and 1993 reveal these tendencies. As Table 1.7 illustrates, from 41 to 70 percent of respondents in the region emphasized economic and social rights in their definitions of democracy. Support for the notion that political features—such as at least two strong political parties and competitive elections, freedom to criticize the government, and minority rights and tolerance—are most important in determining whether a state is democratic was strongest in Bulgaria, the Czech Republic, and among the inhabitants of the former German Democratic Republic.[19] Only among the last group, however,

[19]See Mary E. McIntosh, Martha Abele Mac Iver, Richard B. Dobson, and Steven A. Grant, "The Meaning of Democracy in a Redefined Europe," paper prepared for presentation at the annual meeting of the American Association for Public Opinion Research,

did such conceptions prevail among a majority of the population (Table 1.8).

It follows from these data that a major legacy of communism is the belief that the government is responsible not only for assuring general prosperity for the country, but also for guaranteeing employment and the basic material needs of individual citizens. These responsibilities have become enmeshed in the very definition of democracy for many Russians and Central and Eastern Europeans.

Let us turn now to the "aftermath" of communism, that is, the unintended and frequently negative carryovers from the Soviet period. As the result of living under a communist system, large numbers of citizens in all of these societies have come to distrust public institutions and officials. The Soviet Interview Project asked former Soviet citizens to rate the leaders of various main institutions for competence and honesty (Table 1.9). All leaders, including those of the Academy of Sciences, scored significantly higher on competence than on honesty, which supports the frequent complaint of many citizens of communist states that they were obliged to live a "life of lies." The military scored second highest in both categories: 66 percent of respondents reported that almost all or most military leaders were competent and 36 percent believed that almost all or most military leaders were honest. The leaders of the Academy of Sciences scored nearly the same in each category. The leaders of the local party, local soviet, and local militia received the lowest overall ratings, as the majority of respondents considered only some or hardly any of the leaders of these local organizations to be either competent or honest. The greatest discrepancy between competence and honesty occurred in the case of the KGB, of which 57 percent were rated "competent" and only 14 percent "honest," a 43-point spread. Judging by SIP respondents, the leaders of the principal political and police institutions, including the Politburo, had little or no legitimacy in the eyes of the public, and the integrity of even academic, military, and economic institutions was badly compromised, too.

A December 1991 survey by ROMIR questioned citizens regarding their confidence in various officials, government bodies, and organizations in Russia and the Soviet Union (Table 1.10). Boris Yeltsin and the army scored highest, with 56 and 57 percent of respondents, respectively, having "a great deal" or "a fair amount" of confidence in each.

St. Charles, Illinois, 20–23 May 1993, for detailed information on the surveys and an analysis of their results.

Table 1.9. SIP G1 rating of leaders of institutions for competence and honesty

Question: Here is a list of some institutions that exist in the Soviet Union. I would like you to think about how many of the people in charge of each of them you felt were *honest* during your last normal period [of life in the USSR]. For each one, circle the number under the category that best describes how many of the people in charge were *honest*. Now turn the page over. On this side, think about how many of the people in charge at each of these institutions were *competent*, that is, did their jobs well. Remember, try to think about how you felt during your last normal period. [Same response categories and order of institutions as in the "honesty" question.]

	Politburo	Local party	Local soviet	Local police	Industrial manager	Academy of Science	Military	KGB
Honesty/Integrity								
Almost all (%)	6.9	4.6	4.2	4.4	5.0	10.3	13.2	6.1
Most (%)	9.0	8.9	10.4	7.9	17.6	24.7	22.5	7.5
Some (%)	25.5	34.3	41.8	35.1	50.1	46.5	41.7	24.6
Hardly any (%)	18.2	22.2	23.4	24.9	14.5	8.4	10.9	19.2
None (%)	40.5	30.0	20.2	27.7	12.8	10.0	11.8	42.7
Base N	1,925	2,123	2,193	2,160	2,284	1,921	2,012	1,981
Competence								
Almost all (%)	18.6	10.0	7.0	11.2	11.3	21.7	23.1	28.1
Most (%)	21.7	19.3	19.9	21.5	38.1	44.6	43.1	29.0
Some (%)	35.5	47.9	58.5	48.0	45.7	30.6	30.0	26.9
Hardly any (%)	11.8	13.7	10.1	11.9	3.2	1.0	1.6	7.5
None (%)	12.4	9.1	4.5	7.3	1.7	2.1	2.3	8.6
Base N	1,852	2,045	2,131	2,042	2,276	1,929	1,987	1,918

Source: James R. Millar, "Prospects for Economic Reform: Is (Was) Gorbachev Really Necessary?" in J. J. Lee and Walter Korter, eds, *Political, Economic, and Security Prospects for the 1990s* (Austin, Texas: LBJ School of Public Affairs, 1991), Table 4, 81.

Table 1.10. *Confidence in officials, government bodies, and organizations (Russia, December 1991)*

Question: Now I would like to know how much confidence you have in various officials, government bodies, and organizations. As I read the following list, please tell me whether you have a great deal of confidence, a fair amount of confidence, not very much confidence, or no confidence at all in each one.

	Russian Supreme Soviet (%)	Russian President Boris Yeltsin (%)	USSR State Council (%)	Army (%)	USSR President Gorbachev (%)	KGB[a] (%)	USSR Supreme Soviet (%)
A great deal	9	22	4	24	5	5	3
A fair amount	27	34	12	33	15	19	10
(subtotal)	(36)	(56)	(16)	(57)	(20)	(24)	(13)
Not very much	36	23	30	21	28	25	27
None at all	17	17	27	12	42	28	38
(subtotal)	(53)	(40)	(57)	(33)	(70)	(53)	(65)
DK/NA	11	5	27	10	11	24	23
Total (N = 1,804)	100%	101%	100%	100%	101%	101%	101%

[a]The KGB, briefly reorganized as the Interrepublic Security Service in fall 1991, became two distinct Russian entities in December 1991.
Source: Office of Research, USIA, "Russians Dissatisfied with Political Changes But Still Support Yeltsin," *USIA Research Memorandum,* 6 March 1992, 7. DK = don't know; NA = no answer.

As might have been expected, given the time the questionnaire was fielded, a majority of respondents indicated that they had not very much or no confidence in Mikhail Gorbachev, the USSR Supreme Soviet, and the USSR State Council (70, 65, and 57 percent, respectively). But it is probably significant that a majority of respondents (53 percent) had little or no confidence in either the Russian Supreme Soviet or the KGB.

Surveys conducted in Czechoslovakia, Poland, and Hungary prior to the end of communist rule provide a similar picture of general alienation from the political arena and lack of trust in most public officials and institutions. In Czechoslovakia, for example, research conducted in 1989 by the Institute for Research on Public Opinion before the November revolution found that only one-third of respondents felt that the leading role of the Communist party was necessary; almost 50 percent felt that the party was not needed at all.[20] The results of a 1988 survey conducted by the same institution, which was made public only in 1990, also shed light on citizens' attitudes toward government and their own possibilities to influence politics. Although most of those surveyed indicated that they were willing to participate in an effort to improve their neighborhoods or clean up the environment, very few were either serving or willing to serve as local level officials or members of local government commissions (14 and 24 percent, respectively). The reasons given for lack of interest in such activities, which included low evaluations of the effectiveness of local governments and of citizens' possibilities to influence politics, as well as previous negative experiences with local government, further reflect negative assessments of local-level officials and institutions.[21] Studies of young people conducted in Czechoslovakia in 1989 prior to the revolution also document growing dissatisfaction with the communist political system. Forty-four percent of those surveyed in May 1989, for example, indicated that they felt the existing political system was not democratic. Only 12 percent of respondents felt they had large opportunities to take part in the leadership of society, and more than a third indicated that they had virtually no possibility of participating in decision making on public issues. More than 80 percent stated that they had no influence on the work or policy positions of political organizations. More than 90 percent of those who were sur-

[20]See Jitka Slavíková, "Zpráva z operativního výzkumu č. 89–13" (Prague: Ústav pro výzkum veřejného mínění při Federálním statistickém úřadu, December 1989), 7.

[21]Ružena Navářová, "Občané české republiky o svém vztahu k národním výborům základního stupne," *Národní výbory* (February 1990): 20–21.

Table 1.11. *Confidence in government institutions*

Question: For each of the organizations or institutions I will read to you, please tell me how much confidence you have in it—a great deal of confidence, a fair amount of confidence, not very much confidence, or no confidence at all.

| | Percent saying "a great deal" or "fair amount" of confidence | | | | |
	Poles 1/93	Czechs 11/91	Slovaks 11/91	Hungarians 11/92	Bulgarians 3/93
National government (Council of Ministers)	29	59	34	30	37
Parliament	26	51	30	22	18
Judiciary	NA	35	34	48	33
Army (or armed forces)	72	43	47	46	72

Source: Adapted from Table 4 in Mary E. McIntosh, Martha Abele Mac Iver, Richard B. Dobson, and Steven A. Grant, "The Meaning of Democracy in a Redefined Europe," paper presented at the annual meeting of the American Association for Public Opinion Research, St. Charles, Illinois, 20–23 May 1993. See Table 1.8 for information concerning samples and polling organizations. NA = no answer.

veyed also felt that further decentralization and fundamental economic changes were necessary.[22]

These tendencies have been confirmed by the more systematic survey research on political topics conducted since the end of communist rule. As Table 1.11 illustrates, most Central and Eastern Europeans have only modest levels of confidence in most government institutions. Only in the Czech Republic did a majority of respondents surveyed in the early 1990s indicate that they had a great deal or fair amount of confidence in the national government, defined as the Council of Ministers, or in the national legislature. Interestingly enough, the army was the most trusted institution in Poland, Bulgaria, and Slovakia. Recent surveys conducted by other organizations in several of these countries confirm these trends.[23] Levels of confidence in political institutions in the region at present do not differ very much from those found in more established

[22]Ivan Tomek, "Názory československé mládeže na politický systém ČSSR v letech 1986–1989," *Veřejné mínění v ČSSR*, Prague, 1990. See Laszlo Bruszt, "Without Us But for Us: Political Orientations in Hungary in the Period of Later Paternalism," *Social Research* 55 (Spring-Summer 1989): 43–76; and Stanislaw Kwiatkowski, "Attitudes towards Political Leaders and Institutions," *Report of the Center for Research on Public Opinion*, Warsaw, 1989, for discussion of these tendencies in Hungary and Poland.

[23]See Sharon L. Wolchik, "The Repluralization of Politics in Post-Communist Czechoslovakia," *Journal of Communist and Post-Communist Studies* 26, no. 4 (December 1993): 412–31, for discussion of these trends in former Czechoslovakia and the Czech and Slovak republics between 1990 and 1993.

European democracies, due to recent declines in public trust in institutions in the latter countries. As McIntosh and her coauthors note, however, low levels of confidence are more threatening in Central and Eastern Europe, where democratic governments have only recently been established or reestablished and where there is a much smaller "reservoir of diffuse support" for democratic institutions.[24] Many Central and East Europeans also report low levels of political efficacy and interpersonal trust.[25] As in Russia, support for democratic values is highest among better educated, younger, urban respondents, as well as among men.[26]

The unhappy aftermath of communism also includes a collection of attitudes toward certain kinds of crime and other forms of deviant behavior. It was a well-established fact that participation in quasi-legal and even outright illegal economic activities (*na levo*) was inescapable during the Brezhnev era in the Soviet Union as well as in other communist states, and winking at petty crime was part of the "social contract" of that historical period.[27] A series of surveys conducted by the All-Union Center for the Study of Public Opinion in the fall of 1989 and spring of 1990 revealed an essentially cynical view on the part of the public. Soviet citizens, for example, differed in their evaluations of various kinds of illegal earnings (Table 1.12). Note that reselling goods on the market, whether agricultural or other, and speculation in general were condemned by approximately 75 percent of respondents, a figure equal to the percentage of those who condemned prostitution and surpassed only by the 82 percent who disapproved of overcharging customers. Seventy-one percent of respondents also condemned bribes and "gifts" to officials, but the petty theft of goods, illegal use of state transport, and presents and payments to doctors, nurses, and teachers by contrast were not condemned by a majority of respondents. A subsequent question in the survey helps to explain popular unwillingness to condemn these activities. Some 51 percent of those questioned believed that the growth of black markets and of illegal earnings was caused by "the general deficit of goods and services, the necessity of getting them through illegal means," and 54 percent agreed that it was "sometimes

[24]See McIntosh et al., "The Meaning of Democracy," 8.

[25]See ibid. for discussion of these tendencies. See also AISA, "Výzkum politckých postojů, 15–24 dubna 1992."

[26]See McIntosh et al., "The Meaning of Democracy," and Center for Social Analysis, "Current Problems of Slovakia," Bratislava, March 1993, p. 8, for fuller discussions of these correlations.

[27]See, for example, James R. Millar, "The Little Deal: Brezhnev's Contribution to Acquisitive Socialism," *Slavic Review* 44, no. 4 (Winter 1985): 694–706.

Table 1.12. *Unearned income in the Soviet Union*

Question: How do people around you feel about those who earn money illegally in the following areas?

	Total respondents	Majority condemns	Majority does not condemn	No opinion
Petty theft of goods	1,449	42.9	45.5	11.7
Bribes and "gifts" to officials	1,443	70.8	19.7	9.6
Speculation	1,448	76.2	16.4	7.5
Overcharging customers	1,443	81.6	10.7	8.0
Reselling goods and services	1,443	61.7	29.3	9.6
Illegal use of state transport	1,442	44.7	38.2	17.5
Tips, gratuities	1,429	37.1	40.1	22.9
Prostitution	1,442	75.6	8.1	16.4
Presents and payment to doctors, nurses, and teachers	1,436	47.6	36.4	16.0
Black marketeering (resale of foreign goods)	1,427	57.3	25.4	17.4
Resale of agricultural goods on the market	1,439	74.0	12.4	13.6

Source: "Public Opinion in the Soviet Union," *New Outlook* 1, no. 3 (Summer 1990): 27.

impossible to solve an important problem without using illegal means, even if this causes domestic protests."[28]

Citizens of the former Soviet Union, then, drew a more or less consistent distinction between two kinds of "illegal" economic activity. On the one hand, money grubbing by individuals, such as speculators, middlemen, dishonest salespersons, and corrupt government officials, was viewed as morally reprehensible and completely unacceptable to the majority of respondents. On the other hand, illegal activities by those who were not seeking to get rich, but just to get by economically—who, like almost everyone, were trying to "work the system" to obtain scarce but necessary goods and services—were acceptable because there was no other way to get these goods and services and no one "profited" in a big way from them. The notion that sales effort does not add to the value of goods sold is a Marxian legacy that has been confounded with bribery and corruption and hence represents an unfortunate aftermath of communism for a state that is attempting to introduce a market economy.

Similar attitudes appear to have prevailed in Central and Eastern Europe. As the voluminous literature on the second economies in Hungary and Poland illustrates, many people in both of those societies took

[28]"Public Opinion in the Soviet Union," *New Outlook* 1, no. 3 (Summer 1990): 27–28.

Table 1.13. *Proportion of respondents in
Czechoslovakia who used bribery, gifts,
additional payments, or reciprocal services,
by area, 1988 (percent)*

Purchasing retail goods	75.0
Health care	49.5
Repair and other tradesmen's work	44.5
Purchase and repair of automobiles	37.5
Services	19.0
Activities connected with construction	18.5
Obtaining official actions and permits	18.5
Allocation and exchange of apartments	13.5
Education	13.0
Transportation	9.0
Tourism	7.5
Obtaining scarce books and magazines	6.5
Obtaining tickets to cultural programs	3.0
Purchase of cottages and plots	2.5
Getting favors at work or better job	1.5

Source: Vladimír Hanzl, Marie Ševerová, Vlasta Štěpová, and Jan Žůrek, "Problém nejen morální, ale i
ekonomický," *Hospodářské noviny,* 20 January 1989,
8–9.

for granted participation in such "illegal" activities. Even in Czechoslovakia, which had far tighter restrictions on such activities, many citizens
admitted to having used illegal means (bribery, gifts, additional payments, reciprocal services) to obtain scarce goods or services (Table
1.13). The results of a survey conducted in April 1988 by the Economic
Research Institute in Prague and published in 1989 prior to the revolution found that use of such methods was particularly great in the retail
sector and medicine, as well as in services and in the purchase and
service of automobiles. The fact that only six of two hundred respondents stated that they had never used such means illustrates the extent to
which these activities were widespread.[29]

The surveys cited here and many others conducted over the years,
beginning with SIP, reveal another kind of legacy or aftermath of communism with important implications for reform. Wherever conducted,
these survey results show clear-cut cleavages by generation, educational
attainment, and degree of urbanization. Without exception, support for
reform, for change, and thus for democracy and markets in the former
Soviet Union and postcommunist Central and Eastern Europe comes

[29]See Vladimír Hanzl, Marie Ševerová, Vlasta Štěpová, and Jan Žůrek, "Problém nejen
morální, ale i ekonomický," *Hospodářské noviny,* 20 January 1989, 8–9.

solidly and disproportionately from the younger members of society, the better educated, and the more highly urbanized. These are intersecting variables that reinforce one another. The younger members of former communist societies are the better educated and the more likely also to reside in urban areas. As these members of society are more likely to participate politically, these trends tend to support, for example, Boris Yeltsin in Russia. Ironically, these carryover variables are a result of the success of communist policies in achieving high levels of educational attainment and urban-industrial growth.

Insofar as possible, we have attempted to provide a baseline for examining the social legacies of communism; however, there are many issues for which a baseline is not readily available. In the case of the former Soviet Union, for example, we do not have survey data on attitudes of the various ethnic and national groups prior to glasnost, and we do not know, therefore, whether the strength of these feelings was growing ineluctably over the last decade or so of Soviet rule, or whether perestroika and glasnost themselves precipitated these attitudes. Many analysts of ethnic relations in the Soviet Union during communist rule argue, however, that the impact of modernization and the federal political structure of the Soviet Union increased the political importance of ethnic identity and the incentives for mobilizing citizens around ethnic claims.[30]

Similarly, numerous studies document the existence of negative stereotypes and attitudes toward members of other ethnic groups in a number of Central and Eastern European countries during the communist period as well as the important role of political elites in mobilizing citizens around ethnic identities during that era. In the former Yugoslav state, the more relaxed political climate and federal structure contributed in a very direct way to making ethnicity a key element in political decision making. The country's decentralized economic system and the continued gap in living standards and levels of development in the northern and southern parts of the country also reinforced the role that ethnicity played as a significant source of political division.[31] Political developments as well as survey research illustrate the importance of

---

[30]See Walker Connor, *The National Question in Marxist-Leninist Theory and Strategy* (Princeton: Princeton University Press, 1984). See also Gail Lapidus, "Ethnonationalism and Political Stability: The Soviet Case," *World Politics* 36 (July 1984): 555–80, and Brian Silver, "Levels of Sociocultural Development among Soviet Nationalities: A Partial Test of the Equalization Hypothesis," *American Political Science Review* 68, no. 4 (December 1974): 1618–37.

[31]See Ivo Banac, *The National Question in Yugoslavia: Origins, History, Politics* (Ithaca: Cornell University Press, 1984); Paul Shoup, *Communism and the Yugoslav National*

these factors in increasing the political salience of ethnicity in Czechoslovakia during the communist period.[32]

In the case of the former Czechoslovak state, the results of survey research indicate that many Czechs and Slovaks held negative stereotypes and negative attitudes toward each other prior to the end of communist rule. Members of each group also had very different historical referents and evaluated their joint and individual histories quite differently.[33] A study of nationality relations completed in May 1989 and published in May 1990 in Czechoslovakia illustrates these differences. It also documents a decline over time in perceived friendliness between the two groups. Although the majority of inhabitants in both the Czech Lands and Slovakia felt that relations between the two groups were friendly or rather friendly (69 percent), this proportion was lower than the 79 percent of respondents who evaluated these relations positively in 1983. Each group felt the other to be overrepresented in political positions and, as in earlier studies, members of each group differed in their views of history.[34] There are important historical and cultural distinctions between Czechs and Slovaks, but in contrast to the situation in many parts of the former Soviet Union and former Yugoslavia, there has been little perceived animosity or hatred among members of the two groups.

Most Czechs and Slovaks in fact continued to feel positively about relations between the two groups and to claim that they had good personal relationships with members of the other ethnic group even as their leaders negotiated the end of the common state.[35] The example of Czechoslovakia illustrates the important role that the stresses of the

Question (New York: Columbia University Press, 1968); and Steven Burg, *Conflict and Cohesion in Socialist Yugoslavia: Political Decision Making since 1966* (Princeton: Princeton University Press, 1983).

[32] H. Gordon Skilling, *Czechoslovakia's Interrupted Revolution* (Princeton: Princeton University Press, 1976); Carol Skalnik Leff, *National Conflict in Czechoslovakia: The Making and Remaking of a State, 1918–1987* (Princeton: Princeton University Press, 1988); Sharon L. Wolchik, *Czechoslovakia in Transition: Politics, Economics, and Society* (New York: Pinter Publishers, 1991); Martin Bútora and Zora Bútorová, "Slovakia after the Split," *Journal of Democracy* 4, no. 2 (April 1993); Fedor Gál, "Problém česko-slovenských vztahov po novembri 1989 cez prizmu politiky," in Fedor Gál et al., *Dnešní krize česko-slovenských vztahů* (Prague: Sociologické nakladatelství, 1992); and Sharon Wolchik, "The Politics of Ethnicity in Post-Communist Czechoslovakia," *East European Politics and Societies* 8, no. 1 (January 1994).

[33] See Brown and Gray, *Political Culture and Political Change;* Skilling, *Czechoslovakia's Interrupted Revolution;* David W. Paul, "Czechoslovakia's Political Culture Reconsidered," in Brown and Gray, *Political Culture and Political Change* (London: Macmillan, 1984); and Wolchik, *Czechoslovakia in Transition,* chaps. 2 and 3.

[34] Jan Mišovič, "Názory na vzťahy národov a národností ČSSR," *Informace,* March 1990.

[35] See Wolchik, "The Politics of Ethnicity," for studies illustrating these trends.

economic and political transition have played in increasing ethnic tensions and fueling nationalist movements in postcommunist states. In this case, as in the former Yugoslavia, some of the positive social changes that occurred during the communist era, including urbanization and increases in educational levels, contributed to the ability of ethnic elites to raise ethnic issues in the political arena by increasing the resources at their disposal.[36]

As is true for many of the issues discussed in this volume, the legacy of communist rule in this region has been compounded by developments since the collapse of communism. In both the former Soviet Union and postcommunist Central and Eastern Europe, the political and economic transitions that followed the collapse of communist rule have further fueled nationalist movements. The fate of the former Yugoslav state is the most tragic example of the extent to which this statement is true, but ethnic and national affiliations represent the most powerful self-sustaining forces driving political activity today in many countries of the region.

Marjorie Mandelstam Balzer and Maria Todorova argue (in Chapters 3 and 4) against the misleading notion that it was merely the lifting of the lid of Soviet power that occasioned the explosion of nationalist and ethnic identification and agitation. Balzer argues from empirical data that there were many parallel and intervening variables in the wakening of ethnic consciousness in the former Soviet Union, among them a growing sense of identity. Todorova, in a more theoretical vein, agrees for the case of Central and Eastern Europe. She points out, ironically, that because most of these states did not view themselves as culturally inferior to the Russians, they had experienced a certain sense of superiority while members of the bloc. The reversion to national sovereignty, therefore, also awakens an older sense of inferiority to the West. The economic cost of the loss of the Soviet empire, as "colony," has also been high. Jack Snyder has argued cogently that the idea that ethnic rivalries were seated in age-old, suppressed animosity is superficial. Ethnic conflict can spring and has sprung as much or more from contemporary forces as from remembered wrongs, and it obviously can do so suddenly, as the high rate of interethnic marriages immediately prior to the empire's collapse proves.[37]

[36]See Joseph Rothschild, *Ethnopolitics: A Conceptual Framework* (New York: Columbia University Press, 1981), for an analysis that stresses the importance of these factors.

[37]Jack Snyder, "Nationalism and the Crisis of the Post-Soviet State," *Survival* 35, no. 1 (Spring 1993): 5–26. See also McIntosh et al., "The Meaning of Democracy," for

TRANSITIONAL POLITICS AND
THE RE-CREATION OF THE MARKET

The impact of values and attitudes that developed during the communist era has been compounded by the characteristics of the transition itself. As the chapters in this volume demonstrate, the end of tight political control has allowed a number of old social pathologies to emerge more openly. The opening of borders has also exposed countries, which were formerly shielded to some degree, to foreign influences and problems originating abroad. The uncertainty and need to adjust to change in most areas of life that inevitably attend large-scale political and economic transitions have had psychological as well as political consequences, many of which have fallen disproportionately on women.[38] Coupled with the moral aftermath of communism, which has been eloquently described by numerous Central and Eastern European intellectuals and leaders, these features of the transition have exacerbated many of the problems analyzed in this volume; they have also increased support for nationalistic movements and extremist political groups.

The task of coming to terms with the social legacies and aftermath of communist rule has also been complicated by the nature of transition politics. Competitive elections have legitimized the new governments of most states in the region, and, with a few notable exceptions, large numbers of new leaders have replaced those previously in power. Citizens may now organize with others to make their political views known and to pressure political leaders. They may also participate in the wide variety of political parties, interest groups, and voluntary organizations that have developed in these countries. Yet all of the formerly communist countries share a number of continuing political problems. In each country the political system is still fluid. Constitutional and legal revisions continue, and the competence and authority of various political institutions are still not clearly defined. A stable party system also has yet to develop. Levels of party membership and identification are low, and citizens' political preferences remain volatile. In this situation political leaders, who often enjoy little trust, have been preoccupied with "high politics" and have given relatively little attention to many of the social issues and pathologies discussed in this volume. Those who have

an analysis of conflicting attitudes toward ethnicity in postcommunist Central and Eastern Europe.

[38]See, for example, Valerie Bunce and Maria Csenadi, "Uncertainty in the Transition: Postcommunism in Hungary," *East European Politics and Societies* 7, no. 2 (Spring 1993). See also Wolchik, "The Repluralization of Politics in Post-Communist Czechoslovakia."

attempted to address social issues have been hampered by the lack of resources and the constraints of economic austerity, as well as by the lack of consensus concerning the nature of the problems and an inability to cooperate across partisan lines.

In Central and Eastern Europe, public policy toward social issues was also hindered in the early days after the collapse of communism by a general rejection of socialism in all its forms, specifically, the tradition of direct government involvement and responsibility for helping to resolve social ills. The weakness of what many term "civil society"—that is, a pattern of social organization that includes interest groups, citizens, and voluntary associations—and the lack of economic conditions supportive of pluralism also mean that many of the nongovernmental actors who deal with social problems in other developed societies do not exist or are too weak to be of much help here. As a result, many of the issues discussed in the chapters to follow can be expected to remain troublesome for some time to come.

Although many postcommunist political leaders and economists in the region and abroad have entertained the possibility of starting out with a clean slate and transforming the polities and economies of these formerly communist countries in a relatively short period of time, the premise of the essays collected here is that there is no such thing as a clean slate. The leaders of postcommunist states must deal with the legacies of communism, and they must deal with what Joseph Berliner in the conclusion to this volume calls the "legacies of the legacies of communism." The choices that communist leaders made to value production and defense over environmental concerns and quality health care, to the detriment of urban and interurban infrastructure, leave enormous obstacles that the successor governments will have to overcome at great cost. The values, attitudes, and political and economic behaviors of the population, which represent a complex combination of pre-communist values, Marxist teachings, and the survival techniques that grew out of a culture of permanent scarcity, must be accommodated in the restoration of civil society in these formerly communist societies. As the following chapters demonstrate, the leaders of postcommunist states must also deal with the frequently predictable, but nonetheless intractable, impact of political and economic transitions on social relations and problems.

Part I

Ethnic issues

2

Making up for lost choice: the shaping of ethnic identity in post-Soviet states

PETER JUVILER

A nation is a grand solidarity constituted by the sentiment of sacrifices which one has made and those that one is disposed to make again.

Ernest Renan

The Soviet nation's solidarity had been forged out of sacrifice, confirmed in victory, and backed up by coercion. With time, though, that solidarity eroded. The nation's readiness to sacrifice together for a bright future disappeared, and central authority waned.

During 1988–91, a "parade of sovereignties" in the union republics brought on a "war of laws" between the republics and the center. The Communist party lost its monopoly and central hold over the union in 1990. The failed August 1991 coup, intended to preserve the old union and system, only spurred their breakup. Communist leaders in the republics changed overnight into nationalists. Nationalists new and old then took the final plunge and left the union. On 25 December 1991, President Gorbachev resigned, a little over three weeks after the formation of the Commonwealth of Independent States (CIS) and just four days after its affirmation by eleven former Soviet republics. Kremlin

Research for this work was supported in part by a grant from the International Research and Exchanges Board (IREX), with funds provided by the Andrew W. Mellon Foundation, the National Endowment for the Humanities, and the U.S. Department of State. None of these organizations is responsible for the views expressed. I am indebted also to Priit Jarve and colleagues at the Institute of Philosophy, Sociology and Law, Tallinn, and sister institutes in the two other Baltic republics, which I visited in October 1991; the Russian Intelligentsia for Karabakh and the Society for Russian Culture and other organizers of the Council on Security and Cooperation in Europe (CSCE) parallel conference on nationality relations, in Yerevan; as well as Helsinki Watch and the Lawyers Committee for Human Rights in New York.

guards lowered the red Soviet flag, with its hammer and sickle, and in its place they ran up the white, blue, and red tricolor of Russia, one of the new state flags meant to symbolize a new national identity.

National identity has yet to coalesce out of the welter of ethnic identities that are asserted wherever freedom still prevails in the former Soviet Union. Ethnic identity entails a sense of membership in a community of shared ancestral origins and culture, distinct from other groups in society.[1] Making up for more than seventy years of lost free choice, post-Soviet adherents of democracy and human rights are endeavoring to nurture and protect new, fragile, inclusive, multiethnic national identities. An inclusive ethnic identity leaves room for shared loyalty to a multiethnic political community in which other groups differ in culture ánd language, perhaps race, but still are seen as equal in citizenship, rights, and obligations. Thus far, however, the centrifugal forces still outweigh the centripetal.

The democrats' task is complicated by the social void of the postcommunist era, to which Joseph Berliner refers in the Conclusion to this volume. With the old structures and securities gone, exclusive forms of ethnic identity have surfaced across the former Soviet Union. Exclusive ethnic identity denies the equality, or even the conationality, of other ethnic groups. In its less virulent form, ethnic identity seeks a regional base in partnership with other local nationalities over and against the center. National identity is exclusive when it merges with ethnic identity and associates the national flag and identity with only one dominant ethnic group.

Ethnic identity is the fruit of experience as well as birth.[2] Part of the experience shaping ethnic identity is the worldwide process of state

---

[1]Nathan Glazer and Daniel P. Moynihan, eds., *Ethnicity: Theory and Experience* (Cambridge, Mass.: Harvard University Press, 1975), 1; Louis L. Snyder, ed., *The Dynamics of Nationalism Readings: In Its Meaning and Development* (New York: D. Van Nostrand, 1964), 1–3. "Ethnicity is a type of grouping that is based on some combination of similar ancestral origin, a common history, shared patterns of normative behavior, similar religious commitments, and use of the same language or languages," but not necessarily all of them. James W. Nickel, "Equal Opportunity in a Pluralistic Society," *Social Philosophy and Policy* 5, no. 1 (1988): 105.

[2]Tracy Strong discusses and rejects "thin" unchanging identity, and David Hume pictures identity as "multiple, a bundle of perceptions," complex and changing according to context; see, respectively, Tracy B. Strong, Introduction, and David Hume, "Of Personal Identity," in Tracy B. Strong, ed., *The Self and the Political Order* (New York: New York University Press, 1992), 4, 59–60. Erik Erikson discusses the formation of identity in *Childhood and Society* (New York: Norton, 1950), *Young Man Luther* (New York: Norton, 1993), and *Gandhi's Truth* (New York: Norton, 1993).

building out of empires and old regimes. Identity is shaped also by tradition, by a sense of injustice or threats to security or survival, and by the perception of group interests.[3] In this context communism has bequeathed to the successor states a mixed legacy.

This legacy includes armed conflict in Transcaucasia and Moldova, issues of minority rights in ethnic diasporas, survivalism in the Baltic states, ambiguities and crosscurrents of identity in Central Asia, and relatively inclusive responses to identity crises by the governments of Russia and Ukraine, all constantly under threat of a resurgent extremism.

THE LEGACY

The first legacy of communism for ethnic identity in the former Soviet Union is a multinational land empire that had been violently reclaimed by the Bolsheviks from the ruins of czarist Russian imperialism. The unity of this empire continued to rest on the vitality of the central socialist government.

The second legacy of communism is its destruction of a developing civil society and nascent democracy, which created a near void of local mediation and adjustment processes. Yet except for the alternative of coercion, civil society and democracy are essential for the ultimate resolution of interethnic conflict.[4]

Communism's third legacy has been the official recognition of ethnic dentities that it nurtured and certified in obligatory passports and to which it gave territorial expression by naming regions after indigenous groups. From Central Asia and the Caucasus to the ethnic enclaves of Siberia, Soviet power succeeded in transforming indigenous populations from amorphous settlements of diverse tribes into distinct larger nation-

---

[3]Rupert Emerson, *From Empire to Nation: The Rise to Self-Assertion of Asian and African Peoples* (Boston: Beacon Press, 1960). The veteran diplomat and educator in diplomacy, David B. Newsom, reminds us: "In nations on every continent, including the United States, people who feel their heritage is threatened by the domination of others are seeking recognition. The traditional cohesion of the nation state is being challenged." Newsom, "The World's 'Identity Crisis,'" *Christian Science Monitor* (hereafter *CSM*), 27 February 1991.

[4]Peter Juviler, "Russia Turned Upside Down," in Peter Juviler and Bertram Gross, eds., *Human Rights for the 21st Century* (Armonk, N.Y.: M. E. Sharpe, 1993), 28–59; Roman Szporluk, "The Imperial Legacy and the Soviet Nationalities Problem," in Lubomyr Hajda and Mark Beissinger, eds., *The Nationalities Factor in Soviet Politics and Society* (Boulder, Colo.: Westview Press, 1990), 1–23.

alities. Ethnic cadres got promoted to local leadership in a process of so-called *korenizatsiia* (rooting). Under Stalin they were then purged of unwanted "national communism."[5]

In Central Asia and the Muslim parts of the Caucasus, for example, the often divisive boundary making and the compulsive—and divisive—rewriting of alphabets and redefining of ethnic identities were aimed at thwarting pan-Turanian and pan-Islamic movements. The general purpose of ethnic policy under Stalin was to produce national cultures "socialist in content and national in form."

The fourth legacy of communism is an accumulation of ethnic resentments and separatism suppressed under the tight lid of control. Algiras Prazauskas blamed the tensions quite apparent by 1989 on repressed resentments building up under communist rule without release or chance for mediation.[6]

An Estonian student told this writer at Moscow University in 1959: "The smaller the ethnic group the more nationalist they will have to be to survive. And we are very small!" His compatriots in the room agreed. Nearly thirty years later, I was overwhelmed by the sight and sound of just about one of every seven Estonians, massed on Festival Field, Tallinn, 17 June 1988, to send off delegates to the Nineteenth Party Conference, which they hoped would bring autonomy but did not. The full Festival Field holds 150,000 people—it was full that day. Ethnic Estonians number under one million people by the 1989 census. At that time, the Estonian republic flags they carried were still illegal, so the crowd passed them from hand to hand to obscure any liability among members of the singing, cheering, banner-waving throng.

Years earlier, before perestroika and openness stimulated claims to greater ethnic self-determination, researchers abroad such as Rasma Karklins and Michael Rywkin discerned undercurrents of ethnic resentments and unrest below the surface calm. The discontent they recognized

[5]M. Crawford Young, "The National and Colonial Question and Marxism: A View from the South," in Alexander J. Motyl, ed., *Thinking Theoretically about Soviet Nationalities* (New York: Columbia University Press, 1992), 86–87.
[6]"The forced internationalization . . . excesses in language policy, violation of the principles of social justice and equal rights for all nations—all this aggravated markedly national relations, hampered a natural process of rapprochement of nations and paved the way for the recurrent outbursts of nationalism." Algiras Prazauskas, "National Problems of Renovated Socialism," in *The Revolution Continues: Soviet Society in the Conditions of Restructuring* (Moscow: Social Sciences Today Editorial Board, Nauka Publishers, 1989), 202. Thanks to Frank Bonilla.

prompted Hélène d'Encausse and the late Andrei Amalrik to predict a Soviet breakup.[7]

Repression by Soviet troops and police special forces to disperse protest occurred across the borderlands of the former Soviet Union from Alma-Ata in December 1986 to the "mini-Tiananmen" in Tbilisi on 9 April 1989; repressive actions also occurred in Kokand, Uzbekistan (June 1989), Baku (January 1990), Dushanbe, Tajikistan (February 1990), and the Baltics (between January and July 1991).[8] By 1991, the system tottered nearer to collapse than was generally realized.[9] History has stood Stalin's intentions on their head. The once real iron grip of the central apparatus has become illusory, whereas the once "formal" nationalism in ethnic identity has become all too real.[10]

The fifth legacy of communism is the failure of economic policies at the center. The economic "grand failure" of communism brought on its own decline. Cities became culturally Russian while hinterlands remained Turkic or Iranian. Low out-migration contributed to the unemployment of indigenous nationalities. The unemployment fueled ethnic animosities and resentments, while assimilation failed to produce a civic Soviet identity to prevail over other identities.[11]

Economic hardships, the center's rigidity, and brutal though spasmodic and ultimately ineffectual responses to local unrest brought on

[7]Rasma Karklins, *Ethnic Relations in the USSR* (Boston: Allen and Unwin, 1986); Michael Rywkin, *Moscow's Moslem Challenge: Soviet Central Asia* (Armonk, N.Y.: M. E. Sharpe, 1982). The Soviet attempts at assimilation, of Russian-language training as a means for "the transmission of national values, the identification with a common culture and a common fate," worked with some groups and individuals but, in general, "a policy imposed from the center to reduce national particularism can lead to an unexpected expression of what it sought to destroy." Hélène Carrère d'Encausse, *Confiscated Power: How Soviet Russia Really Works* (New York: Harper and Row, 1982), 279–80, 298–301. Andrei Amalrik foretold the breakup of the USSR and Eastern European sphere during popular discontent caused by the drain of a protracted war with China. Amalrik, *Will the Soviet Union Survive until 1984?* (New York: Harper and Row, 1970), 44–67.

[8]Evidence strongly suggests complicity of the union center, including probably Gorbachev, in these often bloody actions. Human Rights Watch examined in Alma-Ata "official materials setting out plans for 'Operation Snowstorm,' " the military suppression of demonstrations, not unlike means used in the violent breakup of demonstrations in Alma-Ata. Human Rights Watch, *World Report 1992* (hereafter HRW92) (New York: Human Rights Watch, 1992), 527.

[9]Alexander Motyl, *Will the Non-Russians Rebel? State, Ethnicity and Stability in the USSR* (Ithaca: Cornell University Press, 1987), 1–52, 124–70; Alexander Motyl, *Sovietology, Rationality, Nationality* (New York: Columbia University Press, 1990), 195–96.

[10]G. Ch. Guseinov, "Menshinstva v post-imperskom mire," *Korni* (Riga), no. 2 (December 1991): 2.

[11]Karklins, *Ethnic Relations*, 208; Rywkin, *Moscow's Moslem Challenge.*

the destructive speed of the breakup. These factors showed a failure to understand that economic decline coupled with rising nationalism called, already by 1986, for new strategies of reform and reconciliation—these came too late to save the union in any form.[12]

"Gorbachev," wrote Martha Brill Olcott, "consistently stumbled over nationality relations by offering the republics too little too late."[13] Former Foreign Minister and high party official Eduard Shevardnadze wrote of the protracted face-off between center and republics over the Union Treaty: "If we had proposed the treaty three or four years ago, I am certain that the people would have voted for it without hesitation. We were tardy, timid."[14] "Perhaps what was needed for the 'Soviet people' to become a reality," wrote Roman Szporluk, "was for the 'Soviet dream' to become a reality."[15] Controls were lifted inconsistently and grudgingly, generating new frustrations of rising nationalist expectations. Already in 1989, Bohdan Nahaylo and Victor Swoboda's massive study concluded that either democracy or the union would go.[16]

Five essential ingredients for a stable multiethnic community were lacking: equity and equality for all ethnic groups; reasonable economic security; trust in the center and among ethnic groups; legal and political means for settling the legacy of unresolved issues of boundaries and other interests; and a firm, multiethnic, civic identity based on shared values, interests, and loyalties.

Despite these negative legacies, extreme exclusivism and violence have

---

[12]Peter Juviler, "Presidential Power and Presidential Character," *Soviet Union* 16, nos. 2–3 (1989): 245–55; Henry Huttenbach, "Managing a Federation of Multiethnic Republics," *Nationalities Papers* 19, no. 1 (1991): 26–32; Peter Juviler, "Getting to Yes on Self-Determination," *Nationalities Papers* 19, no. 1 (1991): 32–36; and Juviler, "Human Rights after Perestroika: Progress and Perils," *Harriman Institute Forum* 4, no. 6 (June 1991): 1–10.

[13]Martha Brill Olcott, "The Slide into Disunion," *Current History* 90 (1991): 338.

[14]Eduard Shevardnadze, "No One Can Isolate Us, Save Ourselves: Self-Isolation Is the Ultimate Danger," *Slavic Review* 51, no. 1 (1992): 118. On the triple political, economic, and ethnic loss of legitimacy, see also Peter Reddaway, "The End of Empire," *New York Review of Books*, 7 November 1991, 53–59. President Mircea Snegur of Moldova is representative of the viewpoints of many post-Soviet leaders in looking back at the legacy of "territorial dismemberment, ethnic assimilation, organized migration seeking to change the composition of the population of this land, aberrant economic experiments . . . ecological disaster . . . and a social infrastructure incapable of meeting elementary human needs." Vladimir Socor, "Moldova Proclaims Independence, Commences Secession from the USSR," *RFE/RL Report on the USSR* (hereafter *RFE/RL*), no. 42 (1991): 21.

[15]Szporluk, "The Imperial Legacy," 9–10.

[16]Motyl, *Will the Non-Russians Rebel?*; Bohdan Nahaylo and Victor Swoboda, *Soviet Disunion: A History of the Nationalities Problem in the USSR* (New York: Free Press, 1989), 359.

afflicted only a small part of the former Soviet Union.[17] That is no solace for the people involved, nor does it negate the threat of wider violence should interethnic and center-periphery disputes elsewhere not be resolved speedily.

Human Rights Watch notes that exclusionary nationalist ideologies, by "closing the community to diversity and stripping outsiders of essential rights, nourish a climate of often brutal intolerance."[18] According to Elena Lukasheva, head of the Human Rights Sector of the Institute of State and Law, Moscow,

At present a growth of national consciousness is taking place. That is a salutary process. Unfortunately, however, it is often accompanied by the growth of nationalism, intolerance of other peoples who have lived next door for centuries. And that leads directly to the violation of the rights of citizens of non-indigenous nationalities in sovereign national states, and the appearance of hundreds of thousands of refugees. Of course, democracy and human rights are the first to suffer in times of political, economic and national instability.[19]

Though territorial disputes may be settled amicably, they may take violent and chauvinist forms, as in the Transcaucasus.

TRANSCAUCASIA

As long as Soviet power held firm, it enforced peace most of the time between divided or dissatisfied ethnic groups and their republic governments. Once it wavered, battles over borders or degree of self-determination brought tension and violence between Georgians and the minority Abkhazy and South Ossetians, with whose aspirations to autonomy and then separation the Georgians showed little inclination to compromise.[20]

The dispute between Armenia and Azerbaijan over the mainly Armenian-settled enclave of Nagorno-Karabakh, until 1923 part of modern Armenia, brought bloody war. The war produced massive outflows of refugees, totaling over six hundred thousand from Armenia and Azerbaijan; pogroms in Sumgait and Baku, Azerbaijan; gross violations of Armenians' security and rights in Karabakh and the belt of land separating it from Armenia; the apparent participation of Soviet Fourth Army troops; and brutal retaliation by Armenian irregular "freedom fighters."[21]

[17]Paul A. Goble, "Forget the Soviet Union," *Foreign Affairs*, no. 86 (1992): 61.
[18]HRW92, 1.
[19]Elena A. Lukasheva's preface to Juviler and Gross, *Human Rights for the 21st Century*, 8–9.
[20]HRW92, 532–33.
[21]HRW92, 530–32, 534–37.

This intractable conflict had its Soviet origin in Stalin's 1923 decision to transfer Karabakh and intervening land to Azerbaijan from the already truncated Armenia. The conflict flared with Gorbachev's unwillingness to act decisively to assert direct rule over the disputed area early in 1988 and vigorously pursue a settlement.[22]

CONFRONTATION IN MOLDOVA

Losing the Soviet center can both encourage and make more difficult the fostering of a nascent civic culture of rights, democracy, and rule of law. Vladimir Solinar', deputy to the Moldovan Supreme Council, is an ethnic Ukrainian from a village near Chisinau (Kishinev). He explained that he feels he is being forced to choose whether he is just the ethnic Ukrainian he is by descent (with an admixture of Russian cultural identity from his schooling and years of graduate education in Moscow), or Moldovan—the most complex identity of all at present.

The multiethnic pastiche of Moldova, like many other parts of the former Soviet Union, bears the legacy of Stalin's border drawing. About 65 percent of Moldova's population is ethnic Romanian. Russians comprise about 14 percent and Ukrainians about 13 percent of Moldova's population of some 4.3 million. To the south lives a smaller group, the Turkish-Christian Gagauz, about 3.5 percent of the population, who are seeking autonomy within Moldova. The Slavic groups form a majority of 53.7 percent in Trans-Dniestria, a region on the left bank of the Dniester River, with about 60 percent Russian-speakers, that was annexed by Stalin to a truncated Bessarabia in 1945 to form Moldavia.[23] The Soviet citizenship that cemented together the parts of the identity of Deputy Solinar has disappeared. Moscow is in a foreign country.

Tensions between ethnic Ukrainians and other Slavs on the one hand,

---

[22]HRW92, 530–32; on Gorbachev's response, Geoffrey Hosking, *The Awakening of the Soviet Union* (Cambridge, Mass.: Harvard University Press, 1991), 89–91; the Andrei Sakharov Foundation, *Report of a Delegation to Nagorno-Karabakh 3–8 January 1992;* press reports of atrocities by Armenian militias and conversation with a prominent U.S. advocate of human rights in the former Soviet Union, a lawyer recently returned from Nagorno-Karabakh, 17 April 1992.

[23]Of the 600,000 people (out of a population of 4.362 million) who live on the left bank of the Dniester River, a region joined to Moldavia and annexed from the Ukraine by Stalin in 1945, a minority of about 40 percent are Moldovans, 28.3 percent Ukrainians, 25.4 percent Russians, and over 6 percent persons of other nationalities. Vladimir Solinar', "Russophones and Romanists," *Novoe vremia*, no. 37 (1991): 8. On population, see also State Department, *Country Reports on Human Rights Practices for 1992* (Washington, D.C.: U.S. Government Printing Office, 1993), 853.

and the mainly ethnic Romanian Chisinau government on the other hand, created for Solinar' "a crisis of identity; it's like losing yourself."[24]

Foreign observers from the Conference on Security and Cooperation in Europe (CSCE) and foreign nongovernmental organizations have given Moldova a clean bill of health on human rights.[25] But from the viewpoint of ethnic Ukrainian Deputy Solinar', the Moldovan government has not lived up to its pledges to observe the human rights of everyone. He complains of worsening discrimination against Russophones in employment, promotions, and education. The legal establishment of Romanian as the official language in August 1989 and reconversion from Cyrillic to Latin script under pressure from the burgeoning popular front[26] have added to the distrust some non-Romanians have of the Chisinau government's intentions toward them and the possibility of unification with Romania. Hence the declaration of an independent Dniestrian Moldovan Republic on the Dniester River's left bank, the region once part of Ukraine, ready to join in a "union of states." Discontent also inclined leaders and Russophone mass organizations in the Trans-Dniester region to support the August coup and continuation of the Soviet Union.[27]

The Moldovan government and parliamentary majority, however, condemned and nullified the "unconstitutional coup" and confiscated Russophone communist media afterward. Ironically, Vladimir Socor points out, "it was the Moldovans, not Russian residents, who rallied to Yeltsin, 'Democratic Russia,' and the Russian flag; none of these is popular with Moldova's Russian residents."[28]

Parliament unanimously declared the independence of Moldova on 27 August 1991, in a session boycotted by opponents. At the same time, it declared Moldova's adherence to the CSCE accord and United Nations (UN) pacts on human rights.[29] It was to be a troubled independence. On 25 November 1991, armed "worker detachments" seized

[24]Interview with Deputy Vladimir Solinar' of the Moldovan Supreme Council, Moscow, 17 September 1991.

[25]Text of letter by Mircea Snegur, n.d., in *FBIS-SOV-92-071*, 13 April 1992.

[26]Vladimir Socor, "Moldavia Proclaims Independence, Commences Secession from the USSR," *RFE/RL*, no. 42 (1991): 20.

[27]Interview with Deputy Solinar', Moscow, September 1992.

[28]Moldova cracked down on the Communist party and confiscated its property, including *Sovetskaia Moldava*. The paper's assets, including the largest printing press in Moldova, the government transferred to the new pro-Moldovan daily, *Nezavisimaia Moldava*. Vladimir Socor, "Moldavia Defies Soviet Coup, Removes Vestiges of Communism," *RFE/RL*, no. 38 (1991): 21.

[29]Socor, "Moldavia Proclaims Independence," 19.

Moldovan police buildings and other government buildings of the Dubasari district in the Trans-Dniester region. They cut telephone and other communications with the rest of Moldova. Trans-Dniestrians pressured police officers in six districts to quit or to come over to them; women blockaded the railroad station after the arrest of some Trans-Dniestrian leaders.

On 19 November the Russian Republic Supreme Council sent a delegation which found no sign of violation of the human rights of Trans-Dniestrian Russians. In fact, the Russian Supreme Council accused the Trans-Dniestrian leaders of violating the rights of Moldovans in the Trans-Dniester region by restricting their language education. Armed struggle between Moldovan forces and the newly established, armed people's guard flared up before year's end, bringing thirteen reported fatalities on 13 December 1991.[30]

President Mircea Snegur, by no means the most extreme of Moldovan nationalists, wrote to the UN Security Council, CSCE, and member countries of the CIS to request their support in protecting Moldova's independence and territorial integrity against outside intervention. He stated that the declaration of the Trans-Dniester Republic and opposition to Moldovan independence come from a grouping made up mainly of representatives of the communist nomenklatura, the industrial-military complex, and units of the former Soviet army, centered in the industrial eastern part of Moldova.

Fighting intensified in December 1991 with attacks by Trans-Dniestrian irregulars, assisted by thousands of intruding Don and Kuban Cossacks and a sympathetic former Soviet Fourteenth Army, which turned weapons over to the insurgents. Moldova declared states of emergency in Chisinau and in two locations of the Trans-Dniester region as the rebellion grew.[31] "Tens of thousands" of refugees fled the left bank and the right-bank town of Tighnina. For Snegur these attacks reflected not resentment and distrust but rather nothing less than a drive instigated by "extreme rightist and imperialist chauvinist forces from Russia, which view Moldova as a possible bridgehead to reestablish the

[30]HRW92, 538.
[31]Vladimir Solinar', "Nenavist' i strakh na raznykh beregakh," *Novoe vremia*, no. 14 (1992): 18. As violence escalated, Trans-Dniestrians' appeals for help to Russia and Ukraine remained unrequited, except by intruding Cossacks and the army, and nationalists such as Vice-President Aleksandr Rutskoi who supported Trans-Dniestrian independence. Valerii Vyzhutovich, "Rossiiskaia vlast' ne osuzhdaet agressiiu," *Izvestiia*, 10 March 1992.

totalitarian regime and to create a new empire [within] the borders of the former Soviet Union."[32]

National fervor has not eliminated all opportunities for peace. A cease-fire, negotiated 6 April 1992 in Chisinau by the foreign ministers of Moldova, Romania, Russia, and Ukraine, went into effect on 7 April 1992. The first international peacekeeping operation by the CIS took the form of a monitoring commission of CIS representatives.[33] Boris Yeltsin mediated a 21 July 1992 cease-fire arrangement, which provided for a Russian-Moldovan-Trans-Dniestrian peacekeeping force pending settlement of the status of the Trans-Dniester region.[34]

Soviet border making and ethnic labeling had planted seeds of conflict in Moldova. Once Moscow's rule faltered, Moldovans asserted rights to cultural autonomy. This in turn sparked protests among some members of the Slavic minority, who looked outside for support. Then each side accused the other of human rights violations and evil designs.

Should Russia's government turn reactionary, chances of preventing or settling conflicts like that in Moldova would be ruled out. A triumph of imperialist reaction in Russia would also complicate the resolution of issues concerning the rights of Russian-speaking minorities in the diaspora created by the breakup of the Soviet Union.

CALM AND CONFLICT IN THE DIASPORAS

Another divisive territorial legacy of communism has been the creation of diasporas through Soviet policies that deported minority groups and through migrations. Before the breakup of the Soviet Union, Russians shared Soviet citizenship wherever they were. Afterward, the 25 million outside Russia could choose between citizenship in their new states (if this was permitted) or Russian citizenship. Even before the breakup, Russians in the diaspora had begun to feel unwelcome in Central Asia and the Caucasus. By the 1990s this was true also in the Baltic republics and Moldova.

[32]Letter by Mircea Snegur.
[33]*FBIS-SOV-92-071*, 13 April 1992, 50, 54.
[34]Secession in case of Moldovan unification with Romania was supported on 8 April by a resolution of the Sixth Russian Congress of People's Deputies, to the displeasure of Moldovan leaders. *FBIS-SOV-92-069*, 9 April 1992, 57; -072, 14 April, 52; -073, 15 April, 51; -078, 22 April, 38. See also State Department, *Country Reports on Human Rights Practices for 1992*, 847.

The double impact of democratization and liberation of republics from the center has been traumatic for Russian-speaking immigrants in post-Soviet states. They once felt free not to learn the language of their host countries, where Russian enjoyed a favored position (the natives had to learn Russian, not vice versa). Now Russians must learn the local language if they are to work in government or at any job requiring interethnic contact, from sales to medicine. The immigrants once considered themselves Soviet citizens as well as citizens of the republic in which they resided. Now the Soviet citizenship has disappeared and, for some, so has republic citizenship. A new majoritarian democracy led by representatives of formerly subordinate ethnic groups has imperiled minority rights in some areas. The degree and causes of exclusivism (measured by discrimination and hostility) vary greatly.

Secret police archives have revealed, TASS news agency reports, that Stalin deported a total of 3.5 million members of suspect ethnic groups from the Crimea, Caucasus, and other regions. Ten groups were deported in their entirety. Most deported peoples were restored to diminished remnants of their former homelands. That diminution laid the ground for conflict between returning exiles and more recent settlers in their former homelands, as in the conflict between North Ossetians of the Russian Federation and the Ingush seeking to reclaim their former homeland.

The last groups to be getting partial restitution are the Volga Germans (no longer warmly welcome in Germany), Crimean Tatars, Meskhetian Turks from Georgia, and Soviet Kurds. They face various degrees of unwelcome in their homelands, which have tried to use the *propiska* (residence permit) system to block their return.[35] In Crimea, democracy has worked against Tatar minority rights and interstate peace.[36]

At times nondisplaced minority groups have also experienced hostility. Jews are enjoying a cultural rebirth in the former Soviet Union. But if they are now spared most official anti-Semitism, they now experience it unofficially, and the governments appear to pay this little heed. Many Jews, therefore, continue to be doubtful about the tenability of a civic identity within post-Soviet states.

---

[35]Helsinki Watch, *Punished Peoples of the Soviet Union: The Continuing Legacy of Stalin's Deportations* (New York: Helsinki Watch, September 1991).
[36]Serge Schmemann, "Crimea Parliament Votes to Back Independence from Ukraine," *New York Times* (hereafter *NYT*), 6 May 1992.

SURVIVALISM IN THE BALTIC STATES

Baltic nationalists range from moderates (the most inclusive as regards immigrant groups) to extremists (the most exclusive and ready to discriminate against immigrant groups). A rule of thumb, however, is that the more the primary ethnic group has felt threatened demographically by the Soviet-promoted influx of other ethnic groups, the more likely it is to erect legal barriers in the new or renewed state.

Lithuanians look back bitterly to historical Soviet deportations and domination and to violence against them as late as January and July of 1991. A cosmopolitan expert on comparative literature pointed to the statue of Aleksandr Pushkin in central Vilnius and told me that "Pushkin should be moved to the outskirts, leaving only Lithuanian cultural figures in the center. It represents the Russian cultural oppression of Lithuania." She asked angrily another time why I and my Estonian colleague showed so much concern for the resident Poles. Why were we so concerned, when it is "we Lithuanians who have suffered so much"? The identity of ethnic Lithuanian nationalists (and no doubt for nationalists in other republics) is the identity of martyrs abandoned by the West to suffer at the hands of the Soviet oppressor.[37]

Lithuania had been spared the huge influx of immigrants from Russia that inundated Estonia and Latvia in connection with the growth of Moscow-controlled heavy industry in the two republics. Of the population of 3,728,000 in 1989, 80 percent was Lithuanian. The other 20 percent is made up of Russians (9 percent), Poles (7 percent), and smaller proportions of Belorussians, Jews, and other ethnic groups.[38] Because of their strong majority, ethnic Lithuanians did not fear extinction as did the smaller indigenous majority populations of Estonia and Latvia. As a result, the Lithuanian Supreme Council passed an interim citizenship law of 3 November 1989, which gave the option of citizenship to all permanent residents of Lithuania, regardless of length of residency, who registered their assent to citizenship within a two-year period. Fewer than 2 percent of non-Lithuanians remained noncitizens.

The Supreme Council replaced the interim citizenship law with the law of 10 December 1991. The 1991 law recognizes as citizens those who had been citizens of Lithuania before 15 June 1940 and their

[37]Roger Peterson, report to a conference on Soviet cultural studies, Columbia University, 10 April 1992.
[38]Figures on demography cited from Michael Mandelbaum, ed., *The Rise of Nations in the Soviet Union* (New York: Council on Foreign Relations, 1991), in Olcott, "The Slide into Disunion," 340.

children and grandchildren, and also permanent residents under certain conditions.[39] Applicants not qualifying automatically for citizenship must wait ten years for naturalization, have legal employment or a legal income, know Lithuanian and provisions of the constitution, and take an oath of allegiance to the republic. Because of the previous two-year opportunity for automatic citizenship upon registration, the new ten-year residency requirement has nowhere near the impact of even the three-year requirement in Estonia, much less the sixteen-year requirement of the Latvian draft law.

The national survival of Latvia and Estonia was much more endangered than was Lithuania's. Latvia, after all, is about 52 percent ethnic Latvian, and Estonia about 62 percent ethnic Estonian. The political reaction of indigenous majorities in these two formerly occupied states has been to appeal to principles of continuity from "pre-occupation" laws and citizenship. These curtail the rights to citizenship of postannexation immigrants and their children.

The citizenship laws passed or in process follow the principle of automatic citizenship for citizens and residents in the republics at the time of the Soviet invasion in 1940, and their descendants. Of the three Baltic republics, only Latvia (since it lifted the ban on 27 November 1991) did not ban dual citizenship. According to Latvian draft legislative guidelines, citizens as of 17 June 1940 or their descendants qualify for citizenship.

For others, sixteen years of residency are required, save in special cases of meritorious service to the republic. Conditions for naturalization are proof of sixteen years' residency in Latvia, knowledge of the Latvian constitution, readiness to swear allegiance to the Republic of Latvia, and knowledge of spoken Latvian.[40] The 1989 census reports that only a quarter of non-Latvians in the republic speak Latvian, hence

---

[39]Citizenship is automatic for those who became residents between 9 January 1919 and 15 June 1940 and their children and grandchildren, as long as they were residing in Lithuania on 10 December 1991. Most children born of at least one Lithuanian citizen gained Lithuanian citizenship, as well as children born in Lithuania to stateless parents. Republic of Lithuania, Law on Citizenship, 10 December 1991, effective 11 December 1991; Supreme Council of the Republic of Lithuania Resolution on the Procedure for Implementing the Republic of Lithuania Law on Citizenship, 10 July 1991, and its liberal, detailed ways of being considered a permanent resident in Lithuania.

[40]Also eligible, under the Law on Citizenship of 23 August 1919, are those residing in Latvia prior to 1 August 1914 and their descendants, if they have learned a conversational level of Latvian. Also eligible are persons who are granted citizenship by the Supreme Council Presidium on the basis of their "outstanding accomplishments on behalf of the Republic of Latvia." Draft bill passing first reading 9 October 1991, Helsinki Watch fax 17 October 1991.

wide anxiety over the language requirement.[41] All residents, whether or not eligible for citizenship, may stay on as residents.

Along with the citizenship laws, language requirements for citizenship and occupation are deemed essential by their authors if the Latvian ethnic nation is to be preserved. The Russians, who are called members of "the imperial nationality" by one Latvian scholar, do not receive the state assistance for cultural renewal afforded by the Latvian government to resident Ukrainians, Belorussians, Lithuanians, Estonians, Poles, Jews, and so on.[42]

Not all Latvian supporters of a residence requirement would go so far as Visvaldis Latsis of the Movement for the National Independence of Latvia. He explained that he supports citizenship only for those eligible prior to the Soviet occupation, plus their descendants. But past repressions and deportations and present demographic threats of a non-Latvian majority weigh heavily. Chairman Maris Grinblats and Secretary Anita Brence of the Latvian Committee pointed out the statistics of a declining Latvian presence in their own republic. "We were 75.5 percent in 1935, and are no more than half now," they said. Young Deputy Einars Cilinckis, an environmentalist, also talked of the need for legal measures like the residence requirement and language laws to guarantee the survival of the Latvian nation.[43]

Soviet citizenship disappeared along with the union, and for most Russian-speakers in Estonia, republic citizenship was lost as well. According to the refurbished 1938 citizenship law, residents who held citizenship of Estonia on 16 June 1940 (the date of Soviet occupation) acquire Estonian citizenship automatically, along with their descendants, spouses and their children, and a few other special categories of residents.[44]

[41]HRW92, 507–8.

[42]Conversations with Juris Prikulis of the Latvian Academy of Science, in Riga, 4–5 October 1991, and New York City, 29 April 1992.

[43]Interviews: Riga, 5 October 1991 and 4 October 1991, respectively.

[44]An estimated one hundred thousand Russians automatically became Russian nationals for this reason or because they qualified under the revived 1938 citizenship law, as descendants of persons who were citizens of prewar Estonia. The additional special categories automatically qualifying for citizenship include illegitimate children of noncitizen mothers if the father is a citizen and recognizes them, children who are adopted by Estonian citizens, and children born of stateless (and not formerly Soviet) persons in Estonia. Law on Citizenship of 1938, English translation, as amended 11 December 1939 and in effect 16 June 1940, reinstated by resolution of 6 November 1991 and amended by the enabling resolution of the Supreme Council (previous parliament) of 26 February 1992, Articles 3–5; Ministry of Foreign Affairs of the Republic of Estonia Informpress, "Estonian Law on Citizenship"; Resolution of 26 February 1992, points 1, 15.

For the rest of the population of Estonia the path is naturalization. Naturalization requirements include two years of residence before applying plus an additional year's residence in a waiting period before citizenship is granted, knowledge of the Estonian language (a difficult hurdle for many Russian-speakers), and the swearing of an oath of allegiance to the Republic of Estonia and the Constitutional State Order.[45] Exempted from the two-year residence and one-year waiting period are those persons who applied for citizenship prior to the elections to the Estonian Congress in 1990.[46]

The starting date for residency was 30 March 1990.[47] Hence the earliest aliens might apply for citizenship was 1 April 1992, and the earliest they might receive it was 1 April 1993.[48] Not counting children and nonethnic Estonians already citizens, this left about 30 percent of the population—440,000 adult persons—legally disfranchised[49] in the elections of 20 September 1992 to the new parliament, the Riigikogu (State Assembly). When the Riigikogu met on 5 October for the first time in 52 years, Russian-speakers were unrepresented among its 101 deputies.[50]

Estonian defenders of the citizenship law cite the decline in the proportion of Estonians from 88.2 percent in 1939 to 61.5 percent in the 1989 census, with a declining share since. Both the massive immigration and the preindependence campaigns for the primacy of Russian language and culture at the expense of the Estonian culture "together aroused great fears among Estonians, who believed their cultural annihilation to be imminent."[51]

CENTRAL ASIA: TOO FAR FROM HELSINKI?

Bishkek, Kirghizstan, is a lot farther than Moscow is from Helsinki, the center for the CSCE. But Kirghizstan and the four other Central Asian republics are members of the CSCE. They are pledged to uphold the

---

[45]Law on Citizenship, Article 6; Resolution of 26 February 1992, point 15.
[46]Law on Citizenship, Article 7; Resolution of 26 February 1992, points 5 and 6.
[47]Resolution of 26 February 1992, point 5.
[48]Excerpts from the 24 July 1992 "Letter from Mr. Manitski to Mme Lalumiere," courtesy Estonian Foreign Ministry.
[49]*Izvestiia*, 22 September 1992, in *FBIS-SOV-92-189*, 29 September 1992.
[50]Citizenship is required to vote in national elections. Estonian Foreign Ministry, "How the Riigikogu Is Elected" and "Republic of Estonia: Riigikogu Electoral Law," 6 April 1992, with amendments and supplements approved by the Supreme Council on 18 June 1992, unofficial translation, courtesy Estonian Foreign Ministry.
[51]Riina Kionka, "Who Should Become a Citizen of Estonia," *RFE/RL*, no. 39 (1991): 23–24.

equal human rights of all, under the 1975 Helsinki Final Act and later agreements on the humanitarian dimension, as well as through their UN membership and UN treaty obligations. But trouble has been brewing for ethnic relations and rights. In the 1980s, Russians had already begun to feel unwelcome and to leave the area.[52] Beginning in 1985, the region became the scene of many ethnic confrontations, usually among Muslims.

After joining the CIS in December 1991, most of the area remained under regimes headed by ex-communists who were semidemocratic at best. The exception was relatively democratic Kirghizstan, which enjoys considerable freedom under President Askar Akayev. He has taken pains to head off any repetition of the Uzbek-Kirghiz violence in Osh, Fergana Valley, which broke out 4 June 1990 after Kirghiz settlers had been assigned housing plots the previous January on land belonging to an Uzbek collective farm and which claimed 230 lives with 91 missing. The Kirghiz government responded with emergency aid, enforcement measures, and talks between Presidents Islam Karimov of Uzbekistan and Akayev of Kirghizstan to head off violence and settle grievances.[53]

Central Asia has been rife with contradictions, including steadfast adherence to the idea of a union, late-blooming separatism, and the growing influence of orthodox and fundamentalist Islam. There is far from one identity either in the region as a whole or within any republic—and least of all a single fundamentalist identity.

The quite young, Russian-speaking Kirghiz Deputy Timurbek Kenenbaev said that as positive as Kirghizstan feels about keeping up economic and political relations with Russia, of which they voluntarily became a part in the 1860s, they still remember that Russians massacred one hundred thousand Kirghiz during a rebellion in 1916. Later, Russians occupied controlling second posts from the party bureaus on down. The economic collapse of the country caused Kenenbaev to anticipate independence even before the August coup. Kirghizstan under President Akayev, the democratically elected physicist and former head of the Kirghiz Communist party's Science Department, seeks maximum possible technical expertise from the United States and elsewhere. The present leadership of Kirghizstan, one gathers, plans to keep the country a

[52]Karklins showed this in *Ethnic Relations in the USSR.*

[53]Meeting with Beksultan B. Ishimov, chairman, Committee on Defense, National Security and Crime Prevention, Parliament of Kirghizstan; Timurbek O. Kenenbaev, Committee on Legislation, Parliament of Kirghizstan; and Leonid I. Levitin, legal advisor to President Akayev of Kirghizstan, at Patterson Belknap, Webb, and Tyler, New York City, under the auspices of Scott Horton and the Sakharov Foundation, 5 May 1991.

democratic, secular republic very much interested in cooperation with all quarters. It is, however, beset with economic emergency and a potential for intercommunal ethnic conflict.[54]

Authoritative Muslim figures and scholars of Islam see historically a much greater violation of Muslim rights under communism than ever occurred under czarism. The message seems to be that fundamentalism is not inevitable, though it feeds on protest and a sense of discrimination against Muslims and their religion. In former Soviet Central Asia this discrimination includes experiences of religious suppression and isolation,[55] political inequality within the union, economic exploitation, catastrophic unemployment connected with high birthrates and low outmigration, and heedless infliction of an environmental and health catastrophe.[56] Islam, then, is not necessarily exclusive or aggressive in response to discrimination and other wrongs. Many reports from various parts of the world, too many to be coincidental, link various signs of resurgent Islamic fundamentalism with real grievances by its adherents and loss of legitimacy of alternative identities and loyalties.[57]

The states of Central Asia are likely to see their interests lying in close

[54]Conversation with Deputy Kenenbaev; meeting with him and the other two representatives mentioned in note 53, as well as Ambassador Djoumakadyr Atabekov, that day accredited to the United Nations. Arranged by Ed Kline, New York City, 6 May 1992.
[55]"We have many believers in the republic," said Turkmen First Secretary Gapurov, hence the need to keep in mind the broadcasts from Iran on Islamic themes, the "propagation of Islam," seeking "to influence the nationalist struggle and to undermine the ideological and political unity of the Soviet people." D'Encausse, *Confiscated Power,* 305.
[56]Andrei Polonskii, "Islam in the USSR: Its Way of Life and Politics," *Khristianskaia demokratiia* (bulletin of the Christian Democrat International in Eastern Europe), no. 15 (September–October 1991): 14–23; T. Saidbaev, "Rossii ne grozit islamskaia revoliutsiia," *Izvestiia,* 28 November 1991; "The President of the Islamic Center: There Should Be No Privileged Religion," *Pravda,* 3 December 1991, condensed in *Current Digest of the Soviet Press* 43, no. 48 (1991): 13. Numbers in the age group fifteen to twenty-nine increased 10 percent during 1970–89 in Russia, but *237 percent* in Uzbekistan. Cited by Michael Paul Sacks, Harriman Institute, Columbia University, 1 May 1992.
[57]Interview of T. Saidbaev by A. Portanskii, "Rossii ne grozit islamskaia revoliutsiia." Similarly, the growth of Algerian and other North African fundamentalism seems clearly linked with the corruption and failures of the once bright promise of Algerian revolutionary socialism. An Islamic studies center in east-central France seeking to create a Western Islamic identity has to contend with what the secretary general of the Union of Islamic Organizations in France calls a sense of xenophobia against Muslims and exclusion of Muslims from its society. "Many young Moslems who are born and educated in France feel rejected by France, said Secretary-General Ben Mansour." Alan Riding, "Europe's Homebred Imams, Preaching Tolerance," *NYT,* 24 January 1992. Lamis Andoni, "Arabs Foresee Declining Prospects for Democracy," *CSM,* 23 January 1992; Youssief M. Ibrahim, "Algerians, Angry with the Past, Divide over Their Future," *NYT,* 19 January 1992; Jill Smolowe, "An Alarming No Vote; The Fundamentalists' Big Gain Is More a Protest against Socialist Rule than a Mandate for an Islamic Republic," *Time,* 13 January 1992, 28; Mamoun Fandy, "Islamic Victory in Algeria Is a Harbinger," *CSM,* 9 January 1992.

ties with the United States and Europe, but also selectively with other states in the area: Afghanistan, Iran, and Turkey. Persian-speaking, war-torn Tajikistan will be the most likely of all the republics of Central Asia to have close ties with Iran and Afghan fundamentalists. This is especially so if the present Islamist-Democratic opposition coalition overthrows the government of former communists and if the Islamists then come out on top.

Uzbekistan, Kazakhstan, and Turkmenia may well look more to Turkey. They are substituting the Latin alphabet for the Cyrillic script forced on them by the Soviets. Kazakhs and Kirghiz may nurture contacts with China, especially Xinjiang province, where kin minorities such as Uigurs live. Trade is picking up between China and Kirghizstan on their quite open border. The "battle of the typewriters"—import competition between Iranian-made machines with Arabic script and Turkish-made ones with Latin script—makes good press copy; it is likely that both models will sell in Central Asia.

The area will be crisscrossed with Iranian, Arabic, Turkic, and Western influences and models. New regional and national identities will continue to form, responsive to how others react to local statements of aspirations and interests. As yet there is no guarantee that rapid Slavic out-migration will not continue, or even that Muslims will feel comfortable with one another, without enlightened and decisive conflict resolution and leadership from both inside and outside the area.[58] Renewed economic cooperation and recognition of an interdependence among members of the elusive CIS will favor diversity and peace in Central Asia and Russia's influence there.

WHAT IS RUSSIA? WHO ARE RUSSIANS?

To what entity do Russians owe loyalty as soldier or sailor or apparatchik? Do they miss the sense of pride they once felt when Soviet Olympic gold medal winners of all ethnic backgrounds stood proudly for the Soviet anthem? Will the hammer and sickle, still for many a revered flag, ever again fly over anything but protest demonstrations?[59] Have Rus-

---

[58]Claire Messina, "Prospects for Compelled Migrations on the Territory of the Soviet Union," unpublished paper, Harriman Institute, Columbia University, 1992.

[59]The leadership of the former Soviet Union, of Russia, and of Moscow disavowed the celebration of the October Revolution, two months earlier, yet people still turned out for unofficial celebrations on 7 November, the day after Russian President Yeltsin decreed a ban on the Communist party in Russia. Reports in *Pravda,* 9 November 1991, and *CDSP,* 11 December 1991, 1–5.

sians lost forever the comfortable feeling of being a Soviet citizen throughout the realm? The Russian ethnic group does, in fact, most closely identify with the old union. Nearly three-quarters of Russians polled would still vote for a renewed USSR.[60]

The CIS will not soon, if ever, provide a compensating civic identity, given its apparent transience and its limited powers.[61] Vera Filatova and her husband, Nikolai, represent many Russians and other Soviet people who sense a multiple loss of identity. There is confusion over values and traditions:

"Should one try to pay a friend for what used to be a favor . . . and how much in this time of economic madness? Even addressing people on the street is no longer that simple. Should you call them comrade or by the old name *gospodin,* or citizen?" She does not dare predict what might happen next in this country she can no longer name. "What country do I live in? Hmm, that's a tough question—Russia I guess." As for the commonwealth, she says she can't even bring herself to pronounce the unwieldy initials, ess-en-gay.[62]

Ethnic Russians have been reclaiming old place names, old holidays, their Christmas (in 1991 the first one officially celebrated since the Bolshevik takeover in 1917), their Orthodox church. This leads non-Orthodox Christians to wonder about the standing of their churches, Jews to wonder about possible outbursts of anti-Semitism, and neighboring states to wonder about a possible new Russian empire.[63] "The open incorporation of Orthodoxy into the Russian national identity not only further de-Sovietizes Russia, but further separates the Russians from other Soviet [sic] peoples who have their own cultural and religious legacies."[64]

Russia in these times of economic travail and indigenous minority separatism experiences what Roman Szporluk rightly calls "the complex

---

[60]Of Russians polled, 72 percent support the idea of the restoration of the Soviet Union as a union of sovereign states linked at least economically and politically; a plurality of 45 percent agree to military union also. Boris Grushin, "Nazad, k SSSR?" *Novoe vremia,* no. 14 (1992): 19.

[61]Goble, "Forget the Soviet Union," 57.

[62]Anne Garrells reporting from Moscow on National Public Radio, 18 January 1992.

[63]Dmitrii Radyshevskii, "Reporting on Religion in Russia," Kennan Institute, Meeting Report, 13 January 1992. "Statement to the Moscow CSCE Conference on the Human Dimension Presented by the World Conference on Soviet Jewry, Va'ad Confederation of Jewish Organizations and Communities (USSR)," 17 September 1991.

[64]Szporluk, "The Imperial Legacy," 15. See also Serge Schmemann, "Spirit of Christmas Calls Again to Russians," *NYT,* 8 January 1992: the photo shows a beaming Yeltsin—who "says he is not a believer but respects religious traditions"—shaking hands with Patriarch Aleksii II at a service on Russian Orthodox Christmas.

phenomenon of Russian nationalism."[65] The analysis of a recent public opinion poll in *Rossiiskaia gazeta* concluded: "An awareness of the principles of the new Russian statehood is forming with difficulty. What is Russia within the borders of the former RSFSR?"[66] Is it the core of an eventually restored Soviet Union or Russian empire including Finland, as ultranationalists such as Liberal Democratic party leader Vladimir Zhirinovsky advocates? Is it pre-1954 Russia, including the Crimea, as the centrist conservatives and Russian nationalists seek?

The view of the Yeltsin administration seemed to be: preserve a semblance of the post-1954 Russian Federation, with concessions to local autonomy, lest autonomous republics and regions follow the lead of separatist Tatarstan and Chechnia, which stayed out of the new Federal Treaty in 1992.[67]

Ukraine's overwhelming vote for independence on 1 December 1991 ended hopes of Yeltsin and other Russians for a new, confederated union. The new Commonwealth of Independent States, affirmed on 8 December in Minsk and 21 December in Almaty, provides no significant common identity. Now Yeltsin would settle for the Russian Federation, as is, within the commonwealth that it dominates. Its sheer mass and former association with empire keep non-Russian states on the alert against any new Russian imperialism.

Each case of would-be self-determination must be examined, Marjorie Balzer cautions in Chapter 3, in the context of history, the "center-periphery dynamic," and the indigenous leaders. In order of increasing secession-mindedness, Balzer ranked Yakutia (the Yakut-Sakha republic), Buryatia, and Tyva (annexed from China in 1944 and shaken by anti-Russian riots in 1989). She placed Tatarstan and Chechen-Ingushetia as the two most independent-minded of all, a judgment that has been borne out by their opting for separation, pending separate treaty arrangements with Moscow, and by their nonparticipation in the near-miracle new federal treaty signed by all other autonomous republics, provinces, and regions, pending their own separate treaties with

[65]Szporluk, "The Imperial Legacy," 13.
[66]Leontii Byzov, "V predverii reform," *Rossiiskaia gazeta,* 13 December 1991.
[67]On fears in this regard, see interview with Executive Secretary Oleg Rumiantsev of the RSFSR Constitutional Commission, "Natsional'naia politika: Poslednii shans vozrodit' edinuiu gosudarstvennost' Rossii," *Rossiiskaia gazeta,* 15 January 1992; talk by Rumiantsev at Freedom House, New York City, 24 January 1992; *Konstitutsionnyi vestnik,* Moscow, Konstitutsionnaia komissia RSFSR, nos. 8 and 9, October and December 1991. The new constitution, which excluded the Federal Treaty, barely passed in the referendum of 12 December 1993.

Moscow. Of those voting in the Tatarstan referendum, 61.4 percent favored independence in a population that is 48 percent Tatar, 43 percent Russian, and 9 percent other non-Tatar inhabitants.[68]

At stake in the twenty-one autonomous indigenous republics are (1) the future of Russian majorities (mostly) and minorities; (2) the local and central shares in rich natural resources, from Yakutia's diamonds, gold, gas, and oil to Tyumen's large oil reserves and access to Eastern Siberia; (3) the political fate of the Russian leadership, should they lose more of Russia's territory to secession; and (4) peace in Russia, already shattered locally by the conflict between North Ossetians and Ingush seeking to reclaim land in North Ossetia on which they lived before Stalin deported them.[69] The Ossetians appealed to the Soviet and Russian republic governments for protection.[70] Ingush encroachments led to hostilities between Ingush and North Ossetians in November 1992, forcing the Russians to get involved as peacemakers.[71]

Late in 1991, the Chechen and Ingush joined other once-deported Muslim groups—Kabardin, Balkar, Karachay, Cherkess, Abkhaz, along with Ossetians and others—in a meeting of the Third Congress of Mountain Peoples of the Caucasus, which vowed to form its own confederation of independent states.[72] Russia is regaining versions of its identity (which always *was* complex). A shared identity as a multiethnic state remains elusive, even as some of Russia's eighty-eight republics and regions outstrip the center in their pace of economic reform.

UKRAINE: AN INTERNATIONALIST STATE?

By the end of 1991 "communism was dead" in Ukraine as an ideology of state, "but in its place was a romantic nationalism, which—just as

[68] Ann Sheehy, "Tatarstan Asserts Its Sovereignty," *RFE/RL*, no. 14 (1992): 4. Population figures are from Goskomstat SSSR, *Natsional'nyi sostav naseleniia SSSR* (Moscow: Finance and Statistics, 1990) (hereafter Goskomstat SSSR), cited by Robert Lewis, Harriman Institute, Columbia University, 1 May 1992.

[69] The census of 1989 counted 956,879 Chechens and 237,438 Ingush, making up 71 percent of the inhabitants of the area, along with 23 percent Russians and 6 percent other nonindigenous residents. Marjorie Mandelstam Balzer, "Turmoil in Russia's Mini-Empire," *Perspective: A Publication for the Study of Conflict, Ideology and Policy at Boston University* 2, no. 3 (January 1992): 2–3, 7; demographics from Goskomstat SSSR.

[70] HRW92, 539–41.

[71] Human Rights Watch, *World Report 1993* (New York: Human Rights Watch, 1993), 234. For other information on human rights and ethnic conflict in the former Soviet Union, see ibid., 228–51.

[72] Balzer, "Turmoil in Russia's Mini-Empire," 2.

communism was supposed to do—was going to lead Ukraine to its glittering future."[73] This Ukrainian nationalism was inclusive. It nurtured a multiethnic national identity across large parts of the Ukraine. Its government asserted independence as the shared experience of Ukrainians, Russian Jews, Belarussians, Moldovans, Poles, and other ethnic groups who rallied around a common civic identity.[74]

The Ukrainian poet and philologist Oksana Zabuzhko told a Kennan Institute audience in Washington, D.C., on 16 April 1992 that "the real problem nowadays is that of resuming our identity in a very broad sense. I think—I hope—that Ukraine has rid itself of the different forces which were imposed on it and did not permit it to be itself. That's my point: being oneself." The "oneself" of the post-Soviet identity which prevailed into 1992 was not the "oneself" of the Ukrainians shooting at Babyi Yar, or any other exclusivism. Rather it is an identity regained in the very broad sense of membership in a multiethnic nation based on a geographic approximation of historic Ukraine.

The decree of Ukrainian sovereignty on 16 July 1990 pledged "to respect the national rights of all peoples";[75] so far, that appears to be the case. The dwindling Jewish minority received the satisfaction of a solemn speech by President Leonid Kravchuk at Babyi Yar to commemorate the Holocaust and to apologize for Ukrainians' participation in it.

Transcarpathia, the western part of Ukraine annexed in 1945 from Hungary, seeks an agreement with Kiev over a form of autonomy that will guarantee the rights of both Ruthenians and Magyars, in a province with "special self-governing administrative status" and a "Magyar national district" within it.[76] Yet another test of Ukrainian inclusivism will be the resolution of confrontations between the Uniate and Orthodox churches over property the Orthodox received from the repressed Uniates under Stalin.

It is up to leaders of Ukraine and Russia to resist fanning nationalist hostility in their approach to the issue of control over armed forces and the Black Sea fleet, significant portions of which identify with the commonwealth and/or Russia. The ticklish situation in Crimea stirs separatism among the Russian majority there. Meanwhile, returning

[73]Robert Cullen, "Report from Ukraine," *The New Yorker,* 27 January 1992, 57.

[74]*Minority Rights: Problems, Parameters, and Patterns in the CSCE Context* (Washington, D.C.: Commission on Security and Cooperation in Europe), 75.

[75]Ibid., 82.

[76]Alfred A. Reisch, "Transcarpathia's Hungarian Minority and the Autonomy Issue," *RFE/RL,* no. 6 (1992): 17–23.

Tatars look to Ukraine for protection of their right to resettle. If all Tatars returned, they would still comprise only 11 percent of the population. But among Russians—67 percent of the Crimean population— there is discomfort in their view of the Tatar aspirants to land and shelter. Concerned Russians look to nationalists in Russia for support.[77]

CONCLUSION

Among the legacies of communism is what Joseph Berliner (see Chapter 16) dubs a "social void." The social void means actually a double legacy for national identity, as for other aspects of post-Soviet life. There is the legacy of deinstitutionalization under communism and, as Berliner puts it, "the legacy of that legacy," the strain on national and social identities owing to the rapid and economically catastrophic collapse of communism.

Communist rule crushed traditional institutions of civil society and open, legitimate channels of expression and negotiation over ethnic group rights and aspirations. Communism nurtured yet also violated ethnic identity and equality. It shut down channels for pragmatic compromise among contending ethnic groups. Communism's preference for central planning to the exclusion of any legal market brought on an economic decline. That economic legacy to successor states aggravates interethnic and center-periphery tensions. Communism left behind a mixed bag of leaders—some stubborn centrists, and some who are changing into more or less gifted, more or less democratic, and more or less peacemaking nationalists.

Communism's collapse, "the legacy of that legacy" of social void, has shaken or destroyed of individuals' social identities that once were anchored in secure occupations, Soviet ideological beliefs of a defused but still distinctive kind, and Soviet citizenship. In the context of upheaval and transition to new social identities, ethnic group identity provides a haven amid the hardships and uncertainties and loss of unity. Ethnic identity protects against total desperation; it provides a welcome rallying point in times of threats to interests posed by economic calamity and the resultant breakdown of such social identities as occupation, party membership, citizenship, and Soviet nationality.

[77]Cullen gives a firsthand account of this in "Report from Ukraine," 53–56. See also Roman Solchanyk, "Ukrainian-Russian Confrontation over the Crimea," *RFE/RL,* no. 8 (1992): 26–30; demographics for 1989, from Goskomstat SSSR.

The outcome of communism's double legacy is at once an ethnic identity crisis favoring increased tensions and a civic void in institutions for peaceful resolution of such tensions—over self-determination, power, citizenship, and property. Nationalist assertiveness in the former Soviet Union, however, does not justify ethnic-national determinism. Ethnic identity and the nationalism it fosters take a variety of forms depending on the context and responses to them. Preoccupied with ethnic conflict, we may be tempted to ignore the hopeful signs of multi-ethnic unity and reconciliation across large areas of the former Soviet Union. We should remember how far Russia's policies are from Serbia's brutal attempts to unite all its compatriots. But then Soviet Slavs were spared the terrible vendettas and massacres marking relations among the southern Slavs.

Ethnic identity in the former Soviet Union is not something preordained by human nature or by tradition alone. It is being shaped by the difficult social legacy of communism and by the perils and opportunities of the independence brought on by that legacy. Its mix of inclusivism and exclusivism, peace and conflict, ethnic and civic identity will reflect not only setting and tradition but also the choices of political leaders both at home and abroad in their responses to the deep general crisis of post-Soviet society.

3

●━0━●━0━●━0━●━0━●━0━●━0━●━0━●━0━●━0━●━0━●━0━●━0━●━0━●━0━●━0━●━0━●━0━●━0━●━0━●━0

From ethnicity to nationalism:
turmoil in the Russian mini-empire

MARJORIE MANDELSTAM BALZER

The breakup of the Soviet Union into fifteen separate states left academic and policy analysts scrambling to learn lessons from a Soviet "nationalities policy" gone awry. Was the Soviet empire like or unlike other empires? Were regional economic fissures more salient than previously understood? Were historical and cultural substrata predictably reasserting themselves after a mere hiatus of fifty to seventy-five years? Was the development of nationalism, out of a relatively more inchoate, unfocused ethnic consciousness, a predictable phenomenon? As scholars take positions on these critical issues, and as deconstructivist or reconstructivist post-Soviet politics emerge, a further question is being urgently asked. Will the Russian Federation itself survive?

My anthropological approach to Russian Federation survival is to review the political and cultural history of five major republics—Chechnia, Tatarstan, Tyva, Buryatia, and the Sakha republic (Yakutia) (Figure 3.1)—in order to demonstrate the noninevitability of secession movements. Rather than assuming that Russia is an analogue of the Soviet Union, or that Russia's nationality politics consistently resemble the imperial polarizing style of past multiethnic empires, I suspend judgment until specific cases can be described and analyzed. I consider the long-term legacies of communism and short-term aftermaths of Soviet collapse to be intertwined, and both to be potentially positive and negative from the perspective of non-Russian peoples. This view derives from the position that the Soviet so-called system fell apart both "from above" and "from below." Nationalism, only part of the collapse, was both repressed and stimulated historically by Soviet policies, which were man-

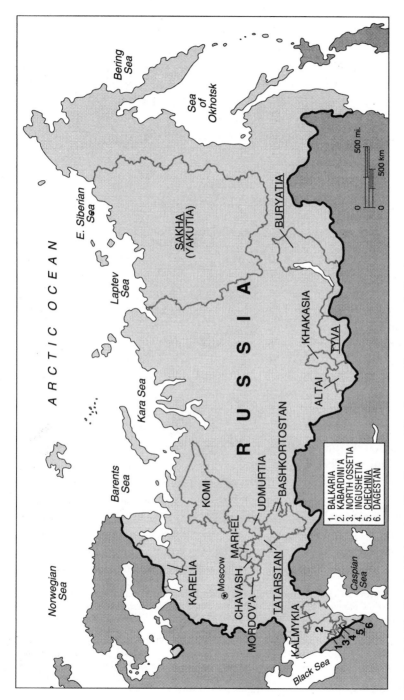

Figure 3.1. The Russian Federation. The five republics featured here are underlined.

ifested differently in various regions, contrary to the superficial assertions of Soviet propaganda and some analysts.[1]

Toward the end of Gorbachev's rule, Yeltsin-leaning intellectuals
criticized Gorbachev's nationalities policies by sarcastically suggesting,
"If he keeps this up, he will have nothing left but Moscow." Their
flippancy revealed an underlying savvy: Various national bids for partial
sovereignty or full independence have been intertwined in the center-
periphery dynamic. Given such complex interactions, each case must be
examined in historical context. Claimed injustices must be reviewed,
indigenous leaders heard, and interrepublic relations assessed before
generalizations can be made about whether a given Russian federal
republic is likely to become a secessionist "nationalist" domino.

One of the conceptual linchpins of any argument stressing center-
periphery interaction is the issue of political polarization and its accompanying psychological ramifications in relation to nationalism. When
key crystallizing political events cause people who had previously
thought of themselves as mildly aware of their ethnic identity to become
dramatically defensive and passionately angered, precisely these people
become the fulcrum of more radical brands of nationalism. Issues of
leadership, land claims, historical grievances, refugees, national chauvinism, and popular front strategy then become mixed to create a potentially incendiary interethnic dynamic. The most obvious cases of nationalist crystallization in recent Soviet history include aftermaths of the
violent April 1989 repression of a peaceful Tbilisi demonstration in
Georgia, the January 1990 troop occupation of Baku in Azerbaijan, and
the January 1991 television tower massacre in Vilnius, Lithuania.

A second, more subtle conceptual issue involves the word "periphery." Any periphery clearly implies the existence of a center, which in
both the Soviet and the Russian context has been Moscow. Yet the
degree to which the inhabitants of "peripheries" accept a marginal view
of themselves varies, by individual, by group, and by situation. Some
prefer the word "frontier," seeing themselves as vanguards and a special

[1]For fieldwork support, I am grateful to the International Research and Exchanges Board
and to the Sakha Ministry of Culture. To sample perspectives on the Soviet demise, see
Edward L. Keenan, "Rethinking the U.S.S.R., Now that It's Over," *New York Times*, 8
September 1991, 3; Paul Goble, "The Imperial Endgame: Nationality Problems and the
Soviet Future," in Harley Balzer, ed., *Five Years that Shook the World* (Boulder, Colo.:
Westview Press, 1991), 91–104; Bohdan Nahaylo and Victor Swoboda, *The Soviet
Disunion: A History of the Nationalities Problem in the USSR* (New York: Free Press,
1990); Marjorie Mandelstam Balzer, "Nationalism in the Soviet Union: One Anthropo-
logical View," *Journal of Soviet Nationalities* 1 (Fall 1990): 4–22.

Table 3.1. *The Russian Federation*

Republics asserting independence and negotiating bilateral treaties with Russia	Republics signing the Federal Treaty, bilateral treaties	Ethnic-based regions, districts
Chechnia	Adyge	Agin-Buryat
Tatarstan	Altai	Ust-Orda
	Balkaria	Buryat
	Bashkortostan	Chukotsk
	Buryatia	Evenk
	Chavash (Chuvashia)	Eveno-Bytantaisk
	Dagestan	Evrei
	Ingushetia	Khanty-Mansi
	Kabardinia	Komi-Permiak
	Kalmykia (Khalmg Tangch)	Koriak
	Karachay-Cherkessia	Nenets
	Karelia	Yamalo-Nenets
	Khakasia	Dolgan-Nenets
	Komi	Taimyr (Nganasan)
	Mari-El (Mari)	
	Mordva	
	North Ossetia	
	Sakha (Yakutia)	
	Tyva	
	Udmurtia	

Sources: "Federativnyi dogovor," ITAR-TASS International Service, 14 March 1992; Ann Sheehy, "The Republics of the Russian Federation," *RFE/RL Research Report*, 5 June 1992, 14. Please note that separate legislatures for Kabardinia and Balkaria were created after the March 1992 Federal Treaty was signed. The Eveno-Bytantaisk district *(raion)* was created within the Sakha republic as a homeland for the Even people in 1989. Several German districts are being formed within Russia, and Cossack districts in the North Caucasus and Siberia are being considered.

breed within a given political context. Others, who are not at the borderlands yet still live far from Moscow, are not in a position to see themselves so romantically. They must deal more pragmatically with their newfound emergence from marginalization into multilateralism and sovereignty, or at least sovereignty claims. A fruitful exercise for readers is to shift their focus from analytical Moscow-centrism to sympathy with, even empathy for, those in periphery or frontier positions. Far from condoning radical, chauvinist, militaristic brands of nationalism, this plea is intended to fracture one's perspective into multiple views in order to create a more in-depth analysis of what is "central" and "peripheral."[2]

[2] My view of nationalism is situational and variable, so that emphasis is placed on multiple forms of nationalism, only some of which are negative and chauvinist. Cf. Eric Hobs-

Eighteen ethnically based republics signed the March 1992 Russian Federal Treaty, consolidating a status upgrade for five republics: the Adyge, Gorno-Altai (now Altai), Ingush (without Chechnia), Karachay-Cherkess, and Khakass. (See Table 3.1.) About thirty-five non-Russian ethnically based political entities (republics and districts, some trying to upgrade their status or divide) are under the jurisdiction of the Federal Treaty. However, non-Russian ethnic groups within Russia are considerably more numerous. Depending on how they are counted, 126 non-Russian groups were represented within Russia in the 1989 census, and some researchers have revised this to about 160.[3] The non-Russian population in Russia, based on the 1989 census, is approximately 30 million, or about 20 percent of the population of Russia (147 million).

The five cases outlined here are in roughly decreasing order of secession-mindedness and turmoil, although the first two cases diverge in approaches and the placement of the last two, relatively quiet cases, could possibly be switched. (See Table 3.2.) Other cases could easily be incorporated into this continuum. As the center-periphery dynamic is constantly changing, some of these other cases—for example, Dagestan, Bashkortostan, Karelia, Mordva, and the republic of Komi—are increasingly salient.

THE CHECHEN REPUBLIC

In the incendiary North Caucasus tier, the Chechen Republic was joined to Ingushetia until 1992. Together they formed the Chechen-Ingush Autonomous Soviet Socialist Republic (ASSR) from 1957 until 1991.

bawm, "The Perils of the New Nationalism," *The Nation* 253 (4 November 1991): 538, 555–56; Ernest Gellner, *Nations and Nationalism* (Oxford: Basil Blackwell, 1983). Since literature on nationalism is reviewed elsewhere in this volume, a summary is not attempted here. But it is crucial to note that the dichotomy between "primordialists" and "modernists" that Anthony D. Smith has presented in *The Ethnic Origins of Nations* (Oxford: Basil Blackwell, 1986), 6–18, is too simplistic. For examples of theoretical discussions of "frontier" and "borderlands" issues, see Alfred J. Rieber, "The Reforming Tradition in Russian History," in Alfred J. Rieber and Alvin Rubinstein, eds., *Perestroika at the Crossroads* (Armonk, N.Y.: M. E. Sharpe, 1991), 3–30; Fredrik Barth, ed., *Ethnic Groups and Boundaries: The Social Organization of Culture Difference* (Boston: Little, Brown, 1969); Robert F. Berkhofer, *The White Man's Indian* (New York: Alfred Knopf, 1978); Calvin Martin, ed., *The American Indian and the Problem of History* (Oxford: Oxford University Press, 1987); Eric R. Wolf, *Europe and the People without History* (Berkeley: University of California Press, 1982).

[3] See L. M. Drobizheva, "Kazhdomu—svoi," *Rodina*, no. 11–12 (1991): 19–22; Irina Krasnopol'skaia, interview with Solomon Bruk, "128 ili 500?" *Soiuz*, no. 16 (April 1991): 14. Statistics here and below are from *Natsional'nyi sostav naseleniia SSSR* (Moscow: Finance and Statistics, 1991).

Table 3.2. *Demographic profiles*

Republic	Population	Percent
Chechen-Ingushetia	1,270,429	
Chechen	734,501	58
Ingush	163,762	13
Russians	293,771	23
Ukrainians	12,637	1
Tatarstan	3,641,742	
Tatars	1,765,404	49
Bashkirs	19,106	0.5
Chuvash	134,221	7
Russians	1,575,361	43
Tyva	308,557	
Tyvans	198,448	64
Khakassians	2,258	0.7
Russians	98,831	32
Ukrainians	2,208	0.7
Buryatia	1,038,252	
Buryats	249,525	24
Evenk	1,679	0.2
Russians	726,165	70
Ukrainians	22,868	2
Sakha (*Yakutia*)	1,094,065	
Sakha	380,242	33
Evenk	14,428	1
Russians	550,265	50
Ukrainians	77,114	7

Source: Natsional'nyi sostav naseleniia SSSR (Moscow: Finance and Statistics, 1991), from the 1989 census. Please note that the major ethnic groups associated with a given republic are included here, but not every ethnic group. Also note that the Tatar and Buryat have substantial populations living outside their republics.

The placing of the Chechen and Ingush together in an autonomous republic was culturally logical (unlike some North Caucasus political matches), for the Chechen and Ingush consider themselves as Nakh, or Nakhchuo, peoples, speaking dialects of one Nakh language (the Veinakh group of the Northeast Caucasian language branch). The Chechen and Ingush are generally less Russified, in linguistic terms and way of life, than many of the peoples of Russia. The terms "Chechen" and "Ingush" derive from Russian designations of the two groups on the basis of their main villages. The names evolved after the mid-nineteenth-century Caucasian Wars, in which the Chechen had fought against the

Russians, whereas most Ingush, sometimes called Western Chechen, sought to remain neutral.[4]

In the 1989 census, the Chechen numbered 956,879 and the Ingush 237,438, or 58 percent and 13 percent, respectively, of the republic's population. The remainder included a large Slavic population (about 25 percent), as well as other North Caucasus peoples. In the early 1990s, relations with local Cossack groups, of Russian and Ukrainian backgrounds, became so tense that several thousand of the Slavic population felt threatened enough to emigrate.

In the spring of 1992, Chechnia formally seceded from Russia, refusing to sign the Federal Treaty and voting in its newly formed parliament to fully restructure its ties to Russia. Ingushetia legally remained in Russia by signing the Federal Treaty. Critical border negotiations and decisions about state property ownership were to be resolved by 1994, according to a Russian Supreme Soviet law adopted on 4 June 1992. But the Chechen government, disputing Ingushetia's split, has not recognized the law. Chechen political status, under a controversially elected president, General Dzhokar Dudaev, was in limbo by 1993. A part of neither the Russian Federation nor the Commonwealth of Independent States (CIS), the Chechen were struggling for international recognition of their Declaration of Independence. Only then, claimed General Dudaev, "can we enter the CIS voluntarily, with the rights of founding members. We do not need to be prodded or forced. . . . Our main goal is the achievement of full political independence."[5] By mid-1993, Chechnia was effectively functioning as an independent state, having warded off a confrontation with Russian troops in fall 1992 over the Ingush-Ossetian border.

Both Chechnia and Ingushetia have a sad legacy as home to two of Stalin's "punished peoples," who were accused en masse of Nazi collaboration during World War II, deported to Central Asia in 1944, and then returned in the 1950s to a cropped territory corresponding neither to their self-defined homelands nor to the territory they inhabited before the war.[6] The Chechen's previous history included a particularly

[4]Ronald Wixman, *The Peoples of the USSR: An Ethnographic Handbook* (Armonk, N.Y.: M. E. Sharpe, 1984), 43–44, 82–83; Ronald Wixman, *Language Aspects of Ethnic Patterns and Processes in the North Caucasus* (Chicago: University of Chicago Press, 1980).

[5]A. Korzun, interview with Dzhokhar Dudaev, "Liniia sviazi luchshe linii ognia," *Komsomol'skaia pravda*, 4 June 1992, 1.

[6]See Alexander Nekrich, *The Punished Peoples* (New York: Norton, 1978); Ralph T. Fisher, review of Alexander Nekrich's *The Punished Peoples*, in *Slavic Review* 41 (Spring 1982): 140–41; James Critchlow, *"Punished Peoples" of the Soviet Union: The Continuing Legacy of Stalin's Deportations* (New York: Helsinki Watch, 1991); and *Anthropology and Archeology of Eurasia* 31, no. 4 (Spring 1993).

brutal (though hardly unique) famine coupled with collectivization in the 1930s, a bitter civil war from 1919 to 1921, and a nineteenth-century history of violent Russian conquest. Indeed, a major culture hero for the Chechen and most other Caucasus mountain peoples remains the Avar leader Shamil, who united various peoples of the Caucasus to fight the Russians for twenty-five years in the mid-nineteenth century.[7] Although some Soviet history books contained attempts to present the acquisition of the North Caucasus by the Russian empire as peaceful and willing, oral tradition and much local scholarship proclaimed Shamil, an Islamic *imam* (religious leader), to be an anti-Russian freedom fighter locked in a *ghazavat* (holy war) that he lost only after enormous bloodshed.

When the Chechen leader General Dudaev campaigned for divorce from Russia, he exploited some of the painful historical memories of his people, evoking Shamil and also Islamic (Sunni) tradition. Yet his political strategy has been more complex. In his presidential campaign he employed the rhetoric of Islam, yet also advocated state secularism. He insisted on priority rights for the Chechen language, yet backed a Chechen law that makes both Russian and Chechen state languages. He urged cultivating diverse Middle Eastern allies, yet employed a German economic advisor and expressed interest in traveling in the West. Some of his Islamic Path and Veinakh party followers volunteered to fight on the Iraqi side in the 1991 Gulf War. Yet he sought to assure the Russians that he had no intention of misusing Soviet weaponry left on his territory.[8]

Given his Islamic rhetoric, his previous high status in the Soviet force, and his vivid anti-Russian positions, General Dudaev has come symbolize Russians' worst renegade nightmares. The Russian press portrayed him as more of a militaristic, fundamentalist, nationalist riah than was perhaps wise or valid.[9] And Dudaev himself was furth in his polarizing secessionist cause when Yeltsin declared a local sta emergency in fall 1991. After an angry Russian parliamentary de

[7]Dudaev is rumored to have said that if Shamil had been Chechen, he would have lost to the czarist empire. For sources on Shamil, see I. N. Zakharin, *Kavkaz i er* (St. Petersburg: Kolninskii, 1902); Paul Henze, " 'Unrewriting' History—The Problem," *Caucasian Review* 6 (1958): 7–29.

[8]D. Mirzoev, "Dzhokhar Musaevich Dudaev," *Argumenty i fakty,* no. 44 (1991); Sheehy, "Power Struggle in Checheno-Ingushetia," *Radio Free Europe/Radio* (hereafter *RFE/RL*) *Report on the USSR,* 15 November 1991, 20–26; *Center for racy in the USSR Bulletin* 4, 14 January 1991.

[9]See, for example, Irina Dementieva, "After the Round-up," *Current Digest of t Press* 44, no. 18 (1992): 21–22, from *Izvestiia,* 7 May 1992, 3.

Yeltsin and the speaker of the Russian Parliament, Ruslan Khasbulatov, a Russified Chechen, backed down. A few Russian troops in the region were surrounded by Chechen forces and sent packing. But great damage to maintaining the federal tie was done: moderate Chechen who had been hesitating to back Dudaev felt angered enough at the troops to become radicalized and more sympathetic to Dudaev's nationalist positions. This process was then further exacerbated by Russian troops in the region from fall 1992 into 1994.

The crystallization of Chechen nationalism has come from a number of sources, only partially enumerated here. Religious revival has included the restoration of various Sufi sects, some of which do advocate the eventual institution of an Islamic state. Relations with the Ingush have soured due to mutual territorial claims, made even more complex in that some of these are in the Prigorodnyi region of North Ossetia and others in Dagestan. The date of 23 February has become an official memorial to the victims of Stalin's deportation campaigns, with some Chechen seeing the secession movement as vengeance for the deportations of their parents.

Together with a rise in nationalism, internal definitions of national patriotism have become increasingly splintered. The issues of economic privation, ecological destruction, and human rights violations within Chechnia have become so divisive that "ordinary" people have been politicized, some against Dudaev. Armed struggles in the capital of Groznyi and at various munitions depots have resulted in bloodshed and an internally declared state of emergency, periodically lifted and then declared anew. Impeachment moves against Dudaev may succeed, but may not radically modify Chechnia's embittered relations with Russia.

Among the more significant developments, with ramifications for the evolution of a new version of old multilayered regional identities, have been Chechen alignments with their Caucasian neighbors. This included Chechnia's harboring of the fleeing Georgian president Zviad Gamsakhurdia in 1992. But potentially more stable and lasting are developing alliances with other mountain peoples of the Caucasus. Joint assemblies of Chechen, Ingush, Abkhaz, Kabardei, Balkar, Karachay, Adyge (Cherkess), Ossetian, Svan, Lezgin, Avar, Lak, and other Dagestani peoples have met since 1989, resulting in the formation of the Independent Mountain Peoples Confederation.[10]

[10]Not all of the peoples named attended the first session, but by the third assembly in 1991, which elected the Kabardei Yuri Shanibov as confederation president,

THE REPUBLIC OF TATARSTAN

The Tatars present a slightly less anti-Russian, anti-Moscow case than do the Chechen. The Tatar geographic, demographic, and political situation has been less conducive to full secession, and fewer Tatars have been radicalized to the same degree as the Chechen. By 1993, Tatar sovereignty had been expressed in several ways: a 1990 declaration of sovereignty within the Soviet Union; a December 1991 parliamentary resolution unilaterally declaring full membership in the CIS; refusal to sign the March 1992 Federal Treaty; and a narrowly passed March referendum that asked: "Do you agree that the republic of Tatarstan is a sovereign state, subject to international law, building its relations with the Russian Federation and other republics and states on equal terms?"[11] The 1992 Tatarstan constitution proclaims dual citizenship for Tatarstan residents. Negotiations over separate Tatar-Russian bilateral treaties proceeded through 1993, with participants on both sides affirming continued economic cooperation as crucial for this oil-rich and highly industrialized region. A compromise treaty was signed in 1994.

Tatarstan, on the Volga in the heart of Russia, had a Tatar population of 1,765,404 in the 1989 census, constituting only 48.5 percent of that of the republic, whereas Russians were 43.3 percent. The Tatars, however, numbered 6,648,760 in the former Soviet Union, so that nearly 75 percent of the Tatar population lived outside their republic in 1989, indicating a large Tatar diaspora. Although some Tatars have returned to their once substantially larger homeland since 1989 (including a few from abroad), Tatarstan has remained a multiethnic republic with a large Slavic population, much intermarriage, mixed youth gangs, and a legacy of accommodation with Russians. Tatar president Mintimer Shamiev, a former Communist party leader elected in 1991, has thus straddled an awkward line between catering to growing Tatar nationalism and favoring negotiations with the Russians of his republic and

most mountain Caucasus peoples were represented. See Ann Sheehy, "More on Confederation of Mountain Peoples," *RFE/RL Daily Report*, 5 November 1992, 9; "The Chechen Republic," *Express Chronicle*, 24–27 February 1992, 8; Elizabeth Fuller, "Georgia, Abkhazia, and Chechen-Ingushetia," *RFE/RL Research Report*, 23 January 1992.

[11]The referendum margin was 61.4 percent in favor, 37.2 percent against, with a high 82 percent turnout. See Ann Sheehy, "Tatarstan Asserts Its Sovereignty," *RFE/RL Research Report*, 3 April 1992, 1–4; "Tatarstan Announces Joining Commonwealth," *FBIS*, 31 December 1991, 50, from Moscow Radio; "Tatars, Adyge, Bashkirs Assert Sovereignty,"*Current Digest of the Soviet Press* 44, no. 8 (1992): 5–6.

Moscow. The very presence of the Tatar diaspora militates against harsh treatment of Russians inside Tatarstan.

Tatar historical, especially territorial, grievances have played a considerable role in the evolution of Tatar nationalism. In 1936, when Stalin's nationality experts were apportioning union republics to peoples with over a million in population, the Tatars qualified but were denied the status, given their geography and perhaps in retaliation against their already jailed "National Communist" leader Mir-said Sultan-Galiev, who had sought union status in 1922 as well.[12] In the early 1990s, Tatar activists, notably those involved with the Ittifak (Alliance) and Vatan (Homeland) parties, plus the Azatlyk (Freedom) youth movement, staged demonstrations on the main square of the capital, Kazan, demanding secession from Russia and, unrealistically, return of lands that had been under Tatar control before Ivan the Terrible defeated the Khans of the Golden Horde in 1552.[13]

The Tatar ethnic group was in part formed by historical mixing of peoples during the Golden Horde period and before, during Mongol conquests. The Tatars are Turkic, descendants of various Kipchak-speaking groups who mixed with Finno-Ugrians, Bulgars, Slavs, and Caucasians. Within the Tatar group are many local, territorial self-designations. In addition, numerous peoples were misidentified as Tatar by the Russians. The Volga Tatars form the core of the group that was, in the Soviet period, allowed to maintain its small "autonomous republic" since 1920, whereas the Crimean Tatars are among the most famous of the "punished peoples," deported like the Chechen by Stalin as Nazi collaborators.[14]

[12]See A. Ziubchenko et al., "O Tak Nazyvaemoi Sultan-Galievskoi Kontrrevoliutsionnoi organizatsii," *Izvestiia TsK KPSS*, no. 10 (1990): 75–88; Alexandre A. Bennigsen and S. Enders Wimbush, *Muslim National Communism in the Soviet Union* (Chicago: University of Chicago Press, 1979); Azade-Ayşe Rorlich, *The Volga Tatars: A Profile in National Resilience* (Stanford: Hoover Institution Press, 1987).

[13]For example, "Tatarstan—Ploshad' Svoboda Kipet," *Pravda*, 17 October 1991, 1. A fuller review of Tatar ethnic politics is by sociologist Roza N. Musina, "Sovremennye etnosotsial'nye protsessy i etnopoliticheskaia situatsiia v respublike Tatarstan," conference paper for Women in International Security, Prague 1992. See also D. M. Iskhakov and R. N. Musina, eds., *Sovremennye national'nye protsessy v respublike Tatarstan* (Kazan: Academy of Sciences, 1992).

[14]Unlike the Chechen, the Crimean Tatars were not given back their homeland in the 1950s, and have their own strong protest movement. On Tatar ethnic history, see R. G. Kuzeev and Sh. F. Mukhamed'iarov, "Etnoyzykovye sviazi," *Sovetskaia tiurkologiia*, no. 2 (1990): 48–60, translated in *Anthropology and Archeology of Eurasia* 31, no. 1 (1992): 24–39; A. Karimullin, *Tatary: Etnos i etnonim* (Kazan: Academy of Sciences, 1989); Alan W. Fisher, *Crimean Tatars* (Stanford: Hoover Institution Press, 1978); Rorlich, *The Volga Tatars;* Edward J. Lazzerini, "The Volga Tatars in Central Asia,

Within their own republic, the Volga Tatars were able to develop a sense of national identity that evolved from prerevolutionary literary, cultural, merchant, and political traditions focused on the intellectual ferment of Kazan yet incorporating folk values, rituals, and customs. In the Soviet period, this identity was overlaid with some Tatar involvement in energy and manufacturing industries as well as more traditional grain, milk, and meat production. But many Tatars felt that without union status, revenues were escaping to the center, depriving them of resources for education and social programs. Relative prosperity did not compensate for Tatar fears of linguistic and social assimilation, expressed in a 1989 language law requiring Tatar language education for all republic citizens, and provisions in the 1990 Tatar Declaration of Sovereignty and the 1992 Constitution that Tatar was the state language, along with Russian. In 1989, more than a million Tatars declared Russian, not Tatar, their native language.[15]

Like the Chechen, many Tatars are Islamic, but some are proud of a reformist tradition, Jadidism, which at the turn of the century advocated education for women and sponsored a satirical journal called *Kha, Kha, Kha*.[16] Leaders of the renewed Islamic reform movement, echoing the historical leader Ismail Bey Gaspraly (Gasprinski), advocate a sophisticated syncretism of Eastern and European traditions. They support professional women, encourage greater female participation in religious activities within local mosques, and are sometimes voices of calm and compromise when the nationalist anti-Russian debate becomes too shrill and chauvinist. The Tatar and Chechen cases thus illustrate the folly of lumping all Islamic peoples together into one fundamentalist, stereotyped category. Although an Islamic revival movement has occurred in Tatarstan, it has not been a unified focal point of post-Soviet nationalist rhetoric.

Political rhetoric has both reflected and enhanced diverse levels of identity, from highly local to pan-Turkic. Various groups emphasize different aspects of their "national" heritage, and they are not necessarily mutually exclusive. Some, for example, focus on tenth-century Volga

18th–20th Centuries: From Diaspora to Hegemony?" in Beatrice Manns, ed., *Central Asia in Historical Perspective* (Boulder, Colo.: Westview Press, 1993).

[15]This was especially true for Tatars outside their republic. Midkhat Farukshin et al., "Ethnic Tension in the Republic of Tatarstan," manuscript, Kazan, 1992.

[16]I am grateful to Edward Lazzerini for first introducing me to this journal. See also Lazzerini, *The Promise of Some Certainty: Ismail Bey Gasprinski and the Fate of Turkic Culture in Late Imperial Russia,* forthcoming.

Bulgar roots, forming a group called Bulgar-al-jadid, or the New Bulgar. Others, stressing Tatar pride and achievements within the Volga area of their own republic, have organized the Tatar Public Center, a major Tatar activist umbrella organization that had great influence on the wording of the 1992 Constitution. Still others, sometimes in conjunction with the Tatar Public Center, stress the natural cultural, political, and economic alliance of the Volga-Ural Turkic peoples, the Tatars and the Bashkirs, advocating a Tatar-Bashkir confederation.[17]

Finally, many are attracted to the philosophies of pan-Tatarism, the brotherhood of all dispersed Tatar peoples, as well as pan-Turkism. This has been reflected in Volga Tatar leadership in several Tatar and Turkic congresses (for example, in Kazan and Almaty, respectively). A Tatar *majlis* (council) held in Kazan in mid-1992 drew numerous Tatar business leaders and academics from abroad. The western Tatar diaspora, officially condemned for years as bourgeois, nationalist traitors, are now looked to for both economic and spiritual revival.[18] Yet striving for broader Tatar and Turkic cultural, economic, spiritual, and political ties is not the same as expecting political unification in the splintered Turkic world.

Had Tatar street demonstrations been repressed violently by Soviet OMON (emergency militia) troops or, later, by Russian republic forces, the Tatar population could have become considerably more radicalized. Instead, they elected the moderate Mintimer Shamiev and have avoided extensive militarization of Tatar opposition groups. But polarization remains a possibility: some nationalists, demanding a grand *majlis* (Islamic elders council) to supplant the elected parliament, have called for Shamiev's arrest.[19] Russian critics resent Tatar rhetoric and referendum behavior. A Tatar minister, part of the new reformist cultural elite, explained recent dynamics of Kazan-Moscow politics as "our play for greater independence that got a little out of hand. What we really wanted was a Federal Treaty with a looser framework, so individual

[17]Sheehy, "Tatarstan Asserts Its Sovereignty"; Ann Sheehy, "Tatarstan and Bashkiria: Obstacles to Confederation," *RFE/RL Research Report,* 29 May 1992, 33–37; Azade-Ayşe Rorlich, "Tatars or Bulghars? The New Winds of Glasnost Bring Back an Old Apple of Discord," *RFE/RL Report on the USSR,* 4 August 1989, 22–24; "The Tatar Public Centre (TOTs)," *Central Asian Survey* 9, no. 2 (1990): 155–65.

[18]Tatar historian Shamil F. Mukhamed'iarov, personal communication, August 1991. See Serge A. Zenkovsky, *Pan-Turkism and Islam in Russia* (Cambridge, Mass.: Harvard University Press, 1960).

[19]"Tatar Leaders React Stormily to TV Report," *FBIS,* 31 January 1992, 55–56, from a Russian television broadcast of 30 January 1992.

republics could have, within it, separate bilateral treaties. If all the autonomous republics had held out for this, we would have all been better off."[20]

An insight into Tatar-Russian tensions and the need for delicate diplomacy can be glimpsed in a 1992 encounter between the then Russian chairman of the State Committee for Nationalities Policy and members of the Tatar Public Center (TPC):

> Valery Tishkov warned the TPC against any drastic actions against the Russian population of Tatarstan, saying that the point has now been reached beyond which the danger of disintegration in Russia could provoke a wave of protest from the Russian population. . . . TPC activists, hearing the minister's speech, saw undisguised threats in it, and did not fail to tell the guest so, reminding him that Tatarstan is not part of Russia, and never has been. "The struggle we are now waging for Tatarstan's independence," Damir Iskhakov, TPC Political Council chair, stressed, "is a struggle for the liberation of the Tatar people from colonial oppression."[21]

REPUBLIC OF TYVA

Tyva, in the Sayan mountains and the Upper Yenisey basin of Siberia, was a separate country bordering on Mongolia from 1921–44 (called Tannu-Tuva from 1921–26). It nonetheless functioned intermittently as a Soviet client state calling itself a revolutionary "people's democracy," especially after Russian interests in the area were cemented by a 1926 treaty. In 1914 Urianghai Territory, including Tyva, had been placed under a weak Russian commission, after Chinese and Mongol rule over the area disintegrated. The chaos of civil war in the region included attempts by Mongols, pan-Mongol Buryat patriots, and Chinese warlords to retake Tyva, but its independence was declared in 1921. Incorporation into Russia as an autonomous oblast in 1944 meant the loss of some land, many resources (including gold, uranium, and coal), and much dignity. Although limited and uneven collectivization, in the form of "production associations," had begun earlier, massive reorganization of the pastoral economy and settlement of Tyvan herders did not begin

[20]Ramil Khabriev, minister of health of the Tatar republic, personal communication, May 1992.

[21]Dmitrii Mikhailin, "Tatarskii ysyk ne tol'ko v Tatarstane," *Rossiiskaia gazeta,* 11 June 1992, 4. For a sense of the background Valery Tishkov had on Tatarstan, see A. N. Iamskov, ed., *Sovremennye problemy i veroiatnye napravleniia razvitiia natsional'no-gosudarstvennogo ustroistva Rossiiskoi Federatsii* (Moscow: Russian Academy of Sciences, 1992), 34–36, produced for the Russian Parliament by the Institute of Ethnology and Anthropology, which Tishkov directs.

until the late 1940s. Even in the late 1950s, some unaffiliated Tyvan herders were still nomadic on territories they considered theirs by clan usufruct. Tyva did not become an autonomous republic inside of the Russian Federation until 1961.[22]

Tyvan ethnic roots derive from a number of sources and should be considered in a context of diverse local economic adaptations, and as background for a more recent sense of nationalism emerging out of republic politics. The Tyvan people formed from several Turkic groups, as well as Turkified Mongols, Samoydeic-, and possibly Ket-speakers. Tyva (Tuva, Tuba) was used as an ethnonym (self-name) as far back as the seventh century, according to Chinese sources. The Tyvan language, sometimes called Urianghai, is classified as Uigur-Tukui (sometimes Old-Uigur), in the Uigur-Oguz division of Northern Turkic, in the Ural-Altaic language family. It has many loan words from Mongolian, and the Tyvan peoples traditionally used Mongolian and Tibetan literary languages. Tyvan-speakers are related to, and have gone into the formation of, the Soyot (Tyvans assimilated by the Buryats), the Beltir (a Tyvan-Khakass people), and the Todzhans (Tyvan-Tofalars). Soyot, Maad, Oorzhak, and Kuzhuget tribes of the Altai-Sayan mountain region were part of Tyvan groupings, with some of these tribal names surviving in twentieth-century Tyvan sociopolitical subdivisions. Such subdivisions have been particularly significant in the Tyvan case, given their region's series of relatively isolated mountain valleys.[23]

Mongol-Tibetan influence in the region was felt not only through language and politics, but also religion. By the eighteenth century, Buddhism had taken hold, syncretized with earlier traditions of shamanism. Just prior to the formation of the "people's democracy," twenty-two

---

[22]See Toomas Alatalu, "Tuva—A State Reawakens," *Soviet Studies* 44, no. 5 (1992): 881–95; Mergen Mongush, "The Annexation of Tannu-Tuva and the Formation of the Tuvin ASSR," *Central Asian Survey* 12, no. 1 (1993); P. S. H. Tang, *Russian and Soviet Policy in Manchuria and Outer Mongolia, 1911–1913* (Durham, N.C.: Duke University Press, 1959); M. G. Levin and L. P. Potapov, eds., *Peoples of Siberia* (Chicago: University of Chicago Press, 1964), 380–422; L. P. Potapov, *Ocherki narodnogo byta tuvintsev* (Moscow: Nauka, 1969); and Sevyan Vainshtein, *Nomads of South Siberia* (Cambridge: Cambridge University Press, 1980), 39–45, and Caroline Humphrey's Introduction in that volume, 1–36. See also Caroline Humphrey, "Perestroika and the Pastoralists: The Example of Mongun-Taiga in Tuva ASSR," *Anthropology Today* 5, no. 3 (June 1989): 6–10.

[23]See Bernard Comrie, *The Languages of the Soviet Union* (Cambridge: Cambridge University Press, 1981), 45–47; Ronald Wixman, *The Peoples of the USSR: An Ethnographic Handbook* (Armonk, N.Y.: M. E. Sharpe), 201; Levin and Potapov, *Peoples of Siberia*, 380–81; Humphrey, Introduction, in Vainshtein, *Nomads of South Siberia*, 4; and Vainshtein, *Nomads of South Siberia*, 39–45.

khure, or lamaist monastery jurisdictions, existed in Tyva, with the largest Buddhist monasteries being in the Chadan Valley, where Manchu administrative structure was also centered. Tibetan as well as local Tyvan lamas numbering about three thousand ran the daily worship, festivals, and economy of the monasteries. Illustrative of religious syncretism was the cult of *ova,* or *oboo,* found throughout Tyva, Buryatia, and Mongolia, which involved cairns in sacred natural areas, considered to be homes for spirits and ancestors of local social groups, accompanied by Buddhist iconography. *Ova* have been reported through the twentieth century and have had a renaissance of open worship recently, along with some aspects of Buddhism, suppressed after 1929 but revived in the 1980s through the new Buddhist Society of Tyva. By 1993, the republic budget included funds for the construction of two Buddhist *khure.*[24]

Tyvan national identity was formed out of patriotism toward their initial "people's democracy" and subsequent republic, with persecution of religion and closings of monasteries driving religious aspects of cultural-political loyalty well underground. Many Tyvans who strongly identified with Buddhism or with the nobility and merchantry fled abroad after 1921, some assimilating in Mongolia. Historical memory of religious persecution, as well as resentment of sedentarization and collectivization, reemerged in the rhetoric of political reform slowly and tentatively during the late 1980s. One of the rehabilitated heros was Churmit-Dazy, a state leader killed in 1938 in a Stalin-style purge.

A 1980s Tyvan cultural revival movement was led by scholars in the capital, at Kyzyl's Institute of Languages, Literature and History, and by informal folk performance groups. It centered on the regeneration of the Tyvan language and on folklore, especially the great Tyvan tradition of throat-singing. Tyvans passed a mild version of a language rights law in 1989, opening the way for increased Tyvan language training in republic schools for both Russians and Tyvans, but not requiring it. The 1993 constitution of Tyva allows for both Tyvan and Russian as state languages.[25]

[24]Zoia V. Anaiban, "K probleme mezhnatsional'nykh konfliktov," conference paper for Women in International Security, Prague 1992, 14; Vladimir Kornev, "Poznavaia vselennyiu: K 250 Letiiu Buddizma," *Soiuz,* no. 30 (July 1991): 14. See also Vainshtein, *Nomads of South Siberia,* 256, note 4, and note 9 by Caroline Humphrey, 256–57.
[25]Tyva's constitution was passed in fall 1993. I am grateful to the Tyvan musician, folklore group leader, and ecological activist Gennadii Chash for providing background on Tyvan cultural and political trends, in June and July 1987 and June 1991, and to Zoia Anaiban for discussion in September 1992 and November 1993. For an example of a cultural revival project, see S. V. Kozlova, ed., *Soveshchanie po problemam razvitiia*

In 1990, the Tyvans joined what Soviet newspapers were calling the "parade of sovereignties," declaring unilaterally a relatively greater political status (real autonomy) within Russia as the Tyvan Socialist Republic, which their reformists saw as a bid for local economic control analogous to that of a union republic. They agitated for boundary changes (of Krasnoyarsk Kray), ecological clean-up, and a changed taxation structure. Their popular front, with both a moderate wing (accommodate Russians) and a radical wing (Russians should have left yesterday), was accused by local Communist party leaders, especially Grigor Shirshin, of fomenting ethnic pogroms against the Russian population. As the moderate popular front leader Kaadyr-ool Bicheldei, an orientalist and subsequent head of the Supreme Soviet, tried to point out, this was far from the case.[26] Serious interethnic violence occurred in May and July 1990, however, and has broken out intermittently since, exacerbating an already scandalous crime problem in the republic.

Interethnic fighting has been concentrated in areas of high unemployment and relatively recent Russian settlement. Beginning with a possibly provoked dance hall brawl, young Tyvans rampaged in the industrial town of Khovu-Aksy, site of a cobalt plant. In Kyzyl, where Tyvans are a minority, non Tyvan-speaking Russians have been shot by Tyvan youth gangs. In the settlement of Elegest, messages were placed under Russian doors, suggesting that families leave within a month; houses also have been burned or raided there. In addition, at the remote mountain lake of Sut-Khol, three Slavic fishers (one a boy) were murdered, at what may well have been a sacred site.[27]

---

khoomeiia [throat-singing] (Kyzyl: Tyva Ministry of Culture, 1988). See also Aleksandra Lugovskaia, "V plenu konflikta," Soiuz, no. 35 (August 1990): 9, 16; and Ann Sheehy, "Russians the Target of Interethnic Violence in Tuva," RFE/RL Report on the USSR, 14 September 1990, 13–17. See Tyvan sociologist Anaiban, "K probleme mezhnatsional'nykh konfliktov." Tyvans have in general been less linguistically Russified than many Siberians.

[26]See, for example, Lugovskaia, "V plenu konflikta," 16.

[27]Sadly, the dance hall origin for the initial flare-up has been repeated in many areas of Russia, including Northern Siberia. Similar incidents have led some native leaders to suggest local party elites had an interest in stirring trouble so that indigenous youths could be threatened and jailed. For coverage of examples of violence in the Soviet press, see A. Bogdanovsky, "Tuva's Troubles," Current Digest of the Soviet Press 42, no. 27 (1990): 25, from Izvestiia, 3 July 1990, 6; and V. Danilenko, "Situation in Tuva Deteriorates," Current Digest of the Soviet Press 42, no. 31 (1990): 29, from Izvestiia, 3 August 1990, 29. Compare with party leader G. Shirshin's defensive accusations against populist hooligans speculating on nation feelings, in "I Want to Say with All Responsibility," FBIS, 3 October 1990, 192, from Sovetskaia Rossiia, 29 September 1990, 3. See Lugovskaia, "V plenu konflikta," 16; Sheehy, "Russians the Target of Interethnic Violence in Tuva"; M. Ia. Zhornitskaia, "Natsional'naia situatsia v Tuvin-

In 1990 Soviet troops were brought in to quell the disturbances, angering Tyvans even further and creating polarization that led to increased nationalism. Russian refugees, estimated at over ten thousand, have been fleeing since 1990 across the high Altai mountains, although local officials beg skilled workers and professionals to stay. In 1926, Tyvans comprised nearly 80 percent of their state's population, with Russians at nearly 20 percent. In 1989, Tyvans numbered 206,629, and were 64 percent of their republic, with Russians at 32 percent. By 1992, Tyvans were estimated at over 70 percent of a republic population of only about three hundred thousand, with some areas composed nearly solidly of the indigenous nationality.[28]

Numerous interrelated factors have contributed to the exceptionally tense interethnic situation in Tyva, some of which are similar to factors in other regions, but their congruence and mutual reinforcement in the Tyvan context has made Tyva a dramatic case. Extractive central economic policies, large proportions of Russian settlers since 1944, and recent unemployment among Tyvan youths have been coupled with the demise of traditional Tyvan pastoralism under harsh sedentarization programs, the mandatory Russifying education of Tyvans in Soviet boarding schools, and the undermining of Tyvan spiritual values. Urbanization and industrialization have created contexts where newcomer Russian professionals live better (or are perceived to live better) than indigenous Tyvans. Russians also are a perceived linguistic and demographic threat and are blamed for ecological destruction. All this is compounded by a history of quasi-independence, followed by incorporation by Russia, Communist party mismanagement through resented native elites, growth of a (split) opposition intelligentsia, Soviet troop misuse, and a folk memory (made rosy by time) of Mongol cultural and political affinity.

Tyvan regional orientation has increasingly turned toward Mongolia, which is struggling with its own impoverishment and difficult reform politics. In 1992 the more radical wing of the Tyvan Popular Front, renamed Khostug Tyva (Free Tyva), urged a referendum on the repub-

skoi ASSR i Khasskoi AO," Institute of Ethnology and Anthropology, manuscript, Moscow, 1990.

[28]See Robert A. Rupen, "The Absorption of Tuva," in Thomas T. Hammond, ed., *The Anatomy of Communist Takeovers* (New Haven: Yale University Press, 1975), 148–50; and "Tuva Citizens Rally to Support Independence," *FBIS*, 26 June 1992, 70, from INTERFAX, 23 June 1992. The refugee figure is an estimate from Zhornitskaia, "Natsional'naia situatsia v Tuvinskoi ASSR i Khasskoi AO," confirmed by ethnosociologist L. M. Drobizheva, personal communication, September 1992.

lic's "independence and secession from Russia" and demanded a reconstituted Tyvan parliament composed of representatives from traditional
regional "commons." They established a protest *yurt* (traditional felt
tent) in the main square of Kyzyl. By 1993 radical restructuring had been
resisted, and Tyva had a newly elected president, Sherig-ool Oorzhak. It
was a republic with scant enthusiasm for either Yeltsin's April 1993
referendum or his November 1993 constitution.[29]

THE REPUBLIC OF BURYATIA

In contrast to the previous three cases, nationalist politics in Buryatia
have been relatively muted. Local Communist party leaders have maintained a great deal of control into the 1990s, and legacies of territorial,
economic, and political grievances have been played down, though not
ignored, by a cautious and small reform movement. Cultural regeneration has been a focus of movement leaders, who have described themselves as more "patriotic" than "nationalist." Nonetheless, because of
Buryatia's geographical position on the border, its past history of pan-
Mongolic activism, the Buddhist background of some of its people, and
its territorial division under Soviet rule, it presents a case of potential
radicalization depending on how center-periphery politics evolve.

Buryatia was gerrymandered in 1937. The homeland of the Buryats,
surrounding Lake Baikal in Southeast Siberia, was split into the Buryat-
Mongol Autonomous Republic and the Agin and Ust-Orda Buryat autonomous *okrugs*, with interspersed regions considered Russian. About
one-tenth of the better farm and pasture land was absorbed by neighboring provinces. The republic became simply the Buryat ASSR in 1958,
symbolically discouraging Mongol connections. Buryats numbered
421,380 in 1989 but were only 24 percent of their republic population.
This percent would rise if the lands that activists claim became part of
an enlarged Buryat-Mongol republic, but Buryats would probably still
not have a majority. In 1926 the Buryat numbered 237,501 and were
about 48 percent of the Buryat-Mongol Autonomous Republic founded
in 1923, which covered most of the territory that western (Cisbaikal)

---

[29]"Tuva Citizens Rally to Support Independence"; see Ann Sheehy, "Tuvinian Independence Claim Halted," *RFE/RL Daily Report*, 28 July 1992, 4. Moderates argue, thus far
successfully, that the new Tyvan constitution's clause enabling future secession is
enough, without demanding a referendum. Zoia Anaiban, personal communication,
September 1992 and November 1993. See also N. P. Moskalenko, *"Etnopoliticheskaia
situatsia v respublike Tyva,"* Institute of Ethnology and Anthropology, Document 37,
1992.

and eastern (Transbaikal) Buryat pastoralists (herding horses, cattle, sheep, and camels) inhabited before the Revolution.[30]

Buryat cultural orientation developed historically in two different directions, with the western Buryats more fully integrated into the Russian empire and accepting, at least superficially, aspects of Russian Orthodoxy. The eastern Buryats were more oriented toward Mongolia and Tibet, although by the Treaty of Nerchinsk (1689) with China, a substantial portion of the Transbaikal was ceded to the Russian czar. At least some eastern Buryat lamas were proselytizing Buddhism (Lamaism) by the eighteenth century. Buddhist culture gradually took hold in Transbaikalia, both merging with and partially supplanting shamanism through a complex system of magnificent, well-supported monasteries, until the 1930s. By the 1920s, about ten thousand Buryats were lamas, a large number until one realizes these were the priests, doctors, scholars, and artists for a devout population with limited access to other schools and hospitals. Through Buddhism, literacy spread in Mongolian with an adapted Buryat alphabet that allowed for works of considerable range—for example, on Buryat folklore as well as Tibetan curing. Buryat intellectuals, including orientalists such as nineteenth-century Dorzhi Banzarov, ethnographer M. N. Khangalov, twentieth-century linguist lama Agvan Dorzhiev, and the doctor of Tibetan medicine Zhamsaran Badmaev, became known beyond Buryatia and eventually became symbols of a unifying Buryat national pride.[31]

The Mongolic-speaking Buryats, whose roots in Baikalia date at least to medieval times, were traditionally divided into five major tribal affiliations: Bulagat, Khori, Ekhirit, Khongodor, and Tabunut. These had diminished in significance by the twentieth century but remained an

[30]For background on Soviet Buryatia, see I. S. Urbanaeva et al., *Natsional'nyi Vopros v Buriatii* (Ulan-Ude: Academy of Sciences, 1989); Caroline Humphrey, *Karl Marx Collective: Economy, Society and Religion in a Siberian Collective Farm* (Cambridge: Cambridge University Press, 1983); Boris Chichlo, "Histoire de la formation des territoires autonomes· chez les peuples Turco-Mongols de Sibérie," *Cahiers du Monde Russe et Soviétique* 28, nos. 3–4 (1987): 369–80. See K. V. Vyatkina, "The Buryats," in Levin and Potapov,. *Peoples of Siberia*, 203–42. I am grateful to the philosopher and ecology activist Irina S. Urbanaeva and the then Soviet Parliament deputy Sergei Shapkhaev for conversations on reform in Buryatia, 21–26 July 1990, Harrogate, England.

[31]Nicholas N. Poppe, "The Buddhists," in Nikolai K. Deker and Andrei Lebed, eds., *Genocide in the USSR: Studies in Group Destruction* (New York: Scarecrow Press, 1958), 181–92; and N. N. Poppe, ed., *Letopisi khorinskikh buriatov* (Moscow: Academy of Sciences, 1935). See also M. N. Kangalov, "Iuridicheskie obychie u Buriatov," *Etnograficheskoe obozrenie* 4 (1894): 100–142; Humphrey, *Karl Marx Collective*, 402–32; and Caroline Humphrey, "Buryats," in Graham Smith, ed., *The Nationalities Question in the Soviet Union* (London: Longman Press, 1990), 292–93.

aspect of complex self-identities for a people known for memorizing genealogies back seven generations or more. In 1990 a festival contest was won by a young woman who remembered seventeen generations. Early twentieth-century reformists tried to overcome traditional political and social divisions through congresses demanding greater local governance, Buryat native schools, and land reform. Non-Bolshevik leaders, who established the Burnatskom (Buryat National Committee) and founded the 1923 Buryat-Mongol ASSR, envisioned a Mongolic state tolerant of religions, centered in the Russian trading town of Verkhneudinsk, which later became the capital Ulan-Ude.[32]

The Buryat national movement of the 1980s inherited a shattered reform tradition, few remnants of Buddhism, and only a dim awareness of prerevolutionary intellectual flourishing. Buryats of the Academy of Sciences Research Center in Ulan-Ude used the opportunities of glasnost to make public the "blank spots" of histories that included massive looting of about forty Buddhist monasteries, arrest of lamas, and killing of Buryat-Mongol ASSR founders. Hidden family histories of persecution were revealed, and some Buryats began proudly admitting shamanic ancestry. In 1987 the Buryat poet Nikolai Damdinov, in characteristically cautious tones, stressed the importance of returning to Buryat language education in the schools, creating Buryat journals, and supporting Buryat museums. In 1989, S. B. Budaev instituted a Buryat language teaching column in *Pravda Buriatiia,* and the Buryat Culture Center was established, with a broad spectrum of language and spiritual revival goals.[33] Other informal groups included the Geser Society, named for the major Buryat epic, a branch of the People's Front for the Assistance of Perestroika, a school for the revival of shamanism, and Buddhist study circles.[34] One of the deputies elected to the Soviet Parlia-

---

[32]Irina S. Urbanaeva, personal communication, July 1990, on the revival of interest in genealogies. See also Humphrey, "Buryats," 292; K. M. Gerasimova, *Lamaizm i natsional 'no-kolonial'naia politika tsarizma v baikalie v XIX i nachale XX vekov* (Ulan-Ude: Buryat Academy of Sciences, 1957).

[33]The first of the language training articles was "Slovo o Buriatskom ysyke," *Pravda Buriatiia,* 17 January 1990, 4. *Pravda Buriatiia* itself remained quite conservative until mid-1990, when its editorial staff was reformed, according to Sergei Shapkhaev, personal communication, July 1990. For Damdinov's statements, see *Literaturnaia Rossiia,* 24 July 1987. The Buryat paper *Tolon* (Sunrise) has since become a focus of cultural and political revival, and the children's journal *Kharaagsai* (Swallow) has encouraged both young Russians and Buryats to learn Buryat. On tensions over language, see also "Buriat Ethnic Concerns Surface in Ulan-Ude Oblast," *FBIS,* 28 February 1989, 60, from A. Zhdanov, "On a Topical Theme," *Pravda,* 20 February 1989, 2.

[34]See Humphrey, "Buryats," 299–303. The shamanism school was founded by Taras Mikhailov, a scholar of shamanism who has also become a practitioner of aspects of

ment in 1989 from Buryatia was a Buddhist, and a few Buryat students were sent for religious training in Mongolia. The Buddhist *datsan* (monastery) at Ivolga, allowed to reopen after World War II as a showplace for peace initiatives and foreign relations in Asia, has become a center of revitalized Buddhism, as has the monastery at Aginsk, near Chita, which in 1991 welcomed back a sacred statue of Maitreya that had been removed in 1940. Ivolga opened a school with sixty initial spaces in spring 1992, run by one of the young lamas trained in Mongolia. But the most public manifestation of the Buddhist revival was the joyfully received visit of the Dalai Lama to Buryatia in July 1991 for a celebration of "250 years of Buddhism."[35]

In addition to its Buddhist tradition, Buryatia is famous for its ecology movement, which focused on saving Lake Baikal from industrial pollution. The movement began with Russian scientists in the 1960s and became a cause célèbre for Siberian intellectuals, including the writer Valentin Rasputin. Buryats were part of the movement, especially by the late 1980s, but have not considered it an exclusive national issue.[36] On the contrary, international contacts have been courted, stimulated, and shared in the region through Baikal activism.

Cultural and scientific ties have been solidified especially with Mongolia, yet most Buryats disclaim interest in union with Mongolia, despite Russian fears. During the Soviet period, Buryat technical intelligentsia were sent to Mongolia as experts and exemplars of modern socialism. A very different politics guided the All-Buryat Congress held in Ulan-Ude

shamanic curing (from his report to a conference on nationality relations in Yakutsk, June 1991). See also his *Buriatskii shamanizm* (Novosibirsk: Academy of Sciences, 1987).

[35]Scholars of religion all over Russia talked excitedly of this visit, which was well publicized. See, for example, Vladimir Kornev, "Poznavaia vselennyiu," *Soiuz*, no. 30 (July 1992): 14. See also R. E. Pubaev, *Istochnikovedenie i istoriografiia istorii Buddizma* (Novosibirsk: Academy of Sciences, 1986). For a sense of Ivolga before perestroika, see Kevin Klose, "Soviet Buddhist Lamas Dwindle to a Cautious Few," *Washington Post*, 21 March 1978, A12. On recent developments at Ivolga and Aginsk, see *Pravda Buriatiia*, 25 February 1991 and 2 March 1991.

[36]I am following the assessment of anthropologist Caroline Humphrey here, which fits with discussions I have had with several Buryat and Slavic residents of Buryatia. See Humphrey, "Buryats," 300. See also Arnold K. Tulokhonov and Irina Urbanava, "Memorandum: Mezhdunarodnoi konferenstii po ekologicheskim problemam Baikalskogo regiona," a manuscript outlining highlights from the international conference Man at Baikal and His Inhabitance, Ulan-Ude, 1990. Irina S. Urbanaeva's *Chelovek u Baikala i mir tsentral'noi Asii: Filosofsko-istoricheskoe issledovanie* (Ulan-Ude: Scientific Center of Buryatia, 1991) reviews Buryat history and ecology. See S. S. Bukhaev, "*Etnopoliticheskaia i etnokul'turnaia situatsia v respublike Buriatiia*," Institute of Ethnology and Anthropology, Document 42, 1993.

in 1991, which included Bargu Buryats from Mongolia. It unanimously condemned as unconstitutional the 1937 three-way split of the Buryat republic and called for greater "national-cultural autonomy to consolidate the Buryat people."[37] Buryat intellectuals had also sent a letter in August 1990 to the USSR Supreme Soviet requesting return of Buryat lands in Irkutsk and Chita oblasts, but they were rebuffed, given obvious concerns in Moscow about the domino effects of any border changes. Local Cossacks in turn discussed a greater Baikal republic that would place the Buryats in a tiny (9 percent) minority—a position that strained interethnic relations.[38]

As with many autonomous republics, the Buryat ASSR officially declared its sovereignty in 1990, within Russia and the Soviet Union. Buryatia, the third ASSR to create a draft for debate (after Tatarstan and Sakha), passed its declaration in October, despite stormy controversy in a still-conservative republic Supreme Soviet. The declaration asserted that Buryatia was a multinational republic, equal in status to the union republics, reserving the right to suspend or contest laws of the union or of Russia that "violate the interests of the people of Buryatia." All land, natural resources, and economic potential of the republic were declared republic property. Both Buryat and Russian were declared state languages, in this and subsequent legislation.[39]

Interethnic tensions have existed under the surface in Buryatia for many years, surfacing in occasional drunken brawls, in Buryat demands that elected deputies speak the native language, in familial discouragement of interethnic marriages (which are nonetheless common), in ethnic enclaves, in surveys indicating preferences for monoethnic group dorm environments, and in Russian resentment over disproportional Buryat representation in the local government. Buryats have maintained about 50 percent representation, though Russians remain nearly 70 percent of the republic.[40] Moscow control has loosened but has not been elimi-

---

[37]See Ann Sheehy, "All-Buryat Congress in Ulan-Ude," *RFE/RL Daily Report*, 25 February 1991. See also congress coverage in *Pravda Buriatiia*, 21–24 February 1991. Several years earlier, Academy of Sciences ties with Mongolia were renewed. See, for example, "O nauchnykh sviaziakh dvukh akademii," *Pravda Buriatiia*, 15 January 1989, 2.

[38]Iamskov, *Sovremennye problemy*, 49–50.

[39]See *Pravda Buriatiia*, 9 October 1990, 1. For a synopsis, see Ann Sheehy, "Buryatia Adopts Sovereignty Declaration," *RFE/RL Daily Report*, 9 October 1990, 8.

[40]On the surveys and some other indicators of tensions, see A. Pakeev, "Chto stoit za tsiframi?" *Pravda Buriatiia*, 2 February 1989; and Zhdanov, "Buriat Ethnic Concerns Surface in Ulan-Ude Oblast." An attempt to minimalize tensions was evident in an article about a mixed ethnic family: A. Gamov, "Tak vedetsia vekami," *Sovetskaia Rossiia*, 25 January 1989, 3, in which a foster mother explained: "Buryat or Russian—really this is important? We live in the same yurt—that means we are members of the same family."

nated, so when a Moscow choice for the local KGB chief was rejected by both Buryatia's legislature and its prime minister, Vladimir Saganov, central authorities were surprised.[41] Buryats demanded changes in the March 1992 Federal Treaty to ensure control over local resources and primacy of most republic laws.

Admitting he was choosing a potential trouble spot, Boris Yeltsin traveled to Buryatia in May 1992 to reassure local peoples about the economy, the Baikal–Amur rail line, the ecology of Lake Baikal, and their "sovereign" rights within the federation. He also reaffirmed the significance of "the revival of the Buryat people's culture," especially Buddhism, and, at Ivolga, promised support for the restoration of monasteries. He was mostly cheered, but a few protesters from the fledgling Buryat-Mongol People's party waved placards with the slogans "We demand the reunification of the Buryat-Mongol lands" and "No Russia in Buryatia—Buryatia alone."[42] A year later, advocates of separatism or unification with Mongolia were still a minority and gradual economic and political reforms were taking hold.

THE SAKHA REPUBLIC (YAKUTIA)

Yakutia simultaneously declared sovereignty in 1990 and signaled a willingness to compromise with Russia by hyphenating its name to the Yakut-Sakha republic. "Yakut" (a Russian corruption of Evenk) is an outsider's name for the Sakha, who speak the farthest North Turkic language. When the elected Sakha president, Mikhail Nikolaev, accepted the Federal Treaty in March 1992, he signed in the name of "the Sakha republic (Yakutia)," already a signal of the determination to negotiate a more independent path, yet still within the framework of Russia. A further indication of this has been the adoption of a Sakha constitution by a reformist republic legislature, before Russia itself had managed to ratify a constitution. The Sakha republic of Eastern Siberia, while one of

[41]Sergei Trofimov, "Buriatia Rejects Moscow-Named KGB Chief," *FBIS*, 17 January 1991, 85, from TASS. Tiny protests against the local Supreme Soviet have been held by a few Democratic Union activists; see, for example, "The Arrest of Andrei Kapitonov," *Express Chronicle*, 4–10 February 1992, 1.

[42]"Yelstin Arrives in Buriatiia," *FBIS*, 28 May 1992, 52, from ITAR-TASS; and other trip coverage, *FBIS*, 29 May 1992, 43–45, especially "Yeltsin Meets Farmers, Buddhists," from INTERFAX, and "Price Hikes," from Vera Kuznetsova, *Nezavisimaia gazeta*, 29 May 1992, 1. See also "First Siberian Trade Exchange Established," *FBIS*, 8 January 1991, 30, from Vladimir Sbitnev, "Creation of the Baikal Exchange," *Izvestiia*, 28 December 1990; and "Buriatia Endorses Private Land Ownership," *FBIS*, 18 June 1992, 50, from Aleksei Subbotin, ITAR-TASS, 11 June 1992. The Buryat-Mongol People's party was founded in 1990.

the poorest per capita in Russia, has nonetheless been in a position of strength with central authorities because of its vast and underexploited wealth in minerals (gold, diamonds, tin, copper) and energy (oil, gas, coal).[43]

Many Sakha are aware of their Turkic linguistic and cultural roots and fascinated by ethnographic and archeological evidence of a mixed ethnic background that includes local northern peoples (Evenk, Even, Yukagir), plus ancestors who may have come from the area around Lake Baikal, driven north by kin of the Mongolic Buryats.[44] Some compare their current cultural and political revival with that of the Buryats, suggesting that perhaps because of the particularly brutal repression of Buddhism, the Buryats until recently have been more timid than the Sakha. Sakha religion has evolved into a complex blend of Russian Orthodoxy, Turkic cosmology, animism, and shamanism, with a focus on sacred sites and trees associated with traditional patrilineal clan territories. Though shamanism, as elsewhere, was driven underground in the Soviet period, it was not entirely destroyed. It has become one aspect of a Sakha cultural revival, symbolized by the founding of an Association of Folk Medicine. Another group, Kut-Sür (roughly glossed as Soul-Reason), has led a campaign for more general awareness of Sakha ritual and philosophical traditions of "folk wisdom."[45]

The Sakha cultural and spiritual revival began before the Gorbachev era but intensified in the late 1980s, leading to a campaign for rebirth of the Sakha language and literature. Although only 5 percent of the Sakha listed their primary language as Russian in 1989, fear of linguistic Russification, especially in the capital Yakutsk, has led to sharp monitoring of politicians' language abilities, to language legislation mandating more Sakha training in the schools, and to joint "state language" status for Sakha and Russian.[46]

[43]"Deklaratsiia," *Sotsialisticheskaia Iakutiia,* 28 September 1990, 1; "Konstitutsia," *Iakutskie vedomosti,* 27 February 1992, 1–8. Interviews with Sakha leaders in June and July 1991, June and August 1992, February, June, and November 1993.

[44]A. I. Gogolev, *Istoricheskaia etnografiia Iakutov* (Yakutsk: Yakutsk University Press, 1986).

[45]Marjorie Mandelstam Balzer, "Dilemmas of the Spirit: Religion and Atheism in the Yakut-Sakha Republic," in Sabrina Petra Ramet, ed., *Religious Policy in the Soviet Union* (Cambridge: Cambridge University Press, 1993), 231–51. Kut-Sür ideas are expressed in L. Afanas'ev, A. Romanov, R. Petrov, and V. Illarionov, *Aiyy yorehe* (Teachings of the Spirit) (Yakutsk: Sakha Keskile, 1990).

[46]See the language sections of the Declaration of Sovereignty and the Sakha constitution, cited in note 43 above. See also M. Muchin, "Nuzhen li zakon o izykakh?" *Sovety Iakutii,* 18 March 1992, 6. Sakha language newspapers have blossomed; for example, *Keskil, Sakha sire,* and *Sakhaada,* with *Kyym,* the old Communist party paper, adapting somewhat.

Historical memory recovery has been stimulated by a revision of the Soviet propaganda that stressed the peaceful incorporation of Yakutia into the Russian empire in the sixteenth century and belittled the degree of economic efficiency and literacy among prerevolutionary Sakha. The most passionate revisions have focused on twentieth-century figures such as Platon Sleptsov—pseudonym Oiunsky, from the Sakha word for shaman—a revolutionary, folklorist, and founder of the Institute of Languages, Literature and History, who died in Stalin's jails in 1937. Other revered Sakha intelligentsia of the period spanning the Revolution include the writer and ethnographer A. E. Kulakovsky, the ethnographer and activist P. V. Ksenofontov, the dramatist and reformist A. I. Sofronov, the writer N. D. Neustroev, and the jurist-dramatist-politician V. V. Nikiforov, all of whom were punished for nationalism in the Stalin era.[47]

The Sakha republic encompasses territory four times the size of Texas, but the Sakha numbered only 381,922 in 1989 and were 33 percent of their republic population, whereas the Russians were 50 percent. In contrast, Sakha comprised 82 percent of their republic population in 1926, before the massive influx of Russian settlers. The Sakha also claim land (reaching to the Sea of Okhotsk) taken from them during the Stalin era, but this has not been the focus of ethnic politics. Rather, since 1990 groups recovering names of 1920s organizations such as Sakha Keskile (Sakha Perspective) and Sakha Omuk (the Sakha People) have sponsored cultural, ecological, political, and economic rights campaigns.

Sakha Omuk, led by Minister of Culture Andrei Borisov, has functioned as an umbrella organization, bringing diverse groups together. It has been active in the elections of reformist deputies to various levels of legislatures, in the passing of sovereignty legislation, and in the election of the moderate and popular Sakha president Mikhail Nikolaev. Other more radical political groups, including some calling themselves popular fronts or parties, have been less effective in a republic with a majority Slavic population, and an interethnic marriage rate that is greater than the Russian republic average. Many reform leaders stress unifying, not polarizing, the republic population. Thus Borisov explained in 1991, "Sakha Omuk was formed in response to Gorbachev's call for new ideas. It is not a party. Perhaps only now are people ready for another

[47]For example, I. I. Nikolaev and I. P. Ushnitskii, *Tsentral'noe Delo: Khronika Stalinskikh repressii v Iakutii* (Yakutsk: Yakutsk Press for Sakha Omuk and Memorial, 1990); and the journal *Illin* 1, nos. 1 (1991) and 2 (1992). See also A. E. Kulakovsky, *Nauchnye Trudy* (Yakutsk: Institute of Languages, Literature, and History, 1979).

party. Earlier, people were too afraid."[48] By 1993 the Sakha Omuk vice-president, Vladimir Nikolaev, lamented that the group had not been able to goad the republic to a "second stage" of truly effective multiethnic sovereignty: "We are neither a real state nor a colony, but something unclear in-between."[49]

Both political and economic concerns led some of the Slavic population to leave Yakutia in the early 1990s, although not in enormous numbers and often for purposes of claiming citizenship in new CIS states of the Baltic and Ukraine. As in many areas of Siberia, most of these people had come to Yakutia as temporary workers, to make a "long ruble" and then return to their homelands. Precisely such workers are often blamed by Siberians (both of Slavic and indigenous backgrounds) for creating a psychology of immediate gratification that has led to terrible ecological destruction in mining and lumbering areas and to ethnic tension. The cool interethnic climate is exacerbated by Sakha perceptions that the newcomers are better paid and exploit Sakha women.

Tensions between Sakha university students and Russian toughs erupted in spring 1986 (concurrent with my residence in a Yakutsk University dorm). Police mishandling of the fighting led to a street demonstration three days later by several hundred Sakha students, the first of a long line of such demonstrations during the Gorbachev period. Although this incident was the most famous, categorized as "nationalist" in the Russian press, other cases of interethnic conflict were also well known in Yakutia, going back to the late 1970s and even the 1960s. Some also interpreted a street fight in early 1990, in which Sakha youths were shot, as a product of interethnic tension, but it may have been more a reflection of the widespread alcoholism and crime in Yakutsk. Sakha sociologists attribute a general social volatility to a breakdown in morals, begun well before the Gorbachev period, expressed through ethnic scapegoating.[50]

---

[48]Andrei Borisov, interview in Yakutia, June 1991. See "Ustav Sakha Omuk," 10 August 1990, manuscript; P. S. Maksimov, ed., *Mezhnatsional'nye otnosheniia v regione (po materialam Iakutskoi ASSR)* (Yakutsk: Institute of Languages, Literature, and History, 1990).

[49]Vladimir Nikolaev's description of group meetings, in a March 1993 letter to the author.

[50]I was falsely accused of being an outside agitator of the demonstrations and narrowly avoided being deported. Many Sakha, especially students, saw the incident as an effort to introduce perestroika into their republic. Their republic Communist party leader, Iu. N. Prokop'ev, made matters worse by accusing the students of improper nationalist upbringing (for example, in "Internatsional'noe vospitanie—delo vsei oblastnoi partiinoi organizatsii," *Sotsialisticheskaia Iakutii,* 18 May 1986, 2–4). A quota system was intro-

The issue of interethnic tensions is intertwined with that of economic viability in Yakutia, for the Slavic newcomer population has dominated the energy and mining industries, while Sakha Communist party leaders have dominated traditional Soviet political positions. Some of these groups formed an uneasy conservative alliance that welcomed the August 1991 putsch and were thus discredited. Less easy to dismiss were demands for economic rights that reached strike proportions in predominantly Slavic subregions of the republic. President Nikolaev's compelling argument to stave off strikes has been that all will benefit if both Russian and Sakha republic leaders can negotiate successfully with the center for a greater share of Yakutia's phenomenal wealth, while still maintaining the ties that provide food subsidies to the North.[51] This argument has also softened threats of some minority Slavic regionalists to split Yakutia in a North-South divide.

Insistence on resource sharing resulted in a 1992 agreement that the republic can control 32 percent of diamond profits and can deal directly with foreign bidders like De Beers. The South Korean firm Khende has also signed a deal involving the Elgin coal deposits and a branch line off the Baikal–Amur railway. Japanese firms have negotiated for republic lumber and other possible investments. Thus, as Moscow has loosened its economic grip on natural resources, the Sakha have been able to turn quickly toward direct, potentially profitable international contacts, especially in the Far East.[52] The danger for the rural Sakha, uneasily collectivized yet hesitant about privatization, is that they will trade

duced in the university, allowing for greater numbers of Slavic students than had been the case previously, and several student leaders were arrested, but the Russian instigators of the fighting were not punished. Students were officially exonerated only in 1990. For a Sakha sociological perspective, see Uliana Vinokurova, *Tsennostnye orientatsii Iakutov v usloviiakh urbanizatsii* (Novosibirsk: Nauka, 1992); and Uliana Vinokurova, *Bihigi Sakhalar* (We Sakha) (Yakutsk: Sakha Sirineehi, 1992). I am grateful to Uliana Vinokurova for discussions from 1986–93. In November 1993, she described the republic as "in a coma" from both Soviet and post-Soviet politics.

[51]Mikhail E. Nikolaev, "Nuzhen li Rossii sever?" *Nezavisimaia gazeta,* 23 June 1992, 5; P. Shinkarenko, interview with M. Nikolaev, "Almaznyi moi venets," *Rossiiskie vesti,* 2 June 1992, 2. For background on Nikolaev, see *Lider reforma* (Yakutsk: Ilin, 1991), pamphlet.

[52]See Ivan Nikolaev, *Zagadka Mikhaila Nikolaeva* (Yakutsk: Ilin, 1992), pamphlet, especially p. 9, for his claim the republic expects a $646 million investment in 1992–94. Uneasiness over how wealth will be shared surfaced during Ruslan Khasbulatov's 1992 visit to the Udachnyi mine, which produces 80 percent of Russia's diamond output. Workers were leaving the region in radically increased numbers, as shown by applications for moving containers. See "Need for Drastic Action," *FBIS,* 28 January 1992, from "Misfortunes of the Diamond Storehouse," *Rossiiskaia gazeta,* 27 January 1992, 1; interview with M. Nikolaev, *Literaturnaia gazeta,* 1 December 1993, 11.

economic and ecological exploitation by Moscow for similar exploitation by foreigners.

Russian leaders have shown some sensitivity to the political implications of the Sakha republic's wealth. Visitors from Moscow have acknowledged that workers in diamond mines should not have to live in wooden barracks. Central authorities conceded to some Sakha demands during negotiations over the Federal Treaty, and they promised other economic (tax) negotiations, which yielded some results in 1993. Despite internal republic debate over the degree to which the center merely throws the republic a few bones, Yeltsin has been particularly attentive to President Nikolaev, whose leadership role in the Russian Federation Council and overtures to other Russian and former republics have helped give the Sakha republic a high profile. Nikolaev and the republic itself are in the midst of a balancing act, supporting Yeltsin's November 1993 constitution while demanding supplies and credits from the center. The Sakha constitution, as Nikolaev has pointed out, places republic laws above Russian federal ones and has a provision for the republic's "right to leave the Russian Federation."[53] Many Sakha say they would prefer not to exercise that right, unless a major upheaval in the center pushes them into it.

CONCLUSION

Within the Russian Federation, non-Russian populations have shifted in the past decade from mildly politicized ethnic consciousness to various forms of nationalism. But this hardly means each republic is demanding the same degree of separation as the Chechen, Tatar, or Tyva republics. Even these cases are not neatly falling nation-state dominoes, but rather examples of varied responses to constantly changing political and economic conditions and crises. These conditions have helped to foster the crystallization of national identities, the use of nationalist idioms to express a range of differences, the exploration of new sources of influence, and a return to historical regional interconnections.

Population dislocations produced by increasing nationalisms have been considerable and painful, yet thus far more Slavs in "ethnic" republics of Russia are staying than leaving. Of the areas examined here,

[53]P. Shinkarenko interview with M. Nikolaev, "Almaznyi moi venets." On Nikolaev's high profile, a story circulates in Yakutia that during Yeltsin's 1992 trip to Buryatia he twice slipped and said "Yakutia," excusing himself with: "That Nikolaev is sitting heavily in my head," reported in Nikolaev, *Zagadka Mikhaila Nikolaeva*, inside cover.

tensions in the North Caucasus and Tyva have been most serious, resulting in an outflow of embittered Slavic refugees. The Slavic majorities in Tatarstan, Buryatia, and the Sakha republic have also been shrinking, through emigrations and especially due to declining immigration. Emigration has political, psychological, and economic ramifications, often creating ethnic polarization and tragic personal hardships. Yet some of the new emigrants came as only temporary workers, and many other would-be emigrants might stay in their current homes if given better economic opportunities.[54]

The Russians constitute 80 percent of their federal republic, with most of the ethnically based republics coping with a Soviet legacy that has turned their primary (titular) ethnic groups into minorities in their own lands. This demographic situation is an example of both the unintended ramifications of policy and the social legacy of policy, in a more direct, planned, and long-term sense. The communist philosophy that placed social "progress" above "parochial" and "selfish" nationalism led to encouragement of multiethnic republics, of mixed ethnic marriages, of borders drawn and even readjusted to incorporate, not exclude, multiple ethnic groups.

Like many experiments in social planning, especially those dealing with attempts to direct ethnic relations "from above," the Soviet communist version of melting-pot ideology scalded its cooks and in many areas did not even achieve for its people its fallback recipe (propagandized by the late ethnographer Iulian Bromlei) of a metaphorical ethnic salad, a "vinaigrette" of mixed ethnic groups keeping their discrete identities and cultural flavors but tossed compatibly together.[55] On the contrary, the ironic consequence of Soviet ethnic policies was a heightened awareness of ethnicity, including establishment of conditions that led eventually, in extreme cases, to polarization and full-fledged, though not always chauvinist, nationalism. In retrospect, almost everything the Soviet leadership tried to do in the area of nationality relations led to heightened, not repressed, ethnic consciousness. This does not deny the

[54]Estimates of refugee populations in the whole of the post-Soviet deconstructivist world vary wildly (from one to seven million) and require regional and comparative analysis. See P. Rudeev, interview in *Ekonomika i zhizn'*, no. 26 (June 1991): 10; L. Krasnovskii, "Russkie Bezhentsy v Rossii," *Narodnoe Obrazovanie* (August 1990): 21–23; Murray Feshbach, "Soviet Population Movements: Internal, External and Nowhere," Oxford Analytica, 1991; Klaus Segbers, "Migration and Refugee Movements from the USSR: Causes and Prospects," *RFE/RL Report on the USSR*, 15 November 1991, 6–14.

[55]See Iulian V. Bromlei, *Etnosotsial'nye protsessy: Teoriia, istoriia, sovremennost'* (Moscow: Nauka, 1987).

existence of a de-ethnicized Soviet group of mixed background, who combine nostalgia for their lost empire with Soviet-style ethnic liberalism. It simply places them in their proper minority perspective. (Russian nationalists do not have a monopoly on nostalgia for empire.)

Conditions for nationalism were present from the outset of Soviet rule, with an ethnically based republic hierarchical structure that created specific, often contested "autonomous republic" boundaries and supported educated, national (albeit mostly puppet) elites. Conditions were compounded by repressions of national leaders and, in extreme form, by deportations of whole ethnic groups. This succeeded in squelching national cultural and political life only temporarily and unevenly. Nationalism was even exacerbated by more mild and tolerant policies of paternalism that chafed as national elites came to know more about other peoples' human rights struggles both within and outside the Soviet empire. All of this nourished a potential for multiple expressions of ethnic identity, multiple manifestations of political activism, and, by 1990, new constitutions for "sovereign" republics.[56]

The explosion of ethnic and nationalist expression arose not simply out of a newly created post-Soviet societal void, or a thawing of frozen, preexisting pre-Soviet identities, but rather as the result of a cumulative series of dynamic interethnic encounters that evolved throughout the twentieth century. Communism helped shape the form and rhetoric of these encounters and the rationale behind them. Another kind of less hypocritical Russian hegemony would have yielded both similarities and differences.

Non-Russians inside the Russian Federation debate perceived legacies of Soviet-style communism in both negative and positive terms. Negative legacies could alternatively be described as residues of resentment: over linguistic Russification, over economic imbalances, over suppression of spiritual life, over the power habits and outright corruption of party elites still hanging on to power as transformed business personnel, and over a political culture organized to channel communication hierarchi-

---

[56]Yeltsin's former nationality advisor, Russian politician and sociologist Galina Starovoitova, is concerned that misuse of the legal term "sovereignty" can lead to international confusion as to whether republics are claiming independence (personal communication, 2 May 1993). She has suggested several criteria for legitimate secession: (1) a history of self-consciousness as a national group; (2) a demographic majority for that group within currently constituted republic boundaries; and (3) a referendum in which a solid majority votes for unambiguous secession (Kennan Institute, 20 April 1992, and Georgetown University, 13 November 1992). In formulating divorce, Moscow would also have a right to demand adequate legal protection for all minorities, including Russians. Only Chechnia, Ingushetia, and Tyva potentially qualify in this scheme.

cally and discourage communication horizontally between republics without Moscow—to name just a few. More positive assessments frequently include aspects of educational achievements, particularly in rural school and literacy programs; selected urban development and industrial attainments; stimulation of national elites on a fairly extensive scale; ideals of interethnic harmony, even if they have not worked out in practice; increased chances for physical and job mobility; social welfare entitlements and some affirmative action programs for non-Russians, at least in theory if not practice.

In 1985, the republics in Russia (or in the *XSSR*) did not start perestroika from positions of equality in relation to the center: economic conditions varied, the degree of geopolitical boundary and ethnic group correlation varied, and legacies of "punishment" before, during, and after Stalin varied, to name only a few of the most salient dimensions.[57] These differences meant that national groups, and the individuals within them, experienced different degrees of radicalization. Given pan-Soviet problems, similar kinds of formal and informal opposition groups evolved, yet nuances are significant here, too. Ecological activism, for example, has been more tied to national consciousness in the Tyva and Sakha republics than in Buryatia.

Given the situational, dynamic, and sometimes volatile nature of post-Soviet republic politics, Russian (and a few non-Russian) authorities in the center face a delicate dilemma of balancing general legal principles with highly specific negotiated compromises.[58] Leaders of the ethnically based republics that form Russia's Federation Council openly complain that stipulations favoring the republics in the Federal Treaty are ignored. Many are impatient to see a functioning new truly federal Russian constitution that might alleviate the complexities and contradictions of the jerry-built one that qualified at once as a legacy, residue, and after-

---

[57]Iamskov, *Sovremennye problemy,* acknowledges these variable legacies, stressing the "irretrievable" problems caused by the 1922 national-state hierarchical administrative system; greater rights of republics over Russian oblasts are critiqued (see, for example, p. 7); conflicts are seen as (1) over status, (2) territorial, and (3) internal political (11–19).

[58]Constitution debates included resurrecting the idea of Andrei Sakharov that regions and republics have relatively more equal rights and obligations (Galina Starovoitova, 2 November 1993, personal communication). This is also Goskomnats Minister Sergei Shakrai's position. An analysis of the possible dismantling of the entire hierarchical republic-region-district federal structure in stages was in the *Post-Factum* report "Regionalizatsiia rossiiskoi federatsii" (Spring 1992), but is too radical for republic politicians furious at the demise of the Federal Treaty. See also former Minister Valery Tishkov's "O kontseptsii i osnovnykh napravleniia natsional'noi politiki v Rossii" (manuscript, 1992), for concern with individual rather than group civil rights.

math of communist rule. Chechnia has already in effect seceded, and Tatarstan, despite its demographic and geographic situation, has bitterly protested Yeltsin's unitary constitution. Tyva and others claim the moral right to secede, on the basis of historical legacy, but hold back and wait for better offers. They will not wait forever.

By examining specific cases in cultural, demographic, and historical contexts, we discover regional as well as center-periphery interactions. In the Siberian cases reviewed here, tensions have emerged between Russian (sometimes called "Siberiak") regionalist aspirations and indigenous national ones. Far Eastern economic separatism, led by Slavic Siberians often of Communist party backgrounds, has provoked concern among numerous representatives of local nationalities for the protection of their minority rights.[59] Yet the Buryat and Sakha republics present cases in which some of these internal tensions may be managed on the basis of a greater sharing of local resources newly wrenched from central control.

Many republic leaders, following as well as guiding the wishes of their multiethnic peoples, want better deals with Moscow, and are negotiating with government authorities from unaccustomed positions of relative strength. Their effectiveness has varied, given differences in electoral base, popularity, personality, background, republic wealth, and the receptivity to reform of republic parliaments. How the Russian Parliament and the central government manage the details of genuine economic and political power sharing with the republics will make an enormous difference in the potential transformation of Russia from a mini-empire to a relatively and unevenly democratic federal state. A constructive social legacy of Soviet-style communism would be to learn from the mistakes of attempted ethnic engineering.

[59] I am grateful to Evdokiia Aleksandrovna Gaer, then USSR Supreme Soviet deputy (personal communication, November 1991), for perspective on this subject. Samples of Siberian regional reporting include: Victor Serov, "Krasnoiarsk-Moskve: Idu na vy!" *Rossiskie vesti,* 7 July 1992, 2; "Tyumen Votes No Confidence in Russian Government," *FBIS* 3 June 1992, 44, from INTERFAX, 29 May 1992; "Urals, Siberia, Far East Urged to Secede," *FBIS,* 23 January 1992, 83, from TASS, 20 January 1992; "Sakhalin Leads Privatization Process," *FBIS,* 18 June 1992, 49, from ITAR-TASS, 16 June 1992. Compare M. V. Lisauskene, "Politicheskie orientatsii Sibiriakov," *Sotsiologicheskie Issledovanie,* no. 10 (1993): 47–53; Jean Riollot and Elizabeth Teague, "Siberian Separatists Cautioned," *RFE/RL Daily Report,* 23 March 1992, 1–2; Robert Osborn, "Russia: Federalism, Regionalism, and Nationality Claims," in George Ginsburg, Alvin Rubinstein, and Oleg Smolansky, eds., *Russia and America: From Rivalry to Reconciliation* (Armonk, N.Y.: M. E. Sharpe, 1993), 63–86; and Vera Tolz, "Regionalism in Russia: The Case of Siberia," *RFE/RL Research Report* 2 (February 1993): 1–9.

4

●━●

Ethnicity, nationalism, and
the communist legacy in Eastern Europe

MARIA N. TODOROVA

Of the four concepts enumerated in the title of this chapter, Eastern
Europe, despite all the controversy over its identity, seems the easiest to
define. It is appropriate to begin by introducing the terms that are the
basic subjects of this chapter. So many wars have been fought over
nationalism and communism, both real ones and wars fought with
words, that it seems necessary to inspect and display one's conceptual
tools before beginning to use them, that is, to state where one stands in
the theoretical debate.

ETHNICITY

In this text "ethnicity" is used as one side of the self-definition and self-
designation of a person, commitment, ideology, or faith (often secular),
based on a sense of (most often invented) kinship and common historical
experience and, as a rule, a community of language, religion, and customs. Such a definition owes much to Fredrik Barth's interpretation of
ethnic groups as "categories of ascription and identification."[1] It clearly
gives precedence to self-ascription, although I also recognize the importance of ascription by others. Barth had intended this new approach to
ethnicity as a way to overcome the limitations of the score of external or
objective theories related to economic, demographic, and other factors,
and principally the definition of ethnicity as the essential bearing group
of culture (in the broad anthropological sense). Without denying the
relevance of cultural differences, the Barthian interpretation of ethnicity
revolves around the important and useful concept of boundaries: It is

[1]Fredrik Barth, Introduction, in Barth, ed., *Ethnic Groups and Boundaries: The Social
Organization of Culture Difference* (Boston: Little, Brown, 1969), 10.

the delineation of boundaries that defines the ethnic groups, rather than their cultural content. These ethnic boundaries are social in character, although they may coincide with territorial or other boundaries.

The other important element of this definition is that, unlike language, territory, religion, race, and so on—which are essentially "dividers" along one criterion (though this does not imply that they cannot be very complex or ambiguous dividers)—ethnicity is a complicated sum total, an aggregate of different qualifiers, which is used for the demarcation of the ethnic boundary.

Lastly, although these particular sum totals can be recognized and analyzed in concrete historical cases, we cannot "discover" an ethnicity as the resultant of the synthesis of these components. This means that ethnicity cannot exist in the eye of the beholder unless it is explicitly stated in a conscious act of self-definition.

This definition with its restrictions will guide me in positioning myself within the great debate about the problem of the origins of ethnicity and nationalism. Broadly stated, it is the great debate between primordialists or perennialists, on the one hand, and modernists or instrumentalists, on the other.[2]

Emphasizing the importance of "primordial" ties based on kinship, race, territory, language, and religion, the first argument views ethnic communities and nations as essential and natural elements of the historical experience of humanity. According to some proponents of this view, ethnicity and nationalism represent a simple expansion of kinship ties (whether real or fictive) as a genetic mechanism of group solidarity in the struggle for survival.[3] In a similar kind of reasoning, other scholars point out the genetic character of the territorial nature of human beings where a formation like the nation-state would be interpreted simply as a historical invention to indicate the territory of the in-group.[4] A more sociological approach considers language, territory, race, and ethnicity as fundamental social links that predate any complex historical social

[2]For a useful summary of the two approaches, see Anthony D. Smith, *The Ethnic Origins of Nations* (Oxford: Basil Blackwell, 1986), 7–13.
[3]P. Van den Berghe, *The Ethnic Phenomenon* (New York: Elsevier, 1979).
[4]The so-called L.A.M. thesis developed by Konrad Lorenz, Robert Ardrey, and Desmond Morris; see K. Lorenz, *On Aggression* (New York: Harcourt, Brace, and World, 1966), R. Ardrey, *The Territorial Imperative: A Personal Inquiry into the Animal Origin of Property and Nations* (New York: Atheneum, 1966), and D. Morris, *The Naked Ape* (New York: McGraw Hill, 1968).

organization, and are immanent characteristics that have always divided humankind.[5]

Whether these two approaches interpret ethnicity as an extension of kinship or in terms of the territorial imperative of the Lorenz-Ardrey-Morris thesis (the sociobiological view), or else as a basic organizing principle of the human species (the sociological view), these two viewpoints converge in treating ethnicity and nationalism as, essentially, stages of the same perennial phenomenon. In fact, there are significant nuances between the more moderate perennial and the more radical primordial position, but in the long run they present a universalist, or even a fundamentalist, interpretation.[6]

On the other side of the debate is the argument that nations and nationalism have been formed during the modern period, that they are by-products (although in particular circumstances they can also act as builders) of such developments as the rise of the modern secular state and its bureaucracy, of capitalism and industrialization, of mass communication and education. Whether they give precedence to the social, economic, political, or cultural factors in their interpretations, these views converge in treating nations and nationalism as phenomena that are essentially connected to the modern world (regardless of whether they are treated as contingent or deterministic).

In offering what is perhaps the best expressed modernist and instrumentalist approach, Ernest Gellner insists that although "patriotism is a perennial part of human life . . . nationalism is a very distinctive species of patriotism, and one which becomes pervasive and dominant only under certain social conditions, which in fact prevail in the modern world, and nowhere else."[7] He continues:

The great, but valid paradox, is this: nations can be defined only in terms of the age of nationalism, rather than, as you might expect, the other way round. It is

[5]Joshua A. Fishman, "Social Theory and Ethnography: Language and Ethnicity in Eastern Europe," in P. Sugar, ed., *Ethnic Diversity and Conflict in Eastern Europe* (Santa Barbara, Calif.: ABC-Clio, 1980); Clifford Geertz, ed., *Old Societies and New States* (New York: Free Press, 1963); Edward Shils, "Primordial, Personal, Sacred and Civil Ties," *British Journal of Sociology* 7 (1957): 113–45.
[6]The latest work in this line of reasoning belongs to James G. Kellas, *The Politics of Nationalism and Ethnicity* (London: Macmillan, 1991), which aims at presenting one integrated theory of the politics of nationalism and contends that such a theory must begin with human nature (160).
[7]Ernest Gellner, *Nations and Nationalism* (Ithaca, N.Y.: Cornell University Press, 1983), 138.

not the case that "the age of nationalism" is a mere summation of the awakening and political self-assertion of this, that, or the other nation. Rather, when general social conditions make for standardized, homogeneous, centrally sustained high cultures, pervading entire populations and not just élite minorities, a situation arises in which well-defined educationally sanctioned and unified cultures constitute very nearly the only kind of unit with which men willingly and often ardently identify. . . . Under these conditions, though under these conditions *only*, nations can indeed be defined in terms both of will and of culture, and indeed in terms of the convergence of them both with political units.[8]

In fact, even most perennialists do not deny the historians' consensus that nationalism as an ideology as well as the nation-state as a specific type of political organization came into being in the last decades of the eighteenth century, although the presence of national sentiments can be traced among educated elites a century earlier. The divide occurs in the treatment of nationalism as the last in the line of similar manifestations versus the view of it as a unique attribute of modernity.

There is no need to enter the discussion about ethnic communities as primordial groups in a full-fledged manner. Suffice it to say here that the primordial approach seems to trivialize the problem in its search for essentials, such as the innate desire to belong, a reduction to regional and kin connections, and so forth.[9] Although this is essentially true, it makes the definitions redundant and, consequently, inoperative. Even worse, by describing ethnicity in terms of historical characteristics, this approach tends to obscure the historical evolution of the phenomenon. One could readily agree that modern European nations developed on the basis of preexisting ethnic identities, yet this statement only transposes the problem from nationalism to ethnicity. Were ethnicities then ubiquitous, as the "perennialist" believes, or were they also "constructed"?

There has been an attempt to moderate what are seen as the two extremes by adopting a standpoint ostensibly intermediate to that of the perennialists and the modernists.[10] This attempt at compromise clearly

[8]Ibid., 55.
[9]The idea of belonging as the critical element in nationalism is developed especially in the works of Boyd C. Shafer: *Nationalism: Myth and Reality* (New York: Harcourt, Brace, 1955), *Faces of Nationalism: New Realities and Old Myths* (New York: Harcourt, Brace Jovanovich, 1972), *Nationalism: Its Nature and Interpretation*, 4th ed. (Washington, D.C.: American Historical Association, 1976), *Nationalism and Internationalism: Belonging in Human Experience* (Malabar, Fla.: R. E. Krieger, 1982).
[10]Smith, *Ethnic Origins*, 18, espouses a view that "allows one to delineate different patterns of nation-formation, according to the degree to which an ethnic mosaic persisted in the relevant area up to the eve of the era of nationalism."

rejects the primordialist view of ethnicity as natural, but it is also a slight departure from the perennialist view in that it discounts the universality and permanence of the phenomenon by insisting, instead, on its recurring and persistent character.[11] At the same time proponents of this view argue that nations are not simply and solely products of modernity but have developed on the basis of preexisting ethnic identities, and that in modern Europe *ethnie* (or ethnic groups) were reformed into nation-states as a result of the "triple Western revolution . . . in the sphere of the division of labor . . . in the control of the administration, and . . . in cultural co-ordination."[12]

In this line of reasoning *ethnie* are seen as having "emerged and reemerged in different periods in several continents and culture-areas right up to the modern era; and that ethnicity has remained as a socio-cultural 'model' for human organization and communication from the early third millennium BC until today, even if not every 'society' has followed this model of organization."[13]

The most serious, though not direct, criticism of the compromise position affects its treatment of premodern *ethnie* and is based on a historical perspective.[14] As a variety of historians of the premodern and early modern period have argued, ethnic and national consciousness requires "embodiment in working institutions in order to acquire enduring reality."[15] Without such an institutional role or embodiment, "ethnic identity remained formless and fragmentary, expressed in a myriad of ways whose significance is difficult to penetrate and thus available for an almost infinitely flexible exploitation at some later time when institutional practice and ethnic identity converged. . . . Statements about group identity only make real sense in the context of how people organize to give such statements validity."[16]

---

[11]Ibid., 32.
[12]Ibid., 131.
[13]Ibid., 32.
[14]Other critiques expose the caveat of essentialism as well as the problem of circular arguments—for example, using certain ethnic characteristics and ethnic consciousness as proof for the existence of *ethnie,* although designating these characteristics and consciousnesses as "ethnic" rests on the assumption of the existence of the ethnic group. See John Breuilly, review of A. Smith's *Ethnic Origins of Nations,* in *English Historical Review* 103, no. 407 (April 1988): 414–18.
[15]Otto Dann, ed., *Nationalismus in vorindustrieller Zeit* (Munich: Oldenburg, 1986), 77, quoted in Breuilly, review of *Ethnic Origins,* 416.
[16]Ibid., 416–17.

In a particularly picturesque metaphor—in fact rewriting Tom Nairn's simile of nationalism as Janus—Paul James remarks:

History has come to be fractured into antinomious faces. It is "pictured as like the Roman god, Janus, who stood above gateways with one face looking forward and one backwards." One face looks through the veil of the last couple of centuries to the "deep" past, while the other face surveys the sweep from the recent past to the present. Each has a different view as to how history is lived and "reproduced"—one face assumes the primordiality of its grounding forms; the other accentuates the historicity of history and emphasizes its self-conscious, constructed, invented quality. It is an ontological split with fundamental implications for historical method and for political practice. . . . When made explicit, such a position faces the danger of succumbing to the dichotomy of essentializing the distant past and fictionalizing the present and the modern past.[17]

Adopting a standpoint intermediate to that of the perennialists and modernists, as argued by Anthony Smith, is, I believe, an illusion. One can refine the extremes of both positions and articulate them in less than mutually exclusive terms. In the end, however, there remains a profound difference between the two approaches: one is based on a structural view of society which, even when recognizing a long-term evolution, still gives precedence to perennial characteristics, a kind of essentialism; the other favors a diachronic view of society which, although recognizing the existence of long-term structural similarities or even identity (in the sense of identicalness), still gives priority to historical uniqueness. Unless (James's) Janus is professed to be schizophrenic, we have to accommodate him in two bodies.

The many convincing theories about the presence of ethnic communities and ethnic consciousness throughout human history are based primarily on sociological constructs. For any historian, the evidence is far too fragmentary to warrant more than the cautious admission of the existence of occasional sentiments in the ancient Near East and medieval Europe articulated by some individuals in terms strikingly similar to those of modern ethnicity and nationalism.[18]

The crucial criterion should not be the potential presence in the human psyche of the characteristics that identify an ethnicity, but the proof that the combination of these characteristics was dominant as a

---

[17]Paul James, "The Janus Faces of History: Cleaving Marxist Theories of Nation and Nationalism," *Canadian Review of Studies in Nationalism* 18, nos. 1–2 (1991): 13, 18.

[18]For an excellent discussion of the evolution of the Greek *ethnos* from antiquity to the contemporary period, see Roger Just, "Triumph of the Ethnos," in E. Tonkin, M. McDonald, and M. Chapman, eds., *History and Ethnicity* (London and New York: Routledge, 1991), 71–88.

form of group identification (for example, ethnicity) over other forms of group identification (religion, caste, kin, localism, and so on) at any given point of historical time. It seems that we do not possess enough historical evidence, however, to claim this for any period before the modern. The postulate of the perennial, or even only of the recurrent, existence of premodern ethnicities is based on conjecture, in order to give a logical explanation for the obvious relation between ethnicity and nationalism, or else in order to accommodate structurally similar manifestations in the past in a Grand Theory. I prefer to consider historical evidence as the basic criterion. Analysis of the existing premodern historical evidence leads me to subscribe, at least for the time being, to a liberal rendition of the modernist approach.

Further, the historical evidence indicates that ethnicity, too, should be regarded as a product of modernity—that is, of the revolutionizing and intensification in communication, of the crisis in religion and secularization, of economic growth and industrialization. It is further linked to the ideology of what we have come to term romanticism: the search for uniqueness and for the original sources of the differences between peoples, mostly constructed around language, religion, and folklore. In this context ethnicity is particularly associated with the philosophy of Johann Gottfried von Herder, whose significance and influence transcends *das Deutsche Kulturgebiet* and who has been called one of the first, if not the first, writer of Europe to develop a comprehensive philosophy of nationalism.[19] It should be added that in the present classification he is, in fact, the first philosopher of ethnicity, and with his approach to nationality as a cultural organism in search of its *Volksgeist* he is also one of the first primordialists. For all his crucial contributions to the development of nationalism he should not be described as a nationalist, however.

NATIONALISM

This leads to the second important notion. Here nationalism is defined, in a formula perhaps reductionist, as the merger of ethnicity and statehood. The belief that "nationalism is not a nineteenth-century product arising from the union of *natio* and *patria* [in the sense of the political

[19]Robert R. Ergang, *Herder and the Foundations of German Nationalism* (New York: Columbia University Press, 1931); F. M. Barnard, *Herder's Social and Political Thought from the Enlightenment to Nationalism* (Oxford: Clarendon Press, 1965).

nation and the vague notion of fatherland], but rather the result of a working relationship between people and a state,"[20] although a minority view, has its strong exponents. "Nationalism," to quote John Jensen, is "the bonding between people and state that became progressively more strong and important in the later eighteenth and nineteenth centuries. The movement becomes possible as the state penetrates and becomes at one with society: it takes different forms directed by the experience and traditions of different parts of Europe."[21]

Where I differ slightly from this view is in recognizing that there is more than just the amorphous "people" who enter this relationship with the state and produce nations and nationalism. There have been two distinct, although sometimes parallel or coinciding, processes all over modern Europe. One is the gradual formation of a distinct group consciousness defined by different authors as national revival, cultural revival, or rebirth, and which I have termed ethnicity and have explicitly linked with modernity. This process had an uneven chronological development paralleling the uneven process of modernization but, as a whole, flowered in Europe in the eighteenth and nineteenth centuries, with some earlier and some later manifestations.

The other process is the merger of this consciousness with statehood and the creation and development of a new consciousness and ideology: nationalism. Ethnicity and nationalism are not coterminous, although, at least in the European experience, nationalism seems to have evolved around an ethnic nucleus and usually assumes the hypostasis of ethnonationalism.

These definitions signify far more than a purely scholastic debate, because they have important implications for the future development of ethnic and national group consciousness. They are also relevant to the attempt to correlate Marxism and communism with nationalism.

COMMUNISM

In the case of communism, it is important to make a distinction between the ideology of prestate communism, or classical Marxism, and the

---

[20]Roland Sussex, Introduction to Roland Sussex and J. C. Eade, eds., *Culture and Nationalism in Nineteenth-Century Eastern Europe* (Columbus, Ohio: Slavica Publishers, 1985), 5.

[21]John H. Jensen, "National and Cultural Revivals: The Relationship between Them, as Exemplified by Romanian and Serbian Experiences (1780s–1870s)," in Sussex and Eade, *Culture and Nationalism in Nineteenth-Century Eastern Europe*, 78.

communist state praxis with its own discourse. Lest this distinction be seen as an attempt at whitewashing communism as a doctrine, I must support my claim. In the context of the present problem, the history of communism as practice is seen primarily as an adaptation of peripheral European states to the challenge of modernization coming (and imposed) from the West European center. As such it should be classified under the rubric of specific responses to modernization rather than under the heading of ideology or "isms." In its response, however, the practice adopted or appropriated elements of the ideology (mostly the ideas of social justice and equality) and, most important, adopted the self-designation "communism": a clear case of ideological nominalism (a concept developed later in the chapter).

This does not presuppose the exclusive treatment of communism as *only* a modernizing response or an ideology of modernization. It certainly does not preclude the interpretation of communism as a totalitarian system, where the party claims exclusivity. This angle of approach is, however, irrelevant to my main theme.

The crucial distinction between communism as ideology and as practice is in the attitude toward the state, which functions like a litmus test. Whereas the state is the raison d'être as well as the modus vivendi of both nationalism and of practical communism, classical Marxism presents an ambiguous attitude toward the state (although not always explicitly antistate). With the Bolshevik revolution and the building of "real socialism" we see the appropriation of select elements of the Marxist doctrine: namely, its ideas of social equality and justice, as well as its modernizing potential, especially in a drive for industrialization. From the outset, the variety of communism that developed in Russia and was exported after World War II was an ideology of modernization, an attempt to produce a unique way to meet the challenge of a hegemonic West. Both nationalism and state communism responded to the same challenge, becoming tools of modernization. Just as the nation-state was imposed as the gold standard of "civilized" international organization in the nineteenth and twentieth centuries, so also industrialization became the standard for economic progress. Stalin, for example, made no secret of this:[22]

We are going full steam ahead toward socialism through industrialization, leaving behind the age-long "Russian" backwardness. We are becoming a land of

[22]David Mackenzie and Michael W. Curran, *A History of the Soviet Union* (Belmont, Calif.: Wadsworth, 1991), 245.

metals ... automobiles ... tractors, and when we have put the USSR on an automobile and the muzhik on a tractor, let the noble capitalists ... attempt to catch up. We shall see then which countries can be labeled backward and which advanced. (1929)

To slacken the tempo ... would mean falling behind. And those who fall behind get beaten. ...
   We are fifty to a hundred years behind the advanced countries. We must make good this distance in ten years. Either we do it, or they crush us. (1931)

Thus, while not denying the continuity between Marxism and communism, one can agree with Leszek Kolakowski that communism is one possible interpretation of Marxism.[23] I would add that it is the etatist interpretation of Marxism.[24]

The distinction between communist prestate ideology (or Marxism) and etatist communism is relevant when facing the question of the so-called syncretism between nationalism and communism as ideologies.

COMMUNISM AND NATIONALISM

The phenomenon of the coexistence and relationship between communism and nationalism has been extensively treated in the literature with the general conclusion that we are facing a case of ideological symbiosis with specific purposes. This ideological fusion between the "two rival salvation movements of modernization" has been explained by the fact that "Marxism and nationalism, for all their mutual antagonisms, display considerable parallels and convergencies. These meeting points clearly permit a doctrinal syncretism."[25] In what is probably the most extensive articulation of this view, Anthony Smith follows up the structural parallels of the two ideologies to conclude that "Marxists and nationalists can be seen to share a concern for man's alienation and his reintegration and return to his authentic state of being. Both ideologies

---

[23]Leszek Kolakowski, *Main Currents in Marxism*, vol. 3, *The Breakdown* (Oxford: Clarendon Press, 1978), 526.
[24]In addressing the question about the relation between Marxist ideology and state communism we are facing essentially the dilemma between ideology and realpolitik. It is obvious that communism in Russia created the strongest break with traditional nineteenth-century perception and loyalties, and perceived itself strongly, indeed exclusively, in ideological terms. But already from the outset there was a gradual shift to pragmatism and raison d'état, which in Stalin's times became predominant. In Eastern Europe this shift occurred almost at the beginning.
[25]Anthony Smith, *Nationalism in the Twentieth Century* (New York: New York University Press, 1979), 116–27.

adhere throughout to a holistic, naturalistic and libertarian view of man and his destiny."[26]

Without our going into a detailed critique, it suffices to remark that this type of intellectual exercise can be performed on any pair of ideologies that display a structural parallelism simply because of being ideologies. Furthermore, such an exercise would be far more successful in the case of ideologies deriving essentially from the same source, as do liberalism and Marxism from the universalist ideas of the Enlightenment. It is well recognized that the resilience of Marx's theoretical legacy is due, among other factors, to its overall accord with the dominant liberal worldview, which interprets individual action as rational pursuit of interests, despite the fact that Marxism takes this view to its extreme and thus forms what has been aptly called the "hyper-rationalist genre."[27]

Together with liberalism Marxism shares in underestimating, indeed discounting, the political significance of ethnicity and nationalism.[28] The huge blow dealt to the central idea of Marxism with the rejection of proletarian solidarity in favor of ethnonationalism during World War I prompted an attempt at adaptation on the part of Lenin and other communist leaders in favoring the principle of self-determination, including the right to secession. It has to be noted that nowhere in Marx's oeuvre is there even mention of a right to self-determination or support for national liberation.[29] This principle was endorsed by the Communist International, however, and after 1924 all communist parties had to adopt it (although it was not practiced).[30] It became one of the important strategies to appeal to broad segments of the population, but it remained only a strategy. In the end, Lenin failed to develop a general theory of nationalism and left "open the question of the nature and role of nationalism in its relationship with socialism."[31]

That Marxism failed to develop an adequate theory of nationalism has become a truism.[32] But the fact that "Marxists have failed in their efforts at incorporating the reality of nationalism into their theoretical

[26]Ibid., 126.
[27]Gale Stokes, "Lessons of the East European Revolutions of 1989," *Problems of Communism* 40 (September–October 1991): 18.
[28]John F. Stack, Jr., "Ethnic Mobilization in World Politics: The Primordial Perspective," in Stack, ed., *The Primordial Challenge: Ethnicity in the Contemporary World* (New York: Greenwood Press, 1986), 6–7.
[29]Shlomo Avineri, "Toward a Socialist Theory of Nationalism," *Dissent* (Fall 1990): 449.
[30]Stack, "Ethnic Mobilization," 7.
[31]Avineri, "Toward a Socialist Theory of Nationalism," 451.
[32]Ibid., 447–57.

understanding . . . is deeply rooted in the nature of Marxist thought itself."[33] The incompatibility between a cosmopolitan universalist ideology and a particularist romantic creed precludes their theoretical syncretism. What did develop, however, was the undeniable phenomenon of "communist nationalism" in Eastern Europe. In place of the interpretation of the four postwar decades as syncretism between nationalism and communism, or as a series of attempts to appropriate the nationalist potential in order to legitimize the communist discourse, I would argue that ethnicity, nationalism, and etatist communism form one line in the historical development of Eastern Europe from the eighteenth through the twentieth centuries, shaping an almost uninterrupted nationalist continuum.

The hegemony of the classical Marxist doctrine in the immediate post–World War II period in Eastern Europe was only a brief caesura, quickly replaced by the practice of state communism. On the other hand, as already stated, etatist communism appropriated important elements of the Marxist doctrine, and above all appropriated its self-designation, thus legitimizing its claims on the basis of the Marxist discourse (a perfect example of ideological nominalism used for legitimation). So-called Communist nationalism was nothing but a transvestite "ordinary" nationalism which, after 1989, gloats in its newly acquired nudity.

A particularly pertinent example in this respect is the standing of the Bulgarian Socialist party (BSP) (the former Communist party) vis-à-vis the Turks in Bulgaria, and particularly toward the Movement for Rights and Freedoms (otherwise known as the Turkish party). The BSP argued that the presence of the Turkish party (the third political force) in Parliament was unconstitutional, because according to the constitution parties based on religious or ethnic principle are forbidden. This position of the BSP reflects the expediency of playing the nationalist card in the power struggle (the explanation usually advanced). There is also the legacy of the period when the party was identical to the state and considerations of raison d'état were an immediate priority. Ironically,

---

[33] John Ehrenreich, "Socialism, Nationalism and Capitalist Development," *Review of Radical Political Economists* 15, no. 1 (1983): 1–40. It is not the task of this chapter to go into detail about the reasons for the inadequacies of Marxism to comprehend and conceptualize the nationalist phenomenon. In a recent monograph on the problem, Ephraim Nimni pointed out that it was the "joint influences of economic reductionism, evolutionism and eurocentrism . . . which informed the European classical Marxist debates on the national question," and which precluded the formulation of an adequate theory. Nimni, *Marxism and Nationalism: Origins of a Political Crisis* (Concord, Mass.: Pluto Press, 1991), 195.

the socialist party has dropped ideological arguments from its arsenal of legitimization and resorts exclusively to legalistic considerations. Conversely, as will be shown later in the chapter, the former democratic opposition, now in power, increasingly appropriates ideological arguments, most often playing the anti-communist card.

Therefore, in addressing the first question—of the communist legacy regarding the problems of ethnicity and nationalism—I maintain that the legacy of Marxism as ideology is practically irrelevant. The one exception is the possible cathartic psychological effect of an open dialogue on ethnic conflicts, which was taboo in all communist countries; as one author has aptly stated, Eastern Europe was deprived of its *Stunde null* (zero hour) in 1945, the "unique caesura that made new solutions possible in the West."[34] This statement is not so unequivocal, however, when applied to the experience of Western Europe: it is both proved (for example, in French-German relations) and disclaimed (for example, regarding the Irish problem).

The contention that a syncretism did not occur between Marxism and nationalism is, of course, applicable only to Eastern Europe. It is undeniable that there are syncretic Marxist nationalisms in the so-called Third World but, as has been recognized, they are usually "second-wave" nationalisms, and their Marxism is invoked more for its state-building potentialities (so well demonstrated by the practice of etatist communism) than for its social message.[35]

This leads to the second question, which can be formulated in a much more mundane way: Did communism put a lid on nationalism? The popular answer, on the basis of appearances as well as the claims of both communists and nationalists (although, of course, with opposing evaluations), is that it did. I argue here that there was a lid on nationalist discourse, but this is not the same as saying that there was a lid on nationalism.

The domination of the communist discourse (or the language of Marxism-Leninism) reflected primarily power politics and is a tribute to the cold war division of the world. Even in societies where communism had a significant degree of indigenous development (for example, Bulgaria or Czechoslovakia) or even legitimacy (for example, Yugoslavia) and was not necessarily or exclusively seen as an alien import, the "genuine" Marxist discourse was soon replaced by the imagery of na-

---

[34]Stokes, "Lessons of the Revolutions of 1989," 19.
[35]Smith, *Nationalism in the Twentieth Century,* 129.

tionalism translated into an idiosyncratic Marxist slang. To quote Katherine Verdery's apt remark: "In its encounter with Marxism, ['the nation'] proved itself capable of subordinating the latter (Marxism) and subverting its terms. . . . A discourse about unity and continuity—the nation—overwhelmed one about differentiation and change—Marxism."[36] I would dare to paraphrase this statement, as I believe it was the nation-state that subverted the earlier and short-lived utopian attempts to build society on the premise of the priority of class-consciousness. The ongoing conflict between the two discourses, however, reflected a power struggle within the intellectual elite for hegemony.

Verdery elaborates further on the mechanisms of how the national discourse subdued the Marxist one in Romania:

> The paradox is that [the national discourse] achieved its triumph at the initiative of the Party leadership and their protochronist allies, seconded (merely) by those who opposed them. The groups in power adopted this once-hegemonic ideology—so potently instituted beforehand—in order to overcome it, incorporate it, and profit from its strength; they were overcome by it instead.[37]

I take issue with the conclusion that national ideology was adopted in order to be overcome. National ideology was shared throughout by the party leadership, but in Romania it was asserted through different discourses, among which the discourse on "the Nation" became incontestably and officially the most powerful.

In a country like Bulgaria, on the other hand, where official policy was or was presented as one of complete consent with the center, Moscow, the majority of the party leadership and the ruling elite also shared the national ideology. But they articulated it in a much more cautious way, using, to a much greater extent, the hegemonic Marxist discourse for clearly legitimizing purposes.

Persistent grievances, which in other circumstances might have been articulated rightly or wrongly as ethnic, were instead articulated in economic and social terms, since these were considered to be legitimate topics in the "socialist" countries. Commenting on the Yugoslav crisis of 1971, George Klein observes that "many arguments couched in the language of economics thinly concealed nationalistic particularism."[38]

---

[36]Katherine Verdery, *National Ideology under Socialism: Identity and Cultural Politics in Ceausescu's Romania* (Berkeley: University of California Press, 1991), 12.

[37]Ibid., 314.

[38]George Klein, "The Role of Ethnic Politics in the Czechoslovak Crisis of 1968 and the Yugoslav Crisis of 1971," *Studies in Comparative Communism* 8, no. 4 (1975): 349–50.

The change that has occurred after the series of "velvet" revolutions is not the release of the genie of nationalism out of a tightly sealed bottle, but the revision of two constraints: (1) the language of the discourse, for it is no longer necessary to pay lip-service to the dominant socialist jargon, and (2), much more important, the international status quo, for an attempt can be made nowadays without grave risks to realize practically the claims articulated in the discourse. For example, the Yugoslavs watched developments in the Baltics closely, and the bewilderment of Croat and Slovene secessionists was sincere when they asked why they should not be recognized if Estonians, Lithuanians, and Latvians could be. Despite the attempt to depict the Baltic case as legally unique, it was perceived only as a rather weak and unconvincing attempt to legitimize an exception to the status quo without upsetting it radically. It was rightly perceived both by a reluctant Gorbachev and by triumphant nationalist and secessionist groups as a precedent. The subsequent developments in Yugoslavia, the shift in support by the international community from self-determination to territorial integrity, the flagrant inconsistencies of approach to the different republics and minorities only emphasized the power vacuum in the region.

The countries of Central and Eastern Europe seem to be returning to old-time nationalism according to the much abused déjà vu metaphor. In addition, this ideology is being put back into structurally historical terms of relations with the West, and thus the responses toward the West might be reminiscent of the pre–World War II period.

The third question to be addressed is directly linked to the previous two, and it concerns the peculiar twist in the development of East European nationalism during its communist period. It has been suggested, in a structural model of internal colonialism that juxtaposes the economic and the political core, that "it is more vexing for an ethnic group to be politically dominated by those whom it considers to be its economic and cultural inferiors [whereas] the 'convergent' situation, if stable, entails less cognitive dissonance and less relative deprivation, [and] thus is psychologically less humiliating to the subordinated group."[39] Two classical examples of this case are the Basque perspective on the Castilians or the Croatian perspective on the Serbs.

Yet within the former "socialist" world, dominated as it was by

---

[39]Joseph Rothschild, "The Emergence of Contemporary Ethnopolitics," in Nissan Oren, ed., *When Patterns Change: Turning Points in International Politics* (New York: St. Martin's Press, 1984), 71–72.

Moscow, there was an idiosyncratic inversion. Nationalism is a relational ideology; that is, it can be defined only vis-à-vis the other, not per se. Confining the Eastern Europeans behind the Wall limited the scope of their comparative horizon. Much as it seems simplified and overstated, many Eastern Europeans constructed the image of colonial relations with an imperial(istic) center in Moscow, and insisted on it even after the mid-1950s. This view bolstered a positive image of themselves in comparison to Russia, which was construed as the eternal Asiatic barbarian.

In a typically crude aphorism leaked to the press in one of his visits to West Germany, Todor Zhivkov expressed this feeling using a double inversion of the colonial metaphor. He maintained that Eastern Europeans in general and Bulgarians in particular enjoyed the privilege of having such a big colonial empire as the Soviet Union. Members of the opposition to the center took upon themselves the glare and romance of national-liberation, of emancipatory struggle against an inferior foe (unlike the usual anticolonial struggle, where local nationalism had to fight also its own inferiority complex). Theirs was not the defensive and inferiority-ridden nationalism of the pre–World War II period vis-à-vis the West.

The disappearance of the Soviet Union inconveniences East European nationalisms in much the same way that it does the military, the intelligence, and cold war ideologues: it accomplished the destruction (or deconstruction) of the *one* enemy. The radical changes that are taking place seem to point to most unwelcome repercussions, concerning not so much *how* Eastern Europe will transform itself, but the fact that it will not do this in a vacuum (or the quasi-vacuum provided by the communist umbrella). Eastern Europe is being exposed to the West, with the hopeful result that this will entail growing adaptation and integration. Always present, however, is the specter of another possible scenario: merciless marginalization and peripheralization.

Such exposure will, naturally, affect the character of nationalism. From the defensive and inferiority nationalism that it was before World War II, it turned into a superiority nationalism in relation to the Soviet Union and now again is reverting back to its original paradigm.[40] Com-

[40]For reasons of space, this chapter treats Eastern European nationalism only in its opposition to the "big" partners—Western Europe or the Soviet Union. It does not address the important problem of inter–East European relations, the relations between neighboring "socialist" countries, and the relations between neighboring states of opposing social systems, all of which had significant implications for the growth and the specific shape of each nationalism.

munism proved to be an unsuccessful attempt to supersede the effects of an unfavorable placement in the international hierarchy of nation-states through isolationism. Within the new (old) paradigm, the growth of nationalist sentiment seems to be inevitable. After all, as Tom Nairn has pointed out, "in a broader sense nationalism is a necessary condition of tolerable modernization."[41]

Lastly, there is the problem that has been mentioned several times in this chapter: ideological nominalism. Ideological nominalism is constructed very much along the lines of ethnic nominalism, which has been described as

the assignment of ethnic labels to aggregates without commensurate, specific evidence regarding the nature, intensity, comprehensiveness, and continuity of individual identity and group structure. It treats *all* who share *some* of the markers of an ethnic group—residents of a particular region or users of a language—or who sometimes, for some purposes, identify or associate with such a group as if they were members of a continuous, comprehensive, and structurally integral social entity.[42]

In ideological nominalism one can distinguish, too, between self-ascription and outside ascription. An example of the former is the "Marxism" of state-socialism, the attempt to legitimize the program and practice of the self-proclaimed Marxist governments by the general doctrine of Marxism/communism. An example of the latter type are the attempts to delegitimize the effects of *any* alternative agenda by attributing to it, by extension, the characteristics of the practice of the communist regimes. Bulgaria's actions in dealing with the breakup of Yugoslavia are a recent example of such actions.

As is well known, Bulgaria went ahead of the European Community in becoming the first state in the world to recognize not only Croatia, Slovenia, and Bosnia-Herzegovina but also Macedonia as sovereign states. At the same time, in an interview with the German *Süddeutsche Zeitung* on 30 August 1991, the president of Bulgaria, Zhelyu Zhelev, gave the following opinion on the Macedonian question, and Bulgaria's stand toward it:

[41]Tom Nairn, *The Enchanted Class: Britain and Its Monarchy* (London: Radius, 1988), 129–30. This is a more prosaic version of his famous metaphor of nationalism as the Roman god Janus, looking backward with one face to the reassuring past, while the other face glances steadily in the direction of a painful modernity. See Tom Nairn, "The Modern Janus," *New Left Review* 94 (1975): passim.

[42]Martin O. Heisler, "Ethnicity and Ethnic Relations in the Modern West," in Joseph V. Montville, ed., *Conflict and Peacemaking in Multiethnic Societies* (Lexington, Mass.: Lexington Books, 1991), 26.

First, Bulgaria would recognize Macedonia after the referendum in the republic on 8 September, because this was consistent with the principles of Bulgaria's foreign policy on recognizing the right to self-determination.

Second, Bulgaria will not recognize the Macedonian nation since that nation was a fiction fabricated by the Communist International with a certain political goal.[43]

A philosopher like the president would know, of course, that all nations can be viewed as fictions and that they all are constructed with certain political goals. His historical advisors would undoubtedly have enlightened him that this particular fiction was concocted decades before the notion of the Third Communist International was even conceived in the conspiratorial mind of world Bolshevism. Yet this story is particularly evocative in demonstrating how ideological nominalism can be used for delegitimizing purposes.[44]

CONCLUSION

The following cautious conclusions may be hazarded:

1. Ethnicity and nationalism are phenomena attributable to modernity.

2. Communism as ideology and state practice must be distinguished.

3. Communism and nationalism are ideologies that are specific responses and attempts at adjustment to the challenges of modernization; there exists, however, an intrinsic theoretical incompatibility which precludes an organic symbiosis between the two ideologies.

4. Nationalism and etatist communism form an almost uninterrupted line of an evolving but essentially the same continuum in the history of

---

[43]Cited in the *Insider*, no. 11 (1991): 27 (Bulgarian text in *Svoboden narod*, 31 August 1991).

[44]This is not meant to be a critique of the integrity of President Zhelev, as it was perceived by some of the Bulgarian participants at the Social Legacy of Communism conference, where an earlier version of this chapter was read. Clearly, in the circumstances of polarized public opinion and the impending presidential elections (in January 1992, when Zhelev was reelected president after a much contested campaign), it would have been suicidal on the part of any politician to recognize the Macedonian nation. The Macedonian question, which has shaped and pestered Bulgarian political life throughout all of the twentieth century, is still (although happily only) a hot emotional issue. On the contrary, this interview shows President Zhelev becoming an experienced politician who recognizes well the uses of ideological nominalism. On the other hand, the whole episode probably merits analysis in the framework of another problem—the dividing lines between political expediency and intellectual consistency in the larger context of the role of intellectuals in society—but that topic obviously falls outside the scope of the present chapter.

Eastern Europe, which began in the late eighteenth and nineteenth centuries and is far from fulfilled today.

5. A kind of merger is possible, as did take place between the communist practice (which appropriated important features of the Marxist doctrine) and nationalism, on the grounds of a common denominator: the state.

6. In the existence of the Eastern European communist states, the hegemony of the classical Marxist doctrine was a brief caesura in a national continuum of the eighteenth through twentieth centuries; and in this continuum classical Marxism became irrelevant, despite ideological nominalism and the domination of a Marxist idiom.

7. Eastern European communist nationalism or nationalist communism was a peculiar type of psychologically inverted nationalism, in which the idea of a more backward metropolis served as a catharsis from an inferiority complex for a while.

8. The really interesting question is not of ethnicity and communism but of ethnicity and nationalism per se. Why does it persist in the modern and postmodern ages? Rather than look for the legacy of communism in order to explain the intensification of ethnic and national feelings in Eastern Europe, we should approach the Eastern European situation within a European—indeed, a global—framework.

Faced with the problem of the emergence of contemporary ethnopolitics in the global context, Joseph Rothschild has attempted to provide a tentative answer:

Why should the ethnic stereotypes eclipse the other possible candidate-images? ... [T]he answer is a contingent one: in a cross-correspondential system of multiple stratifications, alternative sets of stereotypes, like alternative lines of cleavage, are indeed potentially available; and which will emerge as politically protrusive depends on the context. Nevertheless, that having been said, it must also be said that the current context in the modern developed and developing worlds gives a premium to the ethnic alternative. ... [N]ot only do the historical, political, and structural factors ... give an advantage to the ethnic cleavage in a contemporary conflict situation where alternatives are available, but so does the psychological factor.[45]

Although the answer is tentative, it provides a valuable direction for further research.

---

[45]Rothschild, "Emergence of Contemporary Ethnopolitics," 76–77.

Part II

Deviance and health

5

The social construction of deviance
and the transition from communist rule

ANDREA STEVENSON SANJIAN

"Deviance" is typically defined as "a departure from accepted standards." When the standards are physical—the height of a basketball hoop, say, or the purity of drinking water—then measuring or evaluating deviance is a fairly straightforward task. Even if the standards were to change, they are nonetheless discrete and can be expressed in objective terms. When the context is social or political, however, assessing deviance becomes a much more subjective enterprise.

The problem in such cases is that the "standards" themselves represent a far less reliable benchmark by which deviance can be measured: Not only do standards change, such that some behaviors become acceptable over time while others may become illegitimate, but even whether a behavior is considered deviant or not is often a matter of degree. Yet another source of complexity is the issue of just who is establishing these standards in the first place. Some norms may have deep roots in a society's traditions and be an integral part of the community's self-regulation, regardless of whether they become embodied in law. It is not the laws against murder that deter most people from killing one another, for example, and suicide is usually considered a violation of the acceptable even in societies that do not specifically outlaw it. Societally based standards, in other words, tend to be powerful and enduring, and changes in norms are typically either portents or consequences of social change; indeed, shifting standards are a definitive indicator of social instability.

These deeply rooted norms might be termed "standards from below"

I offer my thanks to Louise I. Shelley, David E. Powell, and Joseph Berliner for their helpful comments on an earlier draft of this chapter.

because they are, in effect, organic to a given society. In contrast, standards may originate instead "from above" and reflect the preferences of those with political power rather than the embedded values of society at large, and may even be contrary to those organic values. The imposition of standards from above is inevitably a formidable challenge for the imposers, since it usually implies either replacing traditional, and hence tenacious, norms with contrary ones, or clinging to obsolete, even empty, principles that society has already rejected. The government of the United States learned this lesson after it continued to impose Prohibition on a public that had decided temperance was far less appealing in practice than in theory, whereas the government of Ireland prefers to evade the lesson and retains its ban on divorce despite the hardships caused by the extralegal dissolution of families.[1] A government seeking to impose new definitions of deviance must thus be willing to employ the full measure of its coercive power, because its objective here is to change the behavior not just of the aberrant few but of the many, who have been officially rendered "deviant" even though by commonsense definition deviance is a minority characteristic.

Though brief and admittedly simplified, this exploration of the concept of deviance raises some important issues for its study within the context of the Soviet Union and its successor states. After a period of social experimentation in the 1920s, Soviet society[2] returned to many of its prerevolutionary traditional standards for the remaining sixty years of Communist party rule, and many of these norms seem to have survived into the post-Soviet period as well. Hence murder, theft of personal property, certain sexual practices, and so on, were, and still are, considered deviant behaviors and violations of social as well as legal norms. Some continuity is to be expected: even in a political system committed to social transformation, some continuity is, or becomes, desirable in the interest of at least minimal stability and because many of the old norms were valuable in their own right. Indeed, one of the Bolsheviks' goals was the creation of a society where many traditional

[1] The Irish example is a somewhat awkward one, since the ban on divorce does reflect the influence of Catholic traditions in Ireland and survives due to a 1986 popular referendum endorsing it. On the other hand, private behavior has proved resistant to public policy, and official action has been unable to stem the de facto breakup of marriages.

[2] For the sake of convenience, I use "Soviet society" as my unit of analysis, even though it no longer exists and even though a good case can be made that one of the main reasons it does not exist is that the Soviet state never fully succeeded in its goal of integrating many diverse societies into a single, seamless Soviet one.

forms of deviance, from theft to drunkenness to prostitution, would be eradicated, the obvious implication being that they should be—that they were as offensive to radicals as they were to reactionaries.

If this were the extent of the Communist party leadership's intentions over the years, then analysis of the social consequences of communism could focus on the simple task of measuring whether, and to what degree, the incidence of such behaviors declined. Since that is a success indicator of their own making—based on their belief that Marxist-Leninist socialism should eliminate the conditions fostering or even forcing people into deviance—it is only fair to evaluate communist regimes on these grounds. However, traditional forms of social deviance were a relatively minor element of the Soviet approach to deviance, insofar as it essentially retained the status quo ante in many respects. Of far greater significance, in the final analysis, was the much more aggressive effort to create entirely new classes of deviance, with the express purpose of transforming not only the Soviet social system but the political and economic systems as well. Now that the economy and the state are once again experiencing radical change, we must ask what kind of social transformation has actually occurred under communism, and what impact it has today on the direction of political and economic change. More specifically, how has the official Soviet construction of deviance affected the transitions to post-Soviet systems and their prospects for success? What is the legacy of this system of deviance, in the sense of "an enduring intergenerational transfer"?[3]

TRADITIONAL FORMS OF DEVIANCE

The first major category of deviance to consider in this regard is deviance "from below": the behaviors that violate traditional standards and to which generations of Soviet leaders were as opposed as the czars and patriarchs before them. It is difficult to measure Soviet success with any precision because the data required for this task are usually unreliable or nonexistent. (In fact, statistics of this nature are notoriously unreliable, wherever collected.) Still, there is little basis to credit Soviet rule with any significant victories over the social problems it confronted.

It must be noted, of course, that the rates for violent crime in the

[3]See Millar and Wolchik, Chapter 1 in this volume, "The Social Legacies and the Aftermath of Communism."

Soviet Union, and especially the anonymous street crime that is so corrosive of public confidence, were typically low compared with most other industrialized societies, though not exceptionally so. This is the case even taking into account official undercounting of most criminal acts.[4] On the other hand, traditional forms of crime against property were rampant. Pilfering from the workplace became especially common-place. It had become so prevalent by the time of Gorbachev's accession to power that it was deviant in only the most formal sense of the word, since the standards it violated were routinely ignored by masses and elites alike.

This widespread lack of respect for both law and society—this real threat of anomie—was most strikingly illustrated by the rise in juvenile delinquency beginning in the late Brezhnev period. In addition to this increase, two trends in the evolving pattern of Soviet delinquency stand out in sharp relief. The first has been the growing involvement of young people in serious crimes of violence. The quickly rising incidence of drug and alcohol abuse, prostitution, gang membership, and petty theft was troubling enough, but the 1980s were also marked by a noticeable rise in the number of juveniles committing armed theft, assault, rape, and even murder. The second very serious trend was an increase in what might be termed motiveless crimes: mindless, often impersonal assaults, sometimes featuring great cruelty and even torture, that netted the per-petrators nothing but perhaps the satisfaction of lashing out.[5] The sig-nificance of these trends lies in the way they illustrate not merely an increase in deviance, but a near collapse of the whole notion of deviance, in the sense that the standards supposedly being violated were actually being rejected in many cases, with no new ones taking their place. Moreover, statistics on juvenile delinquency indicate that the disintegra-tion of social norms has extended into and even accelerated among the youngest generation.

---

[4]Criminal acts committed by party members were not recorded in official figures, for instance, because any proceedings against them would be brought before party disciplin-ary bodies rather than the regular criminal justice system, and the *militsiia* tended to respond to party pressure to keep rates of unsolved crimes low by simply not recording many crimes. Louise Shelley, "Crime in the Soviet Union," in Anthony Jones, Walter D. Connor, and David E. Powell, eds., *Soviet Social Problems* (Boulder, Colo.: Westview Press, 1991), 252–69. See Shelley's essay also for a review of patterns and rates of criminal activity in the Soviet Union's last decade.

[5]See, for example, *Izvestiia*, 5 December 1990, 3, and 6 December 1990, 3; and Iu. I. Bitko and A. S. Lando, "Deviantnoe povedeniie podrostkov," *Sotsiologicheskie issledovaniia* (hereafter *Sots. iss.*), no. 2 (1990): 77–79.

Further evidence of this process is seen in the rates of substance abuse. The scale of the population's problems with alcohol is well known, as are the human, social, and economic costs of alcoholism.[6] It does need to be reiterated, however, that excessive drinking is nominally deviant yet widely practiced, at all levels of society and at rising rates among groups who in the past drank at lower levels, namely women and minors. Here again the Soviet Union was by no means unique—women and minors have been consuming more alcohol in many other countries, too—but this trend contributed to the larger pattern of heavy drinking as the norm, not the deviation.

In contrast, drug abuse was and is unambiguously deviant behavior, and its increasing incidence is considered a serious problem in almost all segments of society. Although the statistics are extremely unreliable, it appears that Soviet performance in preventing drug abuse was no worse than that of other industrial societies, and in terms of the actual rates of drug use, almost certainly better than most.[7] Still, the problem did exist, although until the Gorbachev era the political leadership was unwilling to acknowledge it and to respond to increasing drug use with realistic policies and appropriate levels of funding.[8]

In general, then, seventy years of Soviet rule failed to eradicate these and other traditional forms of deviance. The rates for many of these behaviors not only increased over time, but in some cases seem to have been exacerbated by various specific features of Soviet-style communism. Excessive drinking was deeply ingrained in Russian life long before the 1917 Revolution, for instance, but the oppressive drabness and boredom of life under Soviet rule, together with a number of ill-considered but deliberate policy choices on the part of the leadership, encouraged the practice of drinking as a leisure-time activity (and, as a consequence of alcoholism, a workday activity as well). For example, growth in real income during the post-Stalin period was not accompanied by commensurate growth in consumer goods and services, with the result that vodka

[6]For a review of recent problems and policies relating to alcohol, see Vladimir G. Treml, "Drinking and Alcohol Abuse in the USSR in the 1980s," in Jones et al., *Soviet Social Problems*, 119–36. See also A. I. Rybakov, "Tsennostno-normativnye predstavleniia o potreblenii alkogoliia," *Sots. iss.*, no. 2 (1988): 81–83, and V. E. Khvoshchev, "Interval'noe issledovanie p'ianstva i alkogolizma," *Sots. iss.*, no. 4 (1988): 84–86.

[7]For a discussion of the problems that arise in evaluating Soviet data on drug use, see John M. Kramer, "Drug Abuse in the Soviet Union," *Problems of Communism* 37 (March-April 1988): 28–40.

[8]"Narkomaniia c tochki zreniia sotsiologa, vracha, pravoveda i zhurnalista (obsuzhdenie za 'kruglym stolom' redaktsii)," *Sots. iss.*, no. 2 (1989): 38–51.

and other alcoholic beverages were among the very few reliable outlets for consumer spending. Furthermore, inadequate official attention to the provision of leisure-time activities made alcohol an attractive outlet. Caught in the triple bind of dependence on the huge revenues generated by its monopoly on alcohol, the heavy costs imposed on productivity and health care by alcohol abuse, and the need for investment in treatment and education programs, successive generations of leaders almost always opted for the revenues.[9]

Another example of shifting levels of deviance is the theft of goods from the workplace. It is difficult to believe that the Soviet people would have become so accustomed to pilferage had the economic system been less fraught with distortions—if it could have provided for more of their needs legally, or if the demand for labor in an inefficient economy were not so high that thieving workers were better than no workers at all, and so on. In addition, the weakness of systemic checks on officials made it easy for them to abuse their powers, while the same chronic shortages that frustrated the masses made corruption all the more tempting to elites.

Of particular significance is the extent to which these behaviors have become so customary that the term "deviance" can be applied only advisedly. Excessive drinking and embezzlement, for instance, do violate normative standards, unquestionably, and nobody suggests that such acts are unambiguously good or that they should be encouraged. Yet it is also true that these standards have been routinely ignored, and by very large numbers of people. Moreover, these are not necessarily furtive behaviors. There is little, if any, sense of shame associated with them, nor much of an effort to conceal them except from authorities. The typical attitude is, instead, that it is too bad that these acts are so prevalent but that they are understandable under the circumstances. Perhaps most telling is the Soviet-era adage, "He who does not steal from the state steals from his family." The use of the verb "to steal" makes it clear that this is not desirable behavior, but the overall sense of the phrase is that it is nonetheless necessary behavior.

It is perhaps unreasonable to hold the Soviet system to its own standard and criticize it for not eradicating these traditional forms of deviance when most would agree that the standard was utterly unrealistic in the first place. It is fair, however, to criticize it for creating systemic

[9]Treml, "Drinking and Alcohol Abuse," 126–27.

conditions that further encouraged deviance, however unintentional this may have been, and for leaving a legacy of acceptance of such behavior.[10]

SYSTEM-SPECIFIC DEVIANCE

The Soviet system also battled several classes of deviance entirely of its own devising, offenses that were violations of political standards rather than social ones. They are thus system-specific, in that their objective was the maintenance of a particular political system—in this case the Communist party–led Soviet state. The degree to which the political standards of one system are internalized, however, will have a significant impact on the performance of any successor systems and determine whether the standards will be enduring legacies or merely transitory aftermath.

The standards imposed from above by the political leadership were designed to create a society fully committed to the goals and ideals of that leadership as well as to perpetuate its rule. Some of these new standards turned out to be more inconvenient in practice than they had appeared in prerevolutionary theory, and they eventually degenerated into empty slogans rather than active policy; this was particularly likely when the more normative goals associated with socialism conflicted with its economic imperatives. Such goals included gender equality, which mutated into a strictly formal equity coexisting with the very deliberate exploitation of female labor, and "internationalism," which soon gave way to Russianization and a tolerance for racism and anti-Semitism. Since elites themselves honored these ideals so little over the years, and in some cases actively subverted them, there was a predictable lack of success in transforming popular attitudes.

Those standards that furthered official economic goals or reinforced the Communist party's monopoly on power, however, were promoted much more aggressively. The instruments used in these efforts included both socialization campaigns at all levels of society and new legislation. Ideally, the former would be effective and the public would come to accept the new standards, so that social pressure could be brought

---

[10]Here I differ from James Millar, who in Chapter 1 of this volume suggests that this acceptance of deviance would fit in the category of aftermath, or transitory effects. In addition, my usage of "legacy," in accordance with standard dictionary definitions, does not assume that legacies are generally positive: Consider, for example, the legacy of imperialism or of child abuse.

to bear against violators; in those instances when that pressure was inadequate, the coercive power of the state would serve as a backup, as it did against many traditional forms of deviance.

For analytic convenience it is useful to distinguish between two separate classes of regime-imposed deviance: the economic and the more straightforwardly political, though this framework is only valid if one keeps in mind that even the economic deviations were in large part political. They may have been justified in terms of protecting communal interests and principles, but their fundamental intent was to insure political control of the economy and the population.

Some "economic crimes," that is, those committed in the course of commercial or industrial activities, were identical or analogous to offenses considered deviant virtually anywhere. Thus stealing from the workplace and adulterating goods such as food or pharmaceuticals are not system-specific offenses because they typically breach the acceptable, irrespective of the political system in which they were committed. Even padding production figures or otherwise falsifying economic data to be used by central planners is so obviously a type of fraud that it is clear that this should be illegal (that is, deviant) even if laws against it are only necessary in a centrally planned economy.

What set apart the system-specific economic crimes was the fact that they penalized activities that would only be considered deviant in the context of a Soviet-style economy. Most prominent among these was the web of restrictions on private enterprise, rendering illegal many activities that were permitted and even encouraged in market economies, and making deviants of individuals who might otherwise be considered the mainstays of the system. Among the behaviors that became officially classified as deviant were making a profit for oneself—regardless of the nature of the transaction and despite the fact that all of the elements of the exchange might themselves have been gained through totally lawful means—and paying for the labor of others to produce any goods or services for sale. The only significant exception to this rule was in agriculture, where the output of private plots could be sold at market prices; on the other hand, the many restrictions on what could be sold at kolkhoz markets only reinforced the general stigma against private transactions.

Other economic crimes included parasitism, or refusing to take a job within the state-run economy; acquiring and trading with foreign currency, except under narrowly restricted circumstances; and producing substandard goods at the workplace. The latter is perhaps frowned on almost anywhere, but in most systems the market usually serves as an adequate check against this when the health and safety of consumers is not at stake. The effect of laws such as these was to contribute to the image of economic decision making as off-limits to the average citizen and to convey the message that it is the state that establishes standards for society, not society itself.

In addition to state-established economic deviance, there were rigorously enforced sanctions against political deviance. These covered a wide range of activities but, as with the economic crimes, they too were artificially deviant in the sense that the banned behaviors had not been proscribed by society—or, in many cases, the state—prior to the establishment of communist rule, nor were they typically unacceptable elsewhere at the societal level. Unlike economic deviance, however, they were not necessarily illegal, even though any of them could be if pursued aggressively enough by the nonconformist.

Disseminating "anti-Soviet propaganda," demonstrating against official policies, or otherwise expressing political opinions at odds with those of the leadership was unambiguously illegal, and even criticizing official performance as measured by the state's or party's own standards was a violation of criminal codes. The violator might sometimes avoid prescribed penalties for a particular act of dissidence, of course, but making a habit of this would certainly put one at risk. In any case, more informal methods of expressing official disapproval could also be employed; one might be demoted at work, for instance, or be denied permission to travel, or encounter other forms of bureaucratic obstructionism.

In contrast, however, other forms of officially designated deviance were vigorously discouraged but were not in and of themselves illegal. They represented challenges to the Communist party's self-proclaimed monopoly on the interpretation of sociopolitical phenomena and/or its rejection of pluralist conceptions of politics. This category included practicing religion, expressing nationalism as anything but a cultural artifact within the larger socialist society, and voicing any unorthodox and hence unauthorized approaches to society and politics (for example, feminism or pacifism), even within a fundamentally socialist context.

Again, holding such beliefs was not in itself an illegal act, though as a measure of political unreliability it could, for example, interfere with job advancement. Promoting nonconformist beliefs was a different matter, however, because doing so was taken as a deliberate challenge to the political status quo, and penalties could range from bureaucratic obstructionism to more serious forms of official harassment (such as having one's premises searched) to actual imprisonment or forced exile.

None of these forms of deviance would have any great significance for post-Soviet society if these offenses had remained purely legalistic and if the Soviet people had not come to accept for themselves many of the general standards being officially promoted. To a considerable degree, however, the Soviet system was successful in this effort, at least to the extent of fostering collectiveness as a basic value. This was possible at least in part because it took advantage of a cultural affinity for communalism and for a sort of primitive egalitarianism over self-interested individualism that was already present in much of Soviet society. The effort was much less successful in those regions where communalism was not a traditional cultural trait, such as the Baltics.

This is not to suggest that the collectivist orientation was so strong that the state could rely on normative inducements to deter deviance—far from it: Naked self-interest (with a concomitant disregard for community well-being in many cases) was often a powerful motivator. The existence of a pervasive shadow economy is potent testimony to the fact that neither the normative nor the coercive power of the state was necessarily sufficient to prevent private under-the-counter transactions when legal ones were impossible or unsatisfactory.

On the other hand, the Soviet people proved to be remarkably adept at resisting cognitive dissonance, in that behavior both acceptable and necessary to the individual engaging in it was indeed deviant for almost everyone outside of his or her own circle. This was especially true if one party to a transaction benefited more than another (the more successful one thereby becoming an exploitative speculator), and even more so if the "speculator" was a member of a different ethnic group.

Communalism also surfaced in the tendency to be suspicious of heterodoxy, even though any dinner-table conversation anywhere in the country offered proof of the reality of multiple perspectives on public affairs. These expressions were acceptable only among friends, however, and not only out of fear of official retaliation, for the artificial official phrase "harmony of interests" imposed by Soviet rule contributed greatly to a sense of order and social peace for many people. The best evidence of the degree to which such official values were internalized, and the degree to which their transgression had become deviance, is the initial resistance that met official efforts to introduce reforms that seemed to violate these values. Even recent survey research shows that in no age cohort did a majority of survey respondents agree that "freedom to criticize the government" is an essential, and presumably desirable, component of a democratic state.[11]

THE CONSTRUCTION OF DEVIANCE
AND SYSTEM TRANSFORMATION

The preceding sections sketch the nature of deviance as it was perceived in late Soviet society. What, though, are the implications of this construction of deviance for post-Soviet society? How do commonly held notions of the acceptable affect the prospects for political and economic change? On the basis of the Gorbachev-era transition and the brief period since then, it appears that prevailing conceptions of deviance present significant challenges to the transformation process and constitute a legacy that may be difficult to overcome.

Social deviance. Consider first the more traditional forms of deviance (alcoholism, theft, crimes of violence, and so on). As noted earlier, the social controls inhibiting them have weakened over the years and their incidence has generally been on the increase. At the same time—and as both cause and effect, in some cases—the social institutions that have traditionally helped hold deviance in check have themselves weakened or been undermined. The authority of the family, for example, has been deteriorating for many years, and it can no longer be counted on to restrain its own members, while for some seventy years organized religion could offer neither spiritual solace in support of a good life nor the fear of God to deter a bad one. Instead, only the state and its agents (from the schools to the KGB), together with the Communist party, were in a position to tackle social and legal transgressions.

Over the last several years, however, even the state and the party have been weakened; indeed, by January 1992 both had disintegrated and were replaced by frail new successor states whose power and authority are still being established. Even surviving institutions, such as the police and the underdeveloped social services system, have been caught completely unprepared for this assault on their limited resources and are unable to offer any significant relief. The collapse of formal controls has

[11]Millar and Wolchik, "Social Legacies and Aftermath," Table 1.3.

exacerbated the collapse of social controls, and the result has been a serious increase in both the incidence and the variety of traditional deviance. Midway through 1992, the number of juveniles in police custody was already 23 percent higher than for all of 1991, for example, while the number of crimes committed in the first quarter of 1991 was 16.6 percent higher than in the same period in 1990, which was itself a 17 percent increase over the year before.[12] Within the Russian Federation, crime was up 18 percent in 1991 compared with 1990, with theft and robbery accounting for most of the increase; the total number of crimes reported in Russia in 1991 was approximately the same as the number reported for the Soviet Union as a whole during 1990.[13] The level of violence during the commission of crimes was also up, since the loss of state control over access to guns has meant that more criminals are increasingly well armed. This is especially alarming to a population accustomed to a closely regulated but relatively safe environment. In recent years the rate of premeditated murder and of holdups and muggings involving the use of firearms has risen by nearly a third every six months.[14] Moreover, the unpremeditated, often domestic, violence that usually results from drunkenness is exacerbated now by economic stress. There is thus far no reason whatsoever to believe that these trends will reverse themselves over the short term.

Meanwhile, the Moscow police are contemplating formation of a vice squad to combat the increase in prostitution (prostitutes were involved in twice as many crimes in 1991 as the year before), "depraved acts" such as exhibitionism and corruption of minors (the level of which also doubled in that time period), and the flood of pornographic videotapes suddenly available in the city's video stores.[15] The upsurge in the number of prostitutes is largely the consequence of economic hardship and especially of the disproportionate share of women among the newly unemployed; according to Goskomstat, 71 percent of those who have been laid off are women, though in some oblasts women comprise 80 to 90 percent of the total.[16] The high unemployment rates are a consequence of the economic transition, and many women will almost certainly leave the streets once financial security is available elsewhere. (The fate of the

---

[12]*Izvestiia*, 15 June 1991, 6, and 29 July 1992, 3.
[13]Ibid., 11 January 1992, 6.
[14]Ibid., 29 July 1992, 3.
[15]Ibid., 24 March 1992, 7.
[16]Sheila Marnie, "How Prepared Is Russia for Mass Unemployment?" *RFE/RL Research Report*, 4 December 1992, 44–50.

rising numbers of children and adolescents working in prostitution is less easy to predict.) The most significant point here, though, is the fact that the number of women out of work is grossly out of proportion to their prereform share of the total workforce. Their unemployment may be temporary, but the fact of their unemployment reflects the legacy of exploitation of women under Soviet rule. Rather than fulfilling its early promise of gender equality, the communist regime took advantage of traditional inequality to serve its own economic and social needs.

In addition, the collapse of central coordination of antidrug efforts has vitiated the fight against the production and sale of illegal drugs. This comes at a time when drug abuse is already increasing and when economic hardship has revived Central Asian interest in state-run poppy farms as a source of revenue. The situation was worsened recently as a result of the decriminalization of the use (though not the sale) of "narcotic" substances. The legislature's intention was to provide greater legal protections for civil rights, though appearing as it has in an era when extralegal constraints on drug use are crumbling, the legal reform has complicated an already serious problem. And, as is often the case, one form of deviant behavior contributes to others; the high inflation rates that have accompanied marketization—it now costs drug users as much as three thousand rubles a day to maintain their addiction—force addicts to turn to crime more often than in the past to pay for their drug purchases. The high profits combine with relatively low risk to make drug trafficking a high-growth industry; the number of crimes associated with it (admittedly not the best measure of drug trafficking) rose from 287 in 1984 to 900 in 1991, to about 1,800 in 1992.[17]

Economic deviance. Other forms of criminality have also flourished in the shadow of privatization. Both juveniles and established organized criminals have formed protection rackets, for instance, preying on vulnerable new legitimate entrepreneurs. Professional criminals also use the new legal businesses to launder money made from other criminal activities. There is also a marked increase in the number of connections between organized crime and state officials, facilitating the plunder of former state assets in an environment where questions of ownership are

---

[17]*Izvestiia*, 19 February 1992, 6; *Megapolis-Express*, 16 December 1992, 7, translated in *Current Digest of the Post-Soviet Press*, 13 January 1993, 30. The term "narcotic" tended to be applied very loosely in the USSR, a pattern that continues today; it usually refers to virtually any drug not used for legitimate medical purposes.

usually clouded by uncertainty.[18] Meanwhile, even the most high-minded entrepreneurs have discovered that supply shortages and official obstructionism make totally above-board operations virtually impossible in many cases—one legacy of bureaucratic rule is that *blat* (or influence, e.g., personal connections, bribery, trading favors) remains an everyday practice and a predictable if illicit cost of doing business.

Opportunities for fraud have also proliferated. Sometimes the public is the victim: one swindle combined a pyramid scheme with the sale of stock in nonexistent enterprises, in a con game so unlikely that it depended almost entirely on its victims' utter unfamiliarity with the notion of investing.[19] In other instances the victim is the state, as when new enterprises are fraudulently registered in the name of veterans to take advantage of their tax-exempt status; one pair of brothers evaded nearly eleven million rubles in taxes this way.[20] Some of the fraud violates no existing statutes or else calls for trivial penalties—the body of laws regulating legal private enterprise being still underdeveloped—but clearly constitutes deviance in the public mind.

One factor that figures prominently in attempts to explain the rise in deviant behavior is simple need. The combination of rising prices and worsening shortages generated by reform and economic chaos has brought serious economic hardships to many people, some of whom have no doubt violated traditional standards in the effort to meet very basic needs. These factors cannot account for most of the crime, however, which is often well organized and executed on a large scale and with official connivance. In these cases the more important factors are the legacy of disrespect for authority and of the assumption that any law can and may be evaded with the proper combination of bribes and favors.

The costs of this type of behavior are great and varied. When so many economic transactions involve illegalities, and when they must so often be lubricated by graft, economic affairs are deprived of an essential element of rationality. This makes routine tasks such as budgeting, price setting, and maintaining inventories (already difficult enough in post-Soviet conditions) all the more formidable since it is so hard to predict the costs of criminality. Rather than relieving economic distortions, then,

---

[18]*Pravda*, 21 August 1991, 2. This report was prepared by the KGB's Public Relations Center and published during the August coup, but it is fully consistent with reports in other, somewhat more neutral, sources.

[19]*Izvestiia*, 16 August 1991, 3.

[20]*Moscow News*, 1–8 December 1991, 9.

the introduction of private enterprise into such an anarchic environment only worsens them. Similarly, rubles and even hard currency that could be well spent on investment are diverted instead to payoffs, thus handicapping many new enterprises. Meanwhile, other forms of deviance that are also on the rise—substance abuse, for instance, or prostitution—also divert both money and human resources away from more productive pursuits. And all of this perpetuates the communist-era alienation from authority and loss of faith in the future, which will make the establishment of new forms of authority more difficult.

There are still other costs imposed by rampant deviance of this nature, especially when associated with private enterprise. Here the problem is the persistent public image of the entrepreneur as swindler and exploiter. First created by official propaganda, the image now acquires substance as a result of actual experience with businesspeople who bend rules and principles in the pursuit of profit, even if unwillingly. Then again, one reason why entrepreneurs often take this course is that official interference too often makes it a matter of economic survival. Even leaving aside the need to pay bribes, various units of the government have deliberately acted in restraint of trade by making it virtually impossible to rent business quarters, by denying access to supplies and other resources, by imposing near-confiscatory taxes, or by simply prohibiting some kinds of businesses in order to preserve government monopolies.

This kind of gross interference in economic development and the principles of reform espoused by the majority of the population[21] is greeted not with public outrage, but often with strong (if paradoxical) shows of support. The high prices associated with private enterprise perpetuate the popular image of exploitation, and neither the higher quality and better service often found in the private sector nor news reports of the high real costs of doing business have been able to modify that view. What makes a stronger impression on the public is the constant barrage of other media reports of the criminality that accompanies much private enterprises—glasnost countering perestroika, in effect—all of which reinforces personal experiences with high prices. This has created a vicious circle from which entrepreneurs may never fully extri-

[21]In one recent poll, 68 percent of those surveyed claimed to approve of the privatization of stores and services and 75 percent approved of private ownership of land, although only 39 percent favored privately held factories and banks. Ibid., 7. A poll conducted a year later, cited by Millar and Wolchik, "Social Legacies and Aftermath," shows similar results, with a slightly greater tilt toward public ownership.

cate themselves. (The fact that many private businesses still operate as monopolies themselves allows them to be as abusive to consumers as state enterprises were, which does nothing to improve mass perceptions.) The very high incomes earned even by some of the most honest business people present another political problem, insofar as they violate egalitarian ideals still held strongly in much of the former Soviet Union, and this has generated political pressure to regulate income levels.

The situation is, if anything, worse in the countryside, where values are typically slow to change and where private farming is still often viewed as apostasy. As late as 1992, private farmers have been evicted from state apartments for "treason" to the collective farm system and accused of being kulaks, while large-scale demonstrations protest land redistribution. One new private farmer was harassed by neighbors who connected his well to a high voltage electric line, and when that failed to drive him back to the kolkhoz they broke his skull.[22] Such events remain commonplace. (The exception is in regions such as Armenia, where the cultural preference for private ownership was never extinguished by Soviet rule, and where private agriculture has been almost entirely restored. Here the social and cultural legacy of communism is virtually nonexistent, though the legacy of economic and ethnic mismanagement is obvious.)

Political deviance. Political reform has also been a victim of the Leninist legacy, though the damage seems to have been less extensive and more survivable. At issue is the intolerance of diversity bred by the socialist ideal of a unanimity of interests. This was a more serious problem in the early years of democratic reform, when the sudden outpouring of pluralist-style opinions unleashed by glasnost was often condemned by the public itself as divisive. In those years it often appeared that the reluctance to confront the reality of political diversity seriously jeopardized Soviet prospects for democratization. There is still little tolerance of minority opinion when the opinions are those of social, rather than political, minorities—homosexual rights is still a deviant perspective, for example, and feminism only slightly less so—but, by and large, the former Soviet people seem to be adapting to the notion of pluralism, at least in the abstract, and no longer seem to feel threatened by political pluralism.

[22]*Izvestiia*, 25 February 1992, 8.

Relative tolerance does not, however, always extend to differences involving ethnicity and religion. The enforced conformity under communist rule may have suppressed ancient animosities, but it allowed few opportunities to settle old disputes. These quickly burst back into full fury once authoritarian counterweights were lifted or dissolved, and in the case of ethnicity was the single most important factor in the disintegration of the Soviet state.

"Deviance" was defined earlier as "a departure from accepted standards." The problem here is that the standards for behavior toward one's own group are different from those toward certain other groups. This stipulation not only makes it easier to condemn members of the out-group for behavior that would otherwise be more acceptable (as when Russians are more likely to denounce Jewish or Armenian entrepreneurs as "parasitic speculators" than fellow Russians), it even makes possible the victimization of others by committing acts against them that are normally deviant in the extreme. As the Soviet system disintegrated, this came to include acts of great violence, as in Baku, for instance, or the Fergana Valley, as well as casual harassment. Since then intergroup relations have deteriorated further, even leaving aside those cases that have degenerated into civil war. The principal victims have been Chechens, who are associated in the public mind with business success as well as organized crime, though others from the Caucasus, and sometimes Central Asia, have received the same treatment. This ranges from police beatings as "preventive measures" to demonstrations demanding these groups' expulsion from various cities, to a Minsk city ordinance denying them hotel rooms.[23]

CONCLUSION

Any review of sociopolitical conditions in the period immediately before and after the Soviet collapse leaves the clear impression of a near-total disintegration of the moral order. It is thus scarcely surprising that many former Soviet citizens are skeptical of the merits of their new social contract, in which order and social peace were exchanged for greater personal freedoms. The traditional appeal of authoritarianism—the (often unmet) promise of public order—is not spurious, in other words,

[23]Ibid., 19 March 1992, 3, and 12 August 1992, 3; *Nezavisimaia gazeta*, 26 August 1992, 6; *Moscow News*, 31 May 1992, 3.

and the *strogii rezhim* (strict, or severe, regime) of Soviet communism
did offer some advantages, albeit costly ones.

On the other hand, one must take care not to overstate the effects of
current conditions. For all the public outrage and anxiety, there is little
evidence to be found in public opinion surveys of strong and/or growing
support for a return to authoritarian rule as a solution, and virtually
none for a restoration of communism. This latter view remains very
much a minority position. There may be a widespread nostalgia for a
more orderly past, as well as one where the shops were better stocked,
but this does not translate into a real preference for the pre-Gorbachev
Soviet Union. Such preferences may develop, though it seems that this
would more likely be a consequence of severe shortages, especially of
food, than of social disarray.

Looking at the situation from a comparative perspective also has a
moderating effect on perceptions. It is an unfortunate truth that, for an
industrial and largely urbanized society, crime rates in the former Soviet
Union are simply not that exceptional; what is important about them
for post-Soviet society is their rapid increase and the perception this
increase generates among the public of the precipitous collapse of their
social order. What has occurred in recent years is a form of catch-up,
where rates have gone from relatively low levels to those much more
typical—if perhaps now on the high side—for such a society. Some
statistics, such as those for rape, have even improved since the breakup
of the Soviet Union.[24] Although this analysis will doubtless offer little
comfort to the Muscovite or St. Petersburger, it is still important to keep
the picture in its proper perspective. After all, one need only consider the
following: How many people would feel safer taking the subway in any
major U.S. city than in Moscow?

By the same token, one must remember that crime and similar statistics do not reflect the predictable instability of the transition period
alone. They reflect instead long-term trends that had been developing
long before Gorbachev reached the Politburo. The collapse of communism and the Soviet Union, and the process of reform, has only accelerated these trends, not initiated them. An unstable society in which
respect for authority and for individuals is degraded, and where corruption is rampant and tolerated, is not the consequence of communism's

[24]The number of rapes reported in Russia fell in 1991 compared with a year earlier and
continued to decrease through the first half of 1992. *Izvestiia*, 11 January 1992, 6, and
2 October 1992, 8.

collapse but of communism itself—or at least, of this particular model of communism and the policies associated with it.

"Traditional" crime—theft, murder, and so forth—may not be the most important aspect of deviance for a given society, however, and the social construction of deviance is still a matter of considerable significance for post-Soviet politics. As the Soviet Union's successor states embark on political and economic reform, they are hampered by the fact that seventy years of communist rule successfully promoted certain images of deviance that may have contributed to system maintenance under the ancien régime but are now frankly dysfunctional. It will be difficult, if not impossible, to build democratic political systems and market economies if some of the fundamental prerequisites for both are commonly perceived as violations of community standards. Until the "speculator" is transformed in the popular image into the "businessperson," for example, the command economy will never be transformed into a market economy, and until expressing political opinions is recognized as a form of system maintenance and not disruptive behavior, democratization will be a slow process.

Deviance, though, is mutable by nature and a social construct that reflects not only established norms but social changes, too. There is a negative side to this, illustrated by the slide toward tolerance of many antisocial acts during the last decades of Soviet rule and beyond. The new successor states will need to reinforce social controls against such destructive behaviors as substance abuse, violent crime, prostitution, and the like if their new systems are to stabilize. The positive side of this adaptability is that just as the previous regime was able to socialize the public into accepting its standards, so in theory should the new states be able to establish their own new parameters of the acceptable. As Soviet experience suggests, though, this takes time, even with a leadership that was itself thoroughly committed to its new standards. In contrast, the current political leaders are often ambivalent about some of the values underlying their own reforms and in some cases are even unfamiliar with them. In the end, successful transitions will remain at risk until society's construction of deviance reflects the actual threats to the new systems rather than reflecting the new systems as themselves threats.

6

Crime and the collapse of the Soviet state

LOUISE SHELLEY

The social consequences of the Soviet period may take as long to undo as the political consequences. The legacy of problems of social order and crime cannot be easily remedied. Even though the Soviet Union under the communist system had a lower crime rate than most capitalist societies at comparable levels of economic development, this low crime rate was not sustainable. A social contract existed for many years between the Soviet state and its citizens, who exchanged their personal freedom for a high degree of order and the social guarantees of full employment, housing, low-cost medical care, and education.

During the years of communist rule, there was a trade-off between personal freedom and the crime rate. Once greater personal freedom was allowed under glasnost, the crime rate began to grow rapidly. In the late 1980s, the Soviet state could no longer deliver on one of its fundamental promises to its citizenry—the maintenance of order. Highly visible street crime provided vivid evidence that the social contract between the state and the citizen had broken down. The seemingly pervasive organized crime provided a constant reminder of the new dimensions of Soviet criminality. Soviet authorities, like their counterparts in the democratizing countries of the former socialist bloc, discovered that their police were better prepared to deal with crowd control and to extract confessions than to perform the standard police work needed to apprehend criminals.

Crime rates remained far below those in the United States, but the startling rate of growth exacerbated personal insecurity. As Joseph Berliner suggests in Chapter 16, societies can accustom themselves to consistently high crime rates, but a sudden rise in crime causes anxiety. Individuals in the Soviet Union feared for their lives and, to a lesser degree, their property.[1] Citizens changed their life-styles in response to the crime threat. After years of living in a well-ordered, highly policed society, the unprecedented growth in crime was a visible symbol of societal collapse.

The growth of crime was aggravated by the lack of social planning in the transition away from the communist system and by the simultaneous collapse of the system of centralized control. The crime problems that emerged in the final years of the Soviet period were serious and left an unfortunate and dangerous legacy for the societies emerging from the Soviet Union. The crime legacy is particularly disturbing to a population accustomed to a high degree of societal order.

CRIME CONDITIONS BEFORE PERESTROIKA

During the Soviet period, citizens often lived without fear of crime because no crime statistics were published and the censored newspapers masked the growing crime problem. Most citizens were unaware that crime was growing continuously through the 1980s.[2] The Soviet state, instead, boasted of its safe streets as one of the benefits of the socialist system. Many citizens, therefore, perceived crime control as one of the benefits of their authoritarian system.

Despite the growth in crime, the streets of big cities did remain relatively safe. The low rate of criminality was a consequence of the social system, reduced opportunities for crime commission, and a justice system that made sure that crime did not pay. Crime was controlled, in part, through a system that guaranteed both full employment and a social safety net which provided a minimal standard of care for the citizenry. But crime was also contained by a justice system that compelled close cooperation with the state and showed no mercy for the criminal. As the opening chapter of this volume suggests, when an individual was accused of a crime, the state's rights had precedence over the citizen's. Criminologists theorize that uncertain social and economic conditions increase crime commission. During most of the Soviet period, citizens did not know the economic insecurities of their counterparts in capitalist societies. Economic need was rarely a motivation for crime commission. Organized crime and drug trafficking, which had penetrated many Western countries, were not as prevalent in the Soviet

[1] This is based on a 1990 Ministry of Internal Affairs (MVD) survey of citizens cited in V. Golovin, "Vse ot nervov i prestupnost' tozhe," *Iuridicheskaia gazeta* 14 (1991): 21.
[2] "Volny apatii v more stereotipov," *Sovetskaia militsiia* 8 (1990): 12.

Union, because of its closed borders and the social isolation of the population.

Crime commission rates before perestroika, despite the rise during the preceding decade, remained relatively low in the Soviet Union in comparison to those of Western Europe. Until Brezhnev's death in 1982, there were less than 1.7 million reported crimes annually in the major categories of violent and property crime, in a country with a population of approximately 275 million.[3] Crime rates varied significantly by region of the country, however. In 1980 there were 742 offenses per 100,000 persons in Russia, but only 243 in Uzbekistan per 100,000.[4] The reported crime rate in the Soviet Union was artificially low because police were required to clear 95 percent of all reported crimes;[5] consequently, cases went unrecorded when the police thought there was little likelihood of apprehending the offender. In masking actual rates of crime commission, however, the Soviet police were behaving like the police in many other societies.

The criminalization of numerous areas of Soviet life made many persons criminals in the eyes of the law. Many citizens participated in crimes unique to the socialist system, such as speculation (purchase and resale of goods at a profit) and inflating production figures, because they needed to engage in these activities to survive. James Millar and Sharon Wolchik suggest in this volume that winking at petty economic crime was part of the social contract of the Brezhnev period. As their essay indicates, public opinion surveys of 1989 and 1990 revealed that while the majority of citizens condemned speculation and bribes to officials, there was no such consensus regarding presents and payments to doctors or petty theft of goods. This tolerance for theft, a crime in any society, is an unfortunate legacy for the post-Soviet as well as other postcommunist states. Citizens, by realizing that they need to commit crime to survive, have blurred the lines between law-abiding and criminal behavior. This observation was confirmed by the survey reported in Chapter 1 of this volume. In that 1990 study, a majority of Soviet citizens surveyed responded that illegal means might be necessary to solve an important problem.

Although the majority of Soviet citizens were forced to break the law,

---

[3]V. V. Luneev et al., *Prestupnost' i Pravonarusheniia v SSSR* (Moscow: Iuridicheskaia Literatura, 1990), 10–11.
[4]Ibid., 27.
[5]"What Do the Militia Do?" *Moscow News* 50 (1988): 11.

few were arrested for crimes related to illegal economic activity. Such offenses contributed less than 3 percent of total crime commission.[6] The vulnerability of so much of the population to prosecution increased conformity with the state's objectives because all were aware that they were violating the laws in their daily lives.

In addition, levels of criminality were lower in the Soviet Union compared with other industrial nations, because the opportunities for crime commission were reduced. For example, the absence of significant private property reduced the incentive to steal. The internal passport system and the system of local registration decreased the mobility of the population. The passport system, by channeling citizens away from urban centers to more recently developed cities and smaller communities, gave some of these newly established cities very high crime rates. (These cities were populated disproportionately by youthful males, the most crime-prone group.) Large urban areas, on the other hand, were the beneficiaries of this policy permitting selective urban growth, because police controls over the residences of released offenders resulted in the permanent exile of multiple offenders away from urban centers. Large cities could choose their populations and could remove troublemakers from their environment. The USSR thus had created a geography of crime different from that observed in other industrialized countries, where a direct correlation exists between the degree of urbanization and the level of crime commission.[7]

Crime was controlled not only by eliminating the opportunities for crime commission but also by severely punishing perpetrators. The great criminal law philosopher of the Enlightenment, Cesare Beccaria, suggested that certainty of punishment was more important than its severity. The Soviet authorities, however, eschewed this philosophy: Until perestroika, the Soviet Union provided both certain and severe punishment. Citizens were expected to collaborate with the police. When this collaboration was not voluntary, it might be coerced. The inducements for collaboration were significant, and the costs of failure to collaborate were great. Furthermore, many citizens believed that it was impossible to resist the power of the police because ultimately the law enforcers would prevail over the citizen.[8]

[6]Luneev et al., *Prestupnost' i Pravonarusheniia v SSSR*, 71.
[7]See Louise Shelley, "The Geography of Soviet Criminality," *American Sociological Review* 45 (1980): 111–22.
[8]Yevgeniya Albats, "Shadowy Figures," *Moscow News* 14 (1992): 9.

The pervasiveness of the social control apparatus and its citizen collaborators increased the likelihood of apprehension of criminals. Moreover, once an individual entered the criminal justice system there was
little chance he or she could escape conviction. The police were under
pressure not to release apprehended criminals, the procurators were
expected to charge suspects, and the judges were expected to convict.
Judges, in accordance with Communist party directions, convicted 99.8
percent of defendants. As the draft of the Russian Federation judicial
reform noted, "Citizens for many years believed it was as hard to resolve
their problems through the justice system as it was to protect themselves
from the law enforcers once they fell into their clutches."[9] Consequently,
as Millar and Wolchik point out, a fairer judicial system was one of the
attributes Russian citizens identified with democratization.

There was no leniency shown by the justice system. In addition to the
fact that the majority of convicted offenders were incarcerated, many
individuals who in other societies might have served their sentences in
the community were placed in labor colonies and sent into exile. The
Soviet Union until the late 1980s had a large prison and labor camp
population, estimated at 1.75 million individuals. On a per capita basis
this was a rate of incarceration nearly double that which existed in the
United States, a country that led the industrialized world in its use of
prison as a sanction.[10] Although it is difficult to predict who will commit
crime, the Soviet Union was able to suppress crime by incarcerating
enough individuals that many potential offenders were removed from
circulation. Upon release many offenders were placed under close surveillance by the police within their communities. The internal passport
of all former offenders, carried with them at all times, bore a secret
indication that they had been in labor camp. With such an identifying
mark and enhanced police scrutiny, a significant percentage of offenders
were rapidly returned to confinement.[11]

Many juveniles were institutionalized as well as adults. A large system
of children's homes existed throughout the Soviet Union. Its residents
were children from problem homes or those whose parents had been
deprived of their parental rights. Many of these children, the offspring
of criminals, were institutionalized from birth or early childhood. Not

---

[9]S. A. Pashin, ed., *Kontsepstiia Sudebnoi Reformy v Rossiiskoi Federatsii* (Moscow:
Respublika, 1992), 10.
[10]Viktor Loshak, "Reform of Prisons, Penal Colonies Urged," *Foreign Broadcast Information Service Daily Report* (hereafter *FBIS Daily Report*), 18 May 1988, 63.
[11]A. Vlasov, "Na Strazhe Pravoporiadka," *Kommunist* 5 (1988): 58.

themselves criminals, these children spent their entire youth in these institutions, where they were entirely cut off from society. Many of these youths might have been potential juvenile delinquents but were prevented from crime commission by their confinement, and so their institutionalization helped suppress the crime rate. Even though they might not integrate into the community after their "education" was completed in the children's homes, the encompassing system of penal institutions could ensure further confinement if they did not manage to live crime-free lives.

Under the communist system, this high degree of order was not achieved without cost. The price to the citizenry for their relative safety was restrictive laws, encompassing police powers, and a lack of respect for human rights. The institutional controls could not, however, deter all crime commission. A major aggravating factor of crime commission—the high rate of alcohol consumption among the population—remained. The Soviet Union had a high correlation between alcohol use and criminality.[12] Despite negative consequences for social order and the low labor productivity resulting from the consumption of such large quantities of alcohol, Soviet authorities depended on the revenue from alcohol sales and were hesitant to curb alcohol production. The resultant passivity of the population and the absence of alternative consumer goods may also have been important deterrents to reducing alcohol sales, despite the criminological consequences of excessive alcohol consumption among both men and women.

PERESTROIKA AND CHANGES IN CRIME COMMISSION

During perestroika there was a dramatic change in crime commission. Crime rates grew and criminality became more violent. Organized crime became a central element of the crime picture, bringing a violence and visibility previously unknown to Soviet crime. The sophistication and organization of the criminals exceeded that of the law enforcers. The rapid growth in crime resulted from the political, economic, and social changes that transformed Soviet society. Furthermore, the alcohol prohibition campaign and the efforts made to liberalize the criminal justice system had major impacts on criminality.

In the first year of the Gorbachev period, crime rates dipped tempo-

---

[12]V. N. Kudriavtsev et al., eds., *Kurs Sovetskoi Kriminologii* (Moscow: Iuridicheskaia Literatura, 1985), 318.

rarily, probably a result of the strictly enforced antialcohol campaign launched in 1985.[13] In 1986, nearly 2 million crimes were reported (approximately one-fifth to one-sixth of the number reported in the United States). Crime rates rose slightly in 1988 (while prohibition was still enforced), only to be followed in 1989 by a precipitous rise in crime. This increase was explained by many as a consequence of the enhanced freedom and an incapacity of the police to deal with crime in a rapidly changing society.

Ministry of Internal Affairs (MVD) statistics for 1989 reveal that 3.9 million crime reports were made to the police[14] but only 2.5 million crimes were actually registered (a rate of 849 per 100,000). Registered crime in 1989 rose nearly 32 percent over the previous year,[15] and the growth did not stop there. In the first nine months of 1990, crime rates rose 13 percent while serious crime increased by 20 percent.[16] In the first half of 1991, a 22 percent increase was noted over the previous year.[17] National figures were no longer comparable after the first half of 1991, owing to the independence of the Baltics and dissolution of the Soviet state in December of that year. But the 1991 figures for the republics reveal continued growth in crime. Crime escalated further after the breakup of the Soviet Union.[18] For example, in Russia the crime rate rose by one-third, with an especially large rise in juvenile delinquency in the first three months of 1992.[19]

The Soviet Union's growing crime problem was particularly noticeable in large cities, long known for their low rates of criminality. Foreigners were disproportionately victims of crime in Moscow because they possessed desired foreign currency and technology.[20] Removed from close scrutiny by the KGB, foreigners became the responsibility of the overburdened *militsiia*, who were incapable of protecting them.

[13]V. V. Luneev, "Prestupnost' v SSSR za 1988g statistika i kommentarii kriminologa," *Sovetskoe Gosudarstvo i Pravo* 8 (1989): 85. Table 7 shows an overall drop in alcohol-related crimes of 4.2 percent in 1988 in comparison with 1987.
[14]I. Servetskii, "Komu nuzhen otkaznoi," *Sovetskaia militsiia* 11 (1990): 54.
[15]Luneev et al., *Prestupnost' i Pravonarusheniia v SSSR*, 11. Information is contained in Table 1.
[16]V. Lobachenko, "Ryzhkov Interviewed on Plans to Combat Crime," *FBIS Daily Report*, 9 October 1990, 51.
[17]Pashin, *Kontseptsiia Sudebnoi Reformy*, 8.
[18]In the first three months of 1992, the crime rate rose by more than one-third over that for 1991. See "Russia Targets Jobless Youth in Crime Prevention Drive," *RFE/RL Daily Report*, 21 May 1992, 2.
[19]Ibid.
[20]Esther B. Fein, "With Easing of Soviet Police State, Crime against Foreigners Is Rising," *New York Times*, 6 May 1990, 22.

There was an increase in both the level and the seriousness of criminality. A particular rise was noted in the rate of violent crime, especially in such offenses as premeditated murder, aggravated assault, and rape.[21] More violent crimes were committed, often with guns that had been stolen from military or police stations.[22] Greater organization was observed in crime commission as more bands of criminals were arrested[23] and an increasing number of offenses were committed in groups.[24] The victims of crime were increasingly symbols of state authority, such as police and military personnel. Between January and September 1990, a total of 775 police and MVD troops were killed and an additional 6,799 were wounded.[25]

Since the law did not respond to the development of the market economy, increasingly large numbers of individuals were arrested for speculation.[26] Furthermore, as the first chapter in this volume suggests, citizens did not change their attitude toward speculation but continued to believe the Marxian idea that middlemen do not increase the cost above the value of the goods they sell. Therefore, while the state was encouraging the development of private business through the emergent cooperative movement, the criminal law code was not adjusted to accommodate capitalist activity. Law enforcement against entrepreneurs was stepped up in January 1991 after conservatives assumed control of the Ministry of Internal Affairs.[27] Many individuals convicted of economic crimes during the Soviet period were still held in Russian prisons in mid-1992, although other newly sovereign countries have released those convicted of speculation in the Soviet period.[28]

The growth in crime and the increasing severity of criminality were possibly unavoidable in a period of such rapid social change and per-

[21]Anatolii Alekseev, "Itogi i prognozy," *Sovetskaia militsiia* 5 (1990): 7.

[22]"Srochno kupliu oruzhie," *Sovetskaia militsiia* 9 (1990): 55.

[23]"Council of Ministers Presidium Discusses Crime," *FBIS Daily Report*, 9 October 1990, 50.

[24]Luneev et al., *Prestupnost' i Pravonarusheniia v SSSR*, 17, Table 10.

[25]Dawn Mann, "Crime on the Rise across USSR," *RFE/RL Daily Report*, 6 November 1990, 3.

[26]O. Aksenov, "Spekulant nachinaet i ... vyigryvaet," *Sovetskaia militsiia* 2 (1990): 13–15.

[27]David Remnick, "KGB Given Powers over Businesses," *Washington Post*, 27 January 1991, A1.

[28]Presentation of Misha Paleev of the Committee on Legislation of the Supreme Soviet, 10 July 1992, in Washington, D.C. The procurator general of Kirghizstan said that speculators had been released in her country. In Armenia, according to a senior legal official at the seminar, all speculators except those accused of speculating in medicine and bread had been released.

sonal dislocation. In contrast to their approach to many of the other social problems discussed in this book, Soviet leaders not only failed to anticipate the growth in crime but took steps that exacerbated the problem. Although there are few good formulas to help a society reduce crime, there are certain prescriptions for aggravating crime problems. The Soviet Union in its final years is a textbook case of what policies not to pursue if one wants to reduce or control the level of crime commission. During perestroika the state relaxed its police controls and granted more personal freedom. Yet simultaneous with the reduction of institutional controls that inhibited crime commission, the state policy of full employment—which prevented crimes based on absolute need—was eliminated.

Many other policies were undertaken during perestroika that both inadvertently and deliberately contributed to the growth of certain forms of crime commission. The steps taken to make the justice system more accountable to the law and to humanize the administration of justice inadvertently contributed to the rise in crime. Although senior MVD officials warned that an increase in organized crime would follow the initiation of the antialcohol campaign, their advice was ignored because the Politburo leadership decided that the general benefits of this campaign outweighed the criminological consequences.

During the preperestroika period, when the centralized police system operated with some degree of efficiency, the extensive system of population controls could deter criminality. As noted earlier, the permanent exile of serious offenders from major cities, the absence of a large mobile population, and the tracking of ex-offenders prevented much serious crime. Seasoned offenders, therefore, could not train younger criminals in the large cities. Young men, the most likely to commit crimes, could not obtain residence permits to reside in the major urban communities. With the decline of central authority during perestroika and the transfer of police resources to more pressing problems of ethnic conflict, mass political demonstrations, and economic transition, police officers were left little time to maintain these population controls.[29] Furthermore, the problems of large-scale internal migration, a consequence of rising nationalism, and the large numbers of refugees from areas torn by conflict made efforts to limit population movement ineffective.

Increased civil liberties for defendants, the release of dramatic num-

---

[29] A. Chernenko and A. Chernayaki, "Bakatin Interviewed on Crime 'Crisis,'" FBIS Daily Report, 19 July 1989, 98.

bers of offenders from labor camps with no possibility of legitimate employment, and the launching of the antialcohol campaign in 1985 all contributed to the growth in crime, particularly organized crime. The antialcohol campaign was doomed to failure from the start because a population accustomed to heavy drinking cannot shift to total abstention merely through laws and police controls.

Following the enactment of the prohibition campaign in May 1985, the state tried to destroy the sources of production and to punish the users and sellers of illegally produced alcohol. Between 1986 and 1988, more than 10 million individuals were arrested annually for violations of the antialcohol legislation.[30] At first crime rates were depressed because individuals found it more difficult to procure alcohol. But the advantages of the prohibition did not last long because illegal alcohol production became more sophisticated. Those unable to acquire alcohol turned to cologne and numerous other substances. The police not only pursued alcohol abusers but also monitored the department store lines where perfume was sold.[31]

Licit alcohol production was once dominated by the state. Illegal alcohol had been frequently produced by retired female pensioners who made *samogon* (home brew) to supplement their limited pensions. Once the state ceased producing alcohol, women were pushed out of this activity, and the trade increasingly was dominated by sophisticated entrepreneurs who often had links to organized crime. The prototypical producer of home brew became a young man who differed little in his profile from the usual criminal offender. Indicative of the increasing professionalization of illegal alcohol production was a watchtower set up at a remote distillery by an ambitious bootlegger seeking to detect approaching police through binoculars.[32]

Alcohol sales in the Soviet period contributed a significant proportion of the national budget. Experts estimated that the ultimate cost to the Soviet state of the antialcohol campaign for the years 1985–88 was between fifty and one hundred billion rubles in lost revenues.[33] The loss

[30]Between 1 to 2 percent of these arrests were criminal; the rest were for administrative violations. *Statisticheskie Dannye o Prestupnosti i Pravonarusheniiakh po SSSR* (Moscow: MVD USSR Glavnyi informatsionnyi tsentr, 1989), 19.

[31]Anatolii Rubinov, "Otchevo blagoukhaiut muzchiny, ili o parfiumernom sposobe bor'by s alkogolzmom," *Literaturnaia gazeta,* 12 November 1986, 12.

[32]A. V. Vlasov, "Stop the Home Brewer," *Current Digest of the Soviet Press* 10 (1987): 20–21.

[33]Boris Levin, director of Alcohol Research, Institute of Sociology, Academy of Sciences, in lectures in 1988–90.

of such significant revenues aggravated the national debt and inflation also contributed significantly to the economic crisis that hit the Soviet Union in its final period.

The consequences of the antialcohol campaign were both a fiscal crisis and a rise in police corruption. The police became accessories to organized crime. Like their American counterparts during the Prohibition era, they accepted massive bribes from the homebrewers and themselves became procurers of alcohol.[34]

The transfer of large amounts of capital to organized criminals during this critical period enabled them to launder their profits into the burgeoning movement of business cooperatives.[35] Thus organized crime figures were acquiring the funds to dominate the emerging private sector. Moreover, the money they amassed allowed them to purchase the technology, the cars, and the communication equipment that they needed to run their operations successfully. Hard-pressed economically by the costs of the antialcohol campaign, the state lacked the resources to protect itself from organized crime.

Whereas the government, strained by its budgetary crisis, looked for ways to reduce its expenditures, organized crime, enriched by its revenues from the antialcohol campaign, was poised for growth and could afford to hire personnel. As the following discussion illustrates, future cadres of organized crime could come from two different sources: dismissed police personnel and released inmates. Well-motivated state policies contributed to the increase in dismissed police personnel and released convicts, but these efforts to reduce corruption in law enforcement and humanize corrections also had their negative consequences.

The campaign to eliminate corruption in the justice system, particularly in the MVD, was initiated in the waning period of Brezhnev's rule and was continued by his successors. During these years nearly two hundred thousand people were dismissed from the MVD, most of whom had served in the different branches of the police.[36] At the same time, numerous personnel in the Ministry of Justice and the courts were removed from their positions; some of them were tried and imprisoned. Many professional individuals were purged after KGB techniques were

[34]B. Levin and M. Levin, *Krutoi Povorot* (Moscow: Sovetskaia Rossiia, 1989).
[35]Iurii Shchekochikhin and Aleksandr Gurov, "Lev Pryguul," *Literaturnaia gazeta*, 20 July 1988, 13.
[36]Vlasov, "Stop the Home Brewer," 47.

imported into the Ministry of Internal Affairs by its new chief, Vitali Fedorchuk, a former member of the security apparatus.[37]

This campaign to reduce corruption caused many important effects on crime, but the reduction of criminality was not one of them. The dismissed law enforcement personnel often were recruited by the rapidly growing sector of organized crime. Their knowledge of state law enforcement practices, their training in the use of weapons, and the corrupt environment in which they had worked made it possible for them to transfer their skills readily from the state to the criminal sector.

The mass dismissals also demoralized police personnel and made it increasingly difficult for the remaining staff to perform effectively in a time of rapid societal transition. New cadres were not easily recruited, because under perestroika citizens no longer felt obligated to follow the state's orders. The state directed thousands of workers into the police to compensate for the shortfall of personnel, but many refused to obey.[38] Thousands of positions in the police and investigatorial work remained understaffed because of dismissals and the failure to hire replacement personnel. The ranks of experienced personnel were further depleted by voluntary departures to the more lucrative private security apparatuses.[39]

Compounding the problem of inadequate staffing and untrained personnel was the absence of equipment: police personnel could not respond to reported crimes because they lacked cars, dispatcher systems, radio equipment, or even the gas to run their vehicles. Delays of two or three hours were not infrequent, and when two crimes occurred simultaneously, the wait could be even longer.[40]

The most vivid evidence of this situation was the rapid decline in the number of arrests. Between 1986 and 1988, the number of individuals arrested and detained dropped precipitously from 749,000 to 402,000,[41] whereas the crime rate fell by less than 10 percent in these years when the antialcohol campaign seemed to be initially successful. In addition, the certainty of punishment declined significantly in the 1980s. In 1980, no perpetrator was arrested in 9.7 percent of cases; by 1985, the figure had risen to 17.8 percent. It escalated rapidly under perestroika, reach-

[37]N. Kipman, "O Kompetentnosti i professionalizme," *Sovetskaia militsiia* 4 (1990): 22.
[38]Natalia Dzhalogoniia, "Komu stoiat' na strazhe poriadka," *Moskovskie novosti*, 23 August 1987, 14.
[39]"Militia Losing Experienced Personnel," *FBIS Daily Report*, 9 January 1992, 56.
[40]A. Lazarev, "A kogda lovit' prestupnikov," *Nedelia* 43 (1989): 2.
[41]Chernenko and Chernayaki, "Bakatin Interviewed on Crime 'Crisis,' " 99.

ing 49.4 percent in 1988 and 63.4 percent the following year.[42] The decline in police performance is also evident in other figures. In 1979 every criminal investigator cleared 26 crimes, but by 1989 that figure had fallen to 16.8.[43] Some of this decline could be explained by changes in the recording practices, the rise in crime, and the increased workload of police personnel. But an MVD professor offered an alternative explanation. He suggested that the primary cause was that police personnel had been overcome by "a wave of apathy and lowered discipline."[44] The continual decline in the certainty of punishment probably contributed to the crime increase.

Efforts to humanize the legal system and adhere to legal procedures brought profound changes in the processing of cases under perestroika. The certainty of punishment was reduced further because law enforcement personnel tried to follow established legal procedures. Before 1987, thirteen to seventeen offenders out of every hundred were released during the preliminary investigation. By 1988–89, that figure had jumped to between thirty-six and thirty-seven. Police personnel were releasing not only minor offenders but also those accused of committing more serious crimes. In 1988, three times as many individuals accused of physical assault and more than five times as many individuals accused of rape were released during the investigatory stage than in 1985.[45]

This dramatic change in policy could be attributed, in part, to the reduced pressure on investigators to achieve results. Furthermore, prosecutors or judges in the late 1980s might dismiss cases in which there was inadequate evidence or clear violations of the code of criminal procedure. But critics of police practices suggested that the increased dismissal of charges was an effort to cover up their inactivity or incompetence.[46]

Significant changes in sentencing policy were noted. Increasingly community sanctions were used as alternatives to incarceration. In 1985 in Uzbekistan, 45 percent of the offenders sentenced by the lowest courts were sentenced to confinement; by 1989 that figure had dropped to 29 percent. Many of those who remained in the community were thieves, armed robbers, and even embezzlers of large sums of money.[47] In 1988, national statistics indicated that 82 percent of those sentenced were kept within the community. Community sentences were less likely for serious

[42]Luneev et al., *Prestupnost' i Pravonarusheniia v SSSR*, 19.
[43]"Volny apatii v more stereotipov," 12.
[44]Ibid.
[45]Ibid., 13.
[46]Ibid.
[47]O. Aksenov, "Nabolelo," *Sovetskaia militsiia* 7 (1990): 40.

violent offenders, but even significant numbers of these criminals were not sent to penal institutions.[48]

The increased use of community corrections need not have increased crime rates if an appropriate program of community supervision were in existence. But the Ministry of Internal Affairs made no changes in staffing or policy necessary to accommodate the influx of sentenced offenders in the community. The efforts to humanize sentencing policy merely placed inadequately supervised criminals in the community, a prescription for increased crime rates.

The severity of penal sanctions was reduced even for the most serious of offenders. Whereas in 1990, 223 people were sentenced to death in Russia, the corresponding figure in 1991 was 147. The change in the number of offenders condemned to death was solely a consequence of efforts to humanize punishment. In this time period, the number of capital crimes rose by 20 percent.[49]

In a further effort to humanize corrections, large numbers of individuals were released from penal colonies,[50] and many penal colonies were closed (approximately seven hundred thousand places in labor camps were eliminated). In the past the state, by guaranteeing employment, had forced Soviet enterprises to hire ex-offenders. But in the late 1980s, the Soviet system no longer functioned as before. Ex-offenders were released into a society in economic crisis with no jobs available for them and no unemployment benefits or welfare payments to support them legally. The social safety net had collapsed for these released offenders—already susceptible to crime commission, they had difficulty finding legitimate means of support. The absorption of so many ex-offenders would have been a challenge to any society under the best of conditions, but it was particularly problematic at a time of such major economic transition. Many of the released offenders were hired by organized crime, one of the few expanding sectors of the economy.

CRIME AND THE LEGACY OF THE SOVIET SYSTEM

The communist system left the successor states a crime legacy that will be difficult to address in societies hard-pressed by numerous economic problems and with state institutions in rapid transition. Crime is grow-

---

[48]"Volny apatii v more stereotipov," 13.
[49]Elizabeth Teague, "Use of Death Penalty Drops in Russia," *RFE/RL Daily Report,* 14 April 1992, 2.
[50]"Interior Minister Dismisses Rumours of Planned Pogrom," Soviet Union/0165 BBC Information Service, 31 May 1988, i.

ing in all the countries that emerged from the Soviet Union.[51] The former Soviet Union, like the former states of the Soviet bloc, is discovering that increasing crime rates are one of the unfortunate costs of its newfound freedom.

Crime rates generally rise in periods of political and social transition. Yet there are certain features of the Soviet crime legacy that will give the crime of the new successor states a distinctive character in the future. These include, first of all, the fact that the institutionalization of such significant numbers of citizens in penal colonies during the Soviet period has created many graduates of these "schools for crime." In addition, the criminalization of so much human activity during the Soviet years erased the distinction between law-abiding and criminal behavior for many Soviet citizens. The endemic corruption of the Soviet period will affect the privatization process and the distribution of foreign aid from abroad. The large number of weapons in circulation will make future criminal behavior more violent. The growth of organized crime will be a lasting presence on the post-Soviet scene. In addition, the failure to address the drug problem during the Soviet period may lead to a serious crime problem. The understaffed and poorly trained police and the lack of equipment for law enforcement make it difficult for the emergent societies to combat crime. Taken together, all of these circumstances have left a serious negative legacy for the successor states.

Millions of individuals were incarcerated in labor camps and hundreds of thousands of juveniles were confined in children's homes. These people, longtime residents of institutions, did not know how to function in the general community, let alone in a rapidly changing society. The Soviet policy of Russification channeled many released offenders into Tallinn, where they could get residence permits. As a result, the new government of Estonia is facing a serious crime problem because a significant proportion of their capital's male residents have been in labor camps.[52]

Throughout the Soviet period, many Soviets were forced to break the law through either engaging in small-scale speculation, embezzling small amounts of goods from their workplace, or frequenting the black market. Only by violating the law were they able to obtain consumer goods

[51]The author helped organize a conference in Budapest, Hungary, in June 1992. The resulting volume, Jozsef Vigh and Geza Katona, eds., *Social Changes, Crime and Police* Budapest: Eötvös Lorand University, 1993), revealed a significant rise in crime in almost all of the countries of Eastern Europe.

[52]Discussions with Eduard Raska, director of the new Academy for Public Safety in Tallinn, February 1992.

and medicines that were in short supply.[53] As Millar and Wolchik point out, citizens justified this behavior because the goods and services were necessary and no one was profiting greatly from this illegal activity. Chances of arrest for petty illegal activity were small. Even though citizens knew they were breaking the law, they did not see their behavior as reprehensible—on the contrary, many justified their actions as necessary. Citizens lost respect for the criminal law, a respect that may be hard to reestablish even in states that decriminalize the crimes linked to the socialist economy.

The persistent economic shortages of Soviet life and the severity of the criminal justice system contributed to a high degree of corruption. Individuals with access to desired commodities capitalized on their positions. Citizens threatened with arrest did anything within their means to avoid contact with a criminal justice system where there was little chance of a fair trial or investigation.[54] Efforts to privatize the economy fairly have been hindered by the endemic corruption of officials in many successor states and the pervasive organized crime.[55] Aid from abroad has often benefited officials rather than the citizenry for whom it is intended; numerous reports have surfaced in the Soviet press of foreign aid funds financing private dachas for officials rather than feeding hungry citizens.[56]

The ethnic conflict of the final years of the Soviet period also has contributed to a legacy of violence. Citizens exposed to such a significant degree of violence have acquired an immunity to it. Furthermore, the violence against symbols of Soviet authority—the police and the army—has placed many weapons in circulation. Not only have police stations and army posts been raided, but demobilized military personnel have sold weapons to enhance their incomes or support their drug habits. National groups, particularly in the Caucasus, have imported weapons to further their cause. The cost of arms on the black market has dropped. In a society where guns were once tightly controlled, the increasing number of weapons in circulation has led to many more offenses perpetrated with firearms.[57]

[53]Konstantin Simis, *The Corrupt Society* (New York: Simon and Schuster, 1982).

[54]L. Fisher, "Anatomiia Korruptsii," *Sovetskaia militsiia* 4 (1990): 14–16, interview with V. Rogovin on the Institute of Sociology of the Academy of Sciences.

[55]See, for example, L. Raykova, "Privatization of St. Petersburg Store Described," *FBIS Central Eurasia Report*, 12 June 1992, 40, and Yuriy Shatalov, "Corruption Alleged in Perm Privatization," *FBIS Central Eurasia Report*, 24 June 1992, 70.

[56]See, for example, Andrei Gurkov, "German Relief Aid Abuse in the Urals," *Moscow News* 8 (1992): 8.

[57]"Srochno kupliu oruzhie," *Sovetskaia militsiia* 9 (1990): 55.

The proliferation of weapons has convinced many that the police are not able to control the crime problem. This situation has encouraged many groups in Soviet society to take the law into their own hands. Such actions are particularly evident in the Northern Caucasus, where vigilante groups are operating in place of, or in opposition to, state law enforcers.

Organized crime was not new in the Gorbachev period. But the initiation of the antialcohol campaign, the worsened consumer-good shortages under perestroika, and the increasing economic differentiation with the growth of the cooperative movement led to the proliferation of organized crime. The fifteen-year delay in initiating the fight against organized crime, caused by Soviet authorities' refusal to acknowledge the problem, permitted it to proliferate and infiltrate many aspects of Soviet life.[58]

Organized crime became a major economic force in society. Many of the newly formed businesses were established and are run by organized crime, and the illicit roots of much of the emergent business activity make the establishment of legitimate businesses difficult. The proliferation of criminal groups that prey on the new enterprises through extortion schemes hinder the transition to a market economy. Furthermore, the mafia has managed to buy off many police, limiting the efforts to suppress illegal activities.[59] The heavy involvement of organized crime in the emergent capitalist activity has discredited the market in the eyes of many citizens, who equate the market with illicit activity.

Organized crime figures have already established links with other organized criminals outside of the former Soviet Union. These links are apparent in their efforts to internationalize drug trafficking. The crime networks exist in many of the emergent Central Asian and Caucasian countries where drugs are cultivated. Furthermore, the impoverished status of these countries, particularly since the loss of subsidies from Moscow, has made international drug trade one of the few sources of foreign currency available. The threat of a growing domestic market also exists because of the significant number of domestic addicts.

As in the late Soviet period, the fight against crime is crippled by a law-enforcement apparatus that lacks trained personnel and adequate equipment. Only one-quarter of the criminal investigators have at least

[58]Viktor Turshatov, "Organized Crime," *Moscow News* 39 (1988): 14.
[59]"Registered Crime in 1991 Surpasses 2 Million," *FBIS Daily Report*, 29 January 1992, 32.

five years of experience on the job. Approximately 60 percent of the police vehicles need to be replaced.[60] The new states inherited police forces without such rudimentary equipment as police cars, typewriters, or tape recorders, let alone the technology needed to deal with the increasingly sophisticated and well-equipped personnel of organized crime. The successor states lack the institutions needed to fight crime and in most cases the resources needed to train new cadres or equip their police forces. The institutional collapse of the Soviet social control apparatus leaves for the successor states an unfortunate legacy which can neither transform nor create new democratic institutions.

CONCLUSION

During most of the Soviet period, the state had means to prevent and control crime that were unavailable to Western democratic societies. Soviet law enforcement could be more intrusive in the lives of the citizenry, the criminal-justice system permitted few acquittals and allowed prosecutors and police to dismiss few charges, and there was a near certainty of punishment unmatched by other societies. Complementing the punitive justice system were social controls that limited the possibilities for crime commission. The restrictions on personal mobility, the surveillance of ex-offenders, and the widespread system of informants made it more difficult to commit many forms of crime.

Much of the Soviet Union's previous success in limiting crime was attributable to controls rather than panaceas. Crime increased in the late 1980s because centralized control declined, economic hardship increased, and individuals lost their fear of political authority. Furthermore, as the internal affairs minister explained, "The fight against crime has been adversely affected by the considerable diversion of militia resources, means and attention to the localization of interethnic conflicts and the safeguarding of public order when rallies and demonstrations are held."[61]

The police strained simultaneously to preserve the union and to control crime. The police lost on both counts because nationalism increased and the once-unifying ideology was discredited. With the demise of Marxism, the social contract between the state and the citizenry collapsed. Under perestroika, the state reneged on its long-standing promise

---

[60]"Militia Losing Experienced Personnel," *FBIS Daily Report*, 9 January 1992, 56.
[61]Chernenko and Chernayaki, "Bakatin Interviewed on Crime 'Crisis,' " 98.

to provide order, jobs, and social benefits for all its citizens in exchange for unquestioned loyalty to the state. Instead, citizens gained personal freedom but not the benefits of a Western capitalist society. Rising crime rates became a visible symbol of the collapse of the old order and the painful transition to a nonsocialist future.

The social policies and the transformation of Soviet society in the final years of its existence left a continually worsening crime problem for the successor states. Faced by seemingly more demanding problems of economic and political transformation, the Soviet successor states are ill-equipped to handle the ever more pressing threats to their social order. The presence of large-scale organized crime, the proliferation of weapons among the population, and the lack of employment for many released offenders nearly guarantee further escalation of crime rates. With the collapse of the central institutions of social control, the successor states are in no position to fight crime effectively. Furthermore, the citizens of the former Soviet Union are no longer willing to assist the state in its social control function. Instead, many have taken the law into their own hands. Until the political and economic transformations stabilize the successor states, the crime legacy of the Soviet period will undermine the social order of the newly emergent nations. Rising crime rates will be an important problem they must confront in this difficult period.

Many citizens feel nostalgia for the order of the Soviet system. As Millar and Wolchik suggest, crime control is one of the aspects of the old political system that Soviet citizens most want to keep. The growth and the visibility of post-Soviet crime, therefore, is a challenge to the democratization of the society. Citizens, seeking a more ordered society, may strive to reverse the process of democratization, a process that is not smooth or trouble free. More crime and more serious criminality are not only a legacy of the past but impediments to the development of a better future.

7

Drug abuse in Central and Eastern Europe

JOHN M. KRAMER

The specter of communism no longer haunts Central and Eastern Europe,[1] but the legacy of communist misrule in the region remains. Prominent components of this unwelcome aftermath include an obsolete industrial base, a decaying infrastructure in communications and transportation, a massive degradation of the physical environment, and a cluster of long-neglected and festering social pathologies. How to mitigate, transform, or cope with these social ills has become a preeminent issue of public policy in postcommunist Central and Eastern Europe.

Nonalcoholic drug abuse (hereafter referred to as drug abuse)—which is one of the most neglected social pathologies under communist rule—is the primary focus of this chapter.[2] Communist governments had traditionally contended that "negative" phenomena, including drug abuse, were alien to socialism and could flourish only within the exploitation, moral depravity, and vacuousness of capitalism. The "top toxicologist" in Bulgaria argued in 1983 that "there are no social causes for drug addiction in our country. The young people do not face insoluble social or material problems" as they do under capitalism. Similarly, a Czechoslovak source maintained that "drug addiction is a phenomenon that remains totally alien to our socialist society and the instruments wielded by our system make it possible to bring this matter fully under

[1]"Central and Eastern Europe" herein includes Albania, Bulgaria, Czechoslovakia and its successors, Hungary, Poland, Romania, and the former Yugoslav state.
[2]For an earlier analysis of this subject, see John M. Kramer, "Drug Abuse in Communist Europe: An Emerging Issue of Public Policy," *Slavic Review* 49 (Spring 1990): 19–31. Little else has been published on this subject in English; one exception is David Powell, "Drug Abuse in Communist Europe," *Problems of Communism* 21 (July–August 1972): 31–40.

control."[3] The limited available data on drug abuse throughout the region in the 1960s and 1970s belie these insouciant assessments.

Drug abuse appears to have been especially pronounced in Poland. Researchers at the University of Warsaw estimate that in the early 1970s between fifty thousand and seventy thousand persons used narcotic drugs, although they do not indicate the frequency of such use. By 1980, this figure may have approached three hundred thousand to four hundred thousand.[4] Writing in a publication of the United Nations, a Polish specialist on drug abuse asserted that by the late 1970s opium derivatives were the "predominant" drug substances abused by young people.[5] In 1981, a documentary broadcast on Polish national television warning in graphic and stark detail about the horrors of drug abuse created a sensation among a population unaccustomed to frank discussions of such topics.[6] Overall, however, the regime of Edward Gierek largely kept silent about drug abuse, as well as other social pathologies, as it pursued its "propaganda of success" policy that trumpeted the victories of socialist construction in Poland and minimized or concealed the flaws.[7]

Drug abuse among youth in Hungary was first reported in the late 1960s. By the mid 1970s, one survey of high school students found that 20 percent of the sample had witnessed drug abuse among their peers and 5 percent had used drugs themselves.[8] A Hungarian drug specialist writing in the late 1980s in a Soviet journal reported "intensive narcotization" among specific groups of youths at the beginning of the 1980s. The same specialist also found widespread abuse of tranquilizers and other soporific substances during the 1970s. Between 1971 and 1980, daily per capita consumption of tranquilizers increased from 6 to 11 tablets; the respective figures for other soporific substances were 13 and

[3]The comments of the Bulgarian toxicologist are carried in *Narodna mladezh* (Sofia), 13 April 1983, in *Foreign Broadcast Information Service–East Europe Daily Report*(hereafter *FBIS-EEU*), 14 April 1983, p. C2. *Veda a zivot* (Prague), no. 8 (1983), as reported in *Radio Free Europe–Situation Report* (hereafter *RFE-SR*) (Czechoslovakia), 13 September 1983, carries the remarks of the Czechoslovak official.
[4]The Warsaw University data were presented at an international conference in Amsterdam, as reported in the *Manchester Guardian* (England), 11 February 1980.
[5]M. E. Sokalska, "Legal Measures to Combat Drug-Related Problems in Poland," *Bulletin on Narcotics* 36 (July–September 1984): 20.
[6]For details about the documentary, including its impact on the population, see *RFE-SR* (Poland), 29 May 1981.
[7]For an elaboration of this argument, see ibid.
[8]*Nepszabadsag* (Budapest), 10 October 1985, in *FBIS-EEU*, 21 October 1985, F5.

27.5.[9] Even the Hungarian Council of Ministers in an official report in 1978 acknowledged the "growing interest of youths in narcotics and in pharmaceuticals and chemicals that have a narcotic effect."[10] The daily paper of the Hungarian Socialist Workers (Communist) party, citing "well-informed" sources, estimated that approximately ten thousand persons were abusing drugs at the beginning of the 1980s.[11] Yet the Hungarian regime—often reputed to be the most "liberal" in Eastern Europe—more typically concealed the problem of drug abuse. In 1976, it prohibited the broadcast of a television documentary on the subject, and in 1981 it similarly prohibited the publication of an article that allegedly described in "too graphic detail" the life of a Hungarian drug addict.[12] As late as 1987, one source contended that "official records on drug addiction are nonexistent in Hungary."[13]

Published materials on drug abuse during these years in Czechoslovakia, Yugoslavia, and Bulgaria are even more limited and, for other states in the region, nonexistent. A Czechoslovak émigré publication reported that codeine had already become the "national" drug of choice in the 1960s.[14] Consumption of Alnagon, an analgesic drug with a high codeine content, was almost nonexistent before 1963, but consumption increased to 21 pills per 1,000 population per day in 1969 and attained a level of 28 pills in 1975. An official secret report on drug abuse, which was subsequently smuggled to the West, estimated that the number of marijuana smokers among twelve- to thirteen-year-olds had increased by three to five times between 1971 and 1980.[15] In Yugoslavia, the number of drug addicts officially registered with the authorities grew from 250 to 5,000 individuals between 1970 and 1978.[16] The establishment in 1972 of the League to Combat Drug Addiction presumably reflected official concern with this phenomenon.[17] Finally,

---

[9]*Voprosy narkologii* (Moscow), no. 3 (1988): 36.

[10]*Budapesti Nevelo* (Budapest), no. 3 (1979), in *Joint Publications Research Service–East Europe Report—Political, Sociological, and Military Affairs* (hereafter *JPRS-EPS*), 5 September 1985, 45.

[11]*Nepszabadsag*, 10 October 1985, in *FBIS-EEU*, 21 October 1985, F5.

[12]These incidents are reported in *RFE-SR* (Hungary), 25 February 1987.

[13]*Magyar Hirlap* (Budapest), 30 January 1987, in *JPRS–East Europe Report* (hereafter *JPRS-EER*), 16 March 1987, 115.

[14]*Listy* (Rome), no. 5 (1988), in *JPRS-EER*, 10 March 1989, 3.

[15]The official report was acquired by the dissident group Charter 77 and subsequently published abroad. It is reproduced in Charter 77, Document No. 42/83, 30 December 1983.

[16]*RFE–Background Report* (hereafter *RFE-BR*) (Eastern Europe), 13 August 1986, 3.

[17]As reported in Powell, "Drug Abuse in Communist Europe," 39.

Bulgarian sources report only that "in our country drug addiction goes back to the period following 1968."[18] In 1979, there were 412 drug addicts officially registered in Bulgaria compared to 210 addicts in 1971.[19]

Regimes became more forthcoming about acknowledging drug abuse in their societies beginning in the mid-1980s, although to varying degrees. In 1985, Poland became the first state in the region to promulgate a comprehensive law to combat drug abuse.[20] Officials in Czechoslovakia held a press conference in 1987 to publicize their efforts to mitigate the drug problem—an initiative almost unimaginable even several years earlier. In 1988, the Czechoslovak government promulgated national "targets" to combat drug abuse and other social pathologies.[21] Hungary established the Committee on Narcotics (under the auspices of the State Committee against Alcoholism) in 1987 to coordinate its initiatives in this area.[22] The official media in all countries also exhibited greater glasnost on the subject of drug abuse, though once again to varying degrees in different countries. A Czechoslovak source contrasted this new glasnost with the previous policy of official silence:

Until recently we maintained a chaste silence about the symptoms and manifestations of drug addiction in any form or we designated it as a marginal and completely atypical manifestation for our society. However, these positions were an expression of wishes rather than reality while today we are looking at these problems without rose colored glasses.[23]

Two factors seem to account for this greater glasnost. First, the phenomenon—although its exact dimension remained unknown—appeared sufficiently serious to merit an official response that previous silence on the subject inhibited. Second, glasnost had become "politically correct" by then, given the concurrent campaign undertaken by Mikhail Gorbachev in the Soviet Union to discuss and combat a wide range of social pathologies, including drug abuse, that were undermining the moral fabric of socialist society.

[18]*Sturshel* (Sofia), 31 July 1987, in *FBIS-EEU*, 10 August 1987, B3.
[19]*Novo vreme* (Sofia), no. 8 (1979), as reported in *RFE-SR* (Bulgaria), 1 February 1984.
[20]See later section under "Combating Drug Abuse" for a comprehensive discussion of the provisions of the law.
[21]For details of the press conference, see *Rude pravo* (Prague), 8 October 1987, in *FBIS-EEU*, 16 October 1987, 27. The "targets" are discussed in *Lidova demokracie* (Prague), 1 July 1989, in *JPRS-EER*, 19 September 1989, 31–32.
[22]For details of this initiative, see the commentary carried by Radio Budapest, 27 January 1987, as reported in *RFE-SR* (Hungary), 25 February 1987.
[23]*Rude pravo*, 24 June 1987, in *JPRS-EER*, 3 September 1987, 10.

THE SCOPE OF DRUG ABUSE

No one within or without Central and Eastern Europe knows the actual dimensions of drug abuse in the region. As a Polish source, in comments applicable to all states in Eastern Europe, frankly admits: "We can speak only of estimates—in fact, no one can tell us with full responsibility how many addicts there are; probably we shall never know exactly."[24] A similar problem confronts other societies, including the United States. An official with the United States National Institute of Drug Abuse, for example, asserts that "you just can't trust the numbers" when assessing the scope of drug abuse in the United States.[25]

Several factors explain this circumstance. To begin with, terminological imprecision is common worldwide in much of the extant literature on drugs. Terms such as "abuse," "addiction," "dependency," and "misuse" have no universally accepted definitions and often are employed interchangeably.[26] Eastern European sources frequently exhibit this imprecision by referring to all drugs—regardless of their pharmacological qualities—as "narcotics" and all users as "addicts."[27] Whether the addiction or dependency being described is psychological, physical, or both is rarely made explicit.

To mitigate, if not eliminate, terminological confusion, the World Health Organization in 1965 proposed to substitute the term "drug dependence" for "drug addiction" in discourse about this subject. Similarly, the United States National Commission on Marijuana and Drug Abuse recommended (notwithstanding the title of the commission itself) that the term "drug abuse" be deleted from public discussion. "The term has no functional utility," the commission claimed, and "has become no more than an arbitrary codeword for that drug use which is presently

---

[24]Warsaw Television Service, 28 May 1975, in *JPRS-EPS,* 15 July 1985, 69.

[25]Quoted in the *Washington Post,* 10 August 1986.

[26]For an extended discussion of this circumstance, see the Second Report of the National Commission on Marijuana and Drug Abuse, *Drug Abuse in America: Problem in Perspective* (Washington, D.C.: U.S. Government Printing Office, 1973), 121–40. Another treatment of this subject is R. L. Hartnoll, "Current Situation Related to Drug Abuse Assessment in European Countries," *Bulletin on Narcotics* 38 (January-June 1986), especially 71–76.

[27]"Narcotics" are medically defined as central nervous system depressants with analgesic and sedative properties. Under U.S. federal law, narcotics are considered to be addictive drugs that produce physical and psychological dependence and include opium and its derivatives, heroin, morphine, codeine, and several synthetic substances that can produce morphine-type addiction. Under this conception of narcotics, hashish and marijuana would be excluded. See Robert O'Brien and Sidney Cohen, eds., *The Encyclopedia of Drug Abuse* (New York: Facts on File, 1984), 183.

considered wrong."[28] Although this observation has merit, this chapter employs the term "drug abuse" because a term that emphasizes "drug use which is presently considered wrong" has utility for the social scientist who studies public policy and the values of both elites and masses contained therein. Then, too, most individuals possess a commonsense—albeit imprecise—understanding of the behavior that constitutes drug abuse.

In addition, all states encounter difficulties in identifying drug abusers who often have strong personal and professional incentives to conceal their condition from family, acquaintances, and the authorities. This circumstance was especially manifest in communist Central and Eastern Europe, where legal codes often provided severe penalties for the possession, distribution, and, in some states, the use of illegal drugs. The social stigma attached to drug abuse can foster similar behavior among both abusers and their families. In Poland, for example, only a few parents of addicted children are "bold enough" to speak openly of their progeny's condition. Most such parents keep silent "because of strong feelings of guilt and shame vis-à-vis so-called public opinion."[29]

Finally, the still nascent state of empirical research on drug abuse in Central and Eastern Europe prevents the compilation of comprehensive national statistics regarding it. Further, communist regimes—despite the greater glasnost on drug abuse in the post-1985 period—continued to prohibit unrestricted publication of available data.

Overall, the observation of a Czechoslovak émigré source to the effect that "there is nothing else to do but estimate it by extrapolating experiences of a locally limited scope"[30] remains valid when assessing the extent of drug abuse in the region. Yet the available data on drug abuse do permit several tentative generalizations. First, official statistics (which typically include only those individuals registered with the police or medical institutions as addicts) substantially underestimate the extent

[28]The World Health Organization defined "drug dependence" as follows: "A state, psychic and sometimes also physical, resulting from the interaction between a living organism and a drug, characterized by behavioral and other responses that always include a compulsion to take the drug on a continuous or periodic basis in order to experience its physiological effects and sometimes to avoid the discomfort of its absence." Besides being convoluted, this definition is terminologically imprecise as well. For a discussion of this imprecision, see Second Report of the National Commission on Marijuana and Drug Abuse, *Drug Abuse in America*, 126–27; and see page 13 of that volume for the recommendation of the United States National Commission on Marijuana and Drug Abuse.

[29]*Rzeczywistosc* (Warsaw), 5 July 1987, in *FBIS-EEU*, 22 July 1987, 13.
[30]*Listy*, no. 5 (1988), in *JPRS-EER*, 10 March 1989, 3.

of drug abuse. Commenting on this circumstance, a Hungarian source contends that official data reveal only the "tip of the iceberg" about drug abuse in Hungary.[31] A similar observation applies to all states in the region. That nearly 90 percent of all addicts are not registered with the authorities represents a commonly accepted rule of thumb employed among drug specialists in the region.[32] Second, in contrast to the findings in an earlier study on this subject, drug abuse now appears in varying degrees among all socioeconomic groups and educational levels in the population.[33] Third, the acquisition and consumption of drugs in Central and Eastern Europe follow a pattern similar, although not identical, to that in other developed European countries and the United States. The consumption of narcotic drugs, however, appears far less prevalent in Central and Eastern Europe, except perhaps in Poland and Yugoslavia, than in many of these states. That Poland and Yugoslavia constitute an exception to this observation suggests a final generalization: national differences are readily apparent when examining the status of drug abuse in Central and Eastern Europe.

A nation-by-nation examination illustrates the latter circumstance. The caveats contained herein on data about drug abuse should be remembered when assessing the materials presented in this chapter. Albania and Romania are excluded from the analysis because of the paucity of data on the subject.

Bulgaria. Experts "familiar" with "drug addiction" in Bulgaria report that during the 1980s it "visibly increased" and that its extent has now "become alarming."[34] Yet official data seemingly belie these assessments. In 1991, approximately thirteen hundred "addicts"—around two hundred more than in 1989—were officially registered with the authorities.[35] Another source believes that in Bulgaria there are actually upward

---

[31]*Heti Vilaggazdag* (Budapest), 6 September 1987, as reported in *RFE-SR* (Hungary), 25 February 1987.

[32]For an example of a respected Hungarian narcologist using such an estimate, see *Voprosy narkologii*, no. 3 (1988): 37. Other examples employing such an estimate include *Pogled* (Sofia), 10 July 1989, in *FBIS-EEU*, 20 July 1989, 13; *Glos pomorza* (Kozalin), 18 January 1987, in *JPRS-EER*, 27 May 1987, 109; *Narodna armija* (Belgrade), 24 September 1984, in *FBIS-EEU*, 3 October 1984, 17.

[33]In contrast, Powell, "Drug Abuse in Communist Europe," 40, found drug abuse concentrated among the progeny of the urban middle and upper classes.

[34]*Trud* (Sofia), 11 March 1988, in *FBIS-EEU*, 17 March 1988, 9.

[35]Data on officially registered drug addicts in 1991 from *Ateni* (Sofia), 21 August 1991, in *FBIS-EEU*, 28 August 1991, 10. Respective data for 1988 from *Pogled*, 10 July 1989, in *FBIS-EEU*, 20 July 1989, 13.

of twelve thousand "drug addicts," an unspecified number of "victims of 'minor' drug abuse," and some six thousand to seven thousand teenagers who are sniffers of volatile solvents such as glue and paint remover.[36] Approximately thirty-four individuals reportedly "fell asleep forever" from abusing drugs between 1970 and 1990.[37]

Officially registered addicts and abusers are typically male, young, poorly educated, and often unemployed.[38] It remains unclear whether this circumstance accurately reflects the incidence of drug addiction and abuse among different demographic and socioeconomic groups or indicates only the zeal of the authorities in exposing these practices among some groups more than among others. The authorities are particularly alarmed about the spread of drug abuse among youth. Whereas in 1969 individuals between the ages of thirty-five and sixty constituted the "highest percentage" of registered addicts, by 1991 approximately 60 percent of the addicts were under thirty years of age and almost all of them began using drugs before the age of twenty-five.[39] There have even been instances reported of individuals aged ten and younger abusing drugs.[40]

The Czech and Slovak republics. Official data on drug addiction and abuse are contradictory, incomplete, and vary among the organizations reporting them in these countries. In 1988, approximately nine thousand individuals "addicted to nonalcoholic toxicants" were registered with Czechoslovak health care authorities.[41] Yet in 1990 a ranking police official reported that about seven thousand addicts were "on record" with his department.[42] The Ministry of Internal Affairs published statistics in 1991 reporting that there were ten thousand "known" addicts in the country, although the authorities reportedly "believe the real figure could be closer to forty thousand."[43]

The official secret report on drug abuse later published in the West,

[36]*Pogled,* 10 July 1989, in *FBIS-EEU,* 20 July 1989, 13.
[37]*Ateni,* 21 August 1991, in *FBIS-EEU,* 28 August 1991, 10.
[38]Ibid. Another source reports that "90 percent of the drug addicts have elementary education while 30 percent of them do not work or study." *Pogled,* 10 July 1989, in *FBIS-EEU,* 20 July 1989, 13.
[39]*Trud,* 11 March 1988, in *FBIS-EEU,* 17 March 1988; *Ateni,* 21 August 1991, in *FBIS-EEU,* 28 August 1991, 10–11.
[40]See, for example, reports of such incidents in *Sturshel,* 31 July 1987, in *FBIS-EEU,* 10 August 1987, B4.
[41]*Rude pravo,* 14 September 1988, in *FBIS-EEU,* 22 September 1988, 17.
[42]*Lidova demokracie,* 6 February 1990, in *FBIS-EEU,* 8 February 1990, 31.
[43]As reported in *RFE–Report on Eastern Europe* (hereafter *RFE-REE*), 23 August 1991, 35.

as well as limited data published in the official and émigré press, portray a very different situation. The official report, written in 1983, speaks of "tens of thousands" of individuals "addicted" to "hard drugs," without specifying precisely what drugs.[44] A commentary published in 1988 estimated that approximately sixty thousand individuals were then "using narcotic substances," although it provided no data on the incidence of, or the specific substances consumed in, such use.[45] Another government source estimated that in 1983 upward of four hundred thousand persons abused various amphetamines and barbiturates.[46] According to the émigré publication *Listy,* public health officials reported a "severe" increase after 1980 in the abuse of codeine-based derivatives. The approximately ten thousand codeine abusers registered with the authorities in 1989 undoubtedly understate their actual numbers by at least "several times."[47] Finally, children are trying drugs at ever younger ages. Youths aged fifteen to eighteen have predominated among codeine abusers since 1980, whereas individuals aged eighteen to twenty-five constituted the primary abusers before 1980.[48] In one primary school more than twenty children were found to have experimented with drugs, and the authorities report registering addicts "even younger" than nine years of age.[49]

An average of forty drug-related deaths occurred annually in Czechoslovakia prior to the breakup of the federation. This figure excludes drug-related suicides and drug abusers who die after several days of hospitalization for reasons of "breakdown of the organism."[50]

Hungary. Hungarian drug specialists admit that only "very approximate" estimates exist regarding the extent of drug abuse, as systematic survey research on the subject is still in its infancy.[51] In 1990, there were between eight and ten thousand "habitual drug users" known to the police. A senior police official reports that an increasing incidence of drug abuse was a "continuous" but "not large" phenomenon throughout the 1980s. Narcotic drugs such as codeine and morphine and more than fifty pharmaceuticals and medicants "suitable to create a

[44]For a detailed discussion of the report and its contents, see *RFE-SR* (Czechoslovakia), 6 February 1984.
[45]*Mlada fronta* (Prague), 2 June 1988, in *FBIS-EEU,* 7 June 1988, 13.
[46]*Sotsialisticka zakannost* (Prague), no. 7 (1983), cited in *RFE-SR* (Czechoslovakia), 6 February 1984.
[47]*Listy,* no. 5 (1988), in *JPRS-EER,* 10 March 1989, 3.
[48]Ibid.
[49]*Vecernik* (Bratislava), 26 February 1986, in *JPRS-EER,* 4 April 1986, 86.
[50]*Lidova demokracie,* 6 February 1990, in *FBIS-EEU,* 8 February 1990, 31.
[51]*Voprosy narkologii,* no. 3 (1988): 37.

daze" occupy "first place" among the drugs consumed by abusers.[52]

Other sources provide higher estimates of addiction and abuse. A prominent drug specialist, after noting that official data "clearly underestimate" the extent of these phenomena, estimates that by the early 1980s there were "at least" thirty thousand individuals regularly "consuming narcotic substances" in Hungary.[53] If this specialist accurately contends that nearly 90 percent of the drug addicts are unknown to the police, then the estimate on addiction cited in the previous paragraph should be revised to between eighty and one hundred thousand individuals. Other sources speak of forty thousand individuals "addicted to drugs" and upwards of two hundred thousand individuals "in danger" of becoming so. The consumption of unspecified "hard" drugs has reportedly become "common," although the incidence of such consumption remains unpublished.[54] Those who abuse drugs are typically between fifteen and eighteen years of age, and approximately one-third of this group is female.[55] Fifty-five deaths resulting from illegal drug use were recorded between 1973 and 1989, but the actual figure may be considerably higher.[56] One outside report, for example, asserts that thirty-three such deaths occurred in 1984 alone.[57]

Poland. As noted earlier, drug abuse appears to be widespread in Poland. Consumption of narcotic drugs seems far more prevalent in Poland than in other states of Eastern Europe. Writing in a United Nations journal in 1986, a medical specialist on drug abuse estimated that approximately two hundred thousand Poles were then addicted to narcotic drugs.[58] Comparable estimates range from one hundred thousand to six hundred thousand.[59] Estimates of those who abuse, but are not addicted to, drugs vary considerably and are terminologically imprecise. One source, for example, speaks about five hundred thousand persons in

[52] *Magyar Nemzet* (Budapest), 25 May 1990, in *JPRS-EER,* 9 July 1990, 44.

[53] *Voprosy narkologii,* no. 3 (1988): 37.

[54] *Magyar Hirlap,* 2 October 1987, in *FBIS-EEU,* 8 October 1987, 32. Radio Budapest, 12 June 1986, cited in *RFE-SR* (Hungary), 25 February 1987.

[55] *Magyar Tavirati Irada* (hereafter *MTI*) (Budapest), 16 July 1986, in *JPRS-EER,* 7 August 1986, 74.

[56] *MTI,* 10 May 1991, in *JPRS-EER,* 16 May 1991, 43.

[57] *RFE-BR* (Eastern Europe), 13 August 1986.

[58] H. Tobolska, "Problems of Drug Abuse and Prevention Measures in Poland," *Bulletin on Narcotics* 38 (January–June 1986): 100.

[59] A 1991 source estimates that there are one hundred thousand drug addicts between the ages of ten and forty. *Trybuna* (Warsaw), 5 August 1991, in *JPRS-EER,* 4 September 1991, 29. For respective estimates that are far higher see, for example, *Polska Agencja Prasowa* (hereafter *PAP*) (Warsaw), 3 November 1986, in *FBIS-EEU,* 4 November 1986, G9.

1983 who "took drugs," while another account claims that almost a million persons have had "passing contact" with drugs.[60] Data presented at a plenary session of the Commission for Preventing Drug Addiction indicate that "over" 90 percent of the addicts in Poland primarily consume opiates, in particular homemade heroin.[61]

Drug abusers come from all socioeconomic groups. One commentary reports, "It is no longer said that this is only a problem of wild and banal youths. The problem has become quite democratic in its choice of victims and now includes the children of the white collar class, of workers and even rural children."[62] Drug abuse among youths is especially worrisome. Almost two-thirds of drug abusers in Poland are said to be under twenty-one years of age. Epidemiological data gathered under the auspices of the Commission for Preventing Drug Addiction indicate that between 4 and 6 percent of "school age young people" have had "experience" with marijuana and volatile substances.[63] Representatives from a private organization specializing in the treatment of youthful drug addicts estimate (perhaps hyperbolically) that there are approximately twenty thousand youths who have "succumbed to drug addiction" in Gdansk province alone.[64]

Official data indicate that annually approximately one hundred drug-related deaths occur and close to eight hundred persons suffer drug "poisoning." Yet officials admit that the actual number of deaths is far higher, because many addicts die from assorted drug-related illnesses that are not attributed specifically to drugs.[65] The spread of acquired immune deficiency syndrome (AIDS) among drug abusers sharing dirty needles represents a menacing new threat to public health. A physician specializing in AIDS reports that the disease has spread like "wildfire" in the drug community.[66] In 1990, drug addicts comprised approximately 75 percent of the 721 Polish citizens known to be infected with the AIDS virus.[67] These numbers reveal only the "tip of the iceberg" of this phenomenon, one expert contends.[68]

---

[60]*Znaki czasu* (Paris), no. 3 (1986), in *JPRS-EER,* 24 December 1986, 90. *Trybuna rabotnicza* (Katowice), 24 October 1986, in *JPRS-EER,* 26 February 1987, 104.
[61]*Rzeczpospolita* (Warsaw), 28 June 1988, in *JPRS-EER,* 5 October 1988, 59.
[62]*Trybuna rabotnicza,* 24 October 1986, in *JPRS-EER,* 26 February 1987, 104.
[63]*Zdrowie* (Warsaw), no. 12 (1988), in *JPRS-EER,* 14 April 1989, 61.
[64]Ibid. This estimate comes from representatives of MONAR, the Young People's Movement to Combat Drug Abuse.
[65]*Trybuna,* 5 August 1991, in *JPRS-EER,* 4 September 1991, 29.
[66]*Gazeta wyborcza* (Warsaw), 29 August 1989, 53.
[67]Warsaw Domestic Service, 26 February 1990, in *FBIS-EEU,* 28 February 1990, G2.
[68]*Gazeta wyborcza,* 29 August 1989, in *FBIS-EEU,* 5 September 1989, 53.

Claims that the incidence of drug addiction began declining in the late 1980s merit caution. First, the claims point to minimal changes since 1985 in the number of officially registered drug addicts to support their contention.[69] Yet this circumstance may reveal more about declining zeal and effectiveness by the authorities in registering addicts than it does about changes in the incidence of addiction. Then, too, well-documented commentaries exposing major shortcomings in the 1985 law to combat drug abuse seemingly belie contentions that the rigorous enforcement of the law has led to a decrease in addiction.[70]

The former Yugoslavia. Drug abuse appears to have been more prevalent in Yugoslavia than in most of Central and Eastern Europe. In 1986, Yugoslavia had from thirty thousand to forty thousand registered drug addicts.[71] If Yugoslav estimates were accurate that approximately 90 percent of all addicts were not registered,[72] there would then have been around three hundred thousand to four hundred thousand addicts in the country at the time. In contrast, most sources estimate that there were approximately fifty thousand addicts, although a 1986 survey confirmed "the suspicion" that the actual figure may have been more than double the commonly accepted estimate.[73] Belgrade, which reportedly had become "a European center of smugglers, dealers, and addicts of the most dangerous of all drugs, heroin," had more than fifteen thousand addicts in the early 1980s.[74] The treatment of addicts with methadone—found nowhere else in communist Europe on any scale—resulted in substantial numbers (estimated at approximately six thousand individuals in 1983) becoming addicted to this drug.[75]

As elsewhere, youths predominate among users of drugs. In Belgrade,

[69]See, for example, the commentary in *Trybuna ludu* (Warsaw), 23 February 1988, in *FBIS-EEU,* 1 March 1988, 38.

[70]For claims that the 1985 law on drug abuse accounts for the alleged decrease in addiction, see for example, *Zdrowie,* no. 12 (1988), in *JPRS-EER,* 14 April 1989, 61. For a particularly scathing commentary challenging the effectiveness of the drug law, see *Trybuna ludu,* 23 January 1989, in *JPRS-EER,* 17 April 1989, 41–42. This source contends that widespread violations—especially prohibitions against private farmers cultivating poppies—make this law a "worthless document."

[71]*RFE-BR* (Eastern Europe), 13 August 1986.

[72]*Narodna armija,* 20 September 1984, in *FBIS-EEU,* 3 October 1984, I7.

[73]An estimate of the number of addicts is carried by *Tanjug* (Belgrade), 12 January 1986, in *FBIS-EEU,* 13 January 1986, I3. The "suspicion" that this figure may be more than double the commonly accepted estimate is reported in *Narodna armija,* 20 September 1984, in *FBIS-EEU,* 3 October 1984, I7.

[74]*NIN* (Belgrade), 21 November 1982, in *FBIS-EEU,* 8 December 1982, I11.

[75]*NIN,* 24 March 1983, cited in *RFE-BR* (Eastern Europe), 13 August 1986.

surveys indicate that every tenth student tries drugs, every one hundredth student becomes an addict, and at least several addicts are found in each of the city's primary and secondary schools.[76] Many young drug users are the offspring of well-educated, middle-class parents: in one survey approximately one-third of the sample were the progeny of fathers employed in sundry professional positions.[77]

Official statistics indicate that drug-related deaths average thirty to forty per year (at one point, Belgrade reported that nine youths died from overdoses in just one month), but authorities admit that "this is what is known. We can only suspect the rest."[78]

THE ETIOLOGY OF DRUG ABUSE

The nascent state of the etiology of drug abuse in Central and Eastern Europe is obvious. To be sure, outside specialists also advance many conflicting physiological, psychological, and sociocultural hypotheses to explain drug abuse.[79] The unique physical and psychological makeup of each individual probably precludes any definitive explanation for the phenomenon. Marek Kotanski, the charismatic founder and driving force behind the Polish antidrug group MONAR (the Young People's Movement to Combat Drug Abuse), stresses the diverse causes of drug abuse:

I think that there are as many causes of addiction as there are people. Each person has his own reason. For one it might be a broken home, for another a moral crisis, vulnerability to hypocrisy, callousness. Psychological reasons are usually the cause. Dependent people are weaker individuals who don't know how to deal with reality. At a certain point they run across a group of users and try drugs to somewhat ease a stressful situation. Then they do it again a few times, and this is the beginning of it all.[80]

Nevertheless, researchers from outside as well as within the region agree that drugs can become a placebo for adolescents seeking to cope with the emotional insecurities and vulnerabilities typical of their stage in life.

---

[76]*NIN,* 5 November 1984.

[77]*NIN,* 11 October 1981, in *FBIS-EEU,* 3 November 1981, I5.

[78]Data on drug-related deaths from *Tanjug,* 12 January 1986, in *FBIS-EEU,* 13 January 1986, I3. Data on the same subject for Belgrade from *Politika* (Belgrade), 3 October 1981, in *FBIS-EEU,* 3 November 1981, I4. *Narodna armija,* 20 September 1984, in *FBIS-EEU,* 3 October 1984, I7, reports that drug-related deaths are probably far higher than these figures indicate.

[79]A useful summary of these theories appears in O'Brien and Cohen, *Encyclopedia of Drug Abuse,* especially 274–79.

[80]*Zolnierz polski* (Warsaw), 4 February 1990, in *JPRS-EER,* 24 April 1990, 45.

Communist governments prohibited comprehensive empirical research on the etiology of drug abuse. Official commentaries in Central
and Eastern Europe typically combined psychological and sociocultural
explanations for the phenomenon. Alienation, anomie, escapism, hedo-
nism, low self-esteem, and susceptibility to peer pressure were all seen as
psychological factors motivating resort to drugs.[81] "Shortcomings" in
the family, including broken homes, excessive drinking by parents, and
the absence of warm and loving bonds among family members, were
held to lead youths to seek solace in drugs. "In virtually all instances,"
a Czechoslovak source claimed in a representative exposition of this
argument, it is the "fault of the family" that youths abuse drugs.[82] In
contrast, one of the few empirical studies on this subject challenged this
assessment. It concluded that drug addicts "hail from all types of families" and that the reasons for their addictions "are still not quite clear."[83]
Other sources note that the routine use of drugs is embedded in the
traditional culture of some segments of the population and continues to
attract young people to drugs.[84] Other youths are susceptible to Western
media which allegedly promote a hedonistic life-style, including the use
of drugs.[85]

One intriguing question, raised primarily among dissidents and other
unofficial sources, was whether the existing social and political orders
themselves fostered the drug problem; Charter 77, the most significant
dissident group in Czechoslovakia, believed they did. After noting that
the causes of drug abuse were "much the same" in the East and the
West, it asserted that in the former they were aggravated by "drabness,
monotony, and the regimentation of life by the regime."[86] Drug abusers
themselves often offered similar explanations for their behavior. In Poland, abusers explained to a criminologist why they consumed drugs:
"We are looking for a better more colorful world, because the one in
which we live is evil, there are no ideals or aims worth living for."[87] A

[81]Among numerous sources that make this argument, see, for example, *Magyar Hirlap*, 25
April 1985, in *JPRS-EPS*, 14 June 1985, 14.
[82]*Mlada fronta*, 3 April 1984, in *FBIS-EEU*, 5 April 1984, D11.
[83]*Rzeczywistosc*, 5 July 1987, in *FBIS-EEU*, 22 July 1987, 13.
[84]See Powell, "Drug Abuse in Communist Europe," 31, for evidence to support this
argument. Another source making this argument is carried by *PAP*, 18 June 1986, in
FBIS-EEU, 19 June 1986, G6.
[85]For a discussion of this argument, see *Rzeczywistosc*, 18 July 1982, in *FBIS-EEU*, 18
August 1982, G7–8.
[86]Charter 77, Document No. 42/83, 30 December 1983.
[87]*Tygodnik demokratyczny* (Warsaw), 10 February 1985, quoted in *RFE-SR* (Poland), 4
April 1985.

Hungarian abuser provided an equally bleak assessment of why he sought solace in drugs. "Here I simply find that my prospects are hopeless," he explained.[88] One can only speculate about how representative these statements are.

Several emerging developments in postcommunist Central and Eastern Europe may foster drug abuse. First, the still rudimentary capitalist economies in several states are beginning to produce opportunities for private gain and even, in some instances, relative affluence. They are also providing more individuals already predisposed to abuse drugs with the economic wherewithal to do so. Then, too, these economies are likely to begin generating high-pressure jobs whose incumbents—emulating some of their professional counterparts in the West—may use drugs to escape at least temporarily from the tensions and stresses contained therein. In contrast, the differentiated economic and professional rewards associated with capitalism may also produce individuals who use drugs to assuage their frustration at unrealized expectations and envy of peers more successful than they. A Hungarian drug specialist posits the link between drug abuse and an inability to cope with personal failure: "Life has its tensions which we try to escape by withdrawing into our worlds of illusions, and this is the secret behind drug addiction. If I could only instill in people an ability to tolerate failure I could prevent drug use."[89] Finally, some, especially younger Central and Eastern Europeans who are increasingly exposed through personal contact and mass media to Western life-styles that include drug abuse, may see "doing drugs" as socially acceptable and an integral component of a way of life they wish to emulate.

ACQUIRING DRUGS

Drug users in Central and Eastern Europe typically have little difficulty in acquiring psychotropic substances. This is especially the case in Poland. Indeed, a Polish psychiatrist claimed in the mid-1980s (perhaps hyperbolically) that "nowhere is it as easy to buy narcotics as in Poland."[90] Private farmers in Poland cultivate thousands of acres of poppy fields for the production of legal drugs and for culinary purposes, but much of the crop is sold on the black market to organized manufacturers

[88] *Mozgo Villag* (Budapest), May 1985, in *JPRS-EPS*, 5 September 1985, 40.
[89] *Nepszava* (Budapest), 3 February 1989, in *JPRS-EER*, 25 April 1989, 38.
[90] As quoted in *Budapest Domestic Service*, 14 December 1984, in *FBIS-EEU*, 19 December 1984, G7.

and individuals who produce opium-based derivatives from it. Lured by visions of a "poppy 'El Dorado,' " many farmers now cultivate poppies instead of their traditional crops of wheat and sugar beets.[91] Each summer "entire expeditions of native drug addicts" also set off for the Polish countryside to gather poppies for their own use.[92] The Catholic church has sought to discourage these practices by erecting posters in villages declaiming "The Fifth Commandment: Thou Shall Not Kill" and by considering the "strong possibility" of refusing a consecrated burial to Catholic farmers engaged in the drug trade.[93]

Drugs also are easily and often legally obtainable from pharmacies, hospitals, and other medical institutions. In Czechoslovakia, for example, where numerous tranquilizers, sedatives, and other psychotropic drugs are sold legally, many middle-aged individuals, especially women, are afflicted with "codeinism," the abuse of medicaments with a high codeine content. Some women reportedly consume several dozen bottles of codeine-based cough mixture daily.[94] Drugs are obtained illegally from pharmacies and other medical institutions either by theft or by forging of prescriptions.[95] Only in Poland where drugs are easily available in other ways are these practices not widespread.[96]

If allegations in the Polish press are accurate, communist governments themselves may deliberately have been a source of drugs. The Polish samizdat press alleges that officials there seduced youths with drugs to entice them into becoming informers for the security police. "Several tens of thousands" of youths, "demoralized, poisoned by drugs, intimidated, beaten, and blackmailed," are reported to have become informers in this manner.[97]

Amateur and professional smugglers are another, albeit probably limited, source of drugs. Amateur smugglers include the thousands of foreign tourists and students who annually visit the region and may bring drugs with them to sell or to give as gifts. Central and Eastern Europeans returning from abroad may engage in similar practices. Thus

[91]*Trybuna ludu*, 23 January 1989, in *JPRS-EER*, 17 April 1989, 41. A Soviet source suggests that a similar situation may obtain in Bulgaria and Yugoslavia. See *Sovetskoe gosudarstvo i pravo* (Moscow), no. 3 (1989): 100.
[92]*Trybuna ludu*, 23 January 1989, in *JPRS-EER*, 17 April 1989, 41.
[93]These activities are detailed in *RFE-SR* (Poland), 28 October 1986.
[94]*Veda a zivot*, no. 8 (1983), discussed in *RFE-SR* (Czechoslovakia), 13 September 1983. On these practices, see also *Mlada fronta*, 2 June 1988.
[95]*Ateni*, 21 August 1991, in *FBIS-EEU*, 28 August 1991, 11.
[96]Sokalska, "Legal Measures to Combat Drug-Related Problems in Poland," 22.
[97]*Replika* (Warsaw), no. 36 (April 1985) in *RFE-BR* (Polish Underground Extracts), 17 January 1986.

a police official in Hungary recently reported that "some Hungarian tourists are willing to spend their foreign currency on drugs . . . for the smuggler's personal use or for his close friends."[98] Professional drug traffickers move through the region bringing drugs from Asia and the Middle East to other European countries and the United States.[99] Some of these drugs reportedly filter down to the domestic market.[100] Typically, however, professional traffickers have no financial incentive to exchange their wares for the nonconvertible "soft" currencies of the East. As a Hungarian police official asserts in explaining the reasoning of traffickers, "It simply is not good business sense to sell something for forints when one can obtain dollars for it."[101] This reasoning presumably will change to the extent that these states introduce market-based reforms that include the convertibility of their currencies.

Drug users often resort to crime to support their habit. In Czechoslovakia, a 1990 analysis linked drug addiction to male and female prostitution and various forms of crime to support a habit that daily cost approximately three hundred to five hundred koruny (roughly ten to fifteen dollars at the prevailing rate of exchange—an enormous sum given the depressed wages in Czechoslovakia at the time).[102] Over sixteen thousand drug addicts in Poland were reported to have "had a brush with the law" in 1987.[103] Organized criminal gangs also now appear in the illegal drug trade. "Several hundred well-organized gangs" reportedly dominated the distribution and sale of drugs in Czechoslovakia under communist rule.[104] Sources in Poland and Yugoslavia report a similar situation.[105]

COMBATING DRUG ABUSE

Communist regimes, with the partial exception of Poland's, did little to combat drug abuse. "We have been assuming the role of a bystander

[98]*Tallozo* (Budapest), 31 May 1991, in *JPRS-EER*, 28 June 1991, 43.
[99]For a recent discussion of these activities see, among others, *Magyar Nemzet*, 25 May 1990, in *JPRS-EER*, 9 July 1990, 43.
[100]For a discussion of this circumstance, see *RFE-SR* (Hungary), 6 December 1985.
[101]*Magyar Nemzet*, 25 May 1990, in *JPRS-EER*, 9 July 1990, 43. A similar argument is found in *Lidova demokracie*, 6 February 1990, in *FBIS-EEU*, 8 February 1990, 32.
[102]Ibid., 31.
[103]*Rzeczpospolita*, 28 June 1988, in *JPRS-EER*, 22 August 1988, 72.
[104]This assessment comes from the previously cited (note 15) official report on drug abuse in Czechoslovakia that was subsequently smuggled to the West.
[105]For a discussion of organized drug dealers in Poland and in Yugoslavia, see, respectively, *Gazeta wyborcza*, 9 September 1991, in *JPRS-EER*, 9 October 1991, 22; and *Delo* (Ljubljana), 3 March 1984, in *FBIS-EEU*, 9 March 1984, 113.

who merely registers the wave of drug addiction," a Czechoslovak critic charged in remarks applicable to other regimes under communist rule.[106] The limited initiatives these regimes did undertake were often subsumed under laws and institutions concerned primarily with mental health and alcoholism rather than with drug abuse. Not surprisingly, given the urgency of the enormous problems they now confront in establishing democratic polities and market economies, regimes in postcommunist Central and Eastern Europe have also done relatively little to combat drug abuse. Yet the overthrow of communist regimes has permitted freer discussion of the drug problem and of requisite efforts to mitigate it. In Czechoslovakia, for example, opponents criticized as too harsh a law proposed by the government in 1991 that would have classified illegal drug operations as crimes equal to plotting murder.[107] Even in Albania, where discussion of the drug problem was long taboo, the press now regularly prints material on this subject.[108] Free and open discussion constitutes a sine qua non for an effective fight against drug abuse.

Legal and administrative measures predominate among the initiatives that have been undertaken. As noted, in 1985 Poland became the first state in the region to promulgate a comprehensive law to combat drug abuse. Among other things, the law set up the Commission for the Prevention of Drug Abuse; permitted a court to order drug addicts convicted of criminal offenses to undergo up to two years of compulsory treatment for their addiction; provided criminal sanctions for the production and sale, but not the actual use, of illegal drugs; placed restrictions on the cultivation of poppies and hemp; and specified measures to disseminate information, particularly to youths, about the dangers of drugs.[109] The law also established the Drug Addiction Prevention Fund derived from government monies and private contributions to finance antidrug initiatives, especially the construction of drug treatment and rehabilitation centers for adults. The government monies came from taxes levied on the sale of spirits and other alcoholic beverages, a feature that prompted one official to predict that there would be "no shortage

---

[106]*Pruboj* (Prague), 11 April 1986, quoted in *RFE-SR* (Czechoslovakia), 5 September 1986.

[107]For a discussion of the proposed drug law and the ensuing criticisms therein, see *RFE-REE*, 16 August 1991, 38.

[108]This development is discussed in *RFE-REE*, 27 September 1991, 2.

[109]*RFE-SR* (Poland), 4 April 1985, provides a comprehensive summary of the provisions of the law.

of funds for the scheme."[110] The fund apparently encountered difficulties. For one, it failed to spend the considerable monies contained therein. Further, there was a proposal to combine the fund with a similar fund to combat alcoholism, an initiative that was strongly opposed by members of the Commission for the Prevention of Drug Abuse.[111]

Other states in the region place restrictions on access to drugs and provide criminal sanctions for the production and sale, but usually not the use, of illegal drugs. For example, in Bulgaria drugstores that sell narcotic and other soporific drugs are "especially reinforced and equipped with alarm defense systems" and all narcotics are stored in special metal safes.[112] Czechoslovakia, which lacked specific criminal legislation on drugs, prosecuted drug-related offenses under provisions of the 1962 law on alcohol abuse. Those who trafficked in drugs incurred prison terms of two to eight years, and individuals committing crimes while under the influence of drugs were treated as any other criminal would be unless the drug use was judged to constitute a form of mental illness. A quantity of drugs involved in these acts that "may threaten health or life" subjected their possessor to criminal sanctions.[113] The breakup of the Czechoslovak federation calls into question the aforementioned legislation on drug abuse, which presumably would have revised, or replaced entirely, many of the earlier criminal sanctions for drug-related offenses. The Czech government itself in August 1993 approved a new antidrug program which stresses preventive rather than legal measures. In 1987, the Hungarian Supreme Court issued guidelines for the application of criminal sanctions against individuals trafficking in "significant" quantities of illegal drugs. A commentary on the guidelines indicated that courts would classify as "significant" a quantity of drugs "sufficient to endanger the health or life of several persons." Individuals found guilty of trafficking in such quantities were subject to prison terms ranging from one to five and two to eight years.[114]

These measures have evoked widespread criticism since the fall of communist systems. In Hungary, the director of the National Narcotics

[110]The Polish official is quoted in Budapest Domestic Service, 14 December 1984, in *FBIS-EEU*, 19 December 1984, G7.

[111]Materials on these difficulties drawn from *Rzeczpospolita*, 28 June 1988, in *JPRS-EER*, 5 October 1988, 60.

[112]*Ateni*, 21 August 1991, in *FBIS-EEU*, 28 August 1991, 11.

[113]*Svobodne slovo* (Prague), 11 February 1986, in *JPRS-EER*, 10 April 1986, 99.

[114]*Magyar Hirlap*, 20 January 1987, in *JPRS-EER*, 15 May 1987, 45; *MTI*, 20 January 1987, in *FBIS-EEU*, 21 January 1987, F1.

Control Organ finds it "ridiculous" that neither the production nor the possession of illegal drugs is "punished seriously."[115] "We are helpless in the face of Polish regulations" against drugs, contends a ranking police official in Poland specializing in drug-related crime.[116] Such critics frequently blame either the judges—who are alleged to be too lenient in invoking existing legislation against drugs—or, paradoxically, the laws themselves for being insufficiently harsh to deter, incomplete in their list of prohibited acts and drugs, and difficult to apply because of their terminological imprecision.[117] The loopholes in Poland's 1985 drug law that continue to permit the widespread legal cultivation of poppies on private farms have proven especially controversial. Polish authorities promised to close these loopholes completely, but have not yet.[118]

Further, agencies charged with enforcing legislation against drugs often operate ineffectively. Poland provides an example. As a Polish source under communist rule contended, "Discipline in implementing the law is not always our strong point."[119] A 1987 source contended that in Poland "you can count proceedings against traffickers on your fingers." This circumstance "produces bitterness" among parents who worry about their progeny becoming drug abusers.[120] The Society of Parents and Friends of Drug Addicts in Poland, which was founded in 1985, held a press conference where its representatives voiced "bitter complaints" at the alleged laxity of the militia in arresting well-known drug dealers. The representatives asked, "How is this possible? The militia detains small fry street sellers but those who are at the top and earn fortunes always elude arrest. It is common knowledge that there are about 500 drug dens in Warsaw. Why is it that they can operate?"[121]

Specialists dissatisfied with legal measures argue that drug users require therapy and counseling. The director of the Prague Center for Drug Addiction asserted that the "optimal model" of drug treatment "never includes repressive measures."[122] Yet available facilities and

---

[115]*Magyar Nemzet*, 25 May 1990, in *JPRS-EER*, 9 July 1990, 44.

[116]*Gazeta wyborcza*, 9 September 1991, in *JPRS-EER*, 9 October 1991, 23.

[117]For representative commentaries elaborating on these circumstances, see ibid.; Sokalska, "Legal Measures to Combat Drug-Related Problems in Poland," 21; *Magyar Hirlap*, 20 January 1987, in *JPRS-EER*, 15 May 1987, 46; *Rude pravo*, 8 October 1987, in *FBIS-EEU*, 16 October 1987, 27.

[118]*Rzeczpospolita*, 12 March 1990, in *JPRS-EER*, 21 May 1990, 42.

[119]*Trybuna ludu*, 19 June 1986, in *FBIS-EEU*, 25 June 1986, G9.

[120]*Rzeczywistosc*, 5 July 1987, in *FBIS-EEU*, 22 July 1987, 15.

[121]Ibid., 14.

[122]*Lidova demokracie*, 12 October 1987, in *FBIS-EEU*, 16 October 1987, 28.

methods for treatment of drug abusers are woefully inadequate throughout the region. For example, drug abusers in the former Czechoslovakia typically had to wait for up to three years to enter a drug therapy program.[123] Czechoslovakia opened its first specialized drug treatment center in 1988. The center opened with only four employees, no inpatient treatment facilities, and an absence of requisite equipment to perform elementary tasks such as taking and storing blood and urine samples.[124] As in Hungary the few addicts who undergo inpatient treatment usually do so in psychiatric hospitals, where they often share quarters with alcoholics and the mentally ill.[125] Poland devotes only "meager" funds to construct drug treatment facilities.[126] In addition, the limited funds that are allocated for this purpose frequently "migrate" to other projects that officials consider of a higher priority.[127]

There are manifest deficiencies in the treatment that is available to drug abusers. This "treatment" often consists of little more than compelling addicts to go cold turkey through abstinence from drugs.[128] The attitude of many medical personnel toward their patients is also a problem. Thus a Hungarian psychiatrist specializing in drug problems asserted that his colleagues were "inclined to condemn rather than help" those that are addicts.[129] Other sources in Hungary reported that abuses, including instances of "hospital torture," occurred in the treatment of addicts who were "practically at the mercy of the doctors and nurses."[130] Treatment programs often fail to differentiate among drug abusers who vary according to age, sex, state of dependency, and drug of choice. Critics point out that mixing casual (especially youthful) drug users with hardened drug addicts may be an unintended recipe for turning many of the former into the latter.[131]

Critics especially question the efficacy of forcing addicts to undergo compulsory treatment for their condition. Addicts exhibit "mostly a negative attitude" toward compulsory treatment, informs a Czechoslo-

[123]*Lidova demokracie*, 6 February 1990, in *FBIS-EEU*, 8 February 1990, 32.
[124]*Halo sobota* (Prague), 26 November 1988, in *FBIS-EEU*, 7 December 1988, 7.
[125]Ibid., 8, provides a forceful criticism of such practices.
[126]*Gazeta wyborcza*, 20 December 1989, in *FBIS-EEU*, 3 January 1990, 65.
[127]For a description of such practices, see *Rzeczywistosc*, 5 July 1987, in *FBIS-EEU*, 22 July 1987, P13.
[128]For a detailed criticism of this "treatment," see *Elet Es Irodalon* (Budapest), 27 September 1985, in *JPRS-EPS*, 6 November 1985, 21.
[129]*Nepszava*, 2 November 1985, quoted in *RFE-SR* (Hungary), 6 December 1985.
[130]*Mozgo Villag*, May 1985, in *JPRS-EPS*, 5 September 1985, 60.
[131]For a representative criticism of such practices by a Hungarian drug specialist during the communist era, see *Voprosy narkologii*, no. 3 (1988): 38.

vak source in what presumably was an exercise in deliberate understatement.[132] A Hungarian drug specialist, reflecting the attitude of many of his professional peers, contends that treatment can only be successful when an addict voluntarily undergoes it: "I do not believe it is possible to help someone if that person does not realize his problem and does not want to change his addiction."[133] The prospect of compulsory treatment also has the unintended consequence of deterring many addicts from revealing their condition publicly and availing themselves of counseling and emergency services. To mitigate this circumstance, Hungary and Poland established telephone hot lines which drug abusers can use anonymously in times of crisis.[134]

Only in Poland under communist rule were private institutions and support groups actively involved in the fight against drugs. For example, in 1985 concerned adults in Poland established the aforementioned Society of Parents and Friends of Drug Addicts. Members of the society furnished counseling services for both youthful drug abusers and their parents, organized vacation trips for children with drug problems, found gainful employment for former addicts, and staffed crisis intervention teams (known colloquially as "poppy ambulances"). Members publicly criticized alleged defects in legal initiatives against drugs, inefficient use of monies from the Drug Addiction Prevention Fund, and the failure of the state to provide comprehensive free medical treatment for drug addicts.[135]

The Roman Catholic church was also involved in combating drug abuse. As noted, church officials campaigned against private farmers engaged in the drug trade. A priest was a member of the government's Commission on Drug Addiction, and the church ran several therapeutic centers for drug addicts staffed by specially trained priests, monks, and nuns. Faculty at the Catholic University of Lublin conduct research on drug-related issues. Each diocese assigns at least one priest to coordinate antidrug efforts under its sponsorship. Finally, parish priests formed committees of parents of drug users to provide counseling services and disseminate information about the dangers of drugs.[136]

[132]*Rude pravo*, 8 October 1987, in *FBIS-EEU*, 16 October 1987, 27.
[133]*Nepszava*, 3 February 1989, in *JPRS-EER*, 25 April 1989, 38.
[134]*MTI*, 16 July 1986; *Kurier polski* (Warsaw), 24 November 1986, in *JPRS-EER*, 19 March 1987, 148.
[135]*Rzeczywistosc*, 5 July 1987, in *FBIS-EEU*, 22 July 1987, 13, provides extensive materials on the activities of the society.
[136]These activities are detailed in *RFE-SR* (Poland), 28 October 1986; *Zycie Warszawy* (Warsaw), 16–17 May 1987, in *JPRS-EER*, 7 August 1987, 49.

MONAR was the first—and remains the most prominent—of the private institutions established to combat drug abuse.[137] Currently MO-NAR operates nineteen rehabilitation centers and camps (with facilities for approximately six hundred addicts) that offer addicts extended counseling and therapy for up to two years and a "narcotics ambulance service" that brings a MONAR aide to the home of an addict for counseling and advice. Marek Kotanski, MONAR's founder, claims that 40 percent of the individuals treated at his centers emerge "permanently cured" of their addiction. This claim may be premature, however, since MONAR has existed only since 1981.

Furthermore, Kotanski's methods of treatment engender considerable criticism.[138] Critics charge that MONAR displays an "absolutely inimical attitude towards newcomers, intolerance, aggression" that "scares" many addicts who "give up being helped, although they want treatment very much." In response, Kotanski contends:

We don't attack the person. We attack the addict. He has to understand how very sick he is, how difficult it is for other people to accept his filth. We have to cleanse him of this, break through the layer of his addiction and prove that he is dying. If we adopt the method, "Come Brother, we love you," the whole group will derail.

Equally controversial is Kotanski's use of "protective teams" (that is, informers) of MONAR residents who "monitor" the behavior of their peers "day and night" in the rehabilitation centers. Kotanski argues that the monitoring is essential to give "everyone a sense of security that nothing bad is happening in the facility." After all, Kotanski explains, the patients are "drug addicts ... and absolute trust has not always worked for the good."

The Pure Hearts campaign, designed to establish a foothold for MO-NAR in primary and secondary schools, is one of Kotanski's most prominent initiatives.[139] Students who become Pure Hearts are to assume "positive, creative, and active attitudes" and to display "less anger, less aggression, less boorishness, less indifference," and, more concretely, to give up smoking, which Kotanski believes promotes dependency on drugs. In the summer of 1986, he organized a chain of Pure

[137]Materials in this paragraph are drawn from *Trybuna*, 5 August 1991, in *JPRS-EER*, 4 September 1991, 30; and the interview with Marek Kotanski published in *Zolnierz polski*, 4 February 1990, in *JPRS-EER*, 24 April 1990, 44–46.

[138]All materials in this paragraph drawn from the Kotanski interview, *JPRS-EER*, 24 April 1990.

[139]This campaign is described in detail in *RFE-SR* (Poland), 28 October 1986.

Hearts, similar to the Hands Across America initiative, among young people in several Polish cities to symbolize their mutual strength and faith. Shortly thereafter, he repeated the idea on the national level, receiving extensive coverage in the national media. Kotanski has taken his campaign to other Central and East European states and established chapters of Pure Hearts in what was then Czechoslovakia and in Hungary. The Hungarian group, known as the Movement of Clean Hearts, runs a residential drug treatment clinic with facilities for thirty to forty young drug addicts annually.[140]

Kotanski's latest initiatives include the establishment of a national organization staffed by former drug addicts that seeks to identify and unmask those who produce and traffic in drugs. "We are fed up with the daily brutality and ruthlessness in the drug-addicts' circles as well as with addiction spreading to youngsters," Kotanski asserted in announcing the initiative.[141] Considerable public backlash has developed over Kotanski's recent efforts to help drug addicts infected with the AIDS virus. Reportedly, the four MONAR facilities now housing infected addicts have been objects of "numerous violent acts," including threats of arson, from angry and fearful citizens living nearby. Responding to this "nightmare of unusual intolerance," Kotanski proposed to build a self-sufficient city (to be named Victoria Kotan) to care for infected addicts. Kotanski explains that "the town will be a kind of island for people rejected, alone, ill, people who think differently and cannot accept reality."[142]

Central and East European states have cooperated both among themselves and with other states to combat the drug problem. Before 1985, cooperation with noncommunist states was limited primarily to adherence to the 1961 United Nations Convention on Narcotics and to the 1971 United Nations Convention on Psychotropic Substances. Cooperation to deal with drug-related problems began to accelerate after 1985 as part of Mikhail Gorbachev's foreign policy of "new thinking" by the socialist camp toward the West. For example, the United States Drug

---

[140]For information on the Movement of Clean Hearts, see *Magyar Hirlap*, 2 October 1987, in *FBIS-EEU*, 8 October 1987, 32. This source reports that a seemingly inordinate number of patients at the clinic—six individuals just in the period 1984–87—have committed suicide. The source provides no explanation for these acts, although one might conjecture that at least some of them were efforts to escape the harsh regimen of MONAR's treatment program described herein.

[141]*PAP*, 11 July 1991, in *JPRS-EER*, 19 July 1991, 21.

[142]For details of these initiatives, see *Trybuna*, 5 August 1991, in *JPRS-EER*, 4 September 1991, 30.

Enforcement Agency began training personnel from the Soviet Union and other communist states. Several of these states provided information to noncommunist states, including the United States, that led to the seizure of drugs and the arrest of traffickers.[143] Communist states also participated actively in the 1987 United Nations–sponsored Conference on Drug Abuse. The European communist states, excluding Albania, the German Democratic Republic (GDR), Romania, and Yugoslavia, agreed in 1988 to hold "regular meetings" among themselves on cooperation in "combating drug addiction" and to exchange "operational information" to this same end.[144]

Of course, the most controversial aspect of this subject is the allegation made by the United States that the Soviet Union and other socialist states (especially Bulgaria) engaged in drug trafficking to earn hard currency and undermine the moral fabric of capitalist societies.[145] Information disclosed publicly since the demise of communist rule in Central and Eastern Europe substantiates these allegations. Thus, Bulgarian sources now acknowledge that Bulgaria was a "central actor in trading weapons for narcotics," that the trade was motivated "not only by the desire for profit-making, but also by the determination to destabilize the Western society," and that "billions of dollars" in profit from the trade went to the "top crust" of political leaders.[146] The communist regime of the GDR and its leader, Erich Honecker, personally faced similar allegations. According to the testimony of a high-ranking GDR official who later defected to the West, the GDR regime began engaging in the international drug trade as early as 1962. Allegedly "well-informed" Western intelligence analysts, familiar with this testimony, estimate that Honecker's personal profit from this trade may have approached $75 million over a twenty-year period. A Western commentary on these allegations asserts that "there can be no doubt that from the start of Leonid Brezhnev's rule Moscow knew all about Honecker's perfidy."[147]

Both multilateral and bilateral cooperation between the European postcommunist states and other European states and the United States

[143]For details of these activities, see the *Washington Post,* 21 February 1988, B4.
[144]*Izvestiia* (Moscow), 27 June 1988, 3.
[145]These allegations are detailed in Joseph Douglass, Jr., *Red Cocaine: The Drugging of America* (Dunwoody, Ga.: Clarion House, 1990).
[146]These materials are carried by the official news agency of Bulgaria. See *Bulgarsko Telegrafna Agentsiia* (hereafter *BTA*) (Sofia), 7 March 1990, in *FBIS-EEU,* 21 March 1990, 9; *BTA,* 6 August 1991, in *FBIS-EEU,* 7 August 1991, 5.
[147]All materials on these allegations are drawn from the *Washington Post,* 8 March 1990, A27.

have expanded dramatically in the postcommunist era to combat international drug trafficking. An unprecedented meeting to this end occurred in 1991 between United States intelligence experts, including William Colby, former director of the Central Intelligence Agency, and high-ranking intelligence officials from Russia and all Central and East European states except Yugoslavia.[148] Bulgaria, Hungary, and Yugoslavia cooperated in several international forums with Western states to interdict traffic along the so-called Balkan Route, which brought drugs from Asia through southeastern Europe, Hungary, and (especially) Yugoslavia to the West.[149] Czechoslovakia announced its candidacy for a seat on the United Nations Commission on Narcotic Drugs in mid-1991.[150]

Since the end of communist rule, Central and Eastern European states have also actively pursued bilateral initiatives against drugs with other European states. Bulgaria, undoubtedly eager to improve its image tarnished by allegations of complicity under communist rule in the international drug trade, concluded such agreements with Britain, Germany, and the United States. The latter agreement provides that the United States will train Bulgarian intelligence officers in the fight against illegal drugs, arms smuggling, terrorism, and organized crime.[151] Czechoslovakia signed antidrug pacts with Britain, which called for Britain to help Czechoslovakia establish a national drug intelligence agency and train police officers in drug enforcement techniques and procedures, as well as with the United States.[152]

Even Albania, long the most xenophobic and vituperative anticapitalist regime in the region, has involved itself in such cooperation. Thus Albania recently concluded a wide-ranging agreement with Italy to combat international drug trafficking, organized crime, and terrorism.[153]

---

[148]For details of the meeting, see the *Philadelphia Inquirer*, 19 December 1991, 7.

[149]For example, in 1990 Bulgaria hosted a two-day conference of police officials and drug-trafficking specialists who discussed ways to improve efforts at interdiction along the Balkan Route. Representatives from Bulgaria, France, Germany (FRG), Greece, Hungary, Italy, and Yugoslavia attended the meeting. For details, see *BTA*, 2 June 1990, in *FBIS-EEU*, 5 June 1990, 12. To the same end, Hungary and Yugoslavia participated in meetings of the Vienna Club, which includes Austria, France, Germany, Italy, and Switzerland. *Tanjug*, 23 October 1989, in *FBIS-EEU*, 2 November 1989, 4, elaborates on this participation.

[150]As reported in *RFE-REE*, 28 June 1991, 51.

[151]For an overview of these efforts, including a detailed analysis of cooperation with the United States, see *BTA*, 14 August 1991, in *FBIS-EEU*, 15 August 1991, 16.

[152]The accord with the United States is reported in *RFE-REE*, 16 August 1991, 38. For details of cooperation with Britain, see *Prague Domestic Service*, 23 July 1990, in *FBIS-EEU*, 24 July 1990, 10; *RFE-REE*, 25 October 1991, 32.

[153]Unless otherwise noted, all materials on this cooperation are from *RFE-REE*, 27 September 1991, 3.

Reportedly, Italy fears that routes through Albania could become "modern highways for drug trafficking" to Italy that a "desperate Albania may lack the energy or capacity to combat."[154] Italy is to provide technical training and equipment (valued at upwards of thirty-three million dollars) to Albanian law enforcement personnel, and the two states are to begin joint naval patrols in the Strait of Otranto to interdict drug trafficking and other illegalities. The composition of the Italian delegation at the official signing ceremony for the pact in Tirana—which included the minister of the interior, the high commissioner in charge of combating the mafia, and the respective heads of the national police and the customs service—highlighted the importance Italy attaches to the agreement.

The need for international cooperation with Poland is now manifest as that country becomes an important producer of, and transshipment route for, illegal drugs to other countries. A respected Western source reports that laboratories in Poland produce an estimated 12 percent of the amphetamines illegally sold in Western Europe. The flood of Polish-produced amphetamines entering Sweden has led to a "noticeable drop" in prices on that country's drug market. Polish amphetamines now account for approximately 25 percent of the illegal drugs seized in Sweden.[155] This trade has proven highly lucrative—one kilogram of high-quality amphetamines fetches approximately $15,000 on the Western European market—which is why there is "enormous" competition among Polish producers.[156] Reportedly, Western traffickers are increasingly building production facilities in Poland to export heroin to Western Europe. This move makes "good sense," one source explains, since manufacturers face "far less stiff" penalties for their acts in Poland than in the West and they can produce the drugs more cheaply in Poland, where labor costs are lower and payoffs to sundry public officials are smaller.[157] Finally, a Russian source claims that the "Soviet-Polish mafia" has forged close links wherein the Polish faction serves as a facilitator to bring drugs produced by the Soviet members to market in Western

---

[154]*Corriere della Sera* (Rome), 25 August 1991, as quoted in ibid. These apprehensions may not be unfounded. For a detailed discussion of the activities of the Albanian mafia, including its extensive involvement in international drug trafficking, see *Eastern Europe Newsletter* (London), 10 June 1991, 4.

[155]*Die Presse* (Vienna), 12 July 1990, in *JPRS-EER*, 16 October 1990, 15.

[156]*Gazeta wyborcza*, 9 September 1991, in *JPRS-EER*, 9 October 1991, 22.

[157]*Die Presse*, 12 July 1990, in *JPRS-EER*, 16 October 1990, 15. This source reports that as of 1990 Poland's Ministry of the Interior had assigned only ten officials to antidrug operations.

Europe.[158] Responding to such activities, Poland in 1990 joined Interpol, the international police organization, and in 1991 concluded a bilateral agreement with Germany that included initiatives to combat drug trafficking.[159]

COMMUNISM AND DRUG ABUSE

Authorities in Central and Eastern Europe, surveying the spread of drug abuse in their societies, may well reflect, as Thomas Jefferson once did of political corruption, that "the time to guard against it is before it shall have gotten hold of us. It is better to keep the wolf out of the door than to trust to drawing its teeth and talons after he shall have entered."[160] Indeed, the "teeth and talons" of drug abuse "entered" the region under communist rule, and future efforts to combat this phenomenon must grapple with the legacy bequeathed therein.

This legacy is one of overall neglect and indifference that exacerbated the drug problem by inhibiting an effective response to it. The most pernicious components of this legacy include:

1. An antipathy to frank discussion about the drug problem
2. The ensuing ignorance of many citizens to the dangers of drugs
3. Inadequate or nonexistent data about the scope and composition of the population that abuses drugs
4. An underdeveloped etiology of drug abuse
5. A paucity of human, physical, and fiscal resources devoted to the treatment of drug abuse and addiction
6. Manifest deficiencies in drug-related legislation and enforcement
7. Limited cooperation with other governments to combat drug trafficking and production of illegal drugs

Governments in postcommunist Central and Eastern Europe have begun to mitigate selected components of this legacy of drug abuse. The numerous bilateral and multilateral initiatives they have undertaken

---

[158]*Sovetskaia Rossiia* (Moscow), 21 May 1991. This source asserts—without providing proof in substantiation—that "the Soviet-Polish mafia today constitutes the third most important in Europe in terms of the trade and production of narcotics so far as influence and financial turnover are concerned."

[159]For a discussion of why Poland joined Interpol, see *Polityka* (Warsaw), 13 October 1990, in *JPRS-EER*, 11 December 1990, 16–19. Details of the Polish-German bilateral pact are reported in *RFE-REE*, 15 November 1991, 35.

[160]Thomas Jefferson, *Notes on Virginia* (1782), cited in H. L. Mencken, *A New Dictionary of Quotations on Historical Principles* (New York: Knopf, 1946), 223.

with other governments and international agencies to combat drug trafficking are obvious examples. Similarly, in most countries there is now more open discussion about the drug problem and the feasibility of proposed initiatives to obviate it. This circumstance should facilitate a more sophisticated etiology of drug abuse and efforts to determine empirically the scale and composition of the drug abuse population.

Other components of the legacy will be more difficult to mitigate, especially in the short run. Thus the catastrophic economic situation confronting the postcommunist countries, which is itself one of the most unwelcome legacies of communism, makes it unlikely that in the foreseeable future monies for drug treatment programs and facilities will be made available in requisite amounts. Ironically, the successful revitalization of these economies will itself create a new set of circumstances fostering drug abuse. International drug traffickers will begin to view—as their Western counterparts who trade in legal commodities already do—Central and Eastern Europe as an attractive market to sell their wares, especially in countries whose currencies have become convertible. More Central and Eastern Europeans will probably seek solace in drugs to cope with the strains, tensions, and frustrations that are seemingly inevitable concomitants of a capitalist economy. To be sure, drug abuse is unlikely to displace alcoholism as the preeminent social pathology in the region. Yet the preceding analysis makes clear that "how to cope with the 'drug problem' " will be a question that is increasingly debated in postcommunist Central and Eastern Europe.

8

•━•

Postcommunist medicine: morbidity, mortality, and the deteriorating health situation

MARK G. FIELD

THE RESIDUAL SERVICE

If the British Navy can call itself the Senior Service, the Soviet health-care system before the collapse of the Soviet Union would not even qualify for junior status. Rather, it should have been known as the "residual service," residual in that, as former Health Minister E. I. Chazov complained in a moment of glasnost'-induced candor, the financing of that service came last, after all other expenditures had been met.[1] It had to take whatever was left, which, in the Soviet context, was very little.[2] The low priority accorded medicine (with one major exception, as we shall see later) reflected the fact that in the Soviet scheme of things, medical care did not produce quantifiable industrial, agricultural, or military goods such as machine tools, wheat, automobiles, or tanks. Although it would be possible to justify investments in health as economically sound, and indeed profitable, the argument apparently did not carry the day in higher party and government centers. The health-care system cost money, period. Health personnel consistently received the lowest incomes of all occupational categories, approximately 70 to 75 percent of the national average. Some efforts were made in the mid-1980s to increase earnings for both the physicians and the woefully underpaid nurses, but these brought only token raises. The situation did not change after the collapse of the Soviet system. It was reported in February 1993 that the average income of health personnel in Russia in January of that year was 9,533 rubles, compared with an

[1] E. I. Chazov, "Poiski novogo, zaderzhki v puti," *Meditsinskaia gazeta,* 16 February 1990, 1.
[2] "Health Care," in *USSR '88 Yearbook* (Moscow: Novosti Press Agency, 1989), 264–69.

average of 13,800 in the economy at large (70 percent). The health minister ruefully noted that "physicians receive less than veterinarians."[3]

Equally reflective of the financial starvation of the service, indeed a neglect that some might term criminal, was the fact that the proportion of the gross national product (GNP) earmarked for health care fell from the mid-1960s on, whereas in practically every industrial nation it rose, reaching even crisis proportions in the United States. The United States spends more than 14 percent of its national wealth on health care and the Western European countries about 7 to more than 9 percent, and those figures are rising everywhere. In 1965, the share of Soviet GNP devoted to health care was about 6.6 percent; it fell to 4.1 percent in 1970, and to 3 percent in 1980. Between 1985 and 1989, it hovered at slightly less than 3 percent, then rose to an estimated 3.4 percent in 1989.[4] These figures, however, are slight underestimates because of formally illegal under-the-table payments, which are discussed later in the chapter. In 1988, Health Minister Chazov complained that, on an international scale, the Soviet allocation of the GNP to health care ranked about seventy-fifth among 126 countries. In his memoirs, published in 1992, he explained why he had resigned as health minister in 1990, three years after he had been appointed by Gorbachev. He had realized the "hopelessness [*bezperspektivnost'*] of fighting for a renewal of Soviet health care." He further explained that he had tried to introduce a series of new ideas to reform the system, but that these had collapsed because of a lack of financial support, plus a shortage of enough well-qualified physicians and medical equipment.[5]

If, in addition, we note that in those years Soviet GNP was approximately half that of the United States, we can see the rather large disproportion in health-care spending. Although health expenditures are now said to be out of control in the United States and constitute the core of the American "health crisis," in the Soviet Union they were overcontrolled—a situation that can be explained by the fact that practically all health expenditures were financed by and through the public sector. The government was thus effectively in the position to turn the faucet on and

---

[3]F. Smirnov, "Prioriteti novogo ministra," *Meditsinskaia gazeta,* 19 February 1993, 2.
[4]M. D'Anastasio, "Red Medicine: Soviet Health System despite Early Claims Is Riddled with Failures," *Wall Street Journal,* 18 August 1987, 1. D. Rowland and A. V. Telyukov, "Soviet Health Care from Two Perspectives," *Health Affairs* 10, no. 3 (Fall 1991): 71–86.
[5]E. I. Chazov, *Zdorov'e i vlast': Vospominiania "kremlevskogo vracha"* (Moscow: Novosti Press Agency, 1992), 10.

off, as apparently (again according to Chazov) both Gosplan (the state planning agency) and the Ministry of Finances did. This is a situation that cannot be compared with that of the United States, where a large proportion of such expenditures are channeled through the private sector. But unavailability of funds in the Soviet Union was not the only problem. In many instances there was nothing to buy: Medical equipment, bricks and mortar to repair hospitals, pharmaceuticals, and so on were all "deficit commodities." Thus budget lines were often as useful to hospital directors and clinicians as hundred dollar bills to someone stranded alone in the Sahara Desert or Antarctica. Only a relatively small proportion of hospitals (particularly in the countryside) had been built originally as medical facilities. It was not unusual for hospitals, especially in Central Asia, to be without sanitary facilities. According to Chazov, only 35 percent of rural district hospitals had hot running water, 27 percent had no sewerage, 17 percent had no running water at all.

The one major exception to this bleak picture were the so-called closed facilities reserved for the elites and other more privileged members of Soviet society. It is a general rule and universal that medical care follows the stratification pattern of the social system, and that everywhere, East and West, the elites know how to take care of themselves. As V. M. Lupandin remarked in *Meditsinskaia gazeta:* "There developed two pharmacopoeias, one with aspirins and mustard plasters, and the other with the very latest foreign pharmaceuticals, (including) antibiotics. Some regional party committees already had their own water supply, fed from artesian wells, and separate from the polluted water from the river [destined for ordinary mortals]."[6]

But since, as far as we know, the closed medical facilities were funded primarily by allotments from the Health Ministry, and since they were better equipped and had more personnel than those reserved for the rest of the population, the latter had to make do with but a fraction of already meager resources. Of course, those who did enjoy the use of the special or elite facilities were only a small proportion of the total population. Christopher Davis estimated in 1979 that 0.1 percent of the population (about two hundred thousand persons) had access to elite facilities. If we add to that percentage those served by departmental health services (facilities reserved for members of various bureaucracies, for

[6]V. M. Lupandin, "Rossiiskoe zdravookhranenie: Postupi k novoi kontseptsii," *Meditsinskaia gazeta,* 13 September 1991, 7.

example the armed forces and the secret police), we can add another 5 percent or about 12.7 million persons.[7] The other 95 percent of the population had to content itself with inferior, overcrowded, and understaffed facilities. In Moscow about half of all doctors worked in special or closed polyclinics and hospitals in 1987.[8] No wonder, then, that in a system that claimed it had more doctors per capita than any other country in the world, people had to wait hours, sometimes days, to see an overworked physician who usually had five to seven minutes per patient, with half of that time spent on paperwork. Furthermore, those who enjoyed elite facilities and their amenities did so as a perquisite of rank for which they made no payment. But this is not all; regarding the small proportion of the GNP that went into health care, one caveat is in order: given the nature of shortages characteristic of the Soviet system, and the poor official pay of personnel, corruption was (and probably still is) endemic. Patients in most instances paid considerable sums of money under the table for the care they were supposed to receive free of charge: surgical interventions, deliveries, clean sheets, medications, and so on. Free medical care had become a sick joke. It is impossible to estimate or aggregate these "underground" payments at present, but they undoubtedly increased the proportion of the GNP devoted to health care. A survey of the population some time ago disclosed that-three-quarters of those polled said they had given money to health personnel, presumably to secure better, more personalized attention or as a token of appreciation, or both. As a matter of fact there is the Russian saying "lechitsa darom, darom lechitsa" (to be treated free of charge is to be treated in vain), which suggests that free medical care does no good, or that you get what you pay for. But what is significant is that these payments were made by, or extorted from, the ordinary people, that is, those least able to pay.

HEALTH CARE AND LEVELS OF HEALTH

Before proceeding any further, it is necessary to get a perspective on the relationship between medical care and the health of the population. The conventional wisdom is that the two are related, or correlated—that the

[7]Christopher Davis, "The Economics of the Soviet Health System: An Analytical and Historical Study, 1921–1978," Ph.D. diss., Economics, Cambridge University, 1979.
[8]T. Borich, "For a Limited Circle—Polemical Remarks on Special Polyclinics and Special Hospitals," *Meditsinskaia gazeta*, 5 August 1987, 2, in *Current Digest of the Soviet Press* (hereafter *CDSP*) 39, no. 21 (1987): 2.

better the health-care system, whether in its quality or quantity, or its outreach to the population, the better the health levels of that population. Conversely, the tendency is to blame the health-care system for high levels of health problems or poor health. This tendency is only partly justified. The relationship is more tenuous and not as direct as is assumed, and the health of the population is only partly or perhaps even marginally affected by the efforts of physicians and nurses and the availability of hospitals, clinics, and sophisticated equipment. In fact, social and economic conditions, political situations (international or civil wars), the everyday behavior of the population (smoking, alcoholism, sedentariness), and the environment are much more pertinent to health than is the medical care system per se. Although the United States leads the world in health expenditures, expressed as either a fraction of the GNP or per capita outlays (most of which, incidentally, are incurred in the last year of life and without significant results), U.S. health levels calculated in terms of either life expectancy or age-specific mortality fall behind those of many other nations that spend considerably less. The two major indicators in that context are morbidity and mortality. Morbidity, or the level of sickness or disability, is a slippery measure because definitions of illness and its reporting are subject to interpretation, survey reliability, and data aggregation problems. And there are many different definitions of illness that change over time and often reflect cultural rather than physiological or mental states. Who today thinks of fits of conniption, spinal irritation, or having the vapors, or even neurasthenia, which in an earlier time were common conditions?

Differential diagnosis is of the essence in the clinical picture. The present discussion of the Chronic Fatigue Syndrome, for instance, sometimes called the Yuppie disease, reflects the ambiguity and the cultural impact on the definitions of diseases. If you move from one country to another, you find that doctors talk of conditions you never heard of before, and ignore what you sure felt you had. American doctors perform six times as many coronary bypass operations as their Western European colleagues, for populations that have the same prevalence of the disease. It is therefore with respect to morbidity reporting and aggregating that the old adage of there being white lies, big lies, and statistics applies best. Mortality, by contrast, is a more accurate and certainly a simpler index reflecting its unambiguous binary nature: either you are dead or you are not. There is no differential diagnosis here. Of greater relevance is the obvious fact that although everyone has a differential chance of being affected by this or that illness, the mortality for any population, anywhere, is always 100 percent. People who "have not been sick one day in their life," eat reasonably, and stay fit still die.

Thus the question is not what, but when. In essence, one of the functions of the physician and the health system is to retard the inevitable, to give more years to life, to extend life expectancy. A human being, in cold economic terms, represents an enormous investment so that he or she can become a self-sufficient and productive member of society. An early death, sometimes called a premature death, thus represents a terrible loss in potential life years. And in underdeveloped nations, with high birth and death rates, the accumulation of capital for modernization is hampered by such high rates. But the important point is that these rates are only partly affected by the health-care system. Take, for example, infant mortality—defined as infants delivered alive who die within a year of birth or on their first birthday—a standard measure adopted by most countries and the World Health Organization. It is expressed as the number of deaths per thousand infants born alive. It is quite clear that this metric reflects not only the level of available care, prenatal and postnatal, but also the general socioeconomic situation of the parents, their class, and society as a whole. For example, in the United States, whereas the overall infant mortality is now slightly below ten (a fairly good showing on an international scale), among the black population the index is from two to three or more times higher, and this often for populations that live within walking distances of such great medical centers as Boston, Washington, D.C., or New York. In South Africa, the spread in infant mortality rates between white European, Asiatic, and black populations is even more dramatic. In 1970, for instance, it was 21.6 for whites, 36.4 for Asiatics, and 132.6 for blacks, or more than six times higher for the native black population than for the whites.[9] Infant mortality is first and foremost a social rather than a medical problem, and as an indicator it is a good measure of the social, economic, and political well-being of a population.

The lack of a direct relation between mortality/morbidity and medical care leads some people to question the utility of increased GNP allocations and sometimes to argue that it would be better to downsize the funds going into clinical care, particularly for high technology that

[9]R. M. Coe, *Sociology of Medicine* (New York: McGraw Hill, 1987), Table 2-8, 60.

benefits only a small fraction of the people, and either to rechannel these resources to simpler medical uses that would affect a much larger number of lives (well-baby clinics, for instance) or to use them to improve the overall living conditions of the population (better housing, a clean water supply, employment, health education, and so on). This was precisely the argument presented by A. V. Yablokov, the advisor to President Yeltsin for ecology and the protection of health. In a memorandum submitted to the Security Council of Russia in March 1993, Yablokov suggested that priority in preventing premature mortality should go first to exogenous socioeconomic causes, such as traffic accidents, drownings, suicides, homicides, alcohol (and other) poisonings, and accidents caused by fire. Second priority should go to losses of life and health due to ecologically determined causes, particularly water and air pollution. And third in priority would be the elimination of shortcomings in medical care and the supply of pharmaceuticals.[10]

By the same token, a few theorists have argued that the medical care system did not only not do much to help people but actually inflicted iatrogenic (physician-induced) harm to the health and the lives of people. A leading critic in this vein is Ivan Illich, who has attacked most institutions of modern society as counterproductive. In his *Medical Nemesis,* in the manner of a latter-day Martin Luther, he nailed his theses to the door of the medical establishment.[11] He asserted that the medical priests of today are charlatans, corrupt and dangerous to one's health, and that hospitals present a clear and mortal danger to those who entrust themselves to their dubious ministrations. Human beings, he advised, had to reestablish a direct link to their own health and bodies. We can dismiss Illich's hyperbolic (though not entirely invalid) strictures against modern medicine as part of the nostalgia a Jesuit priest felt seeing the care of the sick and the control of the dying and the hereafter slip through the fingers of the church.

All this, then, is a roundabout way to suggest that some of the health problems suffered by Soviet and post-Soviet society are not entirely due to the shortcomings of its system of socialized medicine or whatever is likely to take its place. I now turn to Soviet medicine itself.

[10]A. V. Yablokov, "The Need for a New Approach to Definition of Priority Health Problems of Population of Russian Federation," report presented to the Security Council of Russia, 17 March 1993, translated by A. Demin (unpublished), 9 pp.
[11]Ivan Illich, *Medical Nemesis* (New York: Pantheon Books, 1976).

THE NOBLE PURPOSE

The history of Soviet socialized medicine may be divided into roughly two phases. The first, from the Revolution to the end of the twenties, was dominated by the ideas of social hygienists and true-blue Marxists whose views were that illness and premature mortality were the product of a "sick" social system (capitalism) and that the advent of socialism and eventually communism would usher in a new period in human history—one that would be increasingly free of the socially produced ills and evils of the former system. The social hygienists also held that the etiology of sickness and early death was to be found in social habits and institutions and should be addressed not primarily through medical care (the treatment of illness after it has occurred) but in the reformation and transformation of society and in the education of the population. This led to the orientation of the Commissariat of Health Protection (founded by a decree of Lenin signed in July 1918) and of medical schools toward a preventive and sociological mode rather than a remedial and medical direction. The "pathologies" they were concerned with were therefore more social than biological: alcoholism, drug addiction, prostitution, industrial hygiene, and so on.[12]

The social hygienists' approach, which fitted well with Marxist theory, constituted at the same time a powerful critique of society and was thus in essence political. It was well and good when applied to capitalism and the early postcapitalist period with its heavy legacy of a contaminated past. But it did not sit well at all with the Stalin regime once the decision had been taken to industrialize under forced draft and to collectivize agriculture. Since the strictures of the social hygienists applied equally well to conditions as they existed in Soviet society, and indeed were exacerbated by Stalin's ruthless programs, they simply could not be tolerated. Thus the emphasis was changed 180 degrees, and the health care system reoriented to the classical clinical and remedial approach. The emphasis was moreover utilitarian or functional: medical care was not so much aimed at reducing pain and making life easier and longer; instead its major purpose was to maintain and repair the capacity of the people to perform their jobs in the economy. Of course, in its manifest or explicit presentation, the provision of medical care at the

[12]S. G. Solomon, "David and Goliath in Soviet Public Health: The Rivalry of Social Hygienists and Psychiatrists for Authority over the *Bytovoi* Alcoholic," *Soviet Studies* 41, no. 2 (1989): 254–75.

expense of the state was depicted as one more example of the dedication of the regime to the well-being and the welfare of the people. This was embodied in a provision of the several Soviet constitutions to the effect that all people were entitled to free and qualified medical attention whenever they needed it. Universal *entitlement*, regardless of ability to pay or any other qualification, has since become standard in most industrialized societies under one type of arrangement or another (health insurance, national health service, and so on) with the signal exceptions of the United States and South Africa. It answers a universal yearning for health security from birth to death, or as some would put it, from the womb to the tomb.

Almost invariably, most studies conducted with former Soviet citizens, either by the Harvard University Project in the 1950s or by the Soviet Interview Project in the 1980s, indicate that the idea of universally available medical care at the expense of society (or the state) was one of the most positive aspects of the Soviet system and its welfare features. What seemed important to these persons was the idea of "entitlement," of a claim against society that, in the time of illness or injury, the individual should have a right, spelled out in the constitution, to medical care at no direct cost. What Soviet citizens resented was the poor quality of that implementation and perhaps the individual's inequality before illness and death.

THE GRAND DESIGN

In 1936, the creation of the All-Union Commissariat (later Ministry) of Health Protection reflected the Soviet commitment to centralization, standardization, and control at the national level that placed practically all medical care and public health under the aegis of the party and the state. The health minister became a member of the cabinet, responsible for the health care of the entire nation, although there were jurisdictional exceptions—for example, the armed forces—but even there the principles were said to be the same. Soviet socialized medicine thus became a huge bureaucratic structure, employing several millions of persons and financed almost entirely from the state budget. Physicians became state employees or bureaucrats, without any corporate power as a profession (for example an independent association of physicians that could represent or defend their interests before the state).[13] The fact that they were

---

[13]M. G. Field, "The Hybrid Profession: Soviet Medicine," in A. Jones, ed., *Professions and the State* (Philadelphia: Temple University Press, 1991), 43–62.

paid by the state (and indeed had been trained at state expense) also made it possible to keep their official incomes at a relatively low level. A former Soviet doctor once recounted that when he worked at a large industrial plant, some of the engineers made fun of the physicians because they were so poorly paid. He had a quick retort: "You see, in our country, you get paid according to the value of the materials you work with. You engineers work with equipment purchased abroad with gold. We doctors only work with poor slobs like you whose worth, obviously, is reflected in our pay."

But one might also wonder at the rationale, besides saving money of course, for paying medical personnel so poorly. I have already suggested one factor: that medicine is not "productive" in the industrial sense. One would thus pay engineers more than doctors or teachers. Also, the nature of the work itself led to a decision, made quite early in Soviet history, that medical care like elementary school teaching could just as well be women's work, and women's work is traditionally paid less than men's. The large proportion of women in medicine (close to 70 percent at the present) may be cause and effect.[14] At the same time, it should be noted that the higher levels of the medical hierarchy in the ministries, in the research institutions, and in the USSR Academy of the Medical Sciences were overwhelmingly staffed by men, with commensurately higher salaries.

Next, given the corrupt nature of the health-care system and the age-old custom of giving additional monies or gifts to health personnel, perhaps the regime reasoned that the poor official incomes would be more than made up by payments under the table, sometimes called "envelope-passing medicine" since the money was usually given in this manner. This logic does not sound unreasonable in light of the payments that were extorted or demanded from patients when the average salary of a physician was in the vicinity of two hundred rubles per month. Here are some excerpts from correspondents' visits in Baku, but probably typical of the general situation in 1987.[15]

An operation here in Baku costs the patient's relatives roughly 500 rubles now . . . no one at the hospital comes right out and demands money but . . . you understand. No one will come near you, and the necessary medicine or whatever won't be found. . . . And this happens not only in the hospitals—in the maternity

[14]K. S. Schecter, "Professionals in Post-Revolutionary Regimes: A Case Study of Soviet Doctors," Ph.D. diss., Arts and Sciences, Columbia University, 1992.
[15]P. Makayenko and L. Manukyan, "Should We Pay for Medical Treatment: National Discussion," *Izvestiia*, 24 September 1987, p. 3, in *CDSP* 39, no. 27 (1987): 22.

home no one will look at a woman until she has paid. . . . A baby costs a lot of
money now, the relatives have to have 500 rubles.

Finally, when trying to understand the neglect of health care by the
authorities, we cannot dismiss the factor of stratification mentioned
earlier: the pampered bureaucracy, the partocracy, and the nomenklatura saw to it that they were well taken care of medically and otherwise.
From the vantage point of the rest of the population, the elite displayed
the insouciance, the Marie Antoinette complex, of an indifferent upper
class or aristocracy.

Whatever the mix of factors, in the last few decades during the period
of stagnation, and exacerbated afterward by the economic slide that
accompanied perestroika, the system of socialized medicine simply deteriorated, suffered from neglect, and was and still is plagued by severe
shortages of capital, equipment, maintenance, and pharmaceuticals, especially antibiotics—in short, all the elements (except personnel) that
constitute a medical care system consonant with the state of the art. And
even the personnel, if we are to believe former Minister Chazov, were in
many instances unqualified to perform the simplest medical tasks.

The deconstruction of Soviet society was thus paralleled by the gradual disintegration of its system of medical care, making a mockery of the
promises embodied in the constitution. Here again I must return to the
medical stratification mentioned earlier and its impact on the nonelite
population. The Soviet population may have been ready to accept the
legitimacy of higher incomes, privileges, and perquisites that go with
rank, with different occupational and political responsibilities. People
had become accustomed to these differences, but medical care involves
more than money and dachas. It touches a series of issues that are
emotionally charged: life itself, pain, or incapacitation. To know that in
the "closed" polyclinics reserved for the upper classes there are antibiotics and other medicines that could save the life of a dear one, one's child,
or oneself, and to realize that these are unobtainable because one is not
a part of the mighty and powerful, could be a source of powerful
antagonism and resentment. Shortly after the advent of perestroika, it
was announced that the Fourth Administration of the Health Ministry,
in charge of elite hospitals and polyclinics, had been disbanded and that
henceforth the ordinary population would have access to these facilities.
This was a gesture aimed at appeasing the people. I doubt that this
transformation really took place on a large scale, except perhaps symbolically. In fact, the elite facilities could accommodate but a micro-

scopic portion of the population. After all, it would have been possible, after the French Revolution, to house all those who lived in Versailles in the slums of Paris—but .it would have been impossible to move all, or almost all, of the Paris population into Versailles.

At any rate, the parallel deterioration of the economy and the health-care system led to a worsening of health indicators including mortality, particularly infant mortality, which as suggested earlier reflects socioeconomic conditions and is very sensitive to changes in these conditions. After the early seventies, infant mortality began to climb and in the last twenty years or so has remained at a national level about two and a half times greater than that of the United States. It would be fair to estimate that in the Central Asian republics, particularly in the countryside, it was likely to be two to four times the national figure. And there is evidence that, in many instances, infant mortality data were fudged or faked to make them look better. For instance, if an infant died at eleven months, it would be reported as one year and one month old, thus removing it from the infant mortality rubric. Chazov with his usual frankness noted in 1988: "We took pride in our system of health care. . . . But we kept quiet about the fact that in infant mortality we ranked 50th in the world after Mauritius and Barbados."[16]

By the same token, the overall mortality rate in the Soviet Union was 40 percent higher than in the United States in 1988, 50 percent for men and 40 percent for women. When disaggregated by selected causes for men and women, the Soviet index was higher in all instances except for female neoplasms (cancers) and female motor accidents (10 percent less in the Soviet Union). It was equal in only one case: female deaths from digestive diseases.[17] Writing a few years ago, a French demographer commented, "One has never seen, in peacetime, a regression of health conditions (as measured by mortality) of such magnitude."[18]

To summarize, the Soviet health-care system suffered, and does even more so today, from a lack of resources, a suffocating bureaucracy and hierarchic structure, an unequal distribution of resources, and neglect and corruption. Indeed, the dislocations, the shortages, the disorganization, the rampant inflation of the recent past can only exacerbate the

[16]E. I. Chazov, "Speech," *Izvestiia* and *Pravda*, 30 June 1988, 4, in *CDSP* 40, no. 27 (1988): 8–9.
[17]D. Rowland and A. V. Telyukov, "Soviet Health Care from Two Perspectives," *Health Affairs* 10, no. 3 (Fall 1991): 71–86.
[18]R. Pressat, "Une évolution anachronique: La hausse de la mortalité en Union Soviétique," *Concours médical*, 21 May 1983, 105, 431.

problems of medical care there and, in tandem with the breakdown of the system in general, place the welfare and the health of the population in double jeopardy. This is amply confirmed by two official reports commissioned by the Yeltsin government and released in early October 1992. One reports on the health of the population,[19] the other on the state of the environment in the Russian Federation.[20] They depict in cold statistical terms the steady deterioration of the health of the population and of the environment in Russia. The birth rate is down, the death rate is up. The number of geographic areas where the death rate is higher than the birth rate was 29 in 1991, an increase of 19 since 1989. The rate of natural increase of the population fell from 5.1 per 1,000 in 1981 to 0.7 per 1,000 in 1991; and in the 29 regions cited it was, as noted, negative; the same general phenomenon was reported for Ukraine in the fall of 1991.[21] Between 1980 and 1991, the level of neonatal morbidity in Russia increased from 82.4 cases per 1,000 live births to 173.7. Estimates are that by the year 2015 only 15 to 20 percent of newborns will be born healthy. The Russian Federation (and presumably the rest of the former Soviet Union) is also beset by a series of environmental problems resulting from the contamination of water, soil, and air, including radioactive contamination. Virtually all of Russia's major rivers, including the Volga, Oka, Kama, Don, and the Kuban and Ob basins, suffer from viral and bacterial contamination on the order of tens to hundreds times greater than norms permissible elsewhere. Only 15 percent of city dwellers breathe air that meets acceptable standards. The situation with respect to health is critical, therefore, if not catastrophic.

Proposals to provide emergency assistance to the former Soviet Union usually bracket, and for good reasons, "food and medicines." Food may be more important than medicines, but medicines certainly come a close second. The solution of the medical problems left by the failures of the Soviet regime will come only with the solution of the economic, social, and political legacies of the Soviet Union. What are the likely trends of events in the near future in this domain?

[19] *Gosudarstvennii doklad o sostoianii zdorov'ia naseleniia Rossiiskoi Federatsii v 1991 godu*, Moscow, 1992. A summary of this report was published in *Nezavisimaia gazeta*, 7 October 1992, 6, and is available in English in *Current Digest of the Post-Soviet Press* 44, no. 41 (1992): 1–5, 20.

[20] *Gosudarstvennii doklad'o sostoianii okruzhaiushei prirodnoi sredi Rossiiskoi Federatsii v 1991 godu*, Moscow, 1992. A summary of this report was published in *Nezavisimaia gazeta*, 7 October 1992, 6, and is available in English in *Current Digest of the Post-Soviet Press* 44, no. 41 (1992): 1–5, 20.

[21] D. Bashikov, "V trevoge poka odni mediki," *Meditsinskaia gazeta*, 18 September 1992, 2.

THE LEGACY

A historian is reputed to have said, "Don't ask me to predict the future; but when it happens, I will be glad to explain why it was inevitable." To forecast future trends in health, health care, and vital statistics in the former Soviet Union would be foolhardy. And yet, the visible legacy of the Soviet era in this area is clear for all to see and will shape to a large extent the evolution of the health situation.

I expect that, at the more general level, the collapse of the Soviet system will bring further political instability and economic hardships. In fact, at the present time the economy is in a free-fall, as a result of a precipitous decline in productivity and production, the lack of an institutionalized wholesale and retail market and exchange mechanisms, and high inflation. The command system in the economy—which, as inefficient as it was, had at least the virtue of ordering the movement of goods and commodities to those who needed them—has disappeared. These trends are likely to increase the risks to which the population is exposed, including shortages of food, with the entire process accompanied by the continued deterioration of the environment through uncontrolled pollution of air, water, and soil.[22] Those most likely to be affected adversely will be women of childbearing age, nursing mothers, children, and the elderly. Not enough vaccines will be produced or procured. In addition, as reported by Murray Feshbach and Alfred Friendly, Jr., many children are already suffering from vitamin deficiency and the effects of environmental problems.[23] The outbreak of epidemics is a distinct possibility, and the toll they will take on morbidity and mortality will be in direct proportion to the economic dislocations and shortages of all kinds. It is to be expected that a deteriorating social, political, and especially economic situation will have devastating effects on the health of the population, which was not in great shape even before the events of August 1991.

The health-care system, weak and poorly supplied to begin with, will further deteriorate, particularly as clinical facilities will continue to face increasing shortages of all kinds (financial resources, equipment, pharmaceuticals, fuel, food, and other items that are in scarce supply). It was announced, for example, in February 1992 that the government budget

[22]M. Feshbach and A. Friendly, Jr., *Ecocide in the USSR: Health and Nature under Siege* (New York: Basic Books, 1992).
[23]Ibid., 52.

would be able to fund only 60 percent of health care in Russia.[24] A year later, it was reported that only 3.8 percent of the governmental budget of Russia had been allocated to health care, only about one-half of the "minimum required."[25] Hospitals, particularly those in the Central Asian republics and in the countryside in general, will increasingly resemble those of a Third World country and will to a large extent depend on assistance from the West. In 1989, one-quarter of children who should have been vaccinated against polio were not; one-fifth were not immunized against diphtheria, nor one-third against whooping cough. If this was the situation before the collapse of the Soviet Union, one can well imagine how much worse the situation is likely to be now.[26]

As the bureaucratic medical system established by the Soviets gradually collapses, it is possible that an increasing number of physicians will set up individual and private group practices and that their relative economic position will rise. This development may also lead, as physicians are liberated from their status as state functionaries and employees, to the formation of independent associations of physicians to represent them, to defend their interests, and to raise their prestige and political power in an increasingly pluralistic and, one hopes, democratic environment. There are already independent physician associations in Russia, Ukraine, the Baltic republics, Azerbaijan, and probably other republics. Some of these will undoubtedly publish their own journals. We may thus see a trend toward the reprofessionalization or the deproletarianization of the medical corps in the direction of self-governing corporate bodies. This development will, of course, take time and money, but it would raise the status of professionals to par with that of their colleagues in the West. It is interesting to note that, in the West, physicians are concerned about becoming bureaucrats and employees and about losing their independence and clinical autonomy as attempts are made to slow down or cap medical costs.[27] Thus cautious visions of "convergence" from different starting points appear on the horizon.

Soviet medicine consistently rejected the idea of private practice (with

[24]S. Helmstadter, "Medical Insurance in Russia," *RFE/RL Research Report*, 31 July 1992, 65–69.

[25]Smirnov, "Prioriteti novogo ministra," 2.

[26]A. Hartman, "Life and Death for Russian Children," *New York Times*, 25 February 1992, A21.

[27]J. D. Stoeckle and S. J. Reiser, "The Corporate Organization of Hospital Work: Balancing Professional and Administrative Responsibilities," *Annals of Internal Medicine* 116, no. 5 (1 March 1992): 407–13.

its connotation of the physician as a businessperson) and the concept of charity, which had no place in the Soviet scheme. With the rebirth of private practice and private initiative, we may well see an increase in charitable and volunteer activities (usually inspired and organized by religious organizations), both in the care of the very poor and in providing assistance at hospitals (regular and psychiatric) in the dual capacity of giving physical help and spiritual, emotional, or psychotherapeutic aid to the sick and dying.

The population will continue, at least for the foreseeable future, to expect that medical care is a right of citizenship, and that an individual unable to pay for his or her care should not be deprived of needed services. This may facilitate the establishment and the acceptance of a variety of schemes, especially health insurance, that will provide coverage for certain designated occupational groups (industrial workers, white-collar employees, and so on) supplemented by some kind of state-sponsored arrangements for those not covered (for example, the unemployed, housewives, students, and retirees). At the same time we may expect the continued existence of stratification and inequalities in the delivery of health services, probably a two-tier arrangement, though the composition of the population in these two (or more) tiers will change. The affluent, the well-connected, and the powerful will, undoubtedly, be able to purchase or otherwise obtain better medical care in better-equipped facilities and with more amenities than the poorer members of the population. In any stratified society, the provision of medical care follows that stratification, and there is no reason to assume that the postcommunist world will escape the pattern. The legacy of universal, though not necessarily equal, entitlement will probably remain. But the manner in which this provision will be implemented will remain an open question for a long time, given the failure of state socialized medicine, Soviet style.

In principle, insurance medicine is likely to replace socialized medicine because it is held to be consonant with the transition to a market economy. According to the law, the Russian population was to be covered by insurance medicine beginning in 1993, but, given the present circumstances of economic disorganization and high inflation and the almost total lack of experience with insurance medicine, this is still a pipe dream. Only a small proportion of the population is currently covered by medical insurance, and most medical services will still have to be paid for from the state budget. As Sarah Helmstadter has stated, "Neither the general public, nor the government nor the medical institutions are prepared economically, structurally, or psychologically for the introduction of medical insurance."[28]

We may also expect changes in the structure of the medical research establishment, particularly the institutions under the control of the Academy of Medical Sciences, now the Russian Academy of Medical Sciences. Although it had been assumed that the academy was relatively free of party dictation, in fact it was not. V. M. Lupandin, in a recent article in the *Meditsinskaia gazeta,* pointed to the fact that three academicians had been closely associated with the punitive use of psychiatry as an example of party control.[29]

These changes will take place slowly and unevenly. I would venture that, in the course of the years to come, the health-care system of the republics will increasingly begin to resemble some of those that have emerged in the post–World War II period, particularly in Western Europe. These systems all seem to embody some kind of mix between private and public initiative and financing; a commitment to the population of universal coverage at no cost at the time of the service, or some kind of cost sharing; and some type of implicit or explicit rationing process in light of the ever expanding demand for services (fueled by demographic changes and by expensive technology that is both labor and capital intensive) and the need to contain exponentially rising costs. It is thus possible that both the pluralistic system of the United States and the socialized medicine that existed in the Soviet Union may meld into some kind of amalgam of insurance medicine and state financing of the type seen in most industrial states. In the former Soviet Union the nature of both the health problems (expressed, for instance, in vital statistics of morbidity and mortality) and the health system will depend to a large extent, however, on the evolution of the societies that emerge from the ruins of the Soviet empire. In health care the process is going to be long and tortuous, and every solution or reform adopted will aim to eliminate some glaring problems of the past and generate new ones for the future. This is indeed a universal phenomenon. Looking at the United States and its plethora of health problems, former Surgeon Gen-

---

[28]Helmstadter, "Medical Insurance in Russia."
[29]Lupandin, "Rossiiskoe zdravookhranenie," 7.

eral C. Everett Koop said of health reform, "If we were all men of good will, which we are not, and if we could agree on how it should be done, which we can't, and if we had the money, which we don't, it would still take 10 years."[30] The same could be said of the situation in the former Soviet Union, but it will probably take much longer.

[30]C. E. Koop, quoted in the *Boston Globe*, 21 December 1991, 42.

9

Health and mortality in Central and Eastern Europe: retrospect and prospect

NICHOLAS EBERSTADT

Over the past generation, demographic data from the Soviet Union and Warsaw Pact Europe have detailed an anomalous and disturbing trend: stagnation, even retrogression, in overall health conditions and general mortality levels. For industrialized countries during peacetime, such an interruption of health progress is unprecedented. It is also unique, being limited—at least to date—to those populations living under governments established with the direct assistance of the Red Army. The pervasive nature of the health crisis within the states of the former Warsaw Pact is all the more striking when one considers the historical and cultural differences that otherwise divide the peoples commonly afflicted.

The epicenter of the Warsaw Pact's health crisis was within the Soviet Union, the first Warsaw Pact state to experience secular increases in mortality for men and women of various ages. It is also on the territory of the former Soviet Union that, by a variety of measures, the deterioration of overall health conditions seems to have been most pervasive and severe. But for the more than 100 million people of what was Warsaw Pact Europe, the reverberations of this long-term health crisis have been far from negligible. Rising death rates have been characteristic of broad segments of the public in all of these countries over the past generation. Moreover, for the region as a whole, overall mortality levels, when appropriately standardized, appear to have been higher at the end of the 1980s than they had been in the mid to late 1960s.

Portions of this chapter draw on a paper presented at the Roger Revelle Memorial Symposium, Harvard University, October 1992. The author thanks Jonathan Tombes for his able assistance in this project. Partial support for this study was provided by the U.S. Institute of Peace; the author alone, however, is responsible for all conclusions and interpretations in this chapter.

196

This chapter explores this grim aspect of communism's social legacy in Central and Eastern Europe.[1] It begins by examining the dimensions of the health crisis that beset Warsaw Pact Europe between the mid-1960s and the revolutions of 1989, tracing its trajectory over that generation. It then examines some of the proximate factors accounting for these perverse health patterns. Deteriorating health conditions have a direct bearing on individual welfare; they also have implications for the states under which these syndromes emerged. Finally, this chapter touches briefly on the health prospects for the populations of the formerly communist states of Central and Eastern Europe now that Warsaw Pact communism has collapsed in the region.

DIMENSIONS OF THE CENTRAL AND EASTERN EUROPEAN HEALTH CRISIS FROM ABOUT 1965 TO ABOUT 1989

Specialists in public health and social affairs are by now familiar with the story of the health crisis in the Soviet Union.[2] From the end of World War II until the early 1960s, health progress in the Soviet Union appears to have been steady, rapid, and general. According to recent estimates by the United Nations (UN) Population Division, for example, the infant mortality rate there fell by more than half in the decade 1950–55 to 1960–65, and overall life expectancy at birth rose by more than five years during that same decade.[3] By the mid-1960s, however, all-union death rates were registering a rise for certain cohorts of men in late middle age. The situation subsequently worsened. By the early 1970s, rising death rates were reported for adult males of almost every age group, for women beyond their childbearing years, and even for newborn infants. Sensitive to the political interpretations of such figures,

[1] Only those Central and Eastern European countries that were formerly part of Warsaw Pact Europe will be surveyed in this chapter; developments in former Yugoslavia and Albania (where trends differed somewhat from the patterns described here) will not be analyzed in this chapter.

[2] See, for example, John Dutton, Jr., "Changes in Soviet Mortality Patterns, 1959–77," *Population and Development Review* 5, no. 2 (1979): 276–91; Christopher Davis and Murray Feshbach, *Rising Infant Mortality in the USSR in the 1970s* (Washington, D.C.: U.S. Bureau of the Census, International Population Reports, Series P-95, No. 74, 1980); Murray Feshbach, "Soviet Health Problems," *Proceedings of the Academy of Political Science* 35, no. 3 (1984): 81–97; Barbara A. Anderson and Brian D. Silver, "The Changing Shape of Soviet Mortality, 1958–1985: An Evaluation of Old and New Evidence," *Population Studies* 43, no. 2 (1989): 243–65; and Murray Feshbach and Alfred Friendly, Jr., *Ecocide in the USSR: Health and Nature under Siege* (New York: Harper Collins, 1992).

[3] United Nations, *World Population Prospects: The 1992 Revision* (New York: UN Department of Economic and Social Development, forthcoming), 202.

Soviet authorities imposed a virtual blackout on mortality statistics for a decade, from the mid-1970s through the mid-1980s. By the final years of the Soviet era, data on mortality in the Soviet Union were once again widely available, although they were not without their defects and shortcomings.[4] Nevertheless, they pointed to a syndrome of broad, severe, and long-term deterioration in the country's public health conditions. According to official data, death rates in the Soviet Union were higher in 1989 than they had been thirty years earlier for a large portion of the country's population: men thirty-five years of age or older and women fifty-five or older.[5] By the UN Population Division's assessment, overall life expectancy at birth was actually slightly lower in the Soviet Union in the late 1980s than it had been in the early 1960s.[6]

Although the health record of the Central and Eastern European states has not occasioned as much commentary as that of the former Soviet Union, there are nonetheless striking parallels between the two. Like the Soviet Union, Warsaw Pact Europe began the cold war with a burst of health progress that encompassed virtually all groups and areas within the region. As in the Soviet Union, rapid and uninterrupted improvements in public health continued only up to the early 1960s. Thereafter, health progress came to a halt for a growing portion of the populations of the Central and Eastern European countries, as it did in the Soviet Union. Long-term stagnation, even decline, in health status came to typify the trends for major segments of each society within the Warsaw Pact alliance.

Health status is a subtle and complex quantity; it cannot be captured in a single, summary statistic. But perhaps the best way to chart the shifting health fortunes of Central and Eastern Europe's various populations is by means of local mortality trends. As an indicator of health conditions, mortality has obvious limitations: death rates cannot speak to the physical state of persons who actually manage to survive from one year to the next.[7] Nevertheless, mortality trends are meaningful in and of themselves, broadly suggestive of attendant changes in health

[4]For one assessment of some of these problems, see Barbara A. Anderson and Brian D. Silver, "Trends in Mortality of the Soviet Population," *Soviet Economy* 6, no. 3 (1990): 191–252.

[5]Comparisons based on data presented in United Nations, *Demographic Yearbook* (New York: United Nations), issues from various years.

[6]United Nations, *World Population Prospects: The 1992 Revision*, 202.

[7]For an extended examination of the distinction between morbidity and mortality trends, see James C. Riley, "The Risk of Being Sick: Morbidity Trends in Four Countries," *Population and Development Review* 16, no. 3 (1990): 403–32.

Table 9.1. *Life expectancy at birth in Eastern Europe,*
ca. 1965–89 (years)

Country	Male	Female
Bulgaria		
1965–67	68.81	72.67
1987–89	68.33	74.70
increment	−0.48	+2.03
Czechoslovakia		
1964	67.76	73.56
1988	67.76	75.29
increment	0.00	+1.73
German Democratic Republic (GDR)		
1967	68.35	73.43
1987–88	69.81	75.91
increment	+1.46	+2.48
Hungary		
1964	67.00	71.83
1989	65.44	73.79
increment	−1.56	+1.96
Poland		
1965–66	66.85	72.83
1988	67.15	75.67
increment	+0.30	+2.84
Romania		
1964–67	66.45	70.51
1987–89	66.51	72.41
increment	+0.06	+1.90

Sources: For GDR 1967: GDR State Statistical Committee, *Statistisches Jahrbuch der Deutschen Demokratischen Republik 1970* (Berlin: Staatsverlag der Deutschen Demokratischen Republik, 1970), 470. For all others: United Nations, *Demographic Yearbook* (New York: UN Department of International Economic and Social Affairs), various issues.

circumstances, and by their nature more reliable and intrinsically comparable than many other data pertaining to health status. In short, there is probably no better first approximation of public health conditions for a population as a whole than those afforded by its mortality trends.

The most comprehensive, and intuitively clear, measure of overall mortality is probably life expectancy at birth. Official "life tables"[8] from the six countries of what was Warsaw Pact Europe provide an initial glimpse at the region's emerging health troubles. As Table 9.1 illustrates,

[8]Life tables are standard demographic constructs that trace survival chances across all ages for males and females in a given population.

between the mid-1960s and the late 1980s overall life expectancy did in fact rise, but just barely: taken together, the unweighted average for males and females is an increase of about one year. In aggregate, these six countries experienced no improvement whatever in male life expectancy at birth in the decades under consideration; two of the six states—Bulgaria and Hungary—actually estimated their male life expectancies to have declined. The situation was better for females, who were estimated to have enjoyed an increase in life expectancy at birth averaging a little more than two years. Yet even these improvements look far from favorable when placed in international perspective. By the UN Population Division's assessment, Warsaw Pact Europe's female gains, in terms of years of life expectancy at birth, were less than half as great as those for the rest of Europe during the period from 1960–65 to 1985–90.[9] Apart from the Soviet Union, no region of the world, by this indicator, is believed to have experienced such a marginal improvement in overall female health status over those decades. Despite its well-publicized economic and social travails, for example, the Latin American and Caribbean region is estimated to have significantly outpaced the six Eastern European countries under consideration in life expectancy improvements for men and women alike during that generation.

What accounts for the region's poor performance in these recent decades? In an arithmetic sense, the answer can be exposed by separating the populations in question into component parts. All Central and Eastern European countries reported steady, if undramatic, declines in their infant mortality rates between the mid-1960s and the late 1980s. But the situation for their noninfant populations was rather different (Table 9.2). In four of these six countries, overall life expectancy at age one was somewhat lower in the late 1980s than it had been several decades earlier; it was lower for males in all countries. For the region as a whole, it appears that such health progress as was achieved between the mid-1960s and the late 1980s can be attributed entirely to improvements in infant mortality; life expectancy at age one for the entire region appears to have been slightly lower at the end of that period than it had been at its beginning.

If general health conditions for Central and Eastern Europe's noninfant populations were characterized by stagnation, the plight of adult groups in particular was marked by pervasive deterioration. As Table

[9] Derived from United Nations, *World Population Prospects: The 1992 Revision,* 192.

Table 9.2. *Life expectancy at ages 1 and 30 in Warsaw Pact region, ca. 1965–89*

Country	Life expectancy at age 1 (years)		Life expectancy at age 30 (years)	
	Male	Female	Male	Female
Bulgaria				
1965–67	70.28	73.81	43.06	45.99
1987–89	68.42	74.64	40.87	46.53
increment	−1.86	+0.83	−2.19	+0.54
Czechoslovakia				
1964	68.44	73.96	41.15	45.84
1988	67.70	75.07	39.73	46.62
increment	−0.74	+1.11	−1.42	+0.78
German Democratic Republic				
1967–68	69.77	74.70	42.46	46.70
1987–88	69.53	75.46	41.67	47.08
increment	−0.24	+0.76	−0.79	+0.38
Hungary				
1964	69.08	73.45	41.74	45.45
1989	65.58	73.86	37.84	45.55
increment	−3.50	+0.41	−3.90	+0.10
Poland				
1965–66	68.98	74.43	41.68	46.46
1988	67.37	75.70	39.60	47.29
increment	−1.61	+1.27	−2.08	+0.83
Romania				
1964–67	68.93	72.53	42.04	45.09
1987–89	67.53	73.13	40.45	45.56
increment	−1.40	+0.60	−1.59	+0.47

Sources: United Nations, *Demographic Yearbook* (New York: UN Department of International Economic and Social Affairs), various issues.

9.2 illustrates, life expectancy at age thirty for males is estimated to have fallen in all six countries of Warsaw Pact Europe. Some of these declines were little short of catastrophic. Hungary, for example, registered a shocking drop of nearly four years. In five of the six states, overall life expectancy was lower in the late 1980s than it had been a generation earlier, and in the GDR—the sole exception to the regional trend—it was only very slightly higher.

Changes in age-specific mortality rates highlight the adverse health trends that befell adults in the region (Table 9.3). During the quarter century between 1965 and the revolutions of 1989, death rates in all of

Table 9.3. *Changes in age-specific death rates for cohorts aged 30 to 69 in Warsaw Pact region, ca. 1965–89 (percent)*

Country and sex	Cohort age							
	30–34	35–39	40–44	45–49	50–54	55–59	60–64	65–69
Males								
Bulgaria (1966–89)	+19	+32	+62	+70	+56	+47	−16	+14
Czechoslovakia (1965–89)	−5	+8	+19	+40	+33	+29	+15	+6
GDR (1965–88)	−5	−8	−5	+7	+3	+1	−15	−17
Hungary (1966–89)	+67	+96	+100	+131	+93	+69	+46	+25
Poland (1966–88)	+9	+17	+36	+51	+47	+38	+23	+6
Romania (1966–89)	+32	+36	+43	+61	+44	+32	+35	+15
Unweighted average	+20	+30	+43	+60	+46	+36	+15	+8
Soviet Union (1965–66 to 1989)	−5	0	+21	+25	+24	+25	+20	+25
Females								
Bulgaria (1966–89)	−11	−15	−10	+4	−4	−4	−7	−6
Czechoslovakia (1965–89)	−13	−23	−14	−9	−10	0	−3	−9
GDR (1965–88)	−12	−15	−14	−12	−12	−10	−16	−17
Hungary (1966–89)	+33	+26	+26	+33	+23	+22	+7	−2
Poland (1965–88)	−27	−25	−9	−9	−2	−1	−3	−14
Romania (1966–89)	−8	+13	+4	−3	0	−2	−3	−3
Unweighted average	−6	−7	−3	+1	−1	+1	−4	−9
Soviet Union (1965–66 to 1989)	−21	−17	−4	−3	+2	+11	+4	+19

Note: All changes rounded to nearest percentage point. Percentages derived from sources.
Sources: For Soviet Union 1965–66: John Dutton, Jr., "Changes in Soviet Mortality Patterns, 1959–77," *Population and Development Review* 5, no. 2 (1979): 276–77. All other data: United Nations, *Demographic Yearbook* (New York: UN Department of International Economic and Social Affairs), various issues.

these countries were up for at least some adult male cohorts; for many of these groups, the increases recorded were dramatic and alarming. In Hungary, for example, death rates for men in their forties fully doubled between 1966 and 1989. The patterns for Central and Eastern European women were less unfavorable. Even so, Hungary reported broad rises in adult female mortality, and both Bulgaria and Romania registered at least some long-term increases in mortality for specific female age groups. On the whole, deterioration of health appears to have been most serious for men and women in their forties and fifties. Poor as the Soviet performance with respect to public health may have been over the past generation, it is worth noting that there appear to be many instances in the Central and Eastern European countries considered here in which specific adult cohorts suffered even sharper reversals than those experienced by contemporaries in the former Soviet Union.

Those reversals are all the more dramatic when viewed against the backdrop of the decades immediately following World War II. Between 1945 and 1965, mortality rate decreases were more rapid in communist than in noncommunist Europe. To many observers, that differential pace of progress seemed to present the possibility that the countries of Soviet-bloc Europe might match, and ultimately surpass, the health performance of "capitalist" Europe. By the mid-1960s, convergence did in fact suggest itself. "Age-standardized mortality rates"[10] emphasize this point (Table 9.4). In 1965–69, according to calculations of the World Health Organization (WHO), mortality rates for WHO's four contemporary members from Warsaw Pact Europe, when standardized against the WHO's "European Model" population, looked to be only slightly higher than those of eighteen countries in Western Europe: for females, the differential was about 8 percent; for males, less than 3 percent.

Yet by the eve of the revolutions of 1989, a great gap had opened up between Eastern and Western Europe. For both males and females, age-standardized death rates were, on an unweighted average, over 40 percent higher in Warsaw Pact Europe. Between the mid-1960s and the late 1980s, Western European age-standardized mortality rates had been falling steadily; overall rates dropped by about 25 percent between 1965–69 and 1989. In Eastern Europe, by contrast, the overall impact

[10] Age-standardized mortality rates provide a summary measure of overall mortality by applying age-specific death rates for a given population against a specifically selected age-sex structure; such adjustments afford a greater comparability across countries and over time.

Table 9.4. *Age-standardized mortality rates in selected Eastern European countries and in Western Europe, 1965–69 to ca. 1989 (deaths per 100,000)*

Country or group	1965–69	ca. 1989	Percent change
Bulgaria			
Males	1,228.4	1,396.6	+13.7
Females	956.8	917.8	−4.1
Czechoslovakia			
Males	1,496.0	1,522.8	+1.8
Females	978.7	888.4	−9.2
Hungary			
Males	1,444.2	1,624.9	+12.5
Females	1,044.5	933.4	−10.6
Poland			
Males	1,388.5	1,498.0	+7.9
Females	922.6	838.5	−9.1
Unweighted average, 4 Eastern European countries			
Males	1,389.3	1,510.6	+8.7
Females	975.7	894.5	−8.3
Unweighted average, 18 Western European countries			
Males	1,344.9	1,041.2	−22.6
Females	903.2	626.9	−30.6
Ratio, selected Eastern to Western European countries (Western Europe = 100)			
Males	103	145	
Females	108	143	

Notes: Mortality rates are standardized against the WHO "European Model" population. Western Europe: Austria, Belgium, Denmark, Federal Republic of Germany, Finland, France, Greece, Iceland, Ireland, Italy, Luxembourg, Netherlands, Norway, Portugal, Spain, Sweden, Switzerland, United Kingdom (England and Wales). Western European figures for 1965–69 do not include Italy. Western European figures for ca. 1989 are for 1989, except Belgium (1986), Italy (1988), Spain (1987), and Sweden (1988).
Sources: World Health Organization, *World Health Statistics Annual* (Geneva: WHO), 1988 edition (1989), Table 12; 1990 edition (1991), Table 10; 1991 edition (1992), Table 11.

of mortality change was to *raise* combined rates of age-standardized mortality somewhat, as secular increases in male death rates more than counteracted for the slight improvements that were registered by females.

Table 9.5. *Age-standardized mortality rates for Eastern Europe and selected other populations, ca. 1989 (deaths per 100,000)*

Country or group	Male	Female	Total population
Bulgaria 1989	1,396.6	917.8	1,141.0
Czechoslovakia 1989	1,522.8	888.4	1,158.0
GDR 1989	1,313.7	828.4	1,014.7
Hungary 1989	1,624.9	933.4	1,229.6
Poland 1989	1,498.0	838.5	1,118.7
Romania 1988	1,462.0	1,051.1	1,240.5
Unweighted average, 6 East European countries	1,469.7	909.6	1,150.4
Unweighted average, 18 West European countries, ca. 1989	1,041.2	626.9	803.1
Unweighted average, 6 selected Latin American countries, late 1980s	1,210.7	819.7	997.2
USSR 1988	1,565.2	915.8	1,159.9
Ratios			
USSR: Eastern Europe	106	101	101
Eastern Europe: Western Europe	141	145	143
Eastern Europe: Latin America	121	111	115

Notes: Mortality rates are standardized against the WHO "European Model" population. For West European countries see Table 9.4. The six selected Latin American countries are Argentina (1987), Chile (1987), Costa Rica (1988), Mexico (1986), Uruguay (1987), and Venezuela (1987).
Sources: World Health Organization, *World Health Statistics Annual* (Geneva: WHO), 1990 edition (1991), Table 10; 1991 edition (1992), Table 11.

A generation of stagnation, and even deterioration, in general health conditions took their toll on Central and Eastern Europe's standing in relation to other areas of the world. By 1989, there was no longer any meaningful comparability in general health conditions between the two portions of divided Europe. Age-standardized mortality rates underscore the contrast. As of 1989, these death rates were higher, for males and females alike, in communist Europe's "healthiest" state (the GDR) than in Ireland—the state then registering the highest levels of overall mortality in noncommunist Europe. By the criterion of age-standardized mortality, in fact, health conditions appeared to be better in any industrialized democracy on any continent than in any Warsaw Pact state.

Health conditions in the communist countries of Central and Eastern Europe also fared poorly in comparison with a growing number of developing countries. Table 9.5 contrasts age-standardized mortality rates for Warsaw Pact Europe around 1989 with an unweighted average for six Latin American countries in the late 1980s: Argentina, Chile, Costa Rica, Mexico, Uruguay, and Venezuela. Mortality levels were by then significantly higher in the former group of countries. On an un-weighted average, female death rates were over 10 percent higher; for males, the differential was over 20 percent. By the end of its communist era, in fact, not even the GDR could claim to have an age-standardized death rate as low as the average for these six Latin American popula-tions. Nor were these the only Latin American countries with health conditions superior to those of Warsaw Pact Europe. WHO judges fifteen territories in Latin America and the Caribbean to have sufficiently complete data to permit computation of their age-standardized mortality rates; by WHO's reckoning, overall mortality by this measure was lower than the Eastern European average in eleven of them, and lower than the GDR's in nine.

Even against the unexacting standard of Soviet performance, age-standardized mortality rates in communist Europe in the late 1980s do not look especially favorable. One must remember that the WHO "European Model" population, against which all death rates in Table 9.5 were standardized, is weighted toward adult working-age groups, and thus toward cohorts registering Eastern Europe's most severe health reversals. Nevertheless, by this particular criterion, overall health levels for certain groups—including females from Bulgaria and Romania, and Hungarians of both sexes—actually appear to have been worse than the Soviet Union's own on the eve of the revolutions of 1989.

The health situation in the European communist countries considered here, then, was characterized by both absolute and relative decline over the past generation. But while Soviet-bloc Europe suffered setbacks in health conditions between the mid-1960s and the late 1980s, this out-come was not the result of a single, unremitting trend. On the contrary: two quite different trends are in evidence during those years. From the mid-1960s through the mid-1980s—roughly from 1965 until 1985—overall rates of age-standardized mortality in these countries were gener-ally rising, with modest declines in female rates being more than offset by the increases for men. Between 1985 and 1989, however, there appears to have been something of a turnaround. After decades of worsening health conditions for men, age-standardized mortality for males suddenly started to improve. Progress in reducing female mortal-

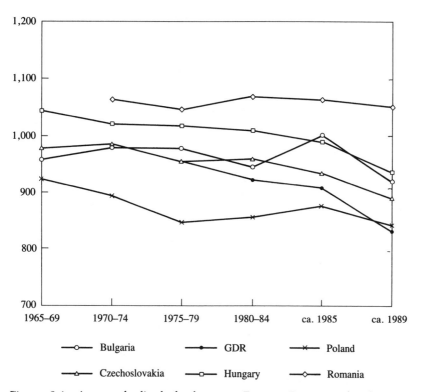

Figure 9.1. Age-standardized death rates, Eastern European females (per 100,000). Mortality rates are standardized against WHO "European Model" population; "ca. 1985" = 1986 (Poland) and 1984 (Romania); "ca. 1989" = 1988 (Romania). From *World Health Statistics Annual* (Geneva: WHO), various editions.

ity, for its part, appears to have accelerated in much of the region (Figures 9.1 and 9.2).

This resumption of broad mortality declines, however, was not enough to draw communist Europe's levels closer to those of non-communist Europe. During those same years, the latter countries were experiencing rapid improvements in mortality rates. Between 1985 and 1989, for example, overall age-standardized mortality fell by more than 11 percent in Austria; in Portugal it dropped by a full 12 percent. Though the region's rate of mortality decline was less rapid overall, it was nonetheless well ahead of that in the European communist states. Thus, even though the European communist countries managed to stabilize and reduce their death rates during the final years of communism,

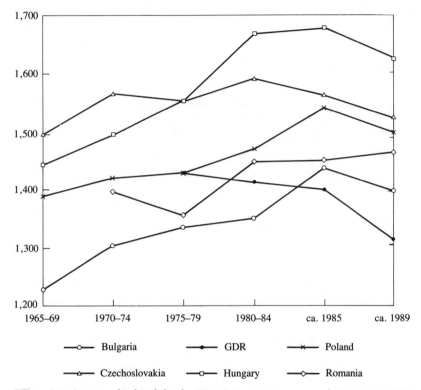

Figure 9.2. Age-standardized death rates, Eastern European males (per 100,000).
See Figure 9.1 for description and sources.

the gap between their health circumstances and those on the other side
of the Iron Curtain apparently continued to widen up to the very collapse of communism itself.

PROXIMATE CAUSES AND UNDERLYING INFLUENCES

How are the peculiar health patterns witnessed by Warsaw Pact Europe
over the past generation to be explained? We may begin by examining a
few hypotheses that do *not* adequately explain the phenomenon.

The first of these theories suggests that the region's rising death rates
were, in large measure, a statistical artifact: a function of improvements
in vital registration systems. This hypothesis can be rejected out of
hand. Death registration remains spotty for infants in several of these

countries—and egregiously incomplete in Romania[11]—but this is not the cohort whose death rates were reported to be on the rise. Throughout the region, by contrast, the mortality data for noninfants, and in particular for adults, seem to have been characterized by nearly universal coverage since at least the mid-1960s.

A second hypothesis argues that rising mortality rates in Central and Eastern Europe are indeed genuine, but that they may be due to factors preceding the communist interlude. By this theory, today's health problems are in large measure a delayed consequence of shocks and stresses suffered during World War II.[12] At first glance, such a "cohort effect" is certainly plausible; excess mortality appears to have been characteristic of certain cohorts of combatant populations that survived the two world wars.[13] But the hypothesis is of little use in explaining the most anomalous and disturbing features of the region's postwar health performance. As we saw in Table 9.3, death rates for Central and Eastern European men in their early forties were, on the whole, much higher around 1989 than around 1965. This is to say that mortality was higher for persons born *after* World War II than for earlier cohorts who lived through it. "Cohort effects," moreover, cannot explain why age-standardized mortality has risen over the past generation in most East European countries even as it was rapidly declining in (for example) Japan—a society that suffered severe wartime losses and endured enormous postwar privation. Nor can this hypothesis cast light on the divergent mortality trends in the GDR and the Federal Republic of Germany (FRG), territories that experienced World War II as a single nation (Table 9.6). Note that, as of 1989, GDR-FRG mortality differentials for younger men and women (ages 15 to 44) were quite similar to those of their older counterparts who had survived World War II (45 and older).

Hypotheses to the contrary notwithstanding, the health problems of the formerly communist countries of Central and Eastern Europe today are all too real; moreover, they appear to reflect the consequence of

[11]See Nicholas Eberstadt, "Health and Mortality in Eastern Europe, 1965–85," *Communist Economies* 2, no. 3 (1990): 349–50.

[12]For one exposition of this hypothesis, see R. H. Dinkel, "The Seeming Paradox of Increasing Infant Mortality in a Highly Industrialized Nation: The Example of the Soviet Union," *Population Studies* 39, no.1 (1985): 87–97.

[13]Shiro Horiuchi, "The Long Term Impact of War on Mortality: Old Age Mortality of the First World War Survivors in the Federal Republic of Germany," *Population Bulletin of the United Nations* 15 (1983): 80–92.

Table 9.6. *Age-specific death rates: GDR and FRG, 1989* *(deaths per 100,000)*

Age	Males			Females		
	GDR	FRG	Ratio (FRG = 100)	GDR	FRG	Ratio (FRG = 100)
0	889.6	845.1	105	618.6	638.8	97
1–4	42.5	43.3	98	38.5	34.3	112
5–14	28.2	21.5	131	15.1	14.6	103
15–24	100.7	87.7	115	42.2	34.6	122
25–34	142.4	113.4	126	63.3	50.2	126
35–44	288.5	214.2	135	129.6	118.7	109
45–54	744.0	571.5	130	353.2	286.0	123
55–64	1,845.2	1,495.3	123	917.2	696.5	132
65–74	4,396.4	3,601.1	122	2,561.7	1,828.5	140
75+	13,578.0	11,340.8	120	10,471.1	8,297.3	126

Source: World Health Organization, *World Health Statistics Annual 1990* (Geneva: WHO, 1991), 226, 228.

events and developments since the advent of communist rule, not just the aftershocks from World War II. But rejecting these hypotheses only begs the question of explanation. If these particular theories are inadequate to account for the region's prolonged health crisis, what factors are responsible for it?

One initial approach to the puzzle is offered by reported cause-of-death patterns for the region's various populations. Such data must be handled with appropriate care;[14] they are, after all, conditioned by an unavoidable element of subjectivity. Specialists have noted variations in diagnosis and coding practices for death certificates among countries in the European Community.[15] Similarly, in a recent experiment in the United States, roughly half of the certificates queried were, upon further investigation, amended with respect to cause of death.[16] We should not expect cause-of-death data from the formerly communist countries of Central and Eastern Europe to attain a higher standard of reliability than that evidenced in the Organization for Economic Cooperation and

[14]As is explained in Lado T. Ruzicka and Alan D. Lopez, "The Use of Cause-of-Death Statistics for Health Situation Assessment: National and International Experiences," *World Health Statistics Quarterly* 43, no. 2 (1990): 249–58.

[15]Zbigniew J. Brzezinski, "Mortality Indicators and Health-for-All Strategies in the WHO European Region," *World Health Statistics Quarterly* 39, no. 4 (1986): 365.

[16]Harry M. Rosenberg, "Improving Cause-of-Death Statistics," *American Journal of Public Health* 79, no. 5 (1989): 563–64.

Development countries—all the more because of the indications that these data were shaped by political considerations under at least some of these regimes.[17] Despite all these qualifications, cause-of-death data may nevertheless afford a view of the proximate causes of the region's health troubles, and by doing so, may be broadly suggestive of the underlying factors propelling large population groups toward reduced life expectation.

Intriguing indications and trends emerge from these data for a variety of reported causes of death: among them, cirrhosis and chronic liver disease (often associated with heavy drinking), lung cancer (heavy smoking), and accidents or injuries (a category defined to include both suicide and homicide). As evocative of broader conditions as such reported causes of death might be, they account for only a relatively minor share of total deaths. On an age-standardized basis, in fact, deaths ascribed to lung cancer, cirrhosis, and suicide accounted for about a tenth of overall male mortality and for less than a twenty-fifth of overall female mortality in Eastern Europe in the mid-1980s.[18] The region's recent mortality patterns and trends, rather, are dominated and indeed shaped by deaths attributed to cardiovascular disease (CVD)—afflictions of the heart and the circulatory system, including ischemic heart disease (heart attacks) and cerebrovascular disease (strokes).

The importance of CVD-attributed deaths in Central and Eastern Europe's health crisis can be seen in Table 9.7. In the late 1960s, according to WHO data, age-standardized mortality rates for deaths ascribed to CVD were quite similar in communist and noncommunist Europe. By around 1989, however, the communist European countries had CVD-ascribed mortality rates vastly higher than Western Europe's: in this particular comparison, over 75 percent higher for men and over 85 percent higher for women. Between 1965–69 and 1989, age-standardized CVD-ascribed mortality had fallen substantially in noncommunist Europe: on average, by about a fourth for men and by about a third for women. In contrast, the communist European countries were subject to an explosion of CVD-ascribed mortality. The region's men suffered an ostensible epidemic of these noncommunicable diseases; in Bulgaria, the increase during the period in question was placed at more than 50 percent. Nor were women spared; most of these countries reported long-term rises in female CVD as well. So severe was the

---

[17]Eberstadt, "Health and Mortality in Eastern Europe, 1965–85," 354.
[18]Derived from ibid., 356.

Table 9.7. *Age-standardized mortality attributed to cardiovascular disease (CVD): Selected Eastern and Western European countries, 1965–69 to ca. 1989 (deaths per 100,000)*

Country or group	1965–69	ca. 1989	Percent change
Bulgaria			
Males	531.3	808.8	+52.2
Females	512.7	595.2	+16.1
Czechoslovakia			
Males	682.4	787.6	+15.4
Females	505.8	507.9	+0.4
Hungary			
Males	747.0	785.7	+5.2
Females	603.0	506.3	−16.1
Poland			
Males	523.6	758.8	+44.9
Females	381.2	465.3	+22.1
Unweighted average			
Males	621.1	785.2	+26.4
Females	500.7	518.7	+3.6
Unweighted average, 18 Western European countries			
Males	601.9	447.0	−25.7
Females	425.7	279.2	−34.4
Ratio, selected Eastern European to Western European countries (Western Europe = 100)			
Males	101	176	
Females	118	186	

Notes: Mortality rates are standardized against the WHO "European Model" population. For Western Europe, see Table 9.4.
Sources: World Health Organization, *World Health Statistics Annual* (Geneva: WHO), 1988 edition (1989), Table 12; 1990 edition (1991), Table 10; 1991 edition (1992), Table 11.

apparent upsurge in cardiovascular mortality that by about 1989, age-standardized CVD-ascribed death rates were on average higher for *women* in the states of communist Europe than for *men* in noncommunist European countries.

Table 9.8 illustrates that the level of mortality attributed to cardiovascular disease by the Soviet bloc countries around 1989 was vastly higher than the rates prevalent in contemporary noncommunist Europe or in economically advanced regions of Latin America. Indeed, the absolute

Table 9.8. *Age-standardized mortality attributed to cardiovascular disease (CVD): Eastern Europe and selected other populations, ca. 1989 (deaths per 100,000)*

Population group or ratio	Male	Female	Total population
Unweighted average,			
Eastern Europe, ca. 1989	774.1	540.9	636.9
USSR 1988	830.9	583.7	672.5
Unweighted average,			
18 Western countries, ca. 1989	447.0	279.2	351.3
Unweighted average,			
6 selected Latin American			
countries, late 1980s	424.5	314.8	364.8
Ratio			
USSR: Eastern Europe	107	108	106
Eastern Europe: Western Europe	173	194	181
Eastern Europe: Latin America	182	172	175
Proportion of overall difference in			
age-standardized mortality			
accounted for by reported			
differences in CVD mortality;			
Eastern Europe vs.:			
Western Europe	76	93	82
Selected Latin American			
countries	135	251	178

Notes: Mortality rates are standardized against the WHO "European Model" population. For Western Europe, see Table 9.4; for Latin America, see Table 9.5.
Sources: World Health Organization, *World Health Statistics Annual* (Geneva: WHO), 1990 edition (1991), Table 10; 1991 edition (1992), Table 11.

level of CVD-ascribed mortality, appropriately standardized, within the Soviet bloc in the 1980s was historically unprecedented. These deaths were by 1989 the principal proximate determinant of overall differences in mortality between the countries of communist and noncommunist Europe. In the two regions, over three-fourths of the mortality differential for males, and over nine-tenths of that for females, were accounted for by differences in death rates attributed to CVD. The same pattern holds for more specific comparisons of countries from the two regions (Table 9.9). On the eve of German reunification, about seven-eighths of the total difference in death rates for males and females alike between the GDR and FRG could be accounted for by their reported differences in CVD mortality.[19]

[19]For a more detailed examination, see Charlotte Hoehn and John Pollard, "Mortality in the Two Germanies in 1986 and Trends 1976–1986," *European Journal of Population* 7, no. 1 (1991): 1–28.

Table 9.9. *Differences in age-standardized cause-of-death structures: GDR versus FRG, 1989 (deaths per 100,000)*

Causes of death	GDR 1989	FRG 1989	Ratio (FRG = 100)	Absolute as % of overall difference
All causes				
Male	1,313.7	1,075.5	122	100
Female	828.4	634.0	131	100
Infectious and parasitic diseases				
Male	5.4	7.8	69	−1
Female	3.3	4.9	67	−1
Malignant neoplasms				
Male	245.5	279.5	88	−14
Female	150.0	166.1	90	−8
Diseases of the circulatory system				
Male	689.1	483.6	142	86
Female	473.8	300.2	158	89
Diseases of the respiratory system				
Male	92.3	77.7	119	6
Female	34.4	28.9	119	3
Chronic liver diseases and cirrhosis				
Male	28.6	29.9	96	−1
Female	10.5	12.4	85	−1
Injury and poisoning				
Male	94.6	61.4	154	14
Female	41.7	27.3	153	7
—of which, suicide and self-inflicted injury				
Male	37.7	22.0	171	7
Female	13.3	8.2	162	3

Note: Mortality rates are standardized against the WHO "European Model" population.
Source: Derived from World Health Organization, *World Health Statistics Annual 1990* (Geneva: WHO, 1991), 380–81.

In proximate terms, it thus appears that the factor mainly responsible for today's gap in mortality levels between postcommunist and other European countries is deaths attributed to cardiovascular disease. CVD-ascribed mortality also appears to be the proximate factor most clearly associated with the region's increases in overall mortality levels over the past generation. (Conversely, the slight declines in overall mortality rates reported for the 1985–89 period are born of reported declines in CVD mortality.) It would seem, then, that the key to explaining the health crisis in postcommunist European countries lies in the distinctive and worrisome movements of the region's CVD-ascribed death rates.

There is much about cardiovascular disease that is poorly, or incompletely, understood at present.[20] Even the relationship between prevalence or severity of CVD and resultant mortality in industrialized countries is a matter of considerable uncertainty. Yet CVD is associated with a variety of identifiable and specific factors. Heavy smoking is one of them. Poor diet, lack of exercise, and obesity are others. Insofar as hypertension bears upon CVD, heavy drinking appears to play a role. And researchers now suspect that psychological stress or emotional strain may have an impact on CVD.[21]

Observers of the scene in the postcommunist countries of Central and Eastern Europe have commented widely on the extent to which these populations are today exposed to these diverse risk factors. Statistical sources strongly suggest that per capita consumption of cigarettes and hard spirits rose dramatically in Eastern Europe between the mid-1960s and the 1980s.[22] No parallel quantitative measure is available for gauging psychological stress or emotional strain, although contemporary literature from the region offers a view of the changing mood of the times. It is, at the very least, quite plausible that people in communist Central and Eastern Europe ran an increasing risk of CVD during their final generation under communism because of a variety of characteristic changes in personal behavior and life-style.

Yet in and of themselves, behavioral factors can only offer an incomplete explanation for changing patterns of health, disease, and death.

[20]Some of these uncertainties are outlined in G. Lamm, *The Cardiovascular Disease Programme of WHO in Europe: A Critical Review of the First 12 Years* (Copenhagen: WHO Regional Office in Europe, 1981).

[21]See, for example, U.S. Department of Health and Human Services, Public Health Service, *Health Consequences of Smoking: Cardiovascular Disease: A Report of the Surgeon General* (Washington, D.C.: U.S. Government Printing Office, 1983); Vaclav Smil, "Coronary Heart Disease, Diet, and Western Mortality," *Population and Development Review* 15, no. 3 (1989): 399–424; Erkki Vartianinen, Du Dianjun, and James S. Marks, "Mortality, Cardiovascular Risk Factors, and Diet in China, Finland, and the United States," *Public Health Reports* 105, no. 5 (1991): 41–46; U.S. Department of Health and Human Services, Public Health Service, *Seventh Report to the Congress on Alcohol and Health from the Secretary of Health and Human Services, January 1990* (Washington, D.C.: U.S. Government Printing Office, 1990); Richard J. Contrada, "Type A Behavior, Personality Hardiness, and Cardiovascular Responses to Stress," *Journal of Personality and Social Psychology* 59, no. 5 (1989): 895–903.

[22]Eberstadt, "Health and Mortality in Eastern Europe, 1965–85," 362–65.

After all, government health policies are framed and pursued on the premise that public interventions can stabilize and reduce overall mortality levels and even insulate the individual from the consequences of his or her own adverse actions. More generally, health and welfare policies undertaken by governments in the modern era are expected to protect vulnerable segments of society, even during times of economic dislocation or crisis.

In retrospect, it is clear that the last generation of "health strategies" and social welfare policies implemented by the communist governments of Central and Eastern Europe failed badly. In the view of its exponents and admirers, the Soviet-style health system—with its universal coverage, its extensive regimen of contacts between medical personnel and the population at large, and its provision that medical treatment costs be borne directly by the state—was a model for the enhancement of public health. Secular increases in national death rates throughout the Warsaw Pact countries speak to the contrary.

Yet they also speak more broadly to the performance of the regimes in question. Mortality conditions are affected by a constellation of social, economic, and environmental factors. Education, housing conditions, and pollution are but a few of the areas bearing on health in which modern governments routinely intervene. For centrally planned economies, where the state arrogates a more far-reaching authority over the social and economic rhythms of life, the correspondence between mortality trends and government performance is presumably all the more comprehensive and direct.

Despite the claims made on their behalf, the fact remains that the Warsaw Pact governments, during their last generation of existence, presided over an extraordinary and unique decline in the well-being of their subjects. Mortality patterns provide incontrovertible proof of this. Yet those same patterns raise questions about the health not only of the citizenry, but of the states that governed them. In the final analysis, the health crisis of the Eastern European peoples during their last generation of communism may be diagnosed as a crisis of the system under which they were living.

SOME IMPLICATIONS OF THE HEALTH CRISIS IN COMMUNIST EUROPE

That long-term increases in death rates are unwelcome should hardly require emphasis—by definition they signify a diminution of public health. They speak to real reductions in individual and social well-being. Moreover, their economic consequences are predictably adverse and wide-ranging. For the consumer, reductions in life expectancy will occasion unanticipated alteration of consumption patterns;[23] for producers it means a smaller and quite possibly more debilitated labor force. Because of the complementary nature of the various quantities together known as "human capital," rising death rates might be expected to have considerable indirect economic repercussions as well.

Not all the implications of Central and Eastern Europe's health crisis, however, concern the populations afflicted by it. These unpredicted, and still largely unexplained, patterns of health reversal also speak directly to the state of our knowledge about, and understanding of, this group of countries during its final generation under communist rule.

The notion that an industrialized society under a stable administrative system and at a time of peace should experience prolonged deteriorations in public health was, to put it mildly, inconsistent with the expectations of outside observers. Yet an entire grouping of such societies, bound together by a tight and far-reaching alliance, was characterized by exactly these sorts of health setbacks. The perverse health trends witnessed throughout the region, indeed, were not only distinctive, but by almost any reading fundamental in their significance. Taken together, these simple but basic facts would seem to frame a compelling case: namely, that conventional Western assessments of Soviet bloc states seriously missed the mark in important respects for at least a generation before their collapse.

What sorts of judgments do the region's health trends suggest? One general tendency surely concerns economic performance. In and of themselves, for example, mortality trends in the region would seem consistent with the proposition that outside studies, with very few exceptions, seriously overestimated levels of per capita output, per capita consumption, and rates of per capita growth of the countries in question during their last generation under communism.

Take the case of the GDR. In 1988, the Central Intelligence Agency's *Handbook of Economic Statistics* placed the GDR's 1987 per capita gross national product (GNP) (in current U.S. dollars) at $12,330—a level almost identical with its estimate for per capita GNP within the

---

[23]Dan Usher, "An Imputation of the Value of Improved Life Expectancy," in Milton Moss, ed., *The Measurement of Social Life and Economic Performance* (Cambridge, Mass.: NBR, 1977), 192–226.

European Community ($12,340).[24] Yet around 1989, age-standardized mortality for men was about 26 percent higher in the GDR than the FRG; for females the difference was about 32 percent. The relationship between mortality levels and productivity levels is admittedly neither tight nor mechanistic. Yet the discrepancy between estimated levels of productivity and actual levels of mortality is glaring and would seem to require explanation. In the absence of a plausible explanation, one is drawn to the conclusion that the GDR's per capita output was dramatically overstated.

Similar questions arise with respect to consumption levels. As we saw in Table 9.5, mortality levels in the communist countries of Central and Eastern Europe around 1989 were typically higher than those recorded in Latin America's more materially advanced societies in the late 1980s. Yet conventional Western estimates at the time indicated that per capita consumption was far higher in the region than in those Latin American societies. Is it possible that levels of per capita consumption could have been far higher in the group of countries whose mortality levels were substantially the worse? In theory, yes; but the juxtaposition is peculiar and requires explanation. In the absence of a convincing explanation, one is drawn to the conclusion that levels of per capita consumption in communist Europe in the late 1980s were not so different from those in various Latin American societies at the time.

Outside estimates of economic growth in Warsaw Pact Europe are subject to parallel questions. As Table 9.10 indicates, official U.S. estimates of per capita growth between 1966 and 1989 were roughly similar for a number of communist and noncommunist European countries. Yet whereas all the noncommunist countries could point to declines in male mortality over those years, the Central and East European communist countries reported increases. In Eastern Europe, as in noncommunist Europe, men made up the bulk of the workforce during this period, and men accounted for the great majority of hours worked in any given year. Could such radically different trends in male mortality be consistent with similar tempos of long-term economic growth? If so, the explanation that would reconcile these contrasting patterns is not immediately evident.

If health trends in Central and Eastern Europe during the period of

---

[24]U.S. Central Intelligence Agency, *Handbook of Economic Statistics 1988* (Washington, D.C.: CIA, 1988), 24–25.

Table 9.10. *CIA estimates of changes in per capita GNP versus WHO estimates of changes in age-standardized male mortality: Selected Warsaw Pact and Western European countries, ca. 1965–89*

Country	Estimated changes in per capita GNP, 1966 to 1989 (percent)	Estimated changes in age-standardized male mortality, 1965–69 to 1989 (percent)
Bulgaria	+61.2	+13.4
Czechoslovakia	+62.7	+1.8
Hungary	+57.3	+12.5
Poland	+62.3	+7.9
Unweighted average	+60.9	+8.9
Netherlands	+63.4	−11.5
Sweden[a]	+61.1	−13.3
Switzerland	+51.6	−27.1
United Kingdom	+63.0	−25.1
Unweighted average	+59.8	−19.4

Note: Mortality rates are standardized against the WHO "European Model" population.
[a] 1988.
Sources: Derived from U.S. Central Intelligence Agency, *Handbook of Economic Statistics* (Washington, D.C.: CIA), 1980 edition, 29; 1990 edition, 44; World Health Organization, *World Health Statistics Annual* (Geneva: WHO), 1988 edition (1989), Table 12; 1990 edition (1991), Table 10; 1991 edition (1992), Table 11.

communist rule appear to argue implicitly for a reassessment of the region's economic performance, they would also seem to merit examination from a political perspective. A striking political coincidence is now evident in communist and formerly communist states. As of 1992, the world's only remaining Marxist-Leninist governments—China, Cuba, North Korea, and North Vietnam—could all claim to have presided over long-term mortality improvements for the populations under their supervision. By contrast, the governments of the Warsaw Pact, all of which collapsed between 1989 and 1991, had each witnessed secular deteriorations in public health conditions over the previous generation.

Is this cleavage an entirely random outcome? Probably not. It would be unwise to overemphasize the role of demographic trends in political developments, yet demographic trends may at times serve as political indicators. The Warsaw Pact countries' long-standing inability to effect mortality decline was arguably a fact of considerable political significance. It bespoke many things, one of which was regime fragility. With the benefit of hindsight, it may be easier now to appreciate just how fragile those regimes were in the years preceding their demise.

HEALTH PROSPECTS AND THE TRANSITION TOWARD A MARKET ORDER

With the collapse of Warsaw Pact communism, the populations of the region are free to experiment with new political and economic arrangements, to embrace new policies, and to identify new social objectives. Although individuals and organized groups will surely differ on the particulars of many postcommunist programs and proposals, the need to improve national health conditions is an objective that is likely to be universally endorsed.

As citizens and officials contemplate health prospects in the new Central and Eastern Europe, they are confronted by two basic questions. First: How heavily are the perverse health patterns from the old communist era impressed upon the region's contemporary populations? Second: Will the economic and social transformations now under way jeopardize the quest for health progress?

That the postcommunist governments of the region must overcome health problems bequeathed to them by the regimes they have replaced is clear enough. Unfortunately, this social legacy of communism looks more troubling as it is examined more closely. Not only are mortality levels throughout the area strangely high, but the pattern of illness and disease they reflect is one that may prove unexpectedly resistant to public health policy interventions.

The formidable challenges posed by the region's health problems are outlined by a simple comparison with materially advanced areas of Latin America. Poland (1989) and Argentina (1987) are presented in Tables 9.11 and 9.12 to frame the contrast, although other combinations could do so just as well. On the whole, mortality in Poland is slightly higher for females than in Argentina and is significantly higher for males. Differentials are greatest for the population conventionally considered to be of working age. Economically inauspicious as higher general levels of mortality may appear, the incidence of Poland's "excess mortality" in relation to Argentina would seem all the more disadvantageous.

Despite Poland's generally higher levels of mortality, Poland does not register higher death rates than Argentina does for all reported categories of deaths. If cause-of-death statistics can be trusted, for example,

Table 9.11. *Ratio of age-specific death rates: Poland 1989 versus Argentina 1987 (Argentina = 100)*

Age group (years)	Male	Female
0	61	59
1–4	67	66
5–14	83	83
15–24	112	63
25–34	147	68
35–44	135	81
45–54	138	103
55–64	127	118
65–74	118	119
75+	110	103
Age-standardized mortality rate, WHO "European Model"	116	100

Source: Derived from World Health Organization, *World Health Statistics Annual* (Geneva: WHO), 1990 edition (1991), 282; 1991 edition (1992), 92.

Poland compares quite favorably with Argentina in its fatalities from certain types of disease, especially those classified as infectious and parasitic. On the other hand, mortality levels ascribed to cancer and cardiovascular diseases are vastly higher in Poland than Argentina.

Taken as a category, infectious and parasitic diseases tend to be amenable to immediate control through discrete, and often relatively inexpensive, public health interventions. Cancer and CVDs, on the other hand, are noncommunicable conditions that tend to be chronic in nature and to reflect physical insults and abuses that have accumulated over the course of a lifetime. Under the best of circumstances, a new regimen of medical and public health policies might be expected to make fewer immediate inroads against cancer and CVD than against infectious and parasitic diseases.

The best of circumstances, moreover, do not obtain in contemporary Poland. In a country at Poland's level of economic attainment, health-care costs must be a consideration in policy, and chronic diseases are especially expensive to treat. (Benefits to health may be expected from less expensive preventative measures, but their impact tends to be greatest in the longer run.) The intrinsic financial problems presented to these postcommunist societies by their disease profiles are exacerbated further by the population structure now characteristic in Eastern Europe. A

Table 9.12. *Differences in age-standardized cause-of-death structures: Poland 1989 versus Argentina 1987 (deaths per 100,000)*

Causes of death	Poland 1989	Argentina 1987	Ratio (age = 100)
All causes			
Male	1,498.0	1,291.7	116
Female	838.5	834.6	100
Infectious and parasitic diseases			
Male	14.2	38.6	37
Female	5.3	26.7	20
Malignant neoplasms			
Male	291.2	232.7	125
Female	154.1	144.7	106
Diseases of the circulatory system			
Male	758.8	603.5	126
Female	465.3	419.7	111
Diseases of the respiratory system			
Male	81.1	95.3	85
Female	28.2	50.7	57
Diseases of the digestive system			
Male	46.9	67.7	69
Female	26.0	36.7	71
Chronic liver disease and cirrhosis			
Male	17.4	22.7	72
Female	6.9	6.4	108
Injury and poisoning			
Male	122.4	86.6	138
Female	34.9	32.5	107
Suicide and self-inflicted injury			
Male	20.9	13.4	156
Female	3.8	4.1	93

Note: Mortality rates are standardized against the WHO "European Model" population.
Source: Derived from World Health Organization, *World Health Statistics Annual 1990* (Geneva: WHO, 1991), Table 11.

generation of fertility near or below the net replacement level has made for populations composed disproportionately of elderly and middle-aged adults—groups most likely to be at risk from cancer and CVD.

The constraints on public health policies for postcommunist Central and Eastern Europe are formidable, but hardly insuperable. To the

Table 9.13. *Age-standardized mortality in Eastern Europe, 1989–90 (deaths per 100,000)*

	Year		Percent change
Country and sex	1989	1990	
Bulgaria			
Males	1,396.6	1,397.3	+0.1
Females	917.8	913.5	−0.5
Czechoslovakia			
Males	1,522.8	1,552.1	+1.9
Females	888.4	874.1	−1.6
Hungary			
Males	1,624.9	1,670.6	+2.9
Females	933.4	955.0	+2.3
Poland			
Males	1,498.0	1,670.6	+1.2
Females	838.5	833.0	−0.7

Note: Mortality rates are standardized against the WHO "European model" population.
Sources: World Health Organization, *World Health Statistics Annual* (Geneva: WHO), 1990 edition (1991), Table 10; 1991 edition (1992), Table 11.

contrary: properly framed and implemented policies, pursued on realistic budgets, should be capable of eliciting steady improvements in general health conditions throughout the region. Indeed, even under the highly questionable public health policies of the region's *anciens régimes,* some general if belated improvements in public health conditions were registered during the second half of the 1980s.

Initial readings from the postcommunist Central and Eastern European countries, however, suggest that the region's health policies have not been adequate to the task of controlling and reducing mortality during the first steps toward a market order. As Table 9.13 details, male mortality rose between 1989 and 1990 in Bulgaria, Czechoslovakia, Hungary, and Poland; in Hungary female mortality rose as well. One may appreciate the potential health stresses attendant upon the revolutions of 1989 without presuming that great economic and social dislocations necessarily result in rising mortality rates. In Latin America and the Caribbean, for example, there is to date no evidence that the widely cited shocks of the debt crisis and "adjustment policies" of the 1980s

Table 9.14. *Reported changes in age-specific death rates in the GDR, 1989–90 (percent)*

	0	1–4	5–9	10–14	15–19	20–24	25–29	30–34	35–39	40–44
Male	−2	+48	+11	+68	+44	+37	+26	+24	+24	+4
Female	−6	+23	+62	+117	+19	+12	+24	−3	+17	+4

	45–49	50–54	55–59	60–64	65–69	70–74	75–79	80–84	85+
Male	+37	+8	+3	0	+4	−15	+16	+5	+2
Female	+18	0	+1	+5	+2	−18	+10	−8	−2

Sources: FRG Federal Statistical Office, *Statistisches Jahrbuch 1991 für das Vereinte Deutschland* (Wiesbaden: Metzler Poeschel Verlag, 1991), 87; unpublished data, Statistisches Bundesamt.

brought about pervasive increases in mortality, even in the most severely affected countries.[25]

More ominous than the upticks in mortality evidenced in the four aforementioned countries are the initial changes registered in the GDR. The East German situation, after all, may be seen as constituting something like the best of all possible postcommunist transitions. With unification, East Germany was subsumed into a stable political order and a highly developed social market economy. Moreover, the German government has been underwriting the unification process with subsidies on a scale unlikely to be repeated in any other postcommunist region. Despite these promising forensics, pervasive increases in death rates for male and female cohorts alike were reported between 1989 and 1990 (Table 9.14).

The general deterioration of health conditions in formerly communist Europe in the immediate aftermath of the 1989 revolutions has widened still further the mortality gap that separates these countries from other European countries. Even if one were to posit an immediate resumption, and acceleration, of mortality declines, it would be many years before these countries could hope to achieve levels characteristic of the rest of contemporary Europe. On the extremely optimistic assumption of a continuing 2 percent per annum decline in age-standardized mortality—a pace to date maintained over time in only a few countries—it would

[25]See, for instance, Kenneth Hill and Anne R. Pebley, "Child Mortality in the Developing World," *Population and Development Review* 15, no. 4 (1990): 657–87.

take more than twelve years for mortality levels in East Germany to reach those registered today in West Germany, and well over twenty years for Hungary's to reach the current average for Western Europe as a whole.

That proposed trajectory, it should be emphasized, is optimistic. It may actually take considerably longer for the postcommunist Eastern European countries to attain the levels of public health evident in the rest of Europe. Thus, like the communist interlude itself, the postcommunist recovery from this aspect of the region's legacy promises to be a historic process.

Part III

Social cleavages

10

Communism's legacy and Russian youth

RICHARD B. DOBSON

Decades of communist rule have left a complex legacy in the former Soviet Union, ranging from unresolved ethnic conflicts and inefficient industrial dinosaurs to acute problems of health care, environmental pollution, and crime. Yet, as James Millar and Sharon Wolchik point out in the first chapter of this volume, it is difficult at present to distinguish between the enduring heritage of communism and the phenomena engendered by its collapse.

This essay focuses on communism's social-psychological legacy—specifically, the extent to which young Russians accept or reject values and beliefs that the communist regime sought to inculcate. I concentrate primarily on Russians who were born between 1960 and 1975 and were between the ages of fifteen and thirty in 1990. This generation had no experience of the October Revolution, collectivization, the Stalinist purges, the Great Patriotic War, or the postwar reconstruction. Indeed, its members were too young to experience the thaw under Nikita Khrushchev or the Soviet-led crushing of the Prague Spring in August 1968. This is a generation molded by more recent events: a succession of infirm communist leaders (Leonid Brezhnev, Yuri Andropov, and Konstantin Chernenko) during the "period of stagnation," the bloody and demoralizing war in Afghanistan (1979–89), and the daring but inconsistent reforms initiated by Mikhail Gorbachev. Whether, and to what degree, these young Russians retain values and beliefs from the communist era is likely to have a significant impact on the shape the new postcommunist society assumes.

Under communist rule, immense energy and resources were devoted to political and civic socialization. The Communist party disseminated

The views expressed in this essay are those of the author—not necessarily those of the U.S. Information Agency or the U.S. Government.

its political messages through the state-controlled media, while placing restrictions on all organizations and socializing agencies, such as churches, that might instill values at variance with the party creed. Communist doctrine permeated the school curriculum, and boys and girls were encouraged to join the official youth groups (the Octobrists, Young Pioneers, and Komsomol). "Communist upbringing" emphasized loyalty to party and state, Soviet patriotism, Marxism-Leninism, and scientific atheism. Success within the system was geared to adherence to the party's norms.[1]

Yet communist ideological indoctrination was never fully successful, and as I shall show, other social forces tended to undercut its effectiveness. These included broad patterns of change, such as urbanization, industrialization, rising levels of education, and increased exposure to the mass media, which produced a society that was more differentiated and less amenable to totalitarian control. It is ironic, as Millar and Wolchik noted earlier, that the communist regime's success in modernizing Soviet society promoted attitudes and values that tended to undermine its foundations.

GENERATIONAL DIFFERENCES IN SUPPORT
FOR COMMUNIST INSTITUTIONS

To understand communism's legacy, it is instructive to review past research on generational differences in attitudes toward Soviet institutions. Results of the Harvard Project on the Soviet Social System, based on interviews with displaced persons following World War II, showed that Russian families underwent a significant transformation in the first two decades of communist rule. In raising their children, parents tended to instill values that would facilitate their children's success within the system, such as achievement and self-expression, while placing less stress on the traditional values of religion, respect for custom, and family heritage.[2] Alex Inkeles and Raymond Bauer pointed out that this value

---

[1] See, for example, Allen Kassof, *The Soviet Youth Program* (Cambridge, Mass.: Harvard University Press, 1967); David Powell, *Antireligious Propaganda in the Soviet Union: A Study of Mass Persuasion* (Cambridge, Mass.: MIT Press, 1975); and Stephen White, "The Effectiveness of Political Propaganda in the USSR," in Erik P. Hoffmann and Robbin F. Laird, eds., *The Soviet Polity in the Modern Era* (New York: Aldine, 1984), 663–90.

[2] Alex Inkeles and Raymond A. Bauer, *The Soviet Citizen: Daily Life in a Totalitarian Society* (Cambridge, Mass.: Harvard University Press, 1961), 210–30. See also Alice S. Rossi, "Generational Differences in the Soviet Union," Ph.D. diss., Columbia University, 1957.

shift appeared to result less from "the direct impact of the conscious family policy of the regime" than from "the other social processes which it initiated—such as mass education and communication, occupational mobility, and employment for women."[3]

The results of the Harvard Project revealed fairly broad acceptance of key features of the social and economic system created by the regime. There was nearly universal support for state-provided education and medical care. Over 80 percent of the displaced Soviet citizens surveyed approved of state employment guarantees and state ownership of heavy industry. In contrast, only a third approved of state ownership of light industry, and even fewer favored collectivized agriculture. Significantly, acceptance of state ownership and planning, state welfare policies, and the regime itself was *stronger* in the younger cohorts, whose members had been born under the Soviet regime, than in the older cohorts.[4]

In subsequent years, various observers called attention to what appeared to be significant changes in Russians' attitudes. In an illuminating essay entitled "The 'New Soviet Man' Turns Pessimist," for example, John Bushnell assessed changes in the outlook of the Soviet urban middle class between the 1950s and 1970s. Drawing on memoirs, press accounts, a smattering of public opinion polls, and his own observations, Bushnell detected growing pessimism among members of the urban middle class. He attributed this increasing pessimism to faltering Soviet economic performance, buttressed by a growing awareness of how much Soviet living standards lagged behind those in other countries.[5] Meanwhile, other sources pointed to rising disaffection among university students, especially after the crushing of the Prague Spring in August 1968.[6]

In the 1980s, the Soviet Interview Project (SIP)—a survey of more than 2,700 émigrés who had left the Soviet Union in the late 1970s—examined attitudes on a wide range of issues. Like the Harvard Project, it found broad public support for state-provided health care, free educa-

---

[3]Inkeles and Bauer, *The Soviet Citizen*, 228.

[4]Rossi, "Generational Differences," 288–89, 294–300; and Inkeles and Bauer, *The Soviet Citizen*, 132–35, 236–38, 242–46, 253–54, 273–74.

[5]John Bushnell, "The 'New Soviet Man' Turns Pessimist," in Stephen F. Cohen, Alexander Rabinowitch, and Robert Sharlet, eds., *The Soviet Union since Stalin* (Bloomington: Indiana University Press, 1980), 179–99.

[6]See, for example, V. T. Lisovskii and A. V. Dmitriev, *Lichnost' studenta* (Leningrad: Leningrad State University Press, 1974), 100–109; and Michael Swafford, "Political Attitudes and Behavior among Soviet University Students," Research Report R-17-79, Office of Research, U.S. International Communications Agency, 20 July 1979.

232   RICHARD B. DOBSON

tion, and state ownership of heavy industry, but little support for state or collective farms.[7] The SIP research, however, revealed generational variations that differed markedly from those in the Harvard Project. Brian Silver found support for "regime norms," such as state ownership and bans on strikes, to be *weaker* among members of the "post-Stalin generation" (born between 1946 and 1960) and persons with higher education than among the older and less-educated segments of the population. Conversely, the post-Stalin generation and the highly educated tended to be *more supportive* of private enterprise and individuals' rights.[8] Although these findings referred to the cohort born between 1946 and 1960, there is reason to believe that the tendencies not only continued but intensified among those born between 1960 and 1975.

FACTORS PROMOTING ATTITUDINAL CHANGE

Let us now look more closely at the changes in Russian society that tended to increase individuals' autonomy and to weaken the regime's ability to instill commitment to communist norms.

Modernization. This broad social process has many facets, including increased urbanization, a shift from agriculture to industry and the service sector, and rising levels of education and media use. Between the 1930s and the 1960s, towns replaced villages as the setting in which most Russians grew up. Meanwhile, educational requirements rose markedly. By the late 1970s, following a decade of rapid educational expansion, the great majority of girls and boys were completing a full, ten-year secondary education. Better educated and predominantly urban, adolescents and young adults enjoyed a higher standard of living and more leisure time than previous generations had. They also tended to have higher expectations for personal success, work satisfaction, and material well-being.

Declining economic growth rates. While young people's demands were rising, the Soviet economy's ability to satisfy them was not increasing at

---

[7] Brian D. Silver, "Political Beliefs of the Soviet Citizen: Sources of Support for Regime Norms," in James E. Millar, ed., *Politics, Work, and Daily Life in the USSR: A Survey of Former Soviet Citizens* (Cambridge: Cambridge University Press, 1987), 109–14.

[8] As Silver pointed out, the two variables, age and education, had independent effects: thus regime norms were rejected most often by members of the post-Stalin generation who had completed higher education. Silver, "Political Beliefs of the Soviet Citizen," 114–22. See also Donna Bahry, "Politics, Generations, and Change in the USSR," in Millar, *Politics, Work, and Daily Life,* 61–99.

a commensurate rate. Rates of growth declined from the mid-1970s, and the communist leadership found it increasingly difficult to deliver food and goods to consumers, to support welfare programs, and to maintain a high level of defense spending.[9] Although the Communist party program adopted under Khrushchev in 1961 claimed that the Soviet Union would overtake and surpass the United States on key economic indices by 1980, the Soviet Union not only continued to lag behind but even lost ground to the United States in areas of advanced technology, such as computers. Shortages became more common as Soviet citizens' incomes increasingly exceeded the supply of available goods. The economic slowdown no doubt increased disillusionment and dissatisfaction, especially among the young, and foreshadowed a crisis for the system.[10]

Peace and the absence of terror. Until the Soviet Union sent its armed forces to fight in Afghanistan in 1979, Russian boys and girls had lived in a time of peace and domestic stability unlike that experienced by older cohorts. Memories of the Great Patriotic War lost their intensity for those born decades after hostilities had ended, and memories of Stalinist terror also became less compelling. Reflecting on the independence displayed by young people in the 1980s, Iurii Shchekochikhin observed: "A new generation, devoid of social fear, had stepped into life. The nightmare of Stalin's terror was not in their genes because they were the first generation in our country whose innocent fathers had not been arrested."[11] For many in this generation, the war in Afghanistan was further proof of the system's rottenness.

Increased travel and communication. Young Russians learned more about the outside world than their parents had. As the ownership of

[9] See, for example, Daniel L. Bond and Herbert S. Levine, "The Soviet Domestic Economy in the 1980s," in Helmut Sonnenfeld, ed., *Soviet Politics in the 1980s* (Boulder, Colo.: Westview Press, 1985), 67–84; Myron Rush, "Impact and Implications of Soviet Defense Spending," in ibid., 131–45; Stephen White, *Gorbachev and After* (Cambridge: Cambridge University Press, 1991), 98–103; and Anders Aslund, *Gorbachev's Struggle for Economic Reform,* expanded ed. (Ithaca: Cornell University Press, 1991), 16–18. Official Soviet figures overstated the amount of economic growth that had occurred. See, for example, Vasilii Seliunin and Grigorii I. Khanin, "Lukavaia tsifra," *Novyi mir* 1987, no. 2: 181–201.

[10] The economist Myron Rush noted before Gorbachev came to power: "If Soviet policies continue on their present course, the USSR seems headed for a crisis in the next decade. What it faces is not a purely economic crisis, but an *economic-political crisis* brought on by the failure of the economy to provide the resources required to sustain at once the welfare state and the Soviet empire in its competition with the West." Rush, "Impact and Implications," 140.

[11] Iurii Shchekochikhin, Foreword, in Nancy Traver, *Kife: The Lives and Dreams of Soviet Youth* (New York: St. Martin's Press, 1989), x.

shortwave radio receivers spread in the 1960s and 1970s, many more young people could (despite periodic jamming) tune in Western radio broadcasts. These broadcasts, more frequent contracts with foreigners, and trips abroad exposed them to Western clothes, music, and life-styles and gave them an intimation of more prosperous, freer lands beyond their borders. Increasingly, the West became a reference point by which young Russians judged their own society. Jeans, rock music tapes, and other goods carrying the West's cachet were coveted and avidly traded on the black market.[12]

Greater international insistence on human rights. Championed by Andrei Sakharov, Aleksandr Solzhenitsyn, and other critics, notions of human rights, the rule of law, and individual freedom spread slowly and unevenly through Russian society. The Soviet Union's 1975 signing in Helsinki of the Final Act of the Conference on Security and Cooperation in Europe (CSCE) contributed to this process. Some Soviet citizens could, and did, demand that their government comply with the human rights provisions of the Helsinki Final Act. Working through the CSCE process, Western governments brought Soviet human rights violations before the court of world opinion and lent moral support to rights activists in the Soviet Union. Western radio broadcasts and samizdat, which relayed information about the regime's human rights abuses to the Russian people, probably had the greatest receptivity among the urban intelligentsia.

The rise of youth subcultures. All of these developments, combined with the example of youth subcultures abroad (a phenomenon most pronounced in the 1960s and early 1970s), contributed to the emergence of distinctive youth subcultures and "informal groups" in Russian cities in the 1980s. Although most nonofficial youth groups were apolitical, they often acquired a political coloring because of the regime's demands for conformity. The proliferation of groups, like the appearance of the

[12]Soviet sociological studies found that young people, especially those who obtained information from foreign sources (e.g., shortwave radio broadcasts, magazines, and films), tended to "evaluate certain elements of life in capitalist countries more highly" than others did. A. A. Voz'mitel', "Nekotorye voprosy differentsirovannogo podkhoda," in A. S. Loginova, comp., *Obshchestvennoe mnenie i lektsionnaia propaganda: Teoriia, metodika, opyt* (Moscow: Znanie, 1986), 88. See also Oleg Manaev, "The Influence of Western Radio on the Democratization of Soviet Youth," in Marsha Seifert, ed., *Mass Culture and Perestroika in the Soviet Union* (New York: Oxford University Press, 1991), 72–91.

dissident movement in the sixties and seventies, pointed to the emergence of a civil society, however embryonic, that was somewhat independent of the regime.[13]

Rock music, though reviled by the authorities, gained a broad following among the young. Between the 1960s and the 1980s, as in much of communist Central and Eastern Europe, rock music acquired the character not only of a generational marker separating the young from the old, but also of a banner of opposition to what was seen as a stultifying and hypocritical system.[14]

THE EFFECT OF THE GORBACHEV REFORMS

The social changes outlined in the previous section, which were well under way before Gorbachev came to power, provided impetus for his reforms.[15] There was surely a growing awareness in the upper echelons of the party not only that the economy was performing poorly, but also that communist ideology had lost its meaning for much of the population. As Robert C. Tucker observed in 1981:

Every society has its real existence in the minds of its members, their sense of constituting together an association with historical significance, of common

[13]On Soviet youth subcultures and informal groups, see Iu. P. Shchekochikhin, "Po kom zvonit kolokol'chik," *Sotsiologicheskie issledovaniia* 1987, no. 1: 81–93; Jim Riordan, ed., *Soviet Youth Culture* (Bloomington: Indiana University Press, 1989); John Bushnell, *Moscow Graffiti: Language and Subculture* (Winchester, Mass.: Unwin Hyman, 1990); and Richard B. Dobson, "Youth Problems in the Soviet Union," in Anthony Jones, Walter D. Connor, and David E. Powell, eds., *Soviet Social Problems* (Boulder, Colo.: Westview Press, 1991), 227–51.

[14]On the spread of rock music, see Pedro [Sabrina Petra] Ramet and Sergei Zamascikov, "The Soviet Rock Scene," Occasional Paper No. 223, Kennan Institute for Advanced Russian Studies, The Wilson Center, Washington, D.C., 1987; Artemy Troitsky, *Back in the USSR: The True Story of Rock in Russia* (Boston: Faber and Faber, 1988); Paul Easton, "The Rock Music Community," in Riordan, *Soviet Youth Culture*, 45–82; Timothy W. Ryback, *Rock around the Bloc: A History of Rock Music in Eastern Europe and the Soviet Union* (New York: Oxford University Press, 1990); and Sabrina Petra Ramet, ed., *Rocking the State: Rock Music and Politics in Eastern Europe and Russia* (Boulder, Colo.: Westview Press, 1944).

[15]Various scholars have sought to explain efforts to reform or transform the Soviet system in terms of the social forces resulting from modernization, especially urbanization, rising levels of education, and the growth of the professional classes. See, for example, Moshe Lewin, *The Gorbachev Phenomenon: A Historical Interpretation*, expanded ed. (Berkeley: University of California Press, 1991); Blair A. Ruble, "The Social Dimensions of Perestroika," in Ed A. Hewett and Victor H. Winston, eds., *Milestones in Glasnost and Perestroika* (Washington, D.C.: Brookings Institution, 1991), 91–103; and Gail W. Lapidus, "State and Society: Toward the Emergence of Civil Society in the Soviet Union," in Seweryn Bialer, ed., *Politics, Society, and Nationality Inside Gorbachev's Russia* (Boulder, Colo.: Westview Press, 1989), 121–47.

participation in a worthwhile collective enterprise. This is what the society's sustaining myth signifies. In the Soviet case . . . the myth no longer sustains more than a small minority, if that. People en masse have stopped believing in the transcendent importance of a future collective condition called "communism." They have stopped believing in the likelihood of the society arriving at that condition and the desirability of trying to achieve it through the leading role of the Communist Party or through themselves as "builders of communism." . . . In a society with an official culture founded on just those beliefs, this spells a deep crisis.[16]

Glasnost and perestroika were designed to reduce repressive bureaucratic controls, spur individual initiative, stimulate economic growth, and reinvigorate the political system. Subjects that had been taboo were now openly debated in the newspapers, on television screens, and in public parks. Suppressed facts about communism's history were brought to light, much like the actual physical remains of victims of Stalinist terror disinterred from mass graves.[17] As glasnost continued to expand, however, public debate acquired a momentum of its own; the authorities could not channel it or turn it off at will.

Popular culture, particularly films, publicized the emerging youth subcultures and the implicit challenge they posed to established standards. For example, Juris Podnieks's film *Is It Easy to Be Young?* provided a jarring view of punks, heavy metal fans, drug addicts, Hare Krishna devotees, and disillusioned veterans home from Afghanistan. The film, which won first prize at the 1987 Tbilisi film festival, sparked heated debate over young people's values and life-styles. Other films of the late 1980s, such as *Dear Elena Sergeevna, Little Vera,* and *The Body,* also portrayed ruthless, troubled, and disoriented young Russians who viewed communist ideology with indifference or derision.

Communist hard-liners found the appearance of unofficial youth groups disturbing, to say the least. They viewed them not only as signs of spreading bourgeois decadence and of laxity in communist control but also as a threat to Soviet rule. As Iurii Solov'ev, who then headed the Leningrad Province Communist Party Organization, said in 1988, "Aping Western 'mass culture' is not exactly innocuous. It is a kind of

---

[16]Robert C. Tucker, "Swollen State, Spent Society: Stalin's Legacy to Brezhnev's Russia," reprinted in Hoffmann and Laird, *The Soviet Polity in the Modern Era,* 62.

[17]In 1988–89 a spate of articles in the Soviet press described the discovery of mass graves and the circumstances surrounding the execution of civilians under Stalin. Kuropaty, a mass grave near Minsk, was one of the most notorious.

time bomb planted under our ideology and morals. Underestimation of such phenomena sometimes leads to the most serious consequences."[18]

The erosion of authority and credibility took its toll on the Komsomol, undercutting its ability to instill Marxist-Leninist values and to foster loyalty to the Communist party. Soviet surveys in this period found that growing numbers of young people were turning away from political education classes and rejecting key elements of the official ideology.[19] According to results of one survey, half the young people polled said they saw no need to evaluate works of literature, art, and music from a "class position" (that is, to evaluate them according to whether they expressed and served the interests of the working class and other "progressive" social forces or of "reactionary" classes).[20] Other surveys revealed "a yawning chasm of pessimism, lack of participation, and skepticism" among Komsomol members.[21]

THE DISINTEGRATION OF THE COMMUNIST WORLDVIEW

In 1988, the head of the Komsomol, Viktor Mironenko, made a telling observation about efforts at political indoctrination:

Unfortunately, dialogue between party and Komsomol workers, teachers, and veterans, on the one hand, and young people, on the other, has often resembled a conversation between the deaf and the mute. The world outlook shaped in this way is *very fragile and disintegrates at its first encounter with real life or the complexity of the historical path covered by our country.*[22] (emphasis added)

---

[18]"Idushchim vosled," interview with Iu. F. Solov'ev by V. Gerasimov and V. Kozhemiako, *Pravda*, 10 March 1988, 2.

[19]See, for example, E. P. Vasil'eva, A. V. Kinsburgskii, L. A. Kokliagina, V. V. Semenova, M. A. Topalov, and V. I. Chuprov, "Otnoshenie studentov k obshchestvennym naukam," *Sotsiologicheskie issledovaniia* 1987, no. 4: 20–24; and I. M. Il'inskii, "Nash molodoi sovremennik (Voprosy mirovozzrensheskogo vospitaniia)," *Sotsiologicheskie issledovaniia* 1987, no. 2: 16–33.

[20]Il'inskii, "Nash molodoi sovremennik," 17.

[21]V. Lukov and G. Inozemtseva, "Kuda vedet krivaia rosta?" *Komsomol'skaia pravda*, 13 February 1988, 2. Results of surveys exploring the opinions of students in higher educational institutions on political issues, nationality relations, and the Komsomol are presented in USSR State Committee on Public Education, Scientific Research Institute of Problems of Higher Education, *Studenchestvo: sotsial'nye orientiry i sotsial'naia praktika. Aktual'nye ocherki (po materialam sotsiologicheskikh issledovanii 1988–1989 gg.)* (Moscow, 1990), translated as "Students' Attitudes toward Socialism, Nationalism, and Perestroika," *Russian Education and Society* 35, no. 4 (April 1993): 9–89.

[22]"Dela ne uspevaiut za slovami," interview with Viktor Mironenko by Y. Evseev and A. Cherniak, *Pravda*, 25 April 1988, 4.

Mironenko's words proved to be prophetic. Revelations about the past and sharp criticism of communism had a strong impact on adolescents, in particular. Addressing a gathering of educators in 1990, the principal of a Moscow school went so far as to claim:

The large number of children's suicides is the consequence of a profound disillusionment as well as the profound upheavals that young people have experienced after seeing the film *Repentance* [*Pokaianie*]. What kind of dialectic is this, when a therapeutic service or psychotherapeutic activity is needed to calm down young people who are ashamed of their past and react fearfully to the future?[23]

He recounted how "a war veteran came to me and cried: 'My grandson insists that his grandfather lived his life in vain, that he was a participant in the creation of the administrative-command [i.e., totalitarian] system.' "[24] Such accusations were no doubt heard in many families.

V. T. Lisovskii, a professor of sociology at Leningrad State University, made similar observations about young people's reactions to the criticism leveled at communist practices:

After I watched the film *We Can't Live This Way* [*Tak zhit' nel'zia*], I was in shock. . . . Our upbringing goes for nothing when young people not only watch but also live under the impression of such films. Consider what conclusions the directors have drawn: "No matter what our propaganda has done, it has always produced the reverse effect"; this is greeted by stormy applause in the audience; the young people are delighted. "Where healthy common sense ends, socialism begins"—stormy applause. "Some kind of Nuremberg Trial should be held for the CPSU"—stormy applause. "Socialism everywhere is a dead end"—stormy applause.[25]

Another participant in the discussion, a professor at the Lithuanian State Pedagogical Institute, decried the fact that "it took just one year . . . to discard the previous ideology, to drive out of young people's minds all the values that we had been inculcating for forty years."[26]

Increasingly, young people gravitated to the "informal groups," political clubs, and civic action organizations that proliferated in the late 1980s.[27] Especially following the April 1986 Chernobyl disaster, there

---

[23]Cited in "Youth and Society" (a roundtable discussion), *Sovetskaia pedagogika* 1990, no. 12, translated in *Russian Education and Society* 34, no. 7 (July 1992): 33.

[24]Ibid.

[25]V. T. Lisovskii, in ibid., 38.

[26]V. P. Bitinas, in ibid., 42.

[27]As one writer observed, the civic action organizations and political clubs were "to a certain degree an elitist movement, especially in Moscow, Leningrad, and a number of other of the largest centers." Activists tended to be "young scientists and scholars (25–35 years old)." Miroslav Buzhkevich, "Demokraticheskoe polovod'e," *Pravda*, 11

was growing awareness of the magnitude of environmental pollution, and of the system's inability to cope with it. Environmental groups gained the support of thousands of young "greens" around the country. Meanwhile, young people were deserting the official youth groups in droves. In 1990, a year before the Komsomol disbanded following the failed coup attempt, some educators frankly acknowledged that "the Pioneer and Komsomol organizations are already lost."[28]

AGE-GROUP DIFFERENCES IN RECENT OPINION SURVEYS

Numerous public opinion polls conducted in Russia and other parts of the Soviet Union leave no doubt that much of the population, and the majority of young Russians, repudiated key features of the worldview that the communists had sought to instill.[29] For example, a survey of 1,050 Russians between the ages of eighteen and twenty-five conducted in six regions of Russia in November 1990 yielded the following startling results:

1. When asked whether seventy years of communist rule had been good or bad for the country, three-quarters of the young Russians said that it had been bad, and about a fifth said it had been good.
2. Asked whether socialism had a future in the Soviet Union, half answered no; a fifth said yes; and the rest were undecided.
3. The overwhelming majority (85 percent) expressed a favorable opinion of private ownership of land, and seven in ten endorsed private ownership of industry and commercial firms.

November 1988, 3. For broader treatments of the growth of nonofficial groups and movements, see S. Frederick Starr, "Soviet Union: A Civil Society," *Foreign Policy* 70 (Spring 1988): 26–41; and Judith B. Sedaitis and Jim Butterfield, eds., *Perestroika from Below: Social Movements in the Soviet Union* (Boulder, Colo.: Westview Press, 1991).
[28]Cited in "Youth and Society," 23.
[29]See Office of Research, U.S. Information Agency (USIA), "Majority of Soviet Adults Disavow 'Old' Communist System," Research Memorandum M-127-90, 14 December 1990; James L. Gibson, Raymond M. Duch, and Kent L. Tedlin, "Democratic Values and the Transformation of the Soviet Union," *Journal of Politics* 54 (May 1992): 329–71; Ada W. Finifter and Ellen Mickiewicz, "Redefining the Political System of the USSR: Mass Support for Political Change," *American Political Science Review* 86, no. 4 (December 1992): 857–74; Richard B. Dobson and Steven A. Grant, "Public Opinion and the Transformation of the Soviet Union," *International Journal of Public Opinion Research* 4, no. 4 (Winter 1992): 302–20; Nikolai P. Popov, "Political Views of the Russian People," ibid., 321–34; and Stephen White, Graeme Gill, and Darrell Slider, *The Politics of Transition: Shaping a Post-Soviet Future* (Cambridge: Cambridge University Press, 1993), 178–92.

4. Six in ten said they favored unrestricted press freedom, whereas one-third called for some restrictions on the media.[30]

Other polls also found that students in secondary school and higher educational institutions had become extremely critical of their society and of institutions created by the communist regime.[31] Judging from a November-December 1990 survey of students in higher education, the majority of Russian students had abandoned Gorbachev and thrown their support to Boris Yeltsin, who promised more radical change.[32]

Further insight into Russians' attitudes can be gained from results of surveys commissioned by the U.S. Information Agency (USIA) in February 1991, December 1991, and June 1992. Each survey was based on personal interviews with nearly two thousand adults (eighteen years of age and older) representative of the adult population of the Russian Federation.[33]

Rejection of the communist system. The February 1991 USIA survey found that young people were more inclined than their elders to reject the Communist party's traditional "leading role" and to affirm the need for multiparty democracy. Seven in ten young people who were eighteen to twenty-nine years old, and an equally large proportion of those thirty to thirty-nine years old, *disagreed* with the statement, "The CPSU is the

[30]The survey, conducted by researchers from the Institute of Sociology of the Soviet Academy of Sciences, was commissioned by *Reader's Digest*. See David Satter, "What Young Russians Really Think," *Reader's Digest* (March 1991): 49–54.

[31]See John P. Robinson et al., "Changing Perceptions of Societal Problems among Soviet Youth," *International Journal of Public Opinion Research* 4, no. 4 (Winter 1992): 335–45; and USSR State Committee on Public Education, *Politicheskie stereotipy studentov i prepodavatel'ei vuzov. Analiticheskaia zapiska po materialam sotsiologicheskogo issledovaniia (noiabr'-dekabr' 1990 g.)* (Moscow and Sverdlovsk, 1991), translated as "Political Stereotypes among Students and Instructors in Higher Education: An Analytical Report Based on Materials of a Sociological Survey (November–December 1990)," *Russian Education and Society* 35, no. 5 (May 1993): 5–31.

[32]"Political Stereotypes among Students," 32–33.

[33]The three surveys were commissioned by the USIA Office of Research. The first of them was conducted by the VP (Vox Populi) Public Opinion Research Service between 15 February and 1 March 1991, with a sample of 1,989 adults; the second, by Russian Public Opinion and Market Research, Ltd. (ROMIR), between 11 December 1991 and 2 January 1992, with a sample of 1,804; and the third, also by ROMIR, between 10 and 21 June 1992, with a sample of 1,800. All three surveys entailed multistage random sampling and the selection of oblasts and sampling points from all geographical zones in the Russian Federation. The potential margin of sampling error was plus or minus 3 percent for each sample; however, it was larger (about 7 percent) for each of the age groups examined. Steven A. Grant, chief of the Russia, Ukraine, and Commonwealth Branch of the USIA Office of Research, and the author had primary responsibility for designing the questionnaires, supervising the execution of the surveys, and analyzing the survey data.

Table 10.1. *Opinion of Soviet socialism (Russia, February 1991)*

Question: There are different opinions about the development of socialism in the USSR. Which of the following views is closest to your own?
—*Socialism in the USSR was flawed from the beginning and could never meet the people's needs.*
—*There were possibilities in Soviet socialism, but these are already exhausted.*
—*Socialism in the USSR is sound and has a future.*

			Age			
	18–29 (N=300)	30–39 (N=476)	40–49 (N=386)	50–59 (N=365)	60+ (N=462)	All (N=1,989)
Socialism:						
Was a mistake (%)	25	21	18	15	11	18
Is exhausted (%)	45	36	34	26	17	31
Has a future (%)	21	32	37	41	48	37
No opinion (%)	9	11	11	18	24	14
Total (%)	100	100	100	100	100	100

only political force capable of governing the country in the decade ahead." Among Russians sixty years of age or older (born before 1932), only half as many disagreed. Conversely, seven in ten young people under thirty agreed that "the Soviet Union needs a real multiparty system," compared to 45 percent of those sixty years and older.[34]

The same survey showed that a large majority of young Russians were disillusioned with the Soviet socialist system (Table 10.1). Overall, half the adults thought that Soviet socialism either was flawed from the beginning and could never meet the people's needs (18 percent) or had exhausted its possibilities (31 percent). Roughly two-fifths felt that socialism was sound and had a future. But the differences among age groups were striking. Seven in ten young people eighteen to twenty-nine years old thought that Soviet socialism had been flawed from the beginning or had exhausted its possibilities; only a fifth felt it had a future. Among persons sixty and older, in contrast, half thought that socialism remained viable.

[34]Some results of the February 1991 survey were presented in Richard B. Dobson, "Looking beyond Communism: A New Generation Enters Russian Politics," *New Outlook* 2, no. 4 (Fall 1991): 16–23. The December 1991 USIA survey showed much the same differentiation among age groups: 62 percent of those in the eighteen to twenty-nine age group agreed that "Russia needs a real multiparty system," compared with only 34 percent of those sixty and older.

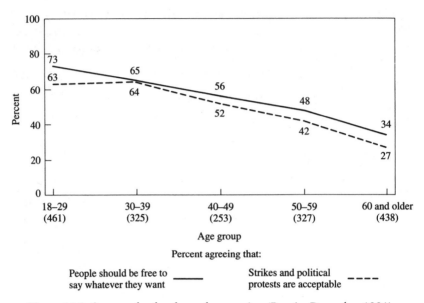

Figure 10.1. Support for freedom of expression (Russia, December 1991).

Support for freedom of expression and protest. Survey data likewise reveal broader support for freedom of expression and political protest among younger Russians. In the December 1991 USIA survey, for example, respondents were asked to select from two statements the one closer to their own opinion. One question was phrased as follows: "Should people be free to say whatever they want, even if what they say increases tensions in society? Or should public order be maintained above all, even if it requires limiting freedom of speech?" A second question asked, "Are strikes, political demonstrations, and other forms of social protest acceptable forms of public conduct? Or should they be avoided as undesirable for social accord?" On both questions, young people tended to endorse free expression (Figure 10.1). They were twice as likely as those sixty and older to say that people should be free to say whatever they want (73 percent versus 34 percent) and to assert that strikes, political demonstrations, and other forms of social protest are acceptable (63 percent versus 27 percent).

Acceptance of economic inequality. Age-group differences extend to the economic sphere as well. In the February 1991 survey, Russians were

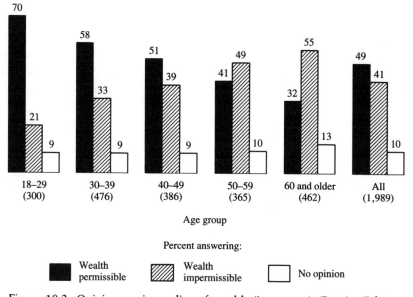

Figure 10.2. Opinion on inequality of wealth (in percent) (Russia, February 1991).

presented with the following question: "Some people say that in principle it is permissible for some people to become very wealthy if their activity contributes to the whole society's well-being. Others maintain that under no circumstances should a person be allowed to get much richer than others because that would be a form of social injustice. Which of these views is closer to your own?" Notwithstanding a common belief that Russians are unwilling to countenance inequalities in wealth, more respondents said that such inequalities were permissible rather than impermissible (49 percent to 41 percent). But as Figure 10.2 demonstrates, there were sharp differences among age groups. More than half of those in the oldest cohort felt that no one should be allowed to become much richer than others. In contrast, seven in ten Russians under thirty considered inequalities in wealth permissible.

Attitudes toward private ownership. Surveys also show consistently that members of the younger generation have a more favorable attitude toward private ownership than their elders. According to the February 1991 survey (Figure 10.3), eight in ten Russians eighteen to twenty-nine years old felt that the state should allow peasants to buy and sell land

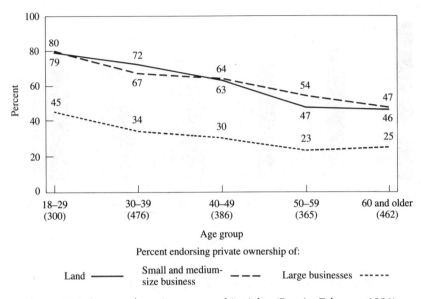

Figure 10.3. Support for private ownership rights (Russia, February 1991).

and to own small and medium-size businesses, such as workshops and restaurants, employing no more than two hundred people. Roughly half of the members of that age group said that the state should allow individuals to own large businesses employing two hundred or more employees. Among those sixty and older, about half approved of private ownership of land and of small and medium-size businesses, but only a quarter endorsed private ownership of large businesses.

When similar questions were asked in December 1991, following the abortive coup attempt and the banning of the Russian Communist party, more Russians expressed support for private ownership rights than had in February. Yet appreciable differences among age groups remained (Figure 10.4). Among those under thirty, nine out of ten said that peasants and other citizens should be able to own, buy, and sell land. Eight in ten thought that individuals should be allowed to own small and medium-size businesses, and six in ten said that citizens should be allowed to be private owners of large businesses employing more than two hundred employees. Among those sixty and older, seven in ten endorsed private ownership of land; half approved of private ownership of small and medium-size businesses; and about a quarter favored private ownership of large businesses.

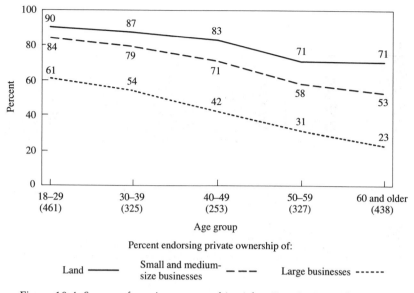

Figure 10.4. Support for private ownership rights (Russia, December 1991).

Another question on the same survey asked Russians to indicate their preference regarding the extent of private and state ownership in the economy as a whole. Among all adults surveyed, a plurality (40 percent) felt that "some enterprises, shops, and farms should be privately owned, and some should be owned by the state." A quarter said that "most enterprises, shops, and farms should be privately owned; state ownership should be limited to only a few necessary industries and services." A fifth thought that "the state should own most or all enterprises, shops, and farms; private property should be kept to the minimum."[35]

As Figure 10.5 indicates, younger Russians more often opted for an economy based on private ownership than did their older compatriots. Two-fifths of those in the youngest cohort thought that most farms and enterprises should be privately owned, and an equal proportion said that some should be owned by the state and some by individuals. The proportion choosing mainly private ownership declined with each successive age group (only 12 percent of those sixty and older chose this type of economy).

[35]Four decades earlier, the Harvard Project had found that the former Soviet citizens surveyed overwhelmingly preferred a "New Economic Policy–type" socialist economy to either a Soviet communist or a capitalist economic system. Inkeles and Bauer, *The Soviet Citizen*, 242–46.

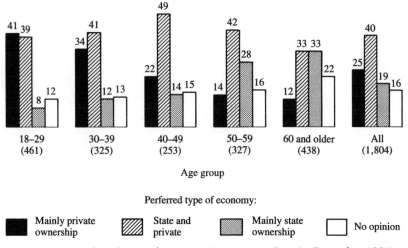

Figure 10.5. Preferred type of economy (in percent) (Russia, December 1991).

Support for state ownership and state welfare guarantees. Although young Russians tend to be more supportive of private ownership than their elders, they certainly do not reject all state ownership, and they broadly favor welfare guarantees. In the December 1991 survey, Russians were asked whether or not they thought that "each of the following should be a main feature of our future social-economic system." The results showed widespread acceptance of state ownership of heavy industry and basic welfare guarantees among all age groups. Among the oldest Russians (sixty and older), 90 percent favored free, guaranteed health care; 87 percent endorsed guaranteed work for all; and 76 percent wanted the state to own most heavy industry. Six in ten desired state ownership of most light industry and wanted to retain state and collective farms. Majorities of the youngest Russians (eighteen to twenty-nine) also wanted guaranteed work for all (69 percent), free health care (65 percent), and state ownership of most heavy industry (60 percent). Less than half (42 percent), however, favored state ownership of most light industry, and just 25 percent thought that state farms and collective farms should be a main feature of the future economic system.

Subsequent surveys confirm that Russians' preference for state or private ownership varies greatly from one sector of the economy to another. Russians interviewed in June 1992 more often said that agriculture should be "mainly" or "exclusively" in the hands of private owners

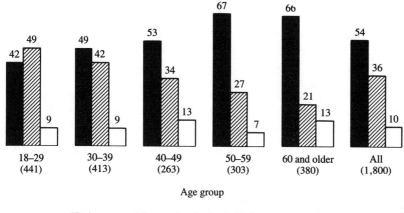

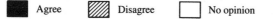

"Its is a great misfortune that the Soviet Union no longer exists."

■ Agree ▨ Disagree □ No opinion

Figure 10.6. Opinion on the Soviet Union's demise (in percent) (Russia, June 1992).

(62 percent) than said the same for shops and food stores (48 percent), the manufacture of consumer goods (31 percent), or heavy industry (9 percent). Russians under thirty years old were consistently more inclined than their elders to favor private ownership in each economic sphere. Majorities of those in the youngest cohort thought that agriculture (76 percent) and shops and food stores (59 percent) should be owned mainly or exclusively by private owners, and nearly half said the same regarding the manufacture of consumer goods. Still, fewer than one in five young Russians favored predominantly private ownership of heavy industry.

Nostalgia for the Soviet past. The disbanding of the Communist Party of the Soviet Union, sudden dissolution of the Soviet Union, and lifting of price controls in 1992 forced Russians to confront a changing, less certain environment. To a considerable degree, people's attitude toward the Soviet Union's demise reflects their attachment to, or rejection of, the communist heritage. (Of course, it also reflects their evaluation of present circumstances.) In the June 1992 USIA survey, Russians were asked whether they agreed with the statement, "It is a great misfortune that the Soviet Union no longer exists." A majority (54 percent) agreed, whereas only about a third disagreed (Figure 10.6). Again, however, the differences among age groups were substantial. Two-thirds of those fifty and older considered the Soviet Union's dissolution a great misfortune. Those under thirty were more evenly divided: two-fifths lamented the Soviet Union's demise, but half did not.[36]

COMMUNISM'S LEGACY: AN UNCERTAIN FUTURE

The evidence that we have reviewed indicates that young Russians have gone further than their elders in repudiating key elements of what communism stood for—not just rule by the Communist party, but also the Soviet socialist model, egalitarianism, and opposition to private property. Young Russians largely view communism as a negative example, and by voicing support for private enterprise, freedom of the press, and political pluralism, they are making a break with the old order. The fact that similar variations among age groups were found in successive surveys suggests that the differences are fairly stable and are likely to persist.[37]

To varying degrees, such age differences exist in other former communist countries as well. Results of the Times Mirror "Pulse of Europe" survey conducted in April and May 1991, for example, found that young people in Russia, Ukraine, Lithuania, Czechoslovakia, Poland, Hungary, Bulgaria, and the former German Democratic Republic all tended to be more supportive of democratic practices and private enterprise than those fifty years of age and older.[38] USIA-commissioned surveys in the countries of Eastern and Central Europe point to the same conclusion. Thus one analysis found negative correlations between age and support for democratic principles not only in Russia, but also in Ukraine, Belarus, Bulgaria, and Poland and among the Slovaks of the former Czechoslovakia.[39]

[36]The young people who agreed or disagreed with this statement tended to differ in their opinions on other issues as well. For example, those who "completely" agreed were twice as likely as those who "completely" disagreed to say that light industry and heavy industry should be mainly or exclusively owned by the state. They were also much less likely to express confidence in Russian president Boris Yeltsin.

[37]At this point, however, we cannot be too certain about the stability of opinion: until there are firm institutional underpinnings (e.g., a sizable private sector, a strong middle class, and democratic political parties that can maintain a following and govern), opinions may be subject to substantial shifts. Future research will enable scholars to determine the degree to which the differences among age groups observed today are associated with life stages (through which successive cohorts pass) or are true generational differences remaining with given cohorts over time.

[38]See "The Pulse of Europe: A Survey of Political and Social Values and Attitudes," final report released by the Times Mirror Center for the People and the Press, Washington, D.C., 16 September 1991.

[39]Support for democratic principles was measured by questions about the importance of freedom to criticize the government and of there being at least two strong parties

Not surprisingly, however, young Russians' rejection of the communist heritage is not complete. Their support for state welfare policies and state ownership of most heavy industry, in particular, shows continuity with the Soviet past and to some extent prerevolutionary traditions as well. The belief that the state should play a major role in the economy and should provide citizens with welfare entitlements appears likely to remain as part of communism's legacy.

Furthermore, young Russians confront a disparity between what they advocate and what they find in the real world, for new institutions are not well developed. They see the need for a multiparty system; yet the numerous parties that have been formed in Russia have few members, no record of representing their constituencies, and little experience in governing. Democratic institutions are not firmly rooted, and whether they will survive the rigors of economic reform remains to be seen. State enterprises (many of which have been geared to military production) still dominate the economy, and many Russians have perhaps "forgotten" what skills private enterprise requires.

Owing to their energy, education, and freedom from communist dogma, young people appear to be relatively well positioned to profit from privatization. And, as Russian president Boris Yeltsin stressed in a June 1992 interview, they appear most willing to seize the new opportunities:

Other countries knew what private property was, but in this country such an understanding had even been erased from the memories of the descendants because we are already down to the second or third generation [since the abolition of private property]. Why is it that today when I go to meet people, young people stand in the front ranks? They understand better what reforms are, they see freedom coming to them, freedom of choice. If you want to make money, you can, because there are now no limits in this respect.[40]

Some young people who have gone into business have been very successful. For example, a twenty-four-year-old college dropout named German Sterligov started a private commodities exchange and named it after his dog, Alisa. The venture was so successful that Sterligov quickly amassed "tens and tens of millions of rubles." As *Washington Post* correspondent

competing in elections. Mary E. McIntosh, Martha Abele Mac Iver, Richard B. Dobson, and Steven A. Grant, "The Meaning of Democracy in a Redefined Europe," paper presented at the annual meeting of the American Association for Public Opinion Research, St. Charles, Illinois, 20–23 May 1993.

[40]Cited in " 'Overwhelming Majority' Backs Reforms, Yeltsin Says," *Washington Post*, 12 June 1992, A28.

David Remnick observed, "It is the Sterligovs of the Soviet Union—young millionaires in their twenties and early thirties—who are the first signs of the absolutely new. They are a half-visible generation of hustler-dissidents, ambitious and vain, free of [communist] ideology and 'slave psychology.' "[41]

Yet young people are also among those most vulnerable to the social and economic dislocations accompanying the transition to a market economy. Students on stipends, like pensioners, may find it difficult to survive on fixed incomes that lag behind inflation. Graduates of educational institutions may face great difficulties in finding employment appropriate for their training, and young workers who lack seniority may be among the first to be laid off by enterprises. The young are also less likely to have accumulated the resources that they can invest in economic ventures.

"Old guard" champions of communist rule and socialism argue that the hardships of transition to a market economy will sour young people on private enterprise and "bourgeois democracy." On the eve of the January 1992 Russian price reforms, Nina Andreeva, the St. Petersburg chemistry professor whose strident attack on glasnost and perestroika caused a sensation in 1988, stated:

Serious shifts are taking place in young people's consciousness. College students' last illusions about entry into a "civilized paradise" and the restoration of capitalist relations are slowly dying. With each passing day, students are beginning to realize more and more clearly that the absolute majority of them will never be millionaires. Moreover, today's student is gradually losing his former confidence in the future, which he used to get from the state system—thoroughly reviled by the "democrats"—of job placement after graduation from a higher educational institution. Hence the look of gloomy despondency on the faces in the lecture halls. The country's three million students know that when they graduate, not only will the majority of them fail to get a job in their field, but they may join the ranks of the unemployed. This is not just a dashing of hopes but a tragedy in a young person's life, one for which the "reformist fathers" should be held accountable.[42]

Although Andreeva's observations no doubt contain a large dose of wishful thinking, the possibility of a backlash cannot be altogether ruled

[41]David Remnick, "Brash New Breed 'Building Empires, Not Evil Ones,' " *Washington Post,* 7 July 1991, A1, A24.
[42]N. A. Andreeva, "Oh Russia, My Russia," *Stolitsa* 1992, no. 1 (January), translated in *Current Digest of the Post-Soviet Press,* 26 February 1992, 14–15. Andreeva's antiperestroika article, first published in *Sovetskaia kul'tura,* 13 March 1988, is reprinted as "I Cannot Forgo My Principles," in Alexander Dallin and Gail W. Lapidus, *The Soviet System in Crisis: A Reader of Western and Soviet Views* (Boulder, Colo.: Westview Press, 1991), 338–46.

out, especially if there is a further erosion in state authority, a continued decline in living standards, mass unemployment, and a widening gap between rich and poor. On balance, however, it appears more likely that young Russians will be an important source of support for privatization, democratic institutions, and individual rights.

Communism has clearly left a deep imprint on the moral and intellectual life of Russia. Indeed, many leading Russian intellectuals contend that communist rule was built on violence and falsehood and led to the moral degeneration of society. Aleksandr Solzhenitsyn, for one, described "the destruction of our souls" as the "most terrible" consequence of communist domination.[43] The sociologist Vladimir Shubkin came to much the same conclusion.[44] And Aleksandr Yakovlev, once a key advisor to Gorbachev and a candidate member of the Politburo, has argued that the systematic persecution of persons who showed initiative and independence led to the "mass *lumpenization*" of society, which in turn "spawned incompetence and irresponsibility."[45]

It is still unclear whether young Russians have, or will find, a "moral compass" with which to navigate the uncharted postcommunist waters. Prominent Russian intellectuals, including Solzhenitsyn and Dmitrii Likhachev, have called on Russians to return to their roots, to repent and reaffirm the core values of Russian culture, frequently associated with Russian Orthodoxy. But young Russians' attachment to precommunist values does not appear strong. The young are much less likely than their elders to say that they are Orthodox believers.[46] Decades of communist rule and social change appear to have created a modern, secular, and in many ways Westernized generation that is neither supportive of communist institutions nor wedded to tradition. What this generation fashions from the elements of Russia's long and troubled history and from more intense interaction with the West will perhaps have a decisive influence on the life of Russia for decades to come.

---

[43] Aleksandr Solzhenitsyn, "Kak obustroit' Rossiiu," *Komsomol'skaia pravda*, 18 September 1990.

[44] See Vladimir Shubkin, "Trudnoe proshchanie," *Novyi mir* 1989, no. 4: 165–84.

[45] Aleksandr Yakovlev, "Social Alternatives in the Twentieth Century," Third Annual W. Averell Harriman Lecture, 15 November 1991 (New York: Harriman Institute, Columbia University, 1992), 26. Like the others cited here, Yakovlev singles out moral renewal as the most essential and challenging task facing Russia.

[46] According to the June 1992 USIA survey, only a quarter of the Russians under thirty, but nearly three-fifths of those sixty or older, professed faith in Russian Orthodoxy. Among the young, as in the adult population as a whole, women were more likely than men to identify themselves as religious believers.

11

The social legacy of communism: women,
children, and the feminization of poverty

GAIL KLIGMAN

The year 1989 marked the formal end of Communist party rule in six
Central and Eastern European countries. Since then, Central and Eastern
Europeans have embarked on uncertain paths toward "recovery" in all
domains of their lives. The institution of democratic practices and of
free-market economies is a goal to which most aspire. How to achieve
them is hotly contested. This draws attention to another critical feature
of the transition, too often ignored by those engaged in crafting this
process: The transition, itself shorthand for the introduction of democratic practices and free markets, also involves ongoing, intense struggles
over the language that shapes identities—be they national, ethnic, or
gendered. Debates over foreign investment, shock therapy, third roads,[1]
or reproductive rights address not only practical concerns about transforming economies but also the very terms through which life opportunities are being defined. The conceptualization of citizenship, as well as
the codification of legal rights and mutual obligations between the state
and its citizens, is fundamental to understanding what "democracy"
means in everyday life and who will benefit from its institutionalization.

In this chapter, I discuss the social legacy of communism as it affects
the lives of women and children during the transition. I begin with a
cursory review of the socialist period, followed by a suggestive discussion about the implications of the transition for women and children. In
the first section, I note structural tensions as they impact on the lives of
women, in particular; in the second, I focus on representations of the

---

[1] See D. Stark, "Privatization in Hungary: From Plan to Market or from Plan to Clan?"
East European Politics and Society 4, no. 3 (1990): 351–92.
    Note that, for considerations of space, footnote citations in this chapter are not meant
to be exhaustive.

female body, as well as bodily practices that shape the "transitional" body politic.

WOMEN, WORK, AND FAMILY:
THE SOCIALIST PAST, THE "TRANSITIONAL" PRESENT

Socialist states were distinctive in their professed ideological dedication to gender equality, which was taken to mean that women should have the right to work.[2] The underlying rationale was that all citizens should contribute to the building of socialism, according to their abilities. In recognition of one of women's "abilities"—childbearing—the socialist state intended to help women enter the economy by providing various forms of social assistance: guaranteed maternity leaves, guaranteed job security, child-care facilities. These entitlements functioned as positive incentives and were progressive in intention if not in their implementation. Unprecedented numbers of women were educated and entered the labor force. However, they tended to be employed in occupations less suited to their educational levels than were those of their male counterparts; furthermore, women's salaries were significantly lower than those of men in similar positions. Susan Gal reports an average 20 percent difference in Hungary, for example.[3] Equal pay for equal work was not realized in socialist states either. In spite of the official discourse about equality, the division of labor as well as the structure of power was distinctly gendered. The core sectors of socialism—the bureaucracy, the state repressive apparatus, and heavy industry—were predominantly populated by males, especially at the top. Women were brought in at lower levels, held clerical functions, worked in light industry and agriculture, or were employed in education, health care, and culture. "Traditional" female roles in the family remained largely feminized

[2] I discussed this at greater length in my article "The Politics of Reproduction in Ceausescu's Romania: A Case Study in Political Culture," *East European Politics and Society* 6, no. 3 (1992): 364–418. For additional references, please refer to this article. I do not herein cite the literature on women under socialism.

[3] For a general summary of data, see, for example, Susan Gal, "Gender in the Post-Socialist Transition: Discourses of Abortion and Reproduction in Hungary," paper presented at the American Anthropology Association meeting, 1991; and M. Fong and G. Paull, "The Changing Role of Women in Employment in Eastern Europe," *World Bank Report*, no. 8213 (1992). See also S. Wolchik, "Women and Work in Communist and Postcommunist Central and Eastern Europe," in H. Kahne and J. Giele, eds., *Women's Work and Women's Lives: The Continuing Struggle Worldwide* (Boulder, Colo.: Westview Press, 1992). For the Soviet Union, see A. Posadskaya, "Changes in the Employment of Women in the Context of Restructuring in the Former USSR," paper prepared for a conference on women and the transition, University of California, Los Angeles, March 1992.

in the broader state division of labor. Although gender equality was ideologically extolled throughout the Eastern bloc, equality was more readily achieved in rhetoric than in practice. Legislation regarding women's rights as workers often came into conflict with women's obligations as reproducers of the labor force, that is, with their roles as mothers.

The "building of socialism" was predicated on a productionist mentality. In theory, socialist transformation incorporated all levels of life, meaning that the population had to be mobilized accordingly. The resultant relation between state policy and demographic factors bore directly on issues of changing gender relations and roles and underscored the contradictory interests of the state and its citizens, especially those of women and children. Romania represented an "extreme case of the generalized pronatalism,"[4] which from the mid-1960s typified the region. Pronatalist policies, aimed at securing an adequate work force to build socialism, formed part of the modernization strategies of these states.[5] Lacking capital intensity, socialist economies relied instead on labor intensity, thereby legitimating official demands for increased population growth.

Women's participation in the national economy and society as workers and mothers through forced egalitarianism, as some have labeled it, created the classic "double" burdens of work in the state sphere and family work in the home.[6] In the case of Romania, the customary double burdens became triple ones when childbearing was declared a patriotic duty.[7] Occupational advances were not coupled with the production of time-saving household devices or with any particular emphasis on changing gender roles within the family. The legacy of patriarchal family relations was not significantly altered and, it may be argued, was further

---

[4]See M. Teitelbaum and J. Winter, *The Fear of Population Decline* (Orlando, Fla.: Academic Press, 1985), 100.

[5]Furthermore, for the 1974 World Population Conference in Bucharest, Ceausescu linked Romanian pronatalism to foreign policy: alignment with the Third World. For a brief summary about pronatalism in Eastern Europe, see, for example, S. Wolchik, "Women and the State in Eastern Europe and the Soviet Union," in S. E. Charlton, J. Everett, K. Staudt, eds., *Women, the State and Development* (Albany: State University of New York Press, 1989), 44–65.

[6]Men were also, if differently, subject to the double burden under socialism through their labor in the second economy. See Kligman, "The Politics of Reproduction"; J. Goven, "Sexual Politics in Hungary: Autonomy and Anti-Feminism," in N. Funk and M. Mueller, eds., *Gender Politics and Post-Communism: Reflections from Eastern Europe and the Former Soviet Union* (New York: Routledge, 1993), 224–40.

[7]Kligman, "The Politics of Reproduction."

exacerbated by the paternalist structure of the socialist state. Moreover, as the Hungarian sociologist Julia Szalai recently pointed out, it was not only women who suffered the contradictions of socialist planning: "Children's needs were painfully subordinated to the political priorities of economic goals."[8] Although child care facilities existed throughout the region, they were unable to accommodate demand. Furthermore, as a result of generalized low investment, these facilities were woefully inadequate with respect to quality. They were often understaffed by poorly trained individuals; they lacked equipment, instructional materials, and so forth.

In the state-controlled public sphere of power, women, like minorities, were present in positions of authority; however, their presence was by and large symbolic, reflecting an operative quota system that paid lip service to the participation of women and minorities in leadership roles.[9] Access to power was stratified. Most persons in positions of power were not in the "inner circle" but, instead, were complicitous with power—they were the "dominated fraction of the dominating class": women did not represent women's interests, just as the workers' unions did not represent workers' interests. That women participated in the public sphere in this manner bears directly on recent developments in the transition.

The socialist state was paternalist;[10] paternalism, in effect, generalized the dependency relations experienced by women and children in the context of the patriarchal family to subordinate men as well. Citizens of the socialist state may be said to have been structurally "feminized" in their relations to the state. This generalized response to state paternalism had various consequences. In the extreme case—Romania in the 1980s—unwanted children were born and abandoned to the care of the paternalist state that had demanded them. That "care," best known as systematic neglect, resulted in institutionalization of the innocent, the rise of an

[8] Julia Szalai, "Some Aspects of the Changing Situation of Women in Hungary," *Signs* 17, no. 1 (1991): 152–70.

[9] Here, it is worth noting the distinction between "presence" and "representation." Jan Gross underscores a similar distinction (between embodiment and representation) in his article "Poland: From Civil Society to Political Nation," in I. Banac, ed., *Eastern Europe in Revolution* (Ithaca: Cornell University Press, 1992), 56–71.

[10] On the paternalist socialist state, see, for example, I. Dolling, "Situation und Perspektiven von Frauenforschung in der DDR," *ZIF Bulletin* 1, no. 1 (June 1990): 1–2; L. Bruszt, " 'Without Us but for Us?' Political Orientation in Hungary in the Period of Late Paternalism," *Social Research* 55, nos. 1–2 (Spring-Summer 1988): 43–76; Kligman, "The Politics of Reproduction."

infant autoimmune deficiency syndrome (AIDS) epidemic, and international trafficking in babies and children through adoption.[11] Extremes aside, throughout the communist countries of Central and Eastern Europe, the paternalist state structured dependency relations, simultaneously encouraging passivity from most members of society. Such patterns of behavior and modes of thinking have been internalized through some forty years of propaganda and everyday practices. They form part of the social legacy of communism that both stimulates as well as impedes the transition.

The euphoria of 1989 has given way to the complexities and traumas provoked by the transition, which are becoming more apparent as some Central and East Europeans balk at yet more economic hardship, rising unemployment and inflation, increasing social differentiation as well as increasing impoverishment for certain segments of society. Explosive ethnic and nationalist tensions reverberate throughout the region. The transition has also bolstered a movement toward what may be called "retraditionalization," a return to traditional values, family life, and religion.[12] For women, this means that their roles in society are being redefined; women's proper place is again supposed to be in the home. Although many find this attractive, economic necessity has not generally made it possible for most women to exit from the wage labor force. In addition to economic insecurity provoked by the transition, women's participation in the polity has been threatened, as have the existence of social assistance provisions for women, children, and families, and the right to personal choice regarding women's reproductive lives.[13]

[11] See Kligman, "The Politics of Reproduction."

[12] See, for example, G. Kligman, "Women and Reproductive Legislation in Romania: Implications for the Transition," in G. Breslauer, ed., Dilemmas of Transition in the Soviet Union and Eastern Europe (Berkeley: Center for Slavic and East European Studies, 1991), 141–66; C. Bohlen, "East Europe's Women Struggle with New Rules, and Old Ones," New York Times, 25 November 1990, 1, 2.

[13] See, for example, M. Fuszara, "Legal Regulation of Abortion in Poland," Signs 17, no. 1 (1991): 117–28; E. Hauser, B. Heyns, and J. Mansbridge, "Feminism in the Interstices of Politics and Culture: Poland in Transition," in Funk and Mueller, eds., Gender Politics, 257–73; S. Gal, "Questions about Women and Gender after Socialism: The Abortion Debate in Hungary," paper presented at the American Anthropological Association annual meeting, November 1991; Szalai, "Some Aspects of the Changing Situation of Women in Hungary," 152–70; D. Rosenberg, "Shock Therapy: GDR Women in Transition from a Socialist Welfare State to a Social Market Economy," Signs 17, no. 1 (1991): 129–51; "Germany and Gender," German Politics and Society 24 and 25 (Winter 1991–92); Wolchik, "Women and Work in Communist and Postcommunist Central and Eastern Europe"; Kligman, "Women and Reproductive Legislation in Romania."

Women in the region, therefore, have not experienced the collapse of communism as necessarily synonymous with the granting of democratic rights and participation in the political public sphere. In the political realm, women have been increasingly marginalized. In contrast to trends elsewhere in Europe, women's participation in the democratically elected parliaments of the postcommunist countries of Central and Eastern Europe reflect the current backlash against them. For example, in Hungary, the number of female parliamentarians initially dropped from 21 percent to 7 percent; in Romania, from 34 percent to 4 percent; in Czechoslovakia, from 30 percent to 9 percent.[14] Many people, male and female, attribute women's decreased representation in the newly elected governments to the widespread disdain caused by their former puppet presences, as mentioned earlier. It is unclear, of course, why men would then be deemed more suitable to deal with the difficult issues confronting these countries, as men were much more culpable for the abuses of state socialism. This facile association of women with evil masks basic structural features of the *process* of transforming the economy and public sphere—that is, the competition for and access to limited resources help create a politics of exclusion, which is also pertinent to concerns about ethnic identity and nationalism. Although women are now visibly underrepresented in the public sphere of governance at a time when multiple voices are struggling to be heard and to make an imprint on the future, women's futures, by and large, are being decided not by women, but by men on behalf of women. This situation has become particularly problematic with respect to the legislation of reproductive rights, to which I shall return later.

For many Central and Eastern European women, although surely not all, the relationship between national liberation and women's liberation is seemingly an inverse one. Indeed, there is no empirical evidence to suggest that the position of women as citizens, workers, and mothers will be radically improved in the near future. Again, unemployment, increasing poverty, and class differentiation are considered to be among the necessary costs of transforming command economies, in which all citizens were expected to participate, into market economies, in which

---

[14]These figures are cited in Gal, "Questions about Women and Gender after Socialism"; similar statistics are presented in Wolchik, "Women and Work in Communist and Postcommunist Central and Eastern Europe." In 1993, of 400 Hungarian parliamentarians, 17 were women; of 200 in the Czech Republic, 20 were women; of 240 in Bulgaria, 32 were women.

profit-oriented goals compete with the demands of labor. Important here are the demographics of the transition. Rising unemployment and growing economic differentiation are experienced differentially, with increasingly negative effects on women and children, regardless of whether women themselves are employed or unemployed. Furthermore, the end of state socialism will probably mean the end of general state subsidies for health, education, and welfare. In consequence of this likely development, some argue that the collapse of communism has introduced civil rights at the expense of economic rights: employment, child care, affordable housing, and access to minimal medical care.

This is where retraditionalization has entered the process of change. The professed return to traditional family roles and religious values that were suppressed under communism coincides with an expressed preference by some political leaders for the return of women to primary roles as wives and mothers. Some women welcome the opportunity to leave their places of work, freeing jobs for men. They would like to see the goal of economic change be the creation of an economy in which women do not have to work. These women would like to be assured that their husbands can support their families (that is, earn a family wage), thereby enabling women to stay at home and raise their children rather than work outside the home in addition to caring for them. This desire is understandable; women in Central and Eastern Europe, as most interviewers learn, are worn out. Indeed, the life choices and careers of many women were determined under very different conditions, for which they are now paying under other conditions and for which they are ill-prepared. Unfortunately, for a majority of women, the matter of choosing to work or to raise families is idealistic in the context of contemporary market economies. Most women, either as members of two-income families or as heads of households, must work to make ends meet. Family incomes have not kept pace with the rising costs of living in the West, let alone in the region.

Hence, the meaning of rising unemployment in Central and Eastern Europe must be analyzed carefully. It cannot be assumed that unemployment rates will be uniformly higher among women than men.[15] At the same time, it is not likely that female wages will be as high as those of

---

[15]Nonetheless, recent unemployment figures for Poland indicate that women comprise approximately 58 percent of the unemployed (Fong and Paull, "Women's Economic Status," 6); 57 percent in the former GDR (Rosenberg, "Shock Therapy," 132); and 85 percent in Romania (Fong and Paull, "Women's Economic Status," 7).

men, despite evidence that women have a higher level of general education than men, which, in turn, suggests that women would be better
positioned to benefit from economic restructuring.[16] Transforming these
economies is fraught with unintended consequences. To illustrate, the
pressures to dismantle the albatrosses of state ownership—heavy industries (steel, mining)—may lead to high unemployment among men, leaving women as primary breadwinners. In that women tended under socialism to occupy less skilled, more poorly paid jobs than men, women
as primary family breadwinners today will most probably translate into
a sharp decrease in their living standards, as well as in future opportunities for their children. The formerly communist countries of Central and
Eastern Europe are both advantageous and disadvantageous for foreign
investment. The region's labor force is generally skilled; however, skilled
labor is also more expensive. Another scenario suggests that in some
sectors of the market, it may be more "profitable" for capitalist firms to
engage female workers because they can be paid lower wages.[17] According to Szalai, part-time female workers in foreign-owned firms in
Hungary currently enjoy higher wages than fully employed men in Hungarian ones.[18] The women are paid in dollars. The advantages for
women in the short run are clear enough, but what this means for future
segmentation and gendering of the division of labor will have to be
carefully studied as the economy continues to change and stabilize.

Combined with diminished and/or disappearing social welfare benefits, the picture for many families does not look rosy. It looks less so for
working mothers still confronted by the contradictory demands of family and wage labor. Retraditionalization theoretically positions women
in their customary roles as caretakers of the young and old; women are
the ones who do what anthropologists call "kin work." Leaving aside

---

[16]In view of the process of restructuring under way, statistical data about the economic
impact on women is more suggestive than conclusive. See, for example, Fong and Paull,
"The Changing Role of Women"; S. Hubner, F. Maier, and H. Rudolph, "Women's
Employment in Central and Eastern Europe, Status and Prospects," paper presented at
ILO conference, "Labor Market and Social Policy Implications of Structural Change in
Central and Eastern Europe," Paris, 1991.

[17]The Asian "miracle" serves as an important comparative lens. See, for example, M.
Brinton, *Women and the Economic Miracle: Gender and Work in Postwar Japan* (Berkeley and Los Angeles: University of California Press, 1992); and especially A. Ong, "The
Gender and Labor Politics of Postmodernity," *Annual Review of Anthropology* 20
(1991): 279–309.

[18]Szalai, public commentary at the conference "Women and Political Transitions in South
America and Eastern and Central Europe: The Prospects for Democracy," held in
Berkeley in 1992.

economic necessity for the moment, it is presumed that women will take up some of the slack that dismantling the socialist welfare state produces: the need to provide care for the young and elderly.[19] But the realities of everyday life do not facilitate this happening as intended. The state is no longer able or willing to subsidize adequately work leaves for family care. In spite of a growing public rhetoric to the contrary, most women must continue to work, which means that they simply take on additional kin work to satisfy their "familial responsibilities." Moreover, generational factors are not insignificant. The birthrate decline has occurred against an increase in life expectancy, and as a result the population has aged. The decrease in child care opportunities, coupled with inflation, unemployment, and increased domestic responsibilities, affects women's participation in the labor force by constraining their possibilities. Generally, women require more flexible schedules in order to meet their multiple demands in different productive and reproductive spheres, which gives rise to structural discrimination in the labor force.

Another factor that must be weighed in deciphering the meaning of unemployment figures is demographic fragmentation due to emigration. Waves of migration from the region to other European countries and to the United States are not new, but unlike trends in the earlier part of the century, many men are now seeking a new life that does not include their wives and children back home. In Poland, for example, the problem of increasing numbers of "social orphans" (children who have at least one living parent) has developed.[20] In 1990, of 14,143 children living in 285 orphanages with a total of 15,678 places, 96 percent were social orphans. The 51 young children's homes with 3,579 places housed 4,399 children up to the age of three.[21] Such statistics have implications for legislating reproduction and the futures of these children. These data

---

[19]The cost of public social services has increased as a result of restructuring; in turn, many of these services have been significantly cut back. See, for example, S. Mayer, "At the End of Playtime: The Cutback of Nursery Schools and Day Care Centers for Socialism's Children Has Begun," *Die Zeit*, 4 May 1990, 100. The structured prioritization of capitalist organization delegates family responsibilities to the private sphere, making most household labor the responsibility of the family on its own. These contradictions are being explicitly felt in Eastern Europe. No matter how inadequate social services were in the former socialist states, the dilemma was at least recognized, though provisions varied considerably.

[20]Social orphans have become most publicly associated with the Ceausescu regime (see G. Kligman, "Abortion and International Adoption in Post-Ceausescu Romania," *Feminist Studies* [Summer 1992]: 405–20). This is not a Romanian problem per se, however, but rather a phenomenon complexly related to poverty. It is an emergent issue in Poland as well as Russia.

[21]See B. Zmijewska, "Born but Unwanted," *Warsaw Voice*, 23–30 December 1990, 10.

(increasingly more common) are also revealing with respect to a social legacy of communism: many husbands do not feel responsibility for their families, assuming instead that the state will take care of them, albeit minimally.[22] The search for work abroad, especially by men, has ironically contributed to a "feminization of poverty" that parallels an earlier feminization of agriculture, which resulted from the heavy industrialization drives that were meant to modernize these economies rapidly.[23] The upheavals of the past few years, despite the enormous jubilation, have contributed to rising divorce rates and the breakdown of the family. These developments have especially been pushing women and children into poverty. According to Hungarian data, young urban families are overrepresented among the poor. Reliance on family grants that enable mothers to stay home with their children is contributing to dependency cycles all too familiar in the United States.[24] Data from elsewhere in the region signal the overrepresentation of female-headed households among the poor. In Poland, of half a million single-parent families recorded in 1990, 91 percent were female-headed. Of these women, 77 percent were employed. The rest were living on benefits, or were supported by their extended families. Approximately 66 percent were living below the poverty line. It was then estimated that every fourth person who should have been paying child support did not.[25] Data from the region challenge some of the typical assumptions about female-headed households living on welfare or below the poverty line. It is impossible to attribute such developments to race as a significant variable. Female heads of household in Poland are by and large white and Catholic. Here it is important to note that the "feminization of poverty" is not racially specific; white women and children are not spared its devastating effects.[26]

[22]See H. Nickel, "Frauen auf dem Spring in die Marktwirtschaft," *Ypsilon* 1, no. 2 (Spring 1990): 26; and Dolling, "Situation und Perspektiven."

[23]On the feminization of agriculture, see, for example, M. Cernea, "Macrosocial Change, the Feminization of Agriculture, and Peasant Women's Threefold Economic Role," *Sociologia Ruralis* 18 (1978): 239–50.

[24]On the feminization of poverty in Hungary, for example, see Szalai, "Some Aspects of the Changing Situation of Women in Hungary."

[25]Zmijewska, "Born but Unwanted"; see also Szalai, "Women and Political Transitions."

[26]On this problematic issue, see, for example (among a broad and diverse literature), D. Pearce, "The Feminization of Poverty: Women, Work and Welfare," *Urban and Social Change Review* (Winter–Spring 1978): 28–36; L. Gordon, ed., *Women, the State and Welfare* (Madison: University of Wisconsin Press, 1990); W. J. Wilson, *Poverty and Family Structure: The Widening Gap between Evidence and Public Policy Issues* (Madison: University of Wisconsin Press, 1985).

THE POLITICS OF THE BODY AND THE BODY POLITIC IN
POSTCOMMUNIST CENTRAL AND EASTERN EUROPE

In view of the centrality of gender, the body, and reproduction under socialism as well as generally in defining the nation itself, it is not surprising that these concerns are currently vital throughout Central and Eastern Europe. I will now turn to varied ways in which the body, especially the female body, has become marked, a focal point of societal attention,[27] as well as vulnerable. The freedom of expression unleashed by the collapse of communism brought pornography into the public sphere; the market was flooded with pornographic materials. Supporters of its dissemination heralded the liberation of the female body for aesthetic "representational" purposes. Some argued that the free circulation of pornography in the public sphere was a visible statement against the prudish mores of the former communists who saturated the public environment with sterile Communist party symbols.[28] In Poland, they also argued that pornography was a means to contest the Catholic church's view of the body as sinful. Still others have invoked more Western, "feminist" arguments about the exploitation of women and the representational degradation of their bodies in public, claiming that the proliferation of pornographic literature and films is but public evidence of the dehumanization and social atomization that is a legacy of communism.[29]

Physicians in the region have noted that this legacy of dehumanization has left too many people with too little respect for their physical and/or mental health. It is only recently that AIDS has been taken seriously. The tragic cases of infant AIDS in Romania drew international attention, but were viewed there and elsewhere as an isolated phenomenon.[30] AIDS

---

[27]This discussion is meant to be suggestive of contemporary currents in everyday life in Eastern Europe; these issues are herein treated briefly.

[28]On reclaiming public space and representation in the public sphere, see, for example, G. Kligman, "Reclaiming the Public: A Reflection on Creating Civil Society in Romania," *East European Politics and Society* 4, no. 3 (1990): 393–438.

[29]I am unable to comment on the dissemination of pornographic materials involving children or men. With regard to the latter, the public legitimacy of homosexual relations varies throughout Eastern Europe; see, for example, J. Borneman, ed., *Gay Voices from East Germany* (interviews by J. Lemke) (Bloomington: Indiana University Press, 1991).

[30]The AIDS epidemic was due to the administration of micro-transfusions of blood to many of these children. The problem of tainted blood was compounded by the lack of disposable syringes as well as the repeated usage of unsterilized ones. See, for example, D. Rothman and S. Rothman, "How AIDS Came to Romania," *New York Review of Books,* 8 November 1990. Lack of contraceptive knowledge and/or usage in many East European countries, the lack of concerted public campaigns about these issues, and

is likely to be on the rise throughout the region, however, due to poor hygienic conditions, increased drug traffic and usage, as well as increased homosexual practices and prostitution without "safe sex." Prostitution has become a means for some women struggling with inflation and unemployment to obtain hard currency and increase their cash flow.[31] It should be emphasized that not all prostitutes are the stereotypical "women of the night." Married women with children often "work" with the full consent of their husbands. Competition has arisen across borders as Romanian and Bulgarian women, for example, sell themselves at cheaper prices in Hungary, Serbia, and elsewhere. Few of these women have been concerned about AIDS and do not insist that their clients use condoms. The increase in prostitution also indicates the easy translation of the "labor value" of the body into entrepreneurial activities.

The vulnerability of women and children has emerged in another context: the private international adoption market. International trafficking in infants and children is partially a result of the legacy of communism, and partially a response to the economic rigors of the transition. Although initially most widespread in Romania, both Poland and Russia have recently joined the ranks of popular sites for those seeking to adopt abroad.[32] Children from these countries are considered among American and European international adoption circles to be particularly desirable because they are white. Adoption is thought to provide a humanitarian road out for some of these children. The adoption of children through legal institutional arrangements is not at issue here. Rather, I refer to the emergence of a private market in what some have labeled "the commerce in human flesh." In Romania, opting for the private adoption process was faster than wading through cumbersome and confusing official bureaucratic procedures; it was also more

increased drug traffic from Asia through this now open corridor to the West have led to increasing numbers of AIDS victims and growing concern. Hence, AIDS in Eastern Europe will spread as a result of poor hygienic and sexual practices common elsewhere.

[31] This was true under socialism as well, although prostitutes had to work more surreptitiously than is the case today, when bodies are openly for sale. For a discussion of prostitution in Hungary during the socialist years, see I. Volgyes, *The Liberated Female* (Boulder, Colo.: Westview Press, 1977). The legacy of the past is such that in Bucharest, prostitutes were frightened that I and a French colleague were secret police come to "bust" them. There was talk about government officials wanting to unionize prostitutes as a means to control sexually transmitted diseases. The prostitutes found such reasons unconvincing; they were certain that authorities wanted to control their wages, as well as continue past surveillance practices under the guise of health control.

[32] See Kligman, "The Politics of Reproduction," for a fuller discussion.

expensive, very arbitrary, and subject to unsavory practices of coercion, corruption, and foreign complicity with these acts. In such cases, the victims of this process were not only foreign adoptive parents but also poor or single Romanian mothers. Poor women are especially vulnerable to the demands of others, some of whom consider their bearing of children to be little more than the means of production that yields a valuable commodity. Hence, in some cases, private adoptions contributed to the exploitation of women's reproductive labor. Given the sharp rise in prices, increasing unemployment, and depressed wages, it is not so difficult to understand why people have been tempted to sell their own, as well as other people's, children. Dealing in babies or children, especially white ones, can be lucrative business. I do not mean to suggest that no women gave up their children freely; for some mothers without the means or the will to support a child, this solved the problem of having to care for the unwanted. For other mothers, however, consent to an adoption was effectively forced in a transaction that was "understood" to be reciprocally beneficial to those involved.[33]

International adoption falls under the scholarly rubric of "the politics of reproduction," which centers attention on the relations between individual, local, and global interests and reproductive practices and public policy.[34] In postcommunist Central and Eastern Europe, debates about reproductive rights and legislation are currently topical, indeed heated. The politics of reproduction involve diverse but related issues including abortion rights or their curtailment, contraceptive options and education, social assistance provisions in the context of developing market economies, and the constitution of rights protected by democratic laws and practices. These debates, especially the ones about abortion, underscore not only the structural similarities characteristic of "the transition" throughout the region, but also the differences that are the result of divergent experiences under socialism. To illustrate, in distinct contrast

[33]The class specificity of socially constructed notions of "mother love" comes into focus in such cases. The "mother love" among the poor may be readily forgotten by those better off in the interest of "helping" or "rescuing" a child. Again, I refer the reader to Kligman, "The Politics of Reproduction," or a version thereof in *Feminist Studies* (Summer 1992). For a comparative discussion of "mother love," see N. Scheper-Hughes, *Death without Weeping: The Violence of Everyday Life in Northeast Brazil* (Berkeley: University of California Press, 1992).

[34]For discussion of this broad topic, see R. Rapp and F. Ginsburg, "The Politics of Reproduction," *Annual Review of Anthropology* 20 (1991): 311–44; and R. Rapp and F. Ginsburg, eds., *The Politics of Reproduction* (Berkeley: University of California Press, forthcoming).

to trends in Poland, Hungary, and Slovakia, where there have been serious moves to restrict abortion, in Romania abortion was fully legalized after the fall of Nicolae Ceausescu's pronatalist regime.[35]

As Gal has noted, "Given the important historical link between the definition of national identity and reproduction, as in the widespread fear of 'national death' through population decline, the differences in ethnic composition in each country, the size and importance of minorities, can also be expected to play important roles" in the debates about abortion and national identity.[36] For example, a typical concern voiced throughout much of the region calls attention to the rising birth rates of Roma, or Gypsies, compared with the declining or negative population figures among Romanians, Hungarians, Czechs, and so forth. Fears about population decline are manipulated to posit that the dominant population is in danger of being overwhelmed demographically, meaning that their authority will be weakened or destroyed. Numbers are used as evidence of strength or weakness.[37]

Theoretical arguments address abstract notions of the family and the nation. Indeed, abortion is one of the means through which nationalist rhetoric is expounded, and has implicit consequences for ethnic groups. Abortion is often raised as a population issue, population being fundamental to constructions of the nation as "imagined community." "Cultural identity" or "cultural autonomy" may be jeopardized by population policies meant to curtail the social reproduction of certain groups (which often gives rise to a counterrhetoric of genocide); relatedly, hegemonic cultural identity or autonomy may be promoted through the formulation of policies that explicitly conjoin cultural identity and reproductive practices (frequently voiced in nationalist terms), resulting in the delegalization of abortion. As Gal has also pointed out, demographic decline is tantamount to cultural decline and, in consequence, a threat to

---

[35] See Kligman, "The Politics of Reproduction."

[36] Gal, "Questions about Women and Gender after Socialism"; E. Huseby-Darvas, " 'Feminism, the Murderer of Mothers': Neo-Nationalist Reconstruction of Gender in Hungary," paper presented at the American Anthropological Association, 1991; O. Supek, "Even the Unborn Are Croats," paper presented at the American Anthropological Association, 1991.

[37] Certain segments of the white South African population have relied on such arguments to bolster their racist positions. The abstract threat of population decline has historically been effective. On the construction of "population" as collective identity, see, for example, M. Shapiro's chapter on "Language and Power," in his *Reading the Postmodern Polity: Political Theory as Textual Practice* (Minneapolis: University of Minnesota Press, 1992), 11–12.

national identity.[38] The "death of the nation" was, and still is, used as an argument against communist internationalism. Romania's dictator, Ceausescu, partially rationalized the stringent pronatalist policies of his regime in these terms. The delegalization of abortion was explicitly embedded in a nationalist rhetoric about self-determination. Ironically these policies, aimed at securing the future of the nation, helped to create a national tragedy measured by the highest maternal mortality statistics in Europe due to illegal abortions and among the highest infant mortality rates in Europe.[39]

Other politically active individuals, in positioning themselves in opposition to communism, currently seek the prohibition of abortion as a means to reinstate the "legitimacy" of motherhood, which was seemingly devalued by the socialist state's ideology of gender equality.[40] An appeal to "rights" broadly interpreted has also been invoked, proclaiming that the communists only considered the rights of women rather than those of the fetus, the husband, and society. Of course, the most extreme cases of banned abortion are found in the regimes in which "rights" were most fully denied and "the family" most heralded, of which Ceausescu's rule was only one of the most recent examples.[41] Heightened attention to reproductive rights—that is, intensified rhetoric about abortion—is predictable when the nation itself is at stake: when who owns it or who represents it is open to question.[42] In the case of

[38]"Death of the nation" is invoked in many contemporary debates about racial and/or cultural genocide. In the case of communist internationalism, the assumed cultural nonspecificity of "worker solidarity" threatened historical and cultural notions of identity, particularly as constituted in modernist discourse. The building of the nation-state theoretically challenged the legitimacy of local, communal relations; at the same time, national identity acquired legitimacy, which internationalism undermines. It is important to note that the transnational relations that are now a customary feature of the late-capitalist, "postmodern" world similarly threaten the sanctity of familiar identities. It is not, then, surprising that "death of the nation" serves as a ground for arguments against social sanctioning of homosexual relationships, which, in turn, confront the Judeo-Christian foundations of Western modernity.

[39]Kligman, "The Politics of Reproduction."

[40]Ibid.; Gal, "Questions about Women and Gender after Socialism"; J. Goven, "The Anti-Politics of Anti-Feminism: State Socialism and Gender Conservatism in Hungary, 1949–90," Ph.D. diss., Political Science, University of California, Berkeley, 1993; Funk and Mueller, Gender Politics. The "new right" antifeminist agenda offers similar arguments; see S. Faludi, Backlash: The Undeclared War against American Women (New York: Crown, 1991).

[41]See, for example, V. de Grazia, How Fascism Ruled Women: Italy, 1922–45 (Berkeley: University of California Press, 1992); C. Koonz, Women in the Fatherland (New York: St. Martin's Press, 1987); G. Bock, "Racism and Sexism in Nazi Germany: Motherhood, Compulsory Sterilization, and the State," Signs 8, no. 3 (1983): 400–421.

[42]See Gal, "Questions about Women and Gender after Socialism."

Central and Eastern Europe, such queries are often directed to concerns about selling the nation to the International Monetary Fund, the World Bank, or the Catholic church, or all three.

These arguments, however, must be interpreted against the realities of everyday life. The discursive interweaving of reproductive rights, or rape as in the tragic case of Bosnia, demographic decline, and national identity plays on popular fears and future dangers: for example, Muslim and/or Roma population explosions. These fears serve to heighten current feelings of uncertainty while masking the structural problems that are provoking them. The demographic threat is one of the rhetorical strategies employed to encourage women to leave the work force; however, the basic problem is economic restructuring, and the consequences of real and rising unemployment.

Although reasons differ, abortion is on the political agenda throughout much of postcommunist Central and Eastern Europe. For Romanian women and men, the fall of the Ceausescu regime embodied "freedom" from the coercion of the paternalist state that forced women to bear children despite the extremely deteriorated conditions of everyday life. Abortion was made fully legal and readily available. Outside media celebrated this liberation, aware of the circumstances in which Romanian unwanted children were "living" like the living dead. The reversal of the antiabortion law was necessary, but it is also problematic. Three years later, abortion still remains the primary method to control family size. In response to an abortion-to-live birth rate of three to one, government and nongovernmental organizations working with the assistance of foreign agencies and individuals have actively begun to promote sex education and family planning. Various efforts in these domains have pointed to a growing recognition that the state must participate responsibly in the protection of its citizens' rights and well-being.[43]

Elsewhere in the region, however, women have found that the right they have long internalized as fundamental to control of their own reproductive cycles is now being challenged by many who simultaneously profess to be supportive of democratic practices. In general, public opinion does not support political moves to restrict abortion. The pace of German reunification was threatened by disparate abortion policies in

---

[43]See Kligman, "The Politics of Reproduction." It should be noted that another social legacy of communism that bears directly on political change is the generalized avoidance of forthright discussion about the state itself.

the two Germanys. What is known as "abortion tourism" unmasks the hypocrisy of the Federal Republic of Germany's law.[44] Attempts to restrict abortion have prompted protests in the Czech lands as well as in Poland, where most citizens oppose curtailment.[45] In Poland, the antiabortion legislation supported by the Catholic church created a women's movement. The conditions of daily life in Poland, as elsewhere, are difficult and will remain so for the foreseeable future. Despite the fact that Poland is overwhelmingly Catholic, abortion is a method of fertility control used by "practicing" Catholics, as is true throughout the Catholic world.[46] Many women surveyed claim they are against abortion for religious reasons, but nonetheless have had them. Such decisions have been, and usually are, weighed in relation to the conditions of daily life.

These conditions have become increasingly difficult, as illustrated in the discussion earlier about the demographics of unemployment, divorce, emigration, and continuing multiple burdens for women. Recounting the real economic costs of having a baby, one woman questioned: "I wonder if any of those screaming murder at me have bothered to count the cost of having a baby. . . . My husband left me when he heard I was pregnant again. What else can I do?"[47] In this context, it is not accidental that Polish women have raised the specter of Ceausescu in their public protests. They have also chanted, "This is Poland, not the

[44]The right to travel abroad to a locale where abortion is legal prompted a national crisis in Ireland over the initial refusal to grant an abortion to a fourteen-year-old who had been raped. The politics of abortion in the United States suggest that abortion tourism will again become a widespread practice of the middle and upper classes; the poor cannot, literally, afford the duplicity. On Germany, see, for example, the following articles in the special issue "Germany and Gender," *German Politics and Society* 24 and 25 (Winter 1991–92): U. Nelles, "Abortion, the Special Case: A Constitutional Perspective," 11–21; D. Birkenfeld-Pfeiffer, "Abortion and the Necessity of Compromise," 122–27; M. Nimsch, "Abortion as Politics," 128–34; T. Bohm, "The Abortion Question: A New Solution in Unified Germany?" 135–41.

[45]On Czechoslovakia, see S. Wolchik, "Women's Issues in Czechoslovakia in the Communist and Postcommunist Periods," in B. Nelson and N. Chowdhury, eds., *Women and Politics Worldwide* (forthcoming). She makes the important point that there is now more room for women and men to express their own preferences. Although women were more likely than men to support "choice" (poll, April 1990), women's Christian groups have organized against abortion. On the debates in Poland, see, for example, Fuszara, "Legal Regulation of Abortion in Poland." There is a growing literature on this particular site of struggle.

[46]For example, in Brazil, where abortion is officially illegal, some four hundred thousand women are admitted to hospitals annually to recuperate from abortion attempts. See J. Brooke, "Brazil Abortions: Illegal in Name Only," *New York Times International,* 21 July 1991, 5.

[47]See Zmijewska, "Born but Unwanted."

Vatican," "God save us from the church," "Fewer churches, more day-care centers." Women from the now destitute textile industry in Lodz carried banners reading, "God gave a baby; who will give for the baby?" Another read, "Poland was enslaved; Polish women will be."[48]

The threat to the right to abortion has spawned women's movements in Central and Eastern Europe. Women are publicly questioning the meaning of democracy and civil society—by and for whom? To be sure, abortion has been, and is, differently linked to questions of nationhood, anticommunism, sexuality, morality, and rights. The control of reproduction is considered essential to concerns about identity and autonomy, whether this control is understood as the control of one's own body (often referred to as biological reproduction) or of the body politic in general (social reproduction). That is partially why abortion is so divisive an issue historically and comparatively.

CONCLUSIONS

Women in Central and Eastern Europe today find themselves with decreased access to the political public sphere that is being formed. This limited access may be as much by choice as a result of the current backlash against women, including their access to employment opportunities. The backlash has engendered, literally, more open discrimination against women in the labor force and workplace. As sketched in this chapter, complex factors have combined to generate the feminization of poverty. The paternalist socialist state appropriated unto itself the patriarchal prerogatives of more traditional family organization in this part of the world. I mentioned earlier that the socialist state's usurping of these patriarchal rights to women's labor and reproduction, as well as to men's labor, threatened and changed the very foundations of social relations. The upheavals unleashed by the collapse of communism, however welcome, have opened a Pandora's box of social problems. The dependency relations long ingrained under communist rule have inhibited many men and women from taking responsibility for their own lives, let alone those of their families.

The social legacy of communism is complicated, as are the social consequences introduced by the transition. As Millar and Wolchik note in the first chapter of this volume, the legacy of communism has created

[48]See E. Hauser, B. Heyns, and J. Mansbridge, "Feminism in the Interstices of Politics and Culture: Poland in Transition," 259.

certain expectations about the obligations of the state to its citizens, which the ABCs of economic reform do not highlight. Nonetheless, the social consequences of democratization and marketization similarly raise questions about the mutual obligations of the state and its citizens. The relationship of the polity to its more vulnerable members—minorities or ethnic groups, women, children, and the elderly—is revealing about the character of the body politic. James Madison understood that a test of democracy lies in the treatment of its minorities, among whom figure women and children. How the various dimensions of societal and biological reproduction are treated in any society dramatically affects the lives of women and children. Whether democracy will be the future of Central and Eastern Europe, or parts thereof, remains to be seen; whether women and children will be equal beneficiaries of democracy's great privileges also remains to be seen. If hope springs eternal, then that may be the best conclusion to be drawn from the legacy of the past and the uncertainties of the present.

12

The religious renaissance in the Soviet Union
and its successor states

DAVID E. POWELL

Everyone now understands that only a revived morality will permit us to overcome the lack of spirituality that destroyed society and will now make us kind
and tolerant of each other.

Leningradskaia pravda, 19 June 1990

People ask me why I, a Christian, am so fundamentally opposed to communism.
Among other things, I must say that communism is the most radical anti-
Christian doctrine and anti-Christian force in world history. The unprecedented
destruction and demolition communism has brought were directed not only
against [Christianity but against] all of society.

Partiinaia zhizn', no. 17 (1990)

I think that during perestroika more children have been baptized than under
Prince Vladimir. . . . The baptism of Russia is continuing.

Argumenty i fakty, no. 29 (1990)

The dramatic shift in government policy toward organized religion is
one of the most important changes introduced by Mikhail Gorbachev
and continued by Boris Yeltsin. Religious beliefs, behaviors, and organizations, which had been exposed to mockery and abuse for more than
half a century, have been freed from interference and persecution.
Equally important, the various agencies that were responsible for polic-
ing religious activities—the Communist party, the Komsomol (the
Young Communist League), the Council on Religious Affairs and Directorate "Z" (the so-called Fifth Directorate) of the KGB—have all been
disbanded.[1]

---

[1] The announcement that the USSR Council for Religious Affairs had "ended its existence"
appeared in *Rossiskaia gazeta*, 5 December 1991. For a discussion of Directorate "Z"
and its demise, see John B. Dunlop, "KGB Subversion of Russian Orthodox Church,"

271

No control mechanisms have been created to replace these institutions; instead, new laws have been fashioned to promote freedom of religion, and the political leadership throughout the former Soviet Union has pledged to protect the rights of believers. The authorities have returned thousands of churches, mosques, and other religious buildings seized by the old regime, and they have not interfered with the construction of new houses of worship. They relaxed and then eliminated antireligious propaganda, legalized religious groups that previously had been banned, allowed clergymen to write for newspapers and participate in television discussions, permitted religious instruction in state and parochial schools, and freed ordinary believers and clergy alike to volunteer their services in hospitals, orphanages, and similar institutions. Copies of the Bible and the Koran are more readily available than ever before, while the number of Jews allowed to emigrate and Muslims allowed to make the pilgrimage to Mecca have increased sharply. Finally, data on the number of religious communities, as well as the number of believers, have been published.

This is an astonishing array of changes, and they have taken place with remarkable alacrity. It was not so long ago—in July 1983—that a plenary session of the party Central Committee declared gravely that "numerous ideological centers of imperialism are striving not only to support, but also to spread religion, and to impart to it an anti-Soviet, nationalistic orientation."[2] In 1985, the year Gorbachev became general secretary of the party, a typical propaganda tract emphasized that "the elimination of vestiges of religion ... is one of the most important components of the party's entire ideological work."[3]

The first steps taken by the Gorbachev administration in the field of religion hardly foreshadowed the "new thinking" that was to become manifest in late 1987 and early 1988. Indeed, at its Twenty-seventh Congress in early 1986, the Communist party adopted rules affirming the obligation of all party members "to carry out a decisive struggle ... with religious ... prejudices ... that are foreign to the socialist way

Radio Free Europe/Radio Liberty Research Report (hereafter cited as *Research Report*), 20 March 1992, 51–53. See also *Moskovskie novosti*, no. 38 (1991): 11.
[2]*Materialy plenuma Tsentral'nogo Komiteta KPSS, 14–15 Iunia, 1983 goda* (Moscow: Izdatel'stvo Politicheskoi Literatury, 1983), 60. Unless otherwise indicated, translations from Russian-language sources are by the author.
[3]I. Y. Bulanyi and I. G. Iavtushenko, *Muzei na obshchestvennykh nachalakh* (Moscow: Profizdat, 1985), 96. For other examples of this sentiment, focusing on the Muslim areas of the country, see *Partiinaia zhizn' Kazakhstana*, no. 2 (1985): 92–94, and no. 12 (1985): 66–69, as well as *Kommunist Uzbekistana*, no. 10 (1985): 94–96.

of life." The congress itself called on party members to engage more energetically in "individual work" with believers—a practice that, in John Dunlop's words, amounts to "singling out religious individuals for criticism and humiliation at public meetings . . . visits by atheist activists at their homes, etc."[4] In fact, no less a figure than Gorbachev himself, in a November 1986 speech, called for "an uncompromising struggle against manifestations of religion."[5]

Furthermore, during the first few years of Gorbachev's reign, the authorities continued to imprison people for their faith and prohibited certain groups, such as the Jehovah's Witnesses, Seventh-Day Adventists, Evangelical Christian Baptists, and Pentecostals, from functioning at all. They also continued to harass, arrest, and/or incarcerate religious dissidents whom they found particularly objectionable or regarded as particularly threatening. Precisely how many people were caught up in the government's punitive system will probably never be known, although millions of men and women certainly belonged to the banned churches.

In addition, the entire population, adults and children alike, continued to be exposed to a steady stream of antireligious propaganda in the schools, media, and their place of work. The creation of new secular rituals and holidays, designed to supplant religious ceremonies and holy days, was said to occupy a particularly crucial place in "the restructuring and spiritual renewal [that was occurring] in all aspects of life" under perestroika.[6] A year and a half before the 1988 celebration marking the millennium of Christianity in Kievan Rus'—an occasion that was to bring church and state together in a mutually beneficial embrace—official propagandists were still warning the populace about the evils of religion, the treachery of clergymen, and the need to eliminate belief in God.

Everything changed and continued to change after Gorbachev's meeting with Patriarch Pimen of the Orthodox church in April 1988. Gorbachev spoke of the church's loyalty and patriotism; he promised that religious people would no longer be treated as pariahs. "Believers," he declared, "are Soviet people, working people, patriots, and they have

---

[4]John B. Dunlop, "Gorbachev and Russian Orthodoxy," *Problems of Communism* 38, no. 4 (July–August 1989): 98. See also David E. Powell, *Antireligious Propaganda in the Soviet Union* (Cambridge, Mass.: MIT Press, 1975), 119–30.
[5]*Pravda vostoka,* 25 November 1986.
[6]*Sovetskaia Rossiia,* 16 February 1986.

every right to express their views with dignity." At the same time, he promised that they would be guaranteed genuine "freedom of conscience" in the future.[7] Six weeks later, Andrei Gromyko, participating in an anniversary celebration marking the millennium, reaffirmed this message, speaking approvingly of the historical role played by the Russian church, as well as the patriotism, humanism, and contributions to peace demonstrated by other churches in the Soviet Union.[8]

We do not know, nor perhaps does he, what persuaded Gorbachev to introduce such a radical shift in official policy. But a variety of motives— his desire for popular support to carry out the policies of glasnost and perestroika, a quest for legitimacy on the part of the regime, the search for an ally in combating the country's social problems, perhaps even a desire to unleash the creative energies of a population alienated by years of restrictions on religious belief and conduct—seem to have persuaded the Soviet leader of the need for change. He took a risk in seeking a rapprochement, possibly even an entente, with organized religion, and the results of his efforts may not have pleased him completely. But he performed a quintessentially democratic act, one that continues to influence events long after the collapse of communism.

RUSSIAN ORTHODOXY

As Gorbachev was making his historic overture to the patriarch, the Communist party's ideological journal, *Kommunist,* was also shifting its attitude toward religion. Once the epitome of "militant Marxism," *Kommunist* in early 1988 called for a more balanced approach to religious issues. As one author put it, "Our task consists in disseminating new thinking to the entire sphere of the study of religion and atheist upbringing, overcoming once and for all dogmatism, primitivism, and reliance on an administrative-bureaucratic style ... which lead to ... violations of the law."[9]

In 1988, the government authorized various Western religious organizations to send a million Bibles to the Soviet Union; other organizations have since added to the total. In late 1988, the journal *V mire knig* published selections from the Gospel of St. Matthew and announced

---

[7] *Izvestiia,* 1 May 1988. Eight months earlier, academician Dmitrii Likhachev urged the authorities to change their attitude toward religion. His statement was the first of its kind to appear in a Soviet newspaper. See *Literaturnaia gazeta,* 9 September 1987.
[8] *Pravda,* 12 June 1988.
[9] *Kommunist,* no. 4 (1988): 115–23.

plans to serialize the entire New Testament.[10] This represented the first time since the Bolshevik revolution that a state publishing house had made religious materials available to readers.[11] Since then, the entire Bible has been published in Russian and several other languages of the former USSR, making it, in *Pravda*'s words, "truly accessible to believers and atheists [alike]."[12]

The decision to make copies of the Bible available may turn out to have been one of the most revolutionary acts of glasnost. Having been denied access to the most basic sources of religious belief and tradition, both urban sophisticates and simple peasants had a very limited understanding of their heritage.[13] Finally given a chance to read the Old and New Testaments, many atheists and agnostics experienced a genuine spiritual awakening. Here are the words of one man from Novosibirsk, writing to *Ogonek* in 1989:

At the age of 30, I have read the Gospels for the first time . . . the text gripped me: I was impressed by the austere power of the words, the elegance of the finely tuned aphorisms, the subtle poetic quality of the images . . . [G]radually I became very angry: what a treasure they have been hiding from me! Who decided, and on what basis, that this was bad for me—and why? . . . I did not run off to church . . . I simply understood that I never was and never will be an atheist.[14]

This is vivid testimony to the power of Gorbachev's "revolution from above." Indeed, exposure to the Gospels and other religious literature seems to have contributed powerfully to a renaissance of faith among the people of the former Soviet Union.

Beginning in 1989, the Soviet government also granted churches and (in some areas) schools permission to organize religious instruction. Latvia was the first republic to offer some form of religious education, and the first Orthodox Sunday school opened in Vilnius in November 1989. The authorities in Vilnius also granted Jewish children permission

[10]*Moscow News*, no. 2 (1989).
[11]See Oxana Antic, "One Million Bibles for the Soviet Union," *Radio Liberty Report on the USSR* (hereafter cited as *Report*), 10 March 1989, 17.
[12]*Pravda*, 9 March 1990.
[13]In the past, atheist activists urged that copies of the Bible be made available to help students become "politically conscious Marxists" and more effective antireligious propagandists; see, e.g., *Komsomol'skaia pravda*, 13 May 1988. In Khrushchev's time, a "humorous Bible" mocking the original was published in an edition of 255,000 copies. See Leo Taksil', *Zabavnaia bibliia* (Moscow: Izdatel'stvo Politicheskoi Literatury, 1964).
[14]*Ogonek*, cited in Christopher Cerf and Marina Albee, eds., *Small Fires* (New York: Summit Books, 1990), 82.

to study Hebrew and Yiddish. By year's end, scores of church Sunday schools were operating in Moscow, Leningrad, and elsewhere, serving thousands of children. In addition, several state schools began to offer optional courses on the history of religion, some of them taught by priests.[15]

The patriarch, at least initially, continued to flatter the regime, suggesting that it had always been solicitous of Orthodoxy. Thus in mid-1988, Pimen declared, "I would describe the interaction of church and state at present as completely normal." The government, he went on, "is doing everything necessary to ensure the vitality of the church, and does its share to meet [the latter's] daily needs."[16] He dismissed assertions that the church had experienced persecution as "lacking in objectivity." Perhaps most striking, he declared that "we always encounter mutual understanding and support on the part of the Council on Religious Affairs"—the very organization that had subjected the church to decades of arbitrariness and oppression.[17]

Still, a great deal of change was evident as the Gorbachev-Pimen meeting approached and, even more, in its aftermath. A church service to mark the millennium of Orthodox Christianity was held at the Bolshoi Theater and broadcast throughout the country. At the same time, millions of television viewers saw the documentary film *The Church*, which portrayed the great contributions Russian Orthodoxy had made to the country.[18] On 26 May 1988, holy relics of several well-known Orthodox saints were removed from the museums of the Kremlin and given over for safekeeping to the church.[19]

So powerful had the momentum for religious freedom become in mid-1988 that an Orthodox church official felt free to say, "No state official should have the right to interfere in the nomination of clergy, in church life, in the organization of congregations and parishes, dioceses, monasteries, libraries, special theological schools and colleges, as well as other institutions . . . believers need for the complete realization of their religious life."[20] Not all of this was possible when he issued his demands, but within a few years virtually all of it had materialized.

Two years earlier, in 1986, the Orthodox church journal *Zhurnal*

---

[15] *Izvestiia*, 29 October 1989.
[16] *Problemy mira i sotsializma*, no. 6 (1988): 79.
[17] Ibid., 80.
[18] *Moscow News*, no. 25 (1988).
[19] *Izvestiia*, 28 May 1988.
[20] *Twentieth Century and Peace*, no. 7 (1988): 43, cited in Dunlop, "Gorbachev and Russian Orthodoxy," 114.

Moskovskoi Patriarkhii had made another revolutionary recommendation. It suggested that priests no longer be required to obtain permission from their local soviet in order to visit "seriously ill" pensioners in their homes, in homes for the elderly, or in penal institutions.[21] In 1988, Pimen himself urged that the church become involved in charitable work.[22] Although this idea made a great deal of sense, any attempt to carry it out would, at the time, have been illegal.

Until 1990, Soviet law did not allow churches a "social mission," and the few volunteer efforts that were undertaken were definitely illegal. After 1988, however, despite the clear language of the law, large numbers of religious organizations and other institutions began to follow the conscience of their members. In 1988, for example, a hospital and a convent, then another hospital and a group of Orthodox church officials, agreed that clergy and ordinary believers could soon begin to aid the sick. A physician connected with one of the agreements explained why he had become involved:

We shall accept everyone. For us, everything is important: a glass of water brought in time, reading to patients, simply talking with them, calming them with a kind word. . . . It is not just that the hospital is short of personnel; we do not have enough tolerance, mercy, and even simple attention to give the patients.[23]

At present, many religious organizations in the former Soviet Union have established programs allowing them to assist needy fellow citizens. Although most of these welfare and charity arrangements were introduced quite recently and are of modest proportions, they have begun to play a significant role in "stabilizing and humanizing [Russian] society."[24] The Orthodox church, the Catholic church, Evangelical Christian Baptists, Seventh-Day Adventists, Pentecostals, and a number of other so-called sects have been especially active in developing such activities. They focus their energies on assisting hospital patients, working with elderly persons living at home and with mentally handicapped children, visiting the inmates of labor camps, and helping to rehabilitate former prisoners.[25] In the summer of 1989, a Baptist chorus was permit-

---

[21]*Zhurnal Moskovskoi Patriarkhii*, no. 1 (1986), Appendix to journal.
[22]*Izvestiia*, 9 April 1988.
[23]*Trud*, 7 June 1988.
[24]Oxana Antic, "Welfare and Charity Programs of Soviet Religious Organizations, 1989–90," *Report*, 30 November 1990, 8.
[25]See, e.g., *Moskovskie novosti*, no. 2 (1988); *Trud*, 7 June 1988; *Ogonek*, no. 38 (1988): 30; Oxana Antic, "Charitable Activities of Churches in the USSR," *Report*, 22 September 1989, 7–9.

ted to stage a concert at a camp for Young Pioneers; after the performance, members of the troupe presented several mini-lectures on religion
and distributed copies of the Bible and the New Testament to campers
and staff.[26] Even more remarkable, members of the Gideon Society have
been allowed to organize Bible readings in Moscow's Second Special
Prison for Criminals, the former Butyrka.[27] Finally, because of the pro-
hibitively high cost of funerals and the spread of poverty among the
masses, the Orthodox church is now offering subsidies to bury the
indigent. Not only is the price thereby made manageable, but "the
relatives of the deceased are spared humiliation and extortion."[28]

Churches in some parts of Russia have "adopted" local hospitals,
day-care centers, or orphanages—occasionally at the request of local
government officials. These arrangements permit members of the congre-
gation to carry out repairs, decorate the premises, purchase furniture or
appliances, set up clubs and workshops, or take children from a shelter
into their homes. A number of concerts have also raised money for
charitable causes.[29] All of this would be impossible were it not for the
1990 Law on Freedom of Conscience and Religious Organizations,
which explicitly authorizes religious groups "to engage in charitable and
philanthropic activities on their own and through foundations."[30]

The church, having been consigned in the 1920s and 1930s to a
virtually parasitic role in society, rejected this arrangement in the late
1980s and, even more so, after 1990. People who wanted to help those
in need finally could do so, and the power of the church grew immeasur-
ably. By April 1991, Patriarch Aleksii (who succeeded Pimen) stated that
"Russia has painfully . . . endured a time of serving false gods,"[31] clearly
implying that that time had ended. Three months later, he could say
without fear of exaggeration that "during the past year, I think that we
truly have been able to extricate ourselves from the state's obtrusive tu-
telage."[32]

In June 1990, religious services were held in St. Isaac's Cathedral in
Leningrad (now St. Petersburg) for the first time in decades. The building
was not actually returned to the Orthodox church—it is supposed to

---

[26]*Sobesednik*, no. 30 (1989).
[27]*Komsomol'skaia pravda*, 6 July 1990.
[28]*Izvestiia*, 6 May 1993.
[29]Antic, "Charitable Activities"; *Izvestiia*, 14 November 1989.
[30]*Pravda*, 9 October 1990.
[31]*Komsomol'skaia pravda*, 16 April 1991.
[32]*Izvestiia*, 10 June 1991.

function instead "both as a temple and as a museum"—but it is now used for major church events.[33] Toward the end of 1991, President Yeltsin signed a decree authorizing the Moscow patriarchate to make use of some of the Kremlin's churches. Responding to an appeal issued jointly by the patriarch and the Moscow city soviet, Yeltsin gave the patriarchate access to some of the country's best-known churches— including the Assumption, Annunciation, and Archangel cathedrals, and the Cathedral of the Protective Veil, better known as St. Basil's (in Red Square).[34]

Among the most joyous changes introduced in recent years is the reinstitution of Christmas, Easter, and certain other Christian holy days as national holidays. With the demise of the Soviet state came the demise of the system of communist holidays, such as 7 November (Revolution Day), 1 May (May Day, the "day of international solidarity of the workers"), and so on. In December 1990, the patriarch wrote to Yeltsin (who was then chairman of the Russian Republic Supreme Soviet), requesting that, beginning in 1991, the first day of Christmas (celebrated on 7 January in the Russian Orthodox faith) and Good Friday be declared public holidays.[35] On 27 December 1990, the RSFSR Supreme Soviet declared Orthodox Christmas a nonworking day.[36]

Most people in the Russian Federation have reacted favorably to the reintroduction of religious holidays. Partly this is an expression of the growing sense of nationalism in Russia, but it also reflects a genuine feeling of religious self-identification, of pride in being part of the Russian Orthodox faith. In the words of *Izvestiia* at Eastertime 1991: "Who would have thought even recently . . . that the capital of our Fatherland, the bulwark of atheism, would dress up for Easter just as it did for the 'red days'—November 7 or May 1?"[37]

Today, the Russian Orthodox church has become a powerful ally of the Russian state and of Boris Yeltsin personally. Before the Russian

---

[33]*Leningradskaia pravda*, 19 June 1990.

[34]*Foreign Broadcast Information Service Daily Report, Central Eurasia* (hereafter cited as FBIS-SOV), FBIS-SOV-91-228, 26 November 1991, 56. In citing this source, I occasionally make minor changes in the translations provided by the service.

[35]*Izvestiia*, 27 December 1990.

[36]*Pravda*, 28 December 1990. At the same time, Ukraine adopted legislation making the first day of Christmas and Easter, as well as Whitsunday, holidays. *Pravda Ukrainy*, 3 January 1991. Christmas is also now celebrated as an official holiday in Belarus, Georgia, and Moldova. See Oxana Antic, "Developments in Church Life," *Research Report*, 3 January 1992, 32.

[37]Cited in the *New York Times*, 8 April 1991.

republic presidential election in June 1991, Patriarch Aleksii spoke out in public on behalf of Yeltsin—and the latter, once he became president, promised to return "all illegally confiscated buildings and other property to the church." During the summer of that year, Aleksii presented a list of properties (buildings, monasteries, icons, and so on) that the church wanted the state to return. Yeltsin's response was immediate and unequivocal: he granted the request unconditionally.[38] In April 1993, the president made arrangements to return additional ecclesiastical properties to the church.[39]

In general, Yeltsin has sought to associate himself more closely with moral questions, simultaneously emphasizing his fidelity to the motherland and to the mother church. On 3 April 1991, for example, he played a prominent role during the Russian Easter service conducted by Patriarch Aleksii at Moscow's Cathedral of the Epiphany.[40] Later that year, he delivered a moving speech on Stalin's destruction of the Cathedral of Christ the Savior—"an unparalleled act of vandalism" as he put it. "The column of dust which rose over the ruins of the church," he declared, "became a sinister symbol of impermissible contempt for Russian sacred objects, a crude trampling of human rights, and monstrous outrages against the feelings of believers—and not only Orthodox believers."[41]

When Yeltsin was sworn in as president of the Russian Federation in July 1991, Aleksii reminded him: "You have taken responsibility for a country that is gravely ill, [one that has experienced] a 70-year destruction of its spiritual system and internal unity." Thus, the patriarch said, the nation's new leader would have to concern himself with Russia's religious, as well as its political, revival:

You bear responsibility not only before the people but also before God. You have accepted not honor, not privileges, but responsibility. As far as the church or religious associations are concerned, we hope that the new President of Russia will promote the return of the church, its age-old sacred places, its churches and cloisters.

Having concluded his remarks, Aleksii made the sign of the cross over the president, signifying in the most vivid way possible his support for the new secular order.[42]

[38] Antic, "Developments in Church Life," 32.
[39] See Radio Moscow, 23 April 1993, in *FBIS-SOV-93-078*, 26 April 1993, 69.
[40] Ibid., 7 April 1991, in *FBIS-SOV-91-067*, 8 April 1991, 38.
[41] Ibid., 5 December 1991, in *FBIS-SOV-91-235*, 6 December 1991, 59.
[42] *Izvestiia*, 10 July 1991.

Since then, the church and the state have continued a kind of dialogue, offering each other mutual support and cooperating in an attempt to revive Russia's sense of spirituality. In the spring of 1993, the patriarch issued his Easter message, calling on the faithful "to do everything to prevent the country from being returned to chaos, ruin and civil war."[43] Yeltsin, celebrating Easter in Vladimir, declared, "I want Russia to remember the traditions of past centuries. I want it to restore truly Russian traditions, [including] religious traditions." His host, Archbishop Eulogii of Vladimir and Suzdal, remarked that the number of Orthodox churches in the two cities had trebled during the previous two years, while several monasteries, seminaries, and Sunday schools had been opened. "Every opportunity has been [afforded] to benefit the souls of Orthodox Christians," he concluded, "and believers are grateful for this . . . to our President Boris Yeltsin."[44] In an odd sort of way, it should be noted, this fulsome praise of the country's top political leader is a vivid example of the social legacy of communism.

A very different expression of communism's legacy is the upsurge in ultranationalist, almost paranoid views in certain church circles—views that remind one of the Stalinist concept of "capitalist encirclement" or of even more pernicious notions. For example, Metropolitan Ioann of St. Petersburg and Ladoga, who, as we shall see, believes fervently in a Jewish and Catholic conspiracy against Russian Orthodoxy, has also accused the U.S. Central Intelligence Agency (CIA) of participating in this plan. According to Ioann, Allen Dulles, the former CIA director, asserted in 1945: "By sowing chaos in Russia, we will imperceptibly supplant their values with false ones and make them believe in those false values." Continuing in the same vein, the metropolitan asked: "What more proof do we need to realize that a base and dirty war—well-funded, carefully planned, unremitting and merciless is a struggle to the death. . . . The entire country . . . is to be destroyed for remaining faithful to its historical mission and its religious devotion."[45]

Despite the presence of "ultras" within the upper ranks of the church, President Yeltsin continues to maintain good relations with Orthodoxy as an institution and with Aleksii as an individual. For example, on 19 August 1991, the first day of the attempted coup d'état against Mikhail Gorbachev, Yeltsin turned to the patriarch with an appeal for support.

[43]Moscow Television, 25 March 1993, in *FBIS-SOV-93-057*, 26 March 1993, 40. See also *Trud*, 17 April 1993.
[44]Radio Moscow, 18 April 1993, in *FBIS-SOV-93-073*, 19 April 1993, 76.
[45]*Sovetskaia Rossiia*, 20 February 1993.

"The tragic events of the past night," he wrote, "oblige me to turn to you and to all believers in Russia." In response, Aleksii challenged the legality of the State Committee for the State of Emergency (the group trying to engineer the coup), demanded that President Gorbachev be given an opportunity to speak, and called on the armed forces "not to permit fraternal blood to be shed." On 21 August he issued an anathema against anyone who had helped organize the coup attempt.[46]

The church continues to experience problems, however; for example, there is a significant shortage of churches and priests. In the final days of the Soviet Union, there were probably only two thousand Orthodox churches in the entire Russian republic, and even a large city such as Sverdlovsk (renamed Ekaterinburg after the fall of the communist regime) had only one or two functioning churches. According to one Orthodox official, "On Sundays and feast days, the churches are so crowded that our worshippers cannot cross themselves."[47] At the same time, the patriarch has declared, the church has an urgent need to train thousands of new priests to meet the needs of the parishioners who will attend these churches as they are opened.

ISLAM

The communist regime was always hostile toward Islam, just as it was toward other denominations. Still, antireligious policy in Central Asia and other areas where the Muslim faith was strong had certain distinctive characteristics. As William Fierman observed, "The regime's aversion to Islam . . . stemmed from both an antipathy to religion in general and to the fear that Islam might unite Muslims in opposition to Soviet rule in particular."[48] From the point of view of Muslim believers, official policy was especially galling because it was devised by outsiders ("infidels"), chiefly Russians, who behaved as conquerors, had little understanding of Islam, and showed little respect for local customs or values.

In the first years of the Gorbachev era, the Central Asian press continued to heap abuse on Islam. Propagandists criticized "the presence of superstition and fantastic notions in the outlook of some people," as well as the harm done by individuals "who preserve harmful survivals of

[46]Oxana Antic, "Church Reaction to the Coup," *Report*, 20 September 1991, 15; and Mark Rhodes, "Religious Believers in Russia," *Research Report*, 3 April 1992, 60.
[47]*Twentieth Century and Peace*, 109.
[48]William Fierman, "Religion and Nationalism in Soviet Central Asia," *Problems of Communism* 38, no. 4 (July–August 1989): 123.

the past" such as religion.[49] An Uzbek ideologist called for "the un-masking of Islamic and other religious ideologies," asserting, "We are for progressive, popular traditions, but we are against harmful ones, including religious traditions. [The latter] must be eradicated."[50] In 1986, the Politburo of the Communist party's Central Committee adopted a secret resolution concerning Muslims and their church; it asserted that "Islam is a hindrance to social and economic development." At the same time, Vladimir Kriuchkov, who was then chairman of the KGB, warned his colleagues about the danger that the Ayatollah Khomeini's revolution in Iran posed for the Soviet Union. He spoke of fundamentalism as "a very dangerous thing, in view of its unscrupulousness and fanaticism."[51]

On 12 May 1988—two weeks after Gorbachev's meeting with Patriarch Pimen—the Tajik party Central Committee called on officials throughout the republic to "intensify the struggle against manifestations of religion and harmful traditions and rituals." Party organizations, the Central Committee went on, "continue to underestimate the increasing significance of . . . atheistic education under conditions of ever deeper democratization." Young people were singled out for particular attention. Government, party, and other official agencies were told to "take steps to improve . . . the atheistic education of young people, developing among them . . . a critical attitude toward religion . . . on the basis of a class-oriented stance."[52]

During the same year, however, Muslims in various parts of the Soviet Union began to speak out against the restrictions Moscow had placed on their religion. Complaining that the consequences of Gorbachev's meeting with the patriarch had not been matched in Central Asia, and that the regime was therefore using a double standard, they demanded equal treatment. Thus the Uzbek writer Emin Usmanov pointed out that although the press had termed the adoption of Christianity in Kievan Rus' "progressive," it "busies itself only with condemning and finding fault with Islam." He continued:

[49]*Tojikistoni Soveti* (Dushanbe), 4 June 1986, translated in *Joint Publications Research Service, JPRS-UPS-86-055*, 21 November 1986, 100. See also *Izvestiia*, 28 November 1991.

[50]*Pravda vostoka*, 24 December 1986. See also *Sotsiologicheskie issledovaniia*, no. 3 (1987): 50–55; *Sovetskaia Kirgiziia*, 29 October 1987; *Sotsialisticheskaia industriia*, 11 February 1988.

[51]*Izvestiia*, 28 November 1991.

[52]*Kommunist Tadzhikistana*, 12 May 1988.

Why have we not tired of looking in a one-sided manner at the dark aspects of Islam and our past culture? . . . Hasn't the time come to speak fairly about both the positive and the negative sides of religion?! . . . Let us explain to the people both aspects of religion, the harmful and the progressive.[53]

Some Soviet analysts continue to regard Islam as "a brake on . . . social and economic development [and a force] perpetuating 'national narrow-mindedness' and ethnic exclusivity." Nonetheless, even they are sensitive to allegations that they have been allowing greater latitude to Christianity than to Islam.[54] As a leading scholar put it in 1991, "The idea of a revival of the Russian people through Orthodoxy is viewed today as something perfectly normal, but when the Muslim people turn to Islam with the same objective, it puts people on guard." The contrast in attitudes, he went on, "is strange, to say the least."[55]

The official response to this controversy has been two-pronged, involving both concessions and heightened militancy. Thus the period between 1988 and 1991, when the Soviet Union finally collapsed, witnessed a considerable easing of policy toward Islam. Media attacks directed against Muslim leaders and against the faith in general occurred less and less frequently, and the authorities allowed considerably greater freedom of worship. Throughout Central Asia, Azerbaijan, and other areas with large Muslim populations, local groups were permitted to open new mosques or to repair and reopen places of worship that had been shut during the Stalin, Khrushchev, and Brezhnev years. Between 1985 and 1990, the number of "working" mosques rose from 392 to 1,103.[56] During the years 1986–91, the number of registered religious communities in Kazakhstan increased fivefold,[57] and in Uzbekistan, the number of mosques grew from eighty-five in 1989 to some four hundred only two years later.[58] There is still a shortage of trained religious leaders, however; in Russia alone, more than five hundred mosques have no imam.[59]

---

[53]Quoted in John Soper, "Kirgiz and Uzbek Writers Express Their Views in Connection with Party Conference," *Radio Liberty Research*, 12 July 1988, 3.

[54]Bess Brown, "Greater Tolerance for Islam?" *Radio Liberty Research*, 1 May 1988, 1, 3. See also *Soiuz*, no. 2 (1991): 11, and *Pravda*, 3 December 1991.

[55]*Izvestiia*, 28 November 1991.

[56]*Argumenty i fakty*, no. 32 (1990). For slightly different figures, see Yasin Aslan, "Mosques Reopened in Azerbaidzhan," *Report*, 10 February 1989, 16.

[57]Radio Moscow, 8 August 1991, in *FBIS-SOV-91-153*, 8 August 1991, 142.

[58]*Krasnaia zvezda*, 10 April 1991.

[59]*RFE/RL News Briefs*, 10–14 May 1993, 6.

The Soviet authorities also granted permission to the government of Saudi Arabia to ship a million copies of the Koran to Muslims in the Soviet Union, and they allowed domestic publishing houses to print Uzbek, Kazakh, and Russian translations of the book. The Russian-language literary journal *Pamir,* the organ of the Tajikistan Writers' Union, began printing the Muslim holy scriptures in 1990.[60] *Islam nuri* (*Ray of Islam*), published in Tashkent, explained the tenets of the Muslim faith to readers, demonstrated how to perform various rituals and ceremonies, provided information about Muslims in other countries, and urged the faithful "to fight against superstition and for religious purity."[61]

At the same time, the influence of "unofficial" Islam spread rapidly. Many of the Sufi brotherhoods, outlawed by the Soviet government, reemerged with "strength, vitality, and dynamism." Underground mosques—which operated out of clubhouses, teahouses, libraries, and private homes—were no longer harassed, and congregants could perform their religious obligations without fear of government interference.[62]

In addition, President Yeltsin, though identifying primarily with the Russian Orthodox church, makes frequent reference to the role of Islam within Russia's pluralistic society. In 1991, for example, on the occasion of the Muslim festival of 'Id ak-Fitr, he expressed his admiration for Islam's "humanistic and moral values,"[63] and the following year, welcoming the holiday of Kuyram Bayram, he articulated his hope that "adherents of Islam will make their weighty contribution to fostering a single Russian community, strengthening civil peace and national accord."[64]

One more positive change in government policy toward Islam should be noted—providing ordinary Muslims with an opportunity to make the pilgrimage, or hajj, to Mecca. For most of the Soviet period, only a handful of Soviet Muslims were granted permission to make the trip, and these people were largely members of the Muslim hierarchy. Even after the death of Stalin in 1953, little changed in this sphere, because

[60]*Izvestiia,* 14 January 1990.
[61]*Pravda vostoka,* 24 May 1990.
[62]Yaacov Ro'i, "The Islamic Influence on Nationalism in Soviet Central Asia," *Problems of Communism* 39, no. 4 (July–August 1990): 50–54.
[63]Radio Rossii, 15 April 1991, in *FBIS-SOV-91-073,* 16 April 1991, 45.
[64]Ibid., 11 June 1992, in *FBIS-SOV-92-113,* 11 June 1992, 33.

Khrushchev pursued a vigorous antireligious policy and Brezhnev was at best indifferent to the expression of religious feelings anywhere in his realm.[65]

After Gorbachev's 1988 rapprochement with religion, however, official attitudes toward the hajj shifted.[66] In 1990, some 1,527 pilgrims were allowed to make the trip, and the number increased the following year to almost 5,000. Far more people wanted to go, of course, but the Soviet and Saudi governments both set limits on the number who could travel and be accommodated. A more complicated problem involved the ever-increasing cost of the journey, as well as the availability of transportation. The extraordinarily high sums demanded of those seeking to make the pilgrimage are said to have caused "mass disorders" and riots, as potential pilgrims in Muslim areas of the Soviet Union expressed their outrage.

Made anxious by such episodes, the government assumed an attitude toward Islam very different from that toward Russian Orthodoxy. From 1986 on, religious and ethnic disturbances occurred regularly in Central Asia, Kazakhstan, and Azerbaijan. According to *Literaturnaia gazeta*, after Kazakh students rioted against the naming of a Russian as the first secretary of Kazakhstan's Communist party, "Muslim fanatics and Sufis penetrated the ranks of the students, manipulating the young people." The head of the republic KGB asserted that "the ringleaders . . . not only fanned religious sentiment but also called for a jihad against the existing system." As late as 1989, the "ringleaders" were said to be receiving support from "foreign representatives of countries following an Islamic ideology." The unnamed foreigners were also accused of making "a major effort to stress holy war as the basic way to conduct a struggle with religious nonbelievers and to spread this concept among adherents of Islam who live in the Soviet Union."[67]

More generally, the policy of increased tolerance for Islam was laden with risk for the Soviet regime. For example, the Islamic Renaissance Party (IRP), established in 1990, pledged "to revive [the religion] in

---

[65]See Walter Kolarz, *Religion in the Soviet Union* (London: Macmillan, 1961), 431; Alexandre Bennigsen and Chantal Lemercier-Quelquejay, *Islam in the Soviet Union* (London: Pall Mall Press, 1967), 178.

[66]The following discussion relies primarily on Ann Sheehy, "Dagestani Muslims Protest against Cost of Pilgrimage to Mecca," *Report*, 28 June 1991, 26–28. See also *Pravda vostoka*, 3 June 1990; *Izvestiia*, 8 June 1991; *Pravda*, 14 September 1991.

[67]Ro'i, "The Islamic Influence on Nationalism," 58–62, and the sources cited therein; *New York Times*, 19 and 21 January 1990. See also *Kommunist Tadzhikistana*, 10 March 1989.

areas from which it [had] been driven out and to spread it to regions where it is altogether unknown or where people have a distorted notion of it." The IRP professed highly conservative beliefs, including the notion that "women must, above all, be keepers of the home and rearers of children."[68] While the Soviet Union still existed, the IRP was actually little more than a loosely knit collection of groups within those republics and regions that had substantial Muslim populations. With the unraveling of the Soviet Union, however, the IRP has been replaced by a number of regionally based Islamic parties. All of them, like their progenitor, continue to pursue a radical Islamic agenda.[69]

The IRP has been recruiting primarily in Tajikistan, the North Caucasus (especially Dagestan and Chechnia), and the Fergana Valley of Uzbekistan.[70] When the communists were still in power, these republican parties were feared by the authorities, who viewed them as potent rivals in an increasingly serious struggle for power. Thus the government refused to allow them to hold meetings, harassed or fined organizers (usually on charges of holding an unauthorized assembly), and, in four of the five Central Asian states, even outlawed the party. But Islamic militants have continued to function, and since the Soviet Union collapsed, the Muslim religion has continued to experience a revival in all of the countries of the area. Most of the region's governments, because of being fearful that organized religion might become a threat to their own power, have sought to contain Muslim influence. Officials assert repeatedly that fundamentalism will not be tolerated, but, oddly enough, they often temper their stern warnings with the reassuring argument that there is no need for concern, since few local citizens would be interested in it anyway.

Thus President Askar Akaev of Kyrgyzstan has declared: "There is no

---

[68] *Izvestiia*, 8 January 1991. This source claimed a membership of ten thousand, primarily in Central Asia and the North Caucasus; another source put the figure at twenty thousand. See *Literaturnaia gazeta*, 8 March 1991.

[69] See Robin Wright, "Islam, Democracy and the West," *Foreign Affairs* 71, no. 3 (Summer 1992): 140, footnote 7. Members of these parties generally are known as "Muslim fundamentalists," but one scholar, Khalid Duran of the Foreign Policy Research Institute in Philadelphia, contends that this term is "a poor substitute for Islamism—the new, messianic ideology whose adherents seek to forcibly impose Islamic rule on non-pious Muslims as well as non-Muslim populations." Because the expression "Islamic fundamentalism" has gained such wide currency, however, it will be used here. See *Near East Report* 37, no. 23 (7 June 1993): 104.

[70] *Izvestiia*, 25 September 1990; *Kommunist Tadzhikistana*, 26 December 1990; *Pravda vostoka*, 1 February 1991; *Literaturnaia Rossiia*, 8 March 1991; *Moskovskie novosti*, 10 March 1991; *Komsomol'skaia pravda*, 23 March 1991.

basis in Kyrgyzstan for fundamentalism; our people are not contaminated with it. . . . We are certainly promoting the revival of religion, but
it serves exclusively to assert moral values in society. We are against
religious interference in how the state is governed."[71] Similarly, President Nursultan Nazarbaev of Kazakhstan has expressed a "sharply negative" view of fundamentalists; their behavior, he says, risks "throwing
the Muslim peoples back into the Middle Ages."[72] Imamali Rakhmonov,
chairman of the Supreme Soviet of Tajikistan, was even more firm when
he spoke in early 1993: "The Tajik people are genuine Muslims, but
they categorically reject Islamic fundamentalism. . . . Every Tajik family
in the last few months has experienced the fruits of this fundamentalism.
. . . The fundamentalists killed and destroyed."[73]

Rakhmonov's remarks require a bit of amplification. For several years
now, Muslim fundamentalists have been waging a bloody civil war
within Tajikistan and have been staging hit-and-run attacks from neighboring Afghanistan. As recently as February 1993, opposition groups in
eastern Tajikistan hung Islamic flags on government buildings, and one
district even went so far as to declare itself "an autonomous Islamic republic."[74]

The Tajik government (aided by Russian, Uzbek, and other forces)
has been trying to contain the radicals, but they have done so at great
cost. The situation is highly complex, of course; it involves not only
local politics, but the concerns of political leaders elsewhere in the
Commonwealth of Independent States (CIS). Pavel Grachev, Yeltsin's
minister of defense, has described the region as "strategically important," a barrier protecting the CIS against the possible spread of
Islamic fundamentalism.[75] According to another source, "In order to
defend itself from a potential adversary, Russia will guard the Tajik-
Afghan border like its own, supporting any regime that agrees to offer
its territory as a buffer zone."[76]

Given the political climate in general, and the turmoil in Tajikistan in
particular, Muslim leaders in the new nations of Central Asia have

[71]*Izvestiia*, 20 March 1992.
[72]Radio Alma-Ata, 16 February 1993, in *FBIS-SOV-93-030*, 17 February 1993, 62.
[73]Radio Dushanbe, in *FBIS-SOV-93-033*, 22 February 1993, 39.
[74]See *RFE/RL News Briefs*, 22–26 February 1993, 9. See also *Pravda*, 4 November 1992, and 6 February 1993.
[75]See *RFE/RL News Briefs*, 8–12 February 1993, 8. See also *Krasnaia zvezda*, 25 May 1993, 3.
[76]*Nezavisimaia gazeta*, 29 April 1993, 3. See also ibid., 13 May 1993; *New Times* (Moscow), no. 47 (1990): 15–16; and *Kommersant-Daily*, 15 December 1992.

disclaimed any interest in constructing states along the lines pursued by Khomeini in Iran. Even in Tajikistan, the country in which Islamic fundamentalism has been most enthusiastically received, the Muslim establishment has been highly critical of a Khomeini-like approach. Akbar Turadzhonzod, the most prominent Muslim leader in Tajikistan, has spoken out in favor of "a democratic secular state in which religion and the state will be separated. . . . To build an Islamic state in the 20th century means to doom the republic to isolation."[77] He also has dismissed fears of an Islamic republic constructed along Iranian lines as "groundless."[78] He has pointed to the fact that Tajiks, unlike Iranians, are Sunni Muslims (and thus do not accept a single imam), that they have been exposed to seven decades of antireligious propaganda, that unity is lacking among both the Muslim faithful and their leaders (there are now reports of armed clashes among rival Muslim groups, some of which are "solved" by the partitioning of mosques), and perhaps most important, that young people have, in the main, "formed liberal views."[79]

Even while disclaiming an interest in establishing an Islamic republic, though, Muslim leaders often use language suggesting that such an arrangement is precisely what they have in mind. In April 1992, Turadzhonzod assured members of the Tajik republic Supreme Soviet that his party did not "seek the destruction of the present state system." Still, because the Communist party played such a prominent role in government, and because it still operated as "a brake on change and the democratization of society," the IRP "is waging a struggle against it." When asked if the party's goal was the establishment of a theocratic regime such as the one that exists in Iran, an IRP spokesman "refused to discuss the question of whether parties which do not profess the values of Islam will be permitted to operate in the republic if the IRP were to gain power."[80]

Only two weeks later, Turadzhonzod used the same sort of elliptical language to hint at his support for a theocracy. "We have no plans to create an Islamic state *by force*," he said. "Unlike the communists, we have no intention of imposing our ideology and system on the country. Of course, if the people favor an Islamic state in a referendum, they

[77] *Komsomol'skaia pravda*, 4 October 1991.
[78] *Izvestiia*, 8 May 1992.
[79] *Komsomol'skaia pravda*, 4 October 1991; Radio Moscow, 4 September 1992, in *FBIS-SOV-92-173*, 4 September 1992, 45.
[80] *Izvestiia*, 23 April 1992.

will have the right to choose that path."[81] This is hardly a ringing endorsement—much less a promise—of a secular future.

Turadzhonzod has been forced to go underground to avoid arrest on charges stemming from his support for the anticommunist opposition.[82] His successor, Imam-Khatib Sharifov, declared in his first speech that "religion will not interfere with state affairs and become involved in politics." That kind of statement is altogether understandable and in keeping with the Muslim establishment's relatively low-key approach to politics. But the mufti's offer of support for the government—which, he contends, is pursuing a policy of peace and stability—closely resembles the unctuous tone adopted by religious leaders in communist times.

Militant Islam has been slow to develop in Kazakhstan, but now is said to be "in the midst of a slow but steady process of gaining strength and gathering momentum for a future 'explosive' involvement in politics." Muslim activists have been operating under the leadership of the Alash Party for the National Independence of Kazakhstan. (The word "alash" is variously translated as "red wolves" and "victors.")[83]

Alash's members oppose the official clergy, especially Ratbek Nysynbaev, the mufti of Kazakhstan, calling him and his confreres hypocrites. In particular, they say the mufti appointed numerous communists and people from the state security agencies to serve as local imams. More important, Nysynbaev is categorically opposed to "the Islamization of political life and, as a result, the activity of religious parties on the territory of Kazakhstan." Like the Islamic parties of Tajikistan, Uzbekistan, and Russia, Alash is radical and often behaves in an intemperate manner; as a result, the Kazakh authorities have said that its activities are unconstitutional. Alash regularly accuses the Nazarbaev government of "violating the rights of the Muslim community." As an alternative, it calls on people to recognize that "enlightened Islam is the only alternative to ethnic and religious conflicts and the most realistic means to ensure peace in the CIS."

THE JEWS

Until the advent of glasnost, the party line stipulated that anti-Semitism did not, indeed could not, exist anywhere in the Soviet Union.[84] This assertion was utter nonsense, of course, but it was not until the Gorba-

[81]Ibid., 8 May 1992 (emphasis added).
[82]RFE/RL News Briefs, 15–19 February 1993, 6.
[83]This and the following paragraph are derived from Nezavisimaia gazeta, 2 July 1992.
[84]Pravda, 22 July 1990.

chev era that the media began to admit that a problem existed and the political leadership tried to do something about redressing old grievances. Thus the authorities have finally acknowledged the full dimensions of Jewish suffering during World War II, taking note of the fact that the Nazis singled out this ethnic group for extermination. President Gorbachev himself, at a ceremony dedicated to the fiftieth anniversary of the German massacre of the Jews at Babi Yar (a ravine outside Kiev), said that "the Jews were among the first Nazi victims, both in our country and in the whole of Europe. ... The Nazis ... used anti-Semitism as a major means to infect people's minds with chauvinism and racism."[85] He declared that "venomous sprouts of anti-Semitism sprang up in the Soviet Union. The Stalin bureaucracy, which publicly dissociated itself from anti-Semitism, in fact used it as a means to isolate the country from the outside world and strengthen its distorted position with the help of chauvinism."[86]

Furthermore, almost a million Jews have been allowed to emigrate from the Soviet Union and its successor states, and another million living in the Commonwealth of Independent States are said to be ready to leave for Israel or the United States.[87] The new Israeli ambassador to the Soviet Union asserted in the fall of 1991 that emigration procedures were already "quite liberal" (in 1990, some 184,000 Soviet Jews had left for Israel) and expressed the hope that the rules would be eased still further.[88]

Similarly, the Soviet Union participated actively in the decision of the United Nations General Assembly to repeal the 1975 resolution which asserted that "Zionism is a form of racism and racial discrimination." By 1991, Soviet political commentators were apologizing for the fact that Moscow "had played a decisive role in securing the adoption of this resolution," a document which, they admitted, had encouraged "a confrontational and hostile attitude toward one of the organization's full-fledged members." One article in *Izvestiia* termed the resolution "clearly unjust with respect to both Jews and Israel," adding that "proclaiming that Zionism [the concept of the Jews' return to their historical homeland] is racism is tantamount to denying Israel's right to exist."[89]

---

[85]Radio Moscow, 23 October 1991, in *FBIS-SOV-91-206*, 24 October 1991, 6.
[86]Ibid., 5 October 1991, in *FBIS-SOV-91-195*, 8 October 1991, 73–74.
[87]Ibid., 20 April 1992, in *FBIS-SOV-92-078*, 22 April 1992, 8.
[88]Ibid., 23 October 1991, in *FBIS-SOV-91-206*, 24 October 1991, 6.
[89]*Izvestiia*, 13 December 1991. For an argument that the *real* problem is "the racist attitude toward Arabs that forms the basis of the ideology and practice of political Zionism," see *Pravda*, 21 December 1991.

This shift in the official Soviet position, along with other changes in the international arena, helped the proposal to repeal the 1975 resolution to pass by a 111-vote majority.

In addition, Jewish books and other artifacts can now be shipped into Russia from abroad. They are no longer confiscated arbitrarily by the customs service. Moreover, some religious books in Hebrew have been published in both the Soviet Union and its successor states. Perhaps most striking, three small yeshivahs have been established in Moscow and St. Petersburg, which means it is no longer necessary for Jewish pupils to go abroad to learn more about their faith.[90]

At the same time, however, there have been a number of profoundly troublesome incidents. The best known involves the January 1990 outburst of a group of *Pamiat'* (Memory) adherents at Moscow's Central House of Writers. Shrieking anti-Semitic epithets, these individuals tried to break up a meeting of liberal writers, denouncing them as Jews, Zionists, and polluters of Russian culture. Remarkably, the Moscow public prosecutor's office instituted criminal proceedings against *Pamiat'* under Article 74 of the RSFSR Criminal Code, which outlaws deliberate actions aimed at "arousing national or racial enmity." Konstantin Ostashvili, the leader and shrillest member of the interlopers, was found guilty of inciting mass hostility toward the Jews. This step, it appears, was unprecedented: It was the first occasion in Soviet history when Article 74 (or its equivalent) was used to pursue anti-Semites.[91] Only three years later, in April 1993, another *Pamiat'* member, who had taken part in a raid on the liberal newspaper *Moskovskii komsomolets*, was given a far less stringent sentence: He was merely put on probation for eighteen months. As a reporter for *Nezavisimaia gazeta* observed after the trial, "The decision confirmed the current tendency of Russian courts to hand down 'milder' sentences."[92] Whether his remarks referred to court cases in general or only to those involving so-called hate crimes, was not clear.

This shift in judicial behavior is, at least in part, reflective of an underlying problem that continues to plague the Jews—their uncertain position in Russian society. Major journals and newspapers, such as *Nash sovremennik, Molodaia gvardiia,* and *Sovetskaia Rossiia,* are

---

[90]Zvi Gitelman, "Glasnost, Perestroika and Antisemitism," *Foreign Affairs* 78, no. 2 (Spring 1991): 155.
[91]Radio Moscow, 12 October 1990, in *FBIS-SOV-90-202*, 18 October 1990, 42.
[92]*Nezavisimaia gazeta,* 27 April 1993.

strongly infused with an anti-Semitic, "nationalist," or "national Bolshevik" content. The articles, novels, novellas, and poetry they contain help to stimulate and reinforce anti-Jewish feelings among a stratum of the intelligentsia that is both prominent and "legitimate."[93]

The prosecutor's office also responded to the publication of the society's program, which urges the "de-Zionization" of the country. According to *Pamiat'*, "Jews and individuals related to them should not be allowed to defend dissertations, receive titles and scientific degrees or enter the ranks of the CPSU. . . . They should not be elected to soviets or to leading party, soviet or other offices."[94] One *Pamiat'* member, speaking up on behalf of Ostashvili at the Moscow city court, proclaimed that "in West Europe people live well because as far back as the Middle Ages they got rid of Jews." He called for deportation of all Jews from the Soviet Union to Israel.[95] Presumably, this is how the term "de-Zionization" is supposed to be understood.

Pamiat', which seems to be more noisy than effective (the organization failed to elect a single legislator in either the 1989 or the 1990 elections, despite vigorous campaigning on behalf of its candidates), was part of an upsurge of anti-Semitism throughout the Soviet Union. Sergei Plekhanov, deputy director of the United States and Canada Institute, observed in 1990 that anti-Semitism was endemic in the Soviet Union. (He called it "one of those diseases of the Russian mind.") But, he added, the phenomenon was on the rise because "at a time of crisis like the one that we're going through, especially in a society like ours, it is just inevitable that ethnic animosities and hatred and conflict flare up."[96]

More generally, greater freedom of religion has been accompanied by increasingly open expressions of anti-Semitism by members of various extremist organizations. In early 1989, for example, *Pamiat'* and other reactionary groups staged a rally at one of Moscow's largest sports arenas. Participants enthusiastically applauded speeches condemning the Jews for having committed numerous "crimes" against the Russian people and for their alleged lack of loyalty to the Soviet Union. Many of

[93]*Pravda*, 22 July 1990. For a more thorough exposition of this point, see Yitzhak M. Brudny, "The Heralds of Opposition to *Perestroyka*," *Soviet Economy* 5, no. 2 (April–June 1989): 162–200. Ostashvili, it should be noted, committed suicide while in jail. See Radio Moscow, 29 April 1991, in *FBIS-SOV-91*, 2 May 1991, 30.
[94]*Literaturnaia gazeta*, 21 February 1990.
[95]Moscow Radio, 25 July 1990, in *FBIS-SOV-90-144*, 26 July 1990, 48.
[96]Ibid., in *FBIS-SOV-90-2-2*, 18 October 1990, 43.

those present carried posters with anti-Jewish slogans or caricatures. One banner proclaimed, "No to Rootless Cosmopolitanism" (a Stalin-era anti-Semitic term) and showed St. George slaying a number of "dragons"—most prominently Leon Trotsky, Yakov Sverdlov, and Lazar Kaganovich, as well as several of Gorbachev's closest advisors, many of whom were Jewish or presented as caricatures of Jews.[97]

In addition, the myth of a Jewish-masonic conspiracy has been resuscitated, *The Protocols of the Elders of Zion* and *Mein Kampf* are available to anyone interested in reading them, and Jews have been accused of an astounding array of evil acts—ranging from the killing of Czar Nikolai II and his family to carrying out the forced collectivization of agriculture, the repressions of the Stalin era, "corrupting Russian culture," and "destroying the ecological system." The magazine *Nash sovremennik* carried an article contending that the Jews themselves were responsible for the mass murders committed at Dachau and Auschwitz, while Valentin Rasputin, a highly respected writer, has alleged that the Jews "killed God."[98]

Evidence of popular hostility against Jews is abundant. A major newspaper reported in early 1990 that, in Kharkov, "several violent attacks were carried out on apartments inhabited by Jews."[99] At about the same time, anti-Semitic leaflets were circulated in Novosibirsk, and most were placed in the mailboxes of Jewish residents of the city. In Kiev, "provocative rumors about 'planned Jewish pogroms' " were disseminated.[100] Rumors and unofficial warnings about pogroms were widely discussed in the press. Although the source of most of these rumors is not clear, both the Ministry of Internal Affairs (MVD) and the KGB denounced them repeatedly. A cynic might wonder whether or not these frequent denials and rebuttals served to remind the Jews—as well as anti-Semites—about the possibility of violence.[101]

Uglier examples of anti-Semitism have been made public in recent years. In 1989, for example, a gang in the small Moldovan town of Orgeev destroyed forty-two graves at the local Jewish cemetery. "They smashed tombstones, destroyed greenery, left excrement on graves,

---

[97]See *Moscow News*, no. 6 (1989). For a representative sampling of letters attacking and defending *Pamiat'*, see *Leningradskaia pravda*, 28 August 1988.
[98]See John and Carol Garrard's letter to the editor, *New York Times*, 27 May 1990, section 4.
[99]*Trud*, 13 February 1990.
[100]Radio Moscow, 14 June 1990, in *FBIS-SOV-90-115*, 14 June 1990, 55.
[101]*Krasnaia zvezda*, 11 February 1990. For a similar statement by the USSR MVD, see Radio Moscow, 21 February 1990, in *FBIS-SOV-90-036*, 22 February 1990, 49.

gouged out the eyes of pictures of the deceased, and left cattle to graze there."[102] The following year, Jewish graves at the Vaganka cemetery in Moscow were desecrated by unknown persons. Swastikas were painted on some twenty gravestones bearing Jewish-sounding names, and nearby trees, pillars, signs, and fences were also daubed with paint. In December 1992, "unknown persons" booby-trapped a synagogue in Kiev; fortunately, there was no explosion, for military personnel were called in to remove two shells and two hand grenades—all of which were set to go off when the door was opened.[103]

Just how frequent such occurrences are is not known, but a Moscow television announcer has asserted that "such instances are becoming more and more frequent in our country."[104] Indeed, as recently as mid-June 1993, a gang of youths smashed windows and drew a swastika on Moscow's main synagogue. The police dismissed the incident as "ordinary hooliganism," rather than anti-Semitism, but how the authorities were able to divine the group's motives was not explained; nor was it made clear why "hooliganism" directed against a place of worship should be treated in such a cavalier manner.[105]

Russia's best-known "anti-Zionist" is a boorish—but clever—political figure named Vladimir Zhirinovskii. The organizer of many nationalist and anti-Semitic rallies in the Soviet Union and Russia, Zhirinovskii and his Liberal Democratic party repeatedly denounce the Jews and blame them for most of Russia's ills. Although many people regard him as a fool or a clown, the country's grave economic difficulties and the humiliations it has been experiencing in recent years might well help him to inflict harm on the Jews.

His views are simple, and he expresses them forcefully. He does not recommend, at least in public, the murder or incarceration of Russia's Jews; he just wants to get rid of them. In a way, his objective is like that of the Serbian nationalists who have been advocating "ethnic cleansing" in Bosnia-Herzegovina. On the rhetorical level, though, he eschews force and violence. In an interview on the *MacNeil/Lehrer News Hour* at

---

[102]Action for Soviet Jewry, *Soviet Jewry Report* (September–December 1989): 4.
[103]*Izvestiia*, 2 December 1992.
[104]Moscow Television, 21 June 1990, in *FBIS-SOV-90-121*, 22 June 1990, 26. Yet another incident of this type took place in late 1991. A group of "extremists" held a rally beside one of the towers of the Kremlin to protest the Jewish festival of Hanukkah. Moscow TASS International Service, 1 December 1991, in *FBIS-SOV-91-232*, 3 December 1991, 39–40.
[105]*New York Times*, 16 June 1993.

the beginning of 1992, Zhirinovskii combined the ingenuous with the disingenuous in asserting:

I am not an anti-Semite myself, but [the Jews'] concept [of politics and economics] is anti-governmental. They do not want to see a great and free Russia. . . . So the best outcome of this process would be a free immigration of Jews out of Russia to Israel.[106]

There is an immense gap between the law which prohibits "propaganda of national hatred" and the "blindness" or, more likely, indifference of those who are entrusted with ensuring that the law is obeyed.[107] Nowhere is this gap so palpable as in the case of the Jews.

By the spring of 1991, Zvi Gitelman, one of America's leading specialists on the "Jewish question" in the Soviet Union and Russia, wrote that anti-Semitism was "more visible today than at any time in the past forty years." He found that grass-roots "Judophobia" among intellectuals and ordinary citizens alike was being expressed more frequently, and in the period since he made his observation, this phenomenon has even gained a kind of legitimacy. Thus the Russian Orthodox church periodical *Moskovskii tserkovnyi vestnik* has referred to former Israeli Prime Minister Menachem Begin as the "Zionist Führer" and accused "Zionists" (that is, Jews) throughout Russia of being "secret agents of Israel."[108]

Similarly, on more than one occasion, Metropolitan Ioann of St. Petersburg and Ladoga has denounced both Jews and Catholics for being, in his words, like "a pack of wild beasts—brutal, greedy, and ruthless."[109] The metropolitan has been especially outspoken on the importance of *The Protocols of the Elders of Zion* (a century-old forgery prepared by the czar's secret police) as a source of insight into Jewish wickedness. While expressing some uncertainty about the authenticity of *The Protocols,* Ioann declared on 20 February 1993 that "world history, as if obeying the command of an invisible dictator, has submissively pursued its capricious course in amazing, detailed correspondence with the plan set forth in their pages."

The metropolitan's writings and sermons have proved to be unsettling to the patriarch. On 25 January 1993—less than a month before Ioann's

[106]*MacNeil/Lehrer News Hour,* 13 January 1992; cited in Jewish Institute for National Security Affairs, *JINSA Security Affairs* (February 1992): 5.
[107]*Pravda,* 22 July 1990.
[108]See Gitelman, "Glasnost, Perestroika and Antisemitism," 153.
[109]The discussion of Ioann's activities is derived from *Sovetskaia Rossiia,* 20 February 1993.

public embrace of *The Protocols*—the patriarch issued a decree forbidding publication of Ioann's writings in church periodicals, because they "have caused an ambiguous reaction on the part of public opinion." If this was a mild rebuke, it was a rebuke nonetheless. But it seems not to have had much of an effect on the metropolitan.

When the chief rabbi of Moscow, Adolf Shaevich, denounced Ioann for "blatant anti-Semitism," the latter's press service simply brushed the allegation aside, suggesting instead that "describing the humble prelate's statements as anti-Semitism is . . . an ill-intentioned provocation that could harm peace between nationalities in Russia." Indeed, the metropolitan himself spoke darkly of "the danger of a revitalized Judaizing heresy that is being brought into the church by priests of Jewish origin," as well as "the terrible imprint that Jewish religious extremism has left on Russia's fate."

An equally distressing episode occurred in May 1993, when the newspaper *Pravda* published an account featuring "Satanic sects," "Western 'preachers,' "—and Jewish ritual murder. According to the article, "The Levites [persons who performed certain sacred rituals in ancient Israel] considered the sacrifice of a gentile on his sacred holiday to be a sign of national and religious might and a solicitation of God's great mercy. The more morally upright the sacrificial victim, the greater God's favor. Therefore, they took children and religious figures to be sacrificed." Just to make sure the message was perfectly clear, the newspaper added that these murders "have continued right up to the present day."[110]

In 1989, some two hundred members of the Congress of People's Deputies, concerned about increasing manifestations of religious and ethnic intolerance, signed a petition asking Gorbachev to condemn anti-Semitism publicly. The petition was not granted.[111] Four years later, in April 1993, Rabbi Shaevich asked President Yeltsin to speak out against "growing and open" anti-Semitism. Yeltsin, too, demurred, arguing that anti-Semitism "on a state level" did not exist in the country. But, as we have seen, it most certainly does exist.

CATHOLICS AND ORTHODOX IN UKRAINE

The Uniate question, which had lain dormant for several decades (except among a relatively small group of militants), was reopened by the Polish pope John Paul II. One of his first acts after assuming his new role in

[110]*Pravda*, 5 May 1993. For a rebuttal, see *Izvestiia*, 7 May 1993.
[111]Gitelman, "Glasnost, Perestroika and Antisemitism," 146.

1979 was to send a letter to Cardinal Iosyf Slipyi, the exiled leader of the Ukrainian Catholic (also known as the Greek Catholic, or Uniate) church. To the intense consternation of political and religious leaders in the Soviet Union, this letter—written in connection with the approaching millennium—praised Ukrainian Catholics for having "endured sorrows and injustices for Christ, preferring fidelity toward the Cross until the last breath of life."[112]

For this and other statements, John Paul was the object of considerable vituperation on the part of Soviet officials. One 1986 article in a Ukrainian propaganda magazine attacked the pope as "a person with extreme anti-Communist views," a man who owed his position to "the most reactionary forces of imperialism."[113] Another source accused him of attempting to exploit the millennium in order to

revive religious feeling among the traditionally believing element of the population and to generate interest in religion among . . . young people and the intelligentsia; to unite under cover of religion discontented anti-Soviet elements who have found refuge abroad; to secure . . . a channel for bourgeois ideological penetration of our country; to revive Uniatism and foment nationalist sentiment.[114]

After Gorbachev came to power, however, Soviet propagandists began to speak differently, and the regime offered the Uniates a number of political concessions. During the period 1986–87, for example, virtually all Ukrainian religious prisoners of conscience were released from incarceration or exile. As a result, the former "catacomb church" became more assertive. Ukrainian Catholic clergymen "held public religious services for large numbers of Uniate believers . . . and collected petitions calling for the reopening of Ukrainian Catholic churches and the complete rehabilitation and legalization of the Church."[115] By the end of the decade, the Greek Catholic church had become a legal entity, thereby fulfilling a nationalist hope long thought impossible to realize—that "believers in our churches will be able to speak with God in Ukrainian."[116]

[112]Cited in Bohdan Nahaylo, "The Prospect for a Papal Visit to the USSR in 1988," *Radio Liberty Research,* 20 November 1986, 6.
[113]*Pid praporom Leninizmu,* no. 18 (1986): 7, cited in ibid.
[114]*Kommunist Ukrainy,* no. 10 (1986): 88–89.
[115]Bohdan R. Biciurkiw, "The Ukrainian Catholic Church in the USSR under Gorbachev," *Problems of Communism* 39, no. 6 (November–December 1990): 7–9.
[116]*Zhovten',* no. 9 (1988): 80, cited in Bohdan Nahaylo, "Ukrainians Object to Moscow Patriarchate's Description of Millennium as Solely 'Russian' Affair," *Radio Liberty Research,* 12 October 1988, 3.

By 1989 their campaign had achieved considerable success, and they were ready to turn their attention to the issue of property rights—*their* property rights. Deprived for decades of their churches and other buildings, they saw it as only fair that they regain what actually belonged to them, which, of course, meant taking it back from the Russian Orthodox church. As one Greek Catholic priest in the Ukrainian city of Lviv put it, "The time of restructuring has come."[117] He might just as well have said, "The time of retribution has come."

Starting in 1989 and continuing well into 1990, Uniates began seizing churches and cathedrals by force. Russian Orthodox officials contended that they, in contrast, preferred to resolve any problem "by peaceful means, in a spirit of brotherly love."[118] But they were willing to return only a handful of buildings. Orthodox spokesmen alleged that Uniates were "flagrantly flouting the rights and dignity of other Christians," using "threats, blackmail, and bribery." Their "un-Christian" rhetoric and behavior were attributed to "encouragement from abroad by nationalist émigré communities and other forces." One commentator asserted that "some people, proclaiming their religion to be more righteous and their church to be more national, are trying forcibly to take back church buildings and property from others whom they consider to be unworthy."[119]

But there is no evidence to support the view that the Uniates considered any other denomination unworthy or their own more righteous; they were simply protesting Stalin's 1946 decision that took away their rights and their property. Their churches and cathedrals had been seized and given to the Russian Orthodox church, they found the situation increasingly intolerable and, miraculously, glasnost and perestroika gave them the opportunity to reclaim what they firmly believed was rightly theirs. (According to one estimate, there were approximately 5,700 Orthodox church parishes in Ukraine in the summer of 1989. Of these, more than half—some 3,000—were in Western Ukraine, and virtually all of the latter were acquired in 1946 when Stalin decided that the Uniates should no longer exist.)[120]

With the transfer—peacefully or otherwise—of thousands of Orthodox churches to the Uniates, the status of Greek Catholic congregations

---

[117]Radio Kiev, 13 March 1990, in *FBIS-SOV-90-067*, 6 April 1990, 101.

[118]Moscow Television, 1 February 1990, in *FBIS-SOV-90-023*, 2 February 1990, 106.

[119]*Pod znamenem Leninizma*, no. 3 (1990): 82–83; *Soiuz*, no. 7 (1990): 16.

[120]Roman Solchanyk, "Church and State Split on Ukrainian Catholic Issue," *Report*, 5 January 1990, 28.

is no longer a major irritant separating Catholics and Orthodox. But if this matter is now "solved," a second set of issues continues to strain the relationship between them. The Russian Orthodox church has been complaining bitterly about the opening of Catholic parishes on Russian territory, the establishment of Catholic bishoprics there, and allegations that the Catholic church is proselytizing in areas that the Russian church considers its own.[121]

At a meeting in 1990, the two sides agreed that "any attempt to convert the believers of one church to another . . . should be ruled out as a distortion of pastoral activity." But what is proselytism? Representatives of the Vatican have asserted that "all pastoral structures that the Catholic church is setting up in the CIS pursue the aim of ministering to the spiritual needs of Catholic believers"; that is, their aim is not to convert Orthodox believers to Catholicism. Nevertheless, the Moscow patriarchate is very concerned with the fact that the number of Roman Catholics in the commonwealth is growing—especially among young people and the intelligentsia. According to one of its statements, "The traditional territories of the Orthodox countries are now seen as 'missionary territories,' and as a result, a network of missions is being set up in them, and all the methods that all Christians have condemned for decades are being used to practice proselytism."[122]

At the end of 1990, Metropolitan Yuvenalii of Krutitskii and Kolomna accused the Ukrainian political leadership of "flouting the rights of Orthodox believers" by protecting and advancing the rights of Catholics. He asserted that the Russian Orthodox church had "left no stone unturned in attempting to solve and regulate the problem of interchurch relations." "Our efforts," he continued, "have come up against a wall behind which are politics, irreconcilability, hostility, and brute force."[123] In April 1991, without offering Russian Orthodox officials any advance warning, the Catholic church suddenly assigned bishops to several cities—Moscow, Novosibirsk, and Karaganda. Responding to this step, Archimandrite Iosif (Pustoutov), who is responsible for the Russian church's relations with Catholicism, expressed considerable irritation. "We aren't against Catholic parishes," he said, "but they must not work to the detriment of the Russian Orthodox church, and they

---

[121]This is a problem affecting other religious denominations as well. For example, Kirghiz and Uzbek Muslims in Central Asia have already clashed with Western Christian evangelists. See *Izvestiia*, 10 April 1992.

[122]*Nezavisimaia gazeta*, 10 April 1992. See also *Izvestiia*, 4 March 1992.

[123]*Sovetskaia kul'tura*, 29 December 1990.

must be oriented toward those [individuals] who have historically belonged to the Catholic faith. . . . We are not imposing our choice, but we object to the creation of parallel missionary structures on our canonical territory."[124] By March 1992, Metropolitan Kirill, head of the Moscow patriarchate's department of external church affairs, said that relations between the two churches had "fallen to their lowest point in the past three years."[125]

In view of these exchanges, it is difficult to see how Roman Catholicism and the various Orthodox churches will be able to meet their announced objective, "full and complete relations that will be neither absorption nor merger, but a meeting in truth and love."[126] Sad to say, religious freedom seems to carry with it the danger of conflict and discord, just as the *lack* of religious freedom did.

To round out the religious picture in Ukraine, we must deal with one further complication. In mid-1989, one of the Russian Orthodox church parishes in Ukraine announced that it was leaving the church and would join the reconstituted Ukrainian Autocephalous Orthodox church. The revival of the Autocephalous church, which had been forced by Stalin to cease functioning in the 1930s, confirmed that Russian Orthodoxy was beginning to lose its grip in Ukraine. Yielding to the pressure of events, the Moscow patriarchate decided in 1991 to give limited internal autonomy to its Ukrainian exarchate, renaming it the Ukrainian Orthodox church. This body still remained part of the Russian Orthodox church, despite the change in name.

Most Ukrainians regarded this step as a thinly veiled attempt on the part of the Russian church to maintain whatever influence it still had in the republic. Ukrainian militants termed the decision "not a religious, but a purely political act." According to a report issued in 1990 by the Ukrainian Supreme Soviet's Commission on Cultural and Spiritual Revival, Moscow's decision "could not help but add tension to the religious situation in Ukraine." The commission characterized the patriarch's decision as indicative of "disregard for the sovereignty of Ukraine, a lack of respect for the national temples of the Ukrainian people, and interference by the Russian Orthodox church in the internal affairs of the republic." Furthermore, the commission's report condemned the "mistaken and essentially chauvinistic treatment by the Russian Ortho-

---

[124]See *Izvestiia,* 30 November 1991.
[125]Ibid., 4 March 1992.
[126]*Nezavisimaia gazeta,* 10 April 1992.

dox Church Synod of Orthodoxy in Ukraine as a 'daughter' church of
the Russian Orthodox church."[127]

Adherents of the Ukrainian Autocephalous Orthodox church became
embroiled in a confrontation with the civil authorities in 1990 over the
issue of church property. The problem grew out of a decision by the
Ukrainian government to allow the Russian Orthodox patriarch to deliver a sermon in Kiev's Cathedral of St. Sofia. Members of the Autocephalous church saw the cathedral as the very embodiment of Ukrainian national identity—and definitely not an appropriate platform for
the Russian patriarch. Their protests were not offered gently, and the
result was multiple fistfights, beatings by the police, and other exchanges
that were, to say the least, far from the model of Christian charity.

The protesters claimed the cathedral as their own—it had, in fact,
belonged to them until 1930, when it was called the Cathedral of the
Primate. They had tried earlier to prevent the patriarch from entering
the building to deliver his message. Indeed, fearing just such a contre-
temps, the Second Congress of Rukh (the Ukrainian nationalist movement) had sent him a telegram earlier urging him not to come. When he
did, the chairman of Rukh's secretariat has stated, "The Russian Orthodox church decided to provoke a confrontation." Moscow was attempting, he said, "to throw a spiritual yoke onto Ukraine," and the
Russian church "is more interested in politics than in faith in God"—
precisely the charge leveled at it by the Uniates.[128] An even more extraordinary series of developments involving Orthodox believers in Ukraine
began to unfold in 1992. Metropolitan Filaret of the Russian church
was forced to resign as metropolitan of Kiev and All Ukraine. (It was
rumored that he was married and had children, and that he had been
compromised by his previous association with the KGB.) Moscow authorized the bishops of the Ukrainian Orthodox church to elect a new
metropolitan, and they selected Vladimir of Rostov and Novocherkassk
to fill the position. But Filaret, despite having been unfrocked, continued
to regard himself as the "true" metropolitan. Almost immediately, he
joined his wing of the Ukrainian Orthodox church to the Ukrainian

---

[127]For the text of the report, see *Kultura i Zhyttya*, 7 December 1990, 7, translated in
JPRS-UPA-91-005, 29 January 1991, 73–77.

[128]*Literaturna Ukraina*, 1 November 1990, translated in *JPRS-UPA-90-072*, 28 December
1990, 81–82; *Kultura i Zhyttya*, 7 December 1990, 75, 76. Similar problems have
arisen in Ivano-Frankovsk and elsewhere in Ukraine. See, e.g., Radio Kiev, 4 March
1992, and *Halychna* (Ivano-Frankovsk), both in *FBIS-SOV-92-645*, 6 March 1992,
45–46.

Autocephalous Orthodox church. Clearly, he was embracing the principle that had been proclaimed previously by President Leonid M. Kravchuk: "An independent state must have an independent church, and we are creating it."[129] From the point of view of Kiev (as expressed by Metropolitan Antony of Pereiaslavl and Secheslavl, one of the leaders of the new Independent United Ukrainian Orthodox church), "an enormous danger is truly hanging over Ukrainian Orthodoxy. That is why we are uniting."[130]

CONCLUDING REMARKS

In the last few years of Gorbachev's reign, party, Komsomol, and government agencies in many localities resisted perestroika's permissive attitude toward religious self-expression. There were frequent reports of recalcitrant town, city, or provincial officials who refused to acknowledge the new rights of the faithful: party activists or the chairmen of local soviet executive committees continued to obstruct groups attempting to register as a religious community, reopen or carry out repairs on a church, and so on. Obviously, it was difficult for bureaucrats who had made a career harassing religious persons and groups to change their behavior. As the writer Aleksandr Nezhny noted, "The contemptuous and dismissive attitude toward anything connected with the church, which has been drummed into us over decades, still controls our consciousness."[131] The problem continues to plague reformers under Yeltsin, too.

Higher-level church functionaries also represent an obstacle to genuine religious freedom. One Western specialist on Russian Orthodoxy has spoken of the "Stalinist-Brezhnevian ecclesiastical nomenklatura that ruled the church since 1943."[132] Similarly, the British historian Geoffrey Hosking has written, "Decades of active persecution alternating with contemptuous manipulation have left it not only numerically reduced but spiritually debilitated. . . . Enfeebled by subservience to an atheist

---

[129]For more on the president's newly acquired religiosity, see Radio Kiev, 31 August 1992, in *FBIS-SOV-92-171*, 2 September 1992, 35, and—even more striking—ibid., 9 April 1993, in *FBIS-SOV-93-068*, 12 April 1993, 50.

[130]*Nezavisimaia gazeta*, 27 June 1992. For additional details, see Jaroslaw Martiniuk, "Religious Preferences in Five Urban Areas of Ukraine," *Report*, 9 April 1993, 52–55.

[131]*Ogonek*, no. 21 (1988), cited in "Church Gains from the Millennium?" *Soviet Analyst* 17, no. 12 (15 June 1988): 6–7.

[132]Vladimir Moss, "Russian Orthodoxy and the Future of the Soviet Union," *Report*, 14 June 1991, 3, 5.

state, the Church is no longer fitted to act as [a] vehicle for [a] religious revival or to promote social solidarity."[133] One group of Orthodox clergy and laymen has even condemned the church leadership as "a remnant of Stalinism" and called on the patriarch "to put an end to an unseemly dependence on an atheist regime and anti-Christian ideology."[134]

In early 1990, the Holy Synod admitted publicly that the government had been interfering in church appointments and in the administration of parishes for many years.[135] The patriarch himself subsequently admitted that "we had to tell lies" and asked for "forgiveness, understanding, and prayer."[136] As we have seen, leading figures in the Islamic faith were also co-opted by the Soviet regime, severely limiting their ability (or their inclination) to represent the needs of ordinary Muslims.

On 20 April 1993, President Yeltsin announced that a department of religious affairs would be set up once again under the Russian government. It is to be headed by a first deputy prime minister and, unlike its predecessor, it is supposed to provide religious communities with "concrete assistance."[137] Unfortunately, this arrangement may not be quite as benign as the president claims. In fact, in November 1992—before Yeltsin's statement—the Presidium of the Russian Federation Supreme Soviet established the Expert Consultative Committee under the Soviet's Joint Committee on Freedom of Conscience, Religion, Charity, and Philanthropy. This organization is responsible for "the collection, processing, and storage of information (a data bank) on the activity of religious and atheistic associations on Russian Federation territory, [and also] analysis of their activity as regards compliance with Russian Federation legislation."[138]

Despite these and other problems, it is clear that organized religion in the Soviet Union and its successor states has done well in the period

---

[133]Geoffrey Hosking, *The Awakening of the Soviet Union* (Cambridge, Mass.: Harvard University Press, 1990), 113, 115.

[134]*Moscow News*, no. 24 (1990): 15.

[135]*Moskovskii tserkovnyi vestnik*, no. 9 (1990): 1, 3, cited in Moss, "Russian Orthodoxy," 3. See also *Moskovskie novosti*, no. 22 (1988), as well as three articles by Aleksandr Nezhny in *Ogonek*, nos. 48 and 49 (1991), and no. 4 (1992).

[136]Cited in Oxana Antic, "Patriarch Aleksii II: A Political Portrait," *Report*, 8 November 1991, 18. For a thorough analysis of penetration of the church by the KGB, see Oxana Antic, "Orthodox Church Reacts to Criticism of KGB Links," ibid., 5 June 1992, 61–63. See also Radio Moscow, 19 November 1991, in *FBIS-SOV-91-224*, 20 November 1991, 31.

[137]*RFE/RL News Briefs*, 19–23 April 1993, 4.

[138]*Nezavisimaia gazeta*, 4 February 1993.

since Gorbachev came to power in 1985. Glasnost, perestroika, and *demokratizatsiia* (democratization) have made it possible to open thousands of churches, mosques, synagogues, and prayerhouses; to build hundreds of others; to allow the church to perform a "social mission," providing help to the very young, the very old, and the very ill; to make Sunday schools and other forms of religious instruction available to young people; to allow clergy access to the mass media; and to give everyone an opportunity to learn the truth about the past conduct and present behavior of various clerics.

This is all to the good. At the same time, though, the shadow of radical Islam hangs over Central Asia, Azerbaijan, and Muslim-inhabited areas of the Russian Federation, and Catholic–Russian Orthodox conflict gives equal cause for uneasiness at the uncompromising policies pursued by some church groups. The picture today is far more encouraging than it was only a decade ago, but it remains highly ambiguous— another legacy of communism. One can hope for less official interference in religious affairs, and one can hope that Yeltsin's propensity to identify with the Orthodox faith does not alienate members of other denominations, but whether or not these hopes are realistic remains to be seen.

Part IV

Labor and elitism

13

~~●━●~~

Elitism in postcommunist Russia:
some interim comments

MERVYN MATTHEWS

The astonishing changes that have taken place in Russia since the late 1980s have affected all layers of society, not least the elite. It is arguable, indeed, that what happens at the topmost level is a pointer to all social transformation; for the elite is likely, by its very nature, to exert a disproportionate influence on the shape and nature of society as a whole. This line of thinking may be distasteful to people of an egalitarian turn of mind, but history seems to have demonstrated its validity. There is certainly no doubt about the determining role that elite groups continue to play in postcommunist Russia.

Analysis of elitism in Russia today is no easy matter. Measuring social phenomena normally requires social stability, hindsight, and adequate information. None of these elements is currently present. One might argue that there is little point in measuring processes that are clearly incomplete and may change direction with little or no warning. For this reason I focus on a few rather specific aspects that I believe to be indicative of major trends. There is no doubt that most of the recognized principles of elite analysis are now appropriate to Russia. Russian society retains, of course, unique features; but many current social processes are predictable, surprising though they may appear at first sight.

For purposes of analysis here, the Russian "elite" is best regarded as a sort of duality—a conglomerate of responsible, highly skilled, well-paid, and often influential occupations, on the one hand, and the corpus of people who can fill them, on the other. At the same time an elite must be a small, exclusive group: The analysis of the Soviet elite I made for the 1970s involved about a quarter of a million employed persons, plus their families.[1] My listing comprised responsible party, state, Komsomol, and trade union officials; managers of large enterprises; the intelligentsia (i.e., academicians, heads of higher educational institutions [VUZy], laboratories, chief doctors, senior legal officials, editors and senior journalists, leaders in the arts and artistic bureaucracy); and senior military, police, and diplomatic personnel.

The principal changes in the occupational structure of the elite that can be observed at present involve the disappearance of several important branches and the appearance of new ones. Gone are the old party, Komsomol, and trade union apparats, as such; some of the state administrations (as enterprises are privatized); a good part of the military officer class, as the Russian army is cut back; and presumably some KGB staff. Russian officials concerned with all-union matters must have been either sacked or transferred to other work. On the other hand, we see the rise of a new business class and of new political, trade union, religious, and criminal elite groupings.

Of course, there are limits to the amount of change one can expect, given the fact that a revolutionary situation has been avoided thus far. The new structure of occupations must in many respects match the old, and in terms of personnel, many old faces will remain. A renewed sociopolitical entity still requires much of the old corpus of knowledge and experience, and former job holders may well do their very best to hang on. It is easier to change one's views than one's job, a principle strikingly demonstrated among former Soviet journalists. If we look at certain categories—such as highly talented artists and scientists—there may have been no turnover whatever.

In this chapter, I primarily consider the occupancy of elitist positions in the legislature; the pattern of change among former Community Party of the Soviet Union (CPSU) officials in a fairly typical provincial town; and the nature of the new business elite. Other topics include: the balance of factors that favor or impede the development of elitism in postcommunist Russia; public attitudes toward elitism—a subject that could never be explored before the advent of glasnost; the fate of the old administratively based privileges; and some more general matters of social differentiation. A complete account of the new elitism would require long study and cannot be attempted here.

---

[1] M. Matthews, *Privilege in the Soviet Union* (London: Allen and Unwin, 1978), 31.

FACTORS AFFECTING ELITE DEVELOPMENT

Since the rejection of Soviet-type rule was initially so forthright, on the surface at least, it seems logical to begin with factors that promoted a new elitism. The egalitarian inhibitions emanating from crude, official Marxism-Leninism largely disappeared, and social differentiation based on personal capability and hard work (à la Gorbachev) acquired the status of an official, if somewhat artificial, norm. This thinking must benefit the more skilled, enterprising, and upwardly mobile. A new unified wage scale for state employees, introduced in January 1993, comprised eighteen steps with a maximum differential of more than one to ten.[2] State decrees have gone some way toward legalizing ownership of the means of production, private enterprise is encouraged at most levels, and extensive plans exist for privatization of state property. High money incomes, earlier considered shameful and carefully excluded from view, are now to some degree acceptable and openly declared; indeed, the tax system has been changed to accommodate them. Obviously, the freeing of prices is less harmful to the rich, and may benefit them if it reduces the demand for scarce food and consumer goods on the part of the poor. The privatization of housing must eventually reduce state control and have the same differentiating effect—apart from which the old elite is already the best housed. Relaxation in the social sphere (discussed later) works mainly to the benefit of the highest earners.[3]

The easing of state control over the information media, both native and foreign, and the encouragement of foreign investment give the elite a better understanding of developments at home and abroad. There is a hitherto unthinkable freedom to associate with foreign cousins. Moreover, the Russian elite now enjoys considerable moral support from its Western counterparts: political leaders are welcomed as part of an international fraternity, amicable efforts are made to train Russian business personnel. Professional and academic fraternization is at an all-time high. All of this seems to be supportive of a healthy, open elitism of the Western variety. No less important is the long-standing and widespread perception that Russian society has always had an elite, even if resented, and would continue to do so.

[2] *Argumenty i fakty,* no. 3 (January 1993).
[3] These generalizations are based on numerous laws and regulations passed after Gorbachev came to power, and listed in the usual official sources, including the serial publications of the Congress of People's Deputies, supreme soviets, and councils of ministers of the Soviet Union and RSFSR. It is impracticable to give a full listing here.

In addition, members of the old elite continue to resist any dismantling of the old structures and changes of staff. This behavior is, as it were, the other side of the same coin. The KGB, Ministry of Defense, and military complex are mentioned often in this respect. The postcommunist organs of state security, for example, have lost their ideological functions, while former capitalist enemies have become sources of national assistance. But the KGB staff was influential enough to force the removal of a new, relatively liberal head (V. V. Bakatin) and actively hindered the exposure of former KGB agents in religious hierarchies. Another much-remarked case concerned freedom of choice of abode, which has been actively opposed by sectors of the old passport bureaucracy.[4]

As for inhibiting factors, the first among them is the opposition of the various central and local bureaucracies to business activity and to the formation of a possibly vigorous "counter-elite" within the business sphere. The opposition varies in character. In the worst cases state officials and directors of enterprises may publicly authorize privatization, but in fact sabotage it. It was recently reported, for example, that the "privatization" of five trusts which between them controlled private housing in Moscow hardly went beyond renaming (as a shareholding society, two companies, and two associations). The old management and restrictive practices were retained.[5] The most anodyne type of bureaucratic impediment entails the tolerance, or manipulation, of private business in order to derive long-term illegal income from it. Corruption of this kind became so widespread that Gavril Popov, the mayor of Moscow, actually hinted that there should, in practice, be some official toleration of it.[6]

The new visibility of the elite has disadvantages as well as advantages. Success stories in the newspapers and in elitist magazines that are too expensive for purchase by the person in the street may foster a certain cohesion, but they also attract the attention of a public that is impoverished, unused to conspicuous consumption, and schooled in the benefits of a supposedly egalitarian society. Criminality is another problem. The shaky legal foundations for private production and services, acute

---

[4]Bakatin was dismissed ostensibly for revealing the secrets of electronic infiltration of the U.S. embassy in Moscow. See M. Matthews, *The Passport Society* (Boulder, Colo.: Westview Press, 1993), chap. 6.

[5]*Kuranty,* 2 April 1992.

[6]See *Argumenty i fakty,* no. 15 (April 1992): 1, for a comment on Yeltsin's decree on the struggle with corruption in state service; *Argumenty i fakty,* no. 14 (April 1992).

shortages of raw materials, and the general vulnerability of the elite mean that it has become an object of attack for the mafia, and indeed may itself have contributed to an expansion of mafiosi groups. Much of the cooperative movement is now said to be under mafia control.

There is, it would appear, a continuing public dislike of elitism in Russia, as demonstrated by a number of social surveys. An investigation conducted by the All-Union Center for the Study of Public Opinion (VTsIOM) in the spring of 1990 showed that although over 80 percent of the respondents were aware of privilege, nearly 70 percent subscribed to the view that "no privileges should exist for anyone, but benefits are needed for people in need (invalids, large families, etc.)." Just under 12 percent thought that a set of legally defined privileges should exist for people in specific jobs; 24 percent thought that privileges should be established for individuals who really deserved them. A survey of attitudes toward private enterprise conducted in December 1990 by the same center showed that 32 percent were against private, individual ownership of small enterprises and 52 percent were against such ownership of large works and factories. Opposition to foreign ownership was higher: 24 percent would not work in a privately owned enterprise and 45 percent did not wish to own an enterprise themselves.[7]

Of course, one would expect to find mixed reactions to privilege anywhere: such is the stuff of left-of-center politics. But from a Western standpoint these figures are high. Long years of administrative privilege and patently unfair elitism, together with a lack of familiarity with more open, merit-based varieties, have left a deep imprint.

It is not easy to assess the impact of the current economic collapse, fierce inflation, and the fragility of law. Such factors are, it is true, socially differentiating, since they tend to hit the poor hardest, while the elite have possessions that retain their real value. Also, the circumstances may provide those having most skill or money with new opportunities for making a fast, if precarious, "buck." Stable elite status, however, usually requires a sound economy, good prospects for business in the longer term, political stability, and good law. Obviously, Russia is a long way from this happy condition. The envy and social tension that economic collapse brings or intensifies are distinctly harmful to elitism. In international terms the Soviet elite was always relatively poor; the

---

[7] *Obshchestvennoe mnenie v tsifrakh*, VTsIOM, *Informatsionnyi bulleten'*, no. 13 (May 1990): 10; no. 9 (1991): 6.

Russian elite has on the whole become poorer. State incomes have not kept up with inflation, many people have suffered from the switch to free prices, and the value of money savings has been sharply reduced.

THE OCCUPATIONAL BACKGROUND OF
RUSSIAN FEDERATION PEOPLE'S DEPUTIES

It is clear that in terms of occupational background the membership of the Russian Congress of People's Deputies is elitist in the traditional Soviet mold. (See Table 13.1.) In other words, the seats are occupied mostly by people who evidently enjoyed privileged positions in Soviet society before the Gorbachev upheaval. The congress was, of course, elected while voting patterns (and selection practices) favorable to the CPSU were still observed and before the impact of perestroika reached the provinces.

The members currently serve on a rotational basis in the Supreme Soviet and have a potent say in the practice of government. In view of the transitional nature of this membership, subsequent elections should in principle reveal more about the involvement of Russian elites in the government of the country.

According to available data, of the 1,063 deputies listed in February 1991, some 812 were at one time members of the CPSU, 238 were "nonparty" in the old sense of the word, and only 13 were listed as members of other political parties. A staunchly conservative bloc could be easily assembled: for example, in the vote on whether people working on the land should have constitutional right to purchase it, 406 deputies voted against. These respondents included 141 representatives of the upper levels of economic and political management, 182 from middle management (including farm directors), 46 lower-grade administrators, 16 workers and peasants, and 21 intellectuals.[8] The occupational pattern that emerges from the data available is shown in Table 13.1.

The breakdown defies proper analysis because some 30 percent of the members were listed as full-time officials in bodies of the congress itself, their earlier associations not being revealed. Moreover, the occupational role of a deputy before election may not always have been directly related to the occupation entered in the list. Nevertheless, it would seem

---

[8]*Spisok narodnykh deputatov RSFSR na 12 fevral' 1991*, Izdanie Verkhovnogo Soveta RSFSR (1991), publication unannounced; *Argumenty i fakty*, no. 15 (April 1992): 1.

Table 13.1. *Occupational background of members of the Russian Congress of People's Deputies*

Occupational background	Number[a]
Leading CPSU officials	38
Middle-grade CPSU officials	15
Heads of subordinate Supreme Soviets	18
Heads of *krai,* oblast, town, and district executive committees, soviets	134
Ministers, deputy ministers	40
Heads of government departments, members of committees and commissions of the Supreme Soviet	305
Heads of various state organizations	35
Heads of scientific and cultural organizations	62
Researchers, engineers, doctors	22
School directors, teachers	5
Journalists	24
Trade unionists	4
Military leaders	24
Police and law officials	27
Directors of collective and state farms	82
Directors of production enterprises	106
Heads of sections in industrial enterprises	43
Heads of sections in agricultural enterprises	4
Directors of private firms, cooperatives	3
Workers, foremen	26
Collective farmers, brigadeers	4
White-collar workers	1
Clergy	1
Others	40

[a]The fact that the absolute total (1,063) is close to a thousand means that each unit can be read as approximately 0.1 percent (i.e., $38 = 3.8$ percent). The categorization used here cannot be other than approximate.

likely that most occupations recorded here predated the election and typically served to promote the candidature.

Starting from the bottom of the social hierarchy, then, the congress contained only twenty-six workers, of whom many were senior, four simple collective farmers, one cleric, and one white-collar employee. Only three persons put themselves down as heads of private enterprises, but this was almost certainly misleading, insofar as some other responsible figures presumably had important business interests, a point we shall return to later. About a quarter of the deputies (245) were heads of production enterprises or sections. It will be noted that about a seventh (134) had responsible positions in lower-level soviets: these must have been experienced or professional politicians when they took their seats. But against this background only some 5 percent of the deputies (53) were full-time CPSU officials.

The configuration of the Russian executive (government) will require investigation in its own right, when, and if, it stabilizes. The existing dual structure is itself the focus of intense political struggle. The old RSFSR Council of Ministers has been replaced by the Presidential Office of Administration with thirty-seven offices and a Presidential Consultative Council of fourteen; the Russian government executive arm contains fifty-eight posts, including twenty-five ministries and twenty committees and agencies.[9] One might also expect these contingents, despite a more liberal complexion, to reveal, when analyzed, strong associations with the former political elite. Numerous individuals of such ilk come to mind, Boris Yeltsin being a prime example.

ELITE CADRES IN THE PROVINCES: THE CASE OF KIROV[10]

The fate of the former CPSU hierarchy at the provincial town level is a matter of interest—if only because about half of the population of Russia lives in such settlements. Kirov is said to be typical of many towns throughout the land.[11] Data were recently collected for fifty-one former CPSU officials in the oblast, town, and district (*raion*) apparatuses, and the pattern to emerge may be summarized as follows.

The total staff of the *obkom* (oblast', or province, committee of the CPSU) was said to be about thirty-five; information is available for twenty-eight of them. Of four secretaries, the first became a member of the Russian Supreme Soviet; the second became general manager of the executive committee of the oblast soviet; the secretary for ideology went back to teaching chemistry at the local pedagogical institute; another joined a sociological agency established within the obkom before dissolution. Of the twenty-four other members, nine became officials in the local soviet, five went into private enterprise, three took responsible jobs in state industry, two got editorial jobs, three took responsible jobs in charitable organizations, and two more went into teaching.

---

[9]See, in particular, *RFE/RL Report on the USSR*, 1 September 1991, 17; *RFE/RL Research Report*, 10 April 1992, 47.

[10]I am grateful to Evgenii Ostanin, lecturer at the Kirov Pedagogical Institute, for collecting this material.

[11]Formerly Vyatka, situated some five hundred miles northeast of Moscow, Kirov is an industrialized rail center, population 421,000.

At the *gorkom* (town, or city, committee of the CPSU) level, the first secretary became director of a section at a local holiday center, while the second secretary became chairman of the local soviet (in which, incidentally, only about a quarter of the deputies belonged to the new democratic bloc). The secretary for ideology became head teacher at a boarding school for handicapped children; of three instructors, two went into charity organizations and one also became a teacher in the previously mentioned boarding school. Of seventeen district secretaries, no less than eleven simply moved into local government, usually taking up minor managerial positions as heads of sections, though two became chairmen of local soviets. Four moved into managerial positions in industrial or transport enterprises, one became a school teacher, and one was said to be unemployed.

The impression this listing conveys is by no means one of a complete rout of the old guard. The old cadres lost power as CPSU officials, but stayed well up in the local administrative hierarchy. The other three most common fates were managerial posts in private or state enterprise, teaching, and somewhat surprisingly, charitable organizations. In any case, a majority of them seemed able to retain a position in the upper reaches of society. There was no suggestion of loss of advantageous housing, for example, or personal property. Maybe some of them deserved a less happy fate, but anyone wishing to see Russia develop liberal values must at least welcome smooth transition.

It is interesting to note in this context that the new chair and deputy chair of the Kirov oblast soviet were not from the CPSU apparatus, though the chairman apparently enjoyed CPSU support. The president's representative was a deputy to the Russian Supreme Soviet and a member of the Democratic Russia movement. Three-quarters of the deputies, as noted, were said not to belong to the democratic bloc.

THE NEW BUSINESS ELITE

One of the most interesting aspects of the current situation is the appearance of a new business elite, though the private sector is still only in the initial stages of formation. Government plans have envisaged the process of "privatization" as taking three years (1992–94), but given progress so far this timetable is optimistic. Probably the best overall measure is the size of the labor force involved: by the end of 1991 this comprised 1.7 million, which was only 2.3 percent of the 73.6 million national labor force.[12] Nevertheless, privatization should eventually extend to many nonstrategic sectors of the economy. At least four mechanisms will be used to promote it: the leasing of state enterprises to private operators; worker-management schemes, under which the employees obtain a share in their own enterprises; the disposal of state enterprises, sometimes disparagingly termed "nomenklatura privatization" since enterprises may pass into the hands of previous managers; and the independent creation of new businesses. Evidently the new business elite, as it forms, will use all of these means.[13]

Any assessment of the size and composition of the new business elite depends on the definitions and measures one uses. The information available is incomplete and somewhat contradictory, but some of the more important data may be mentioned, if only to demonstrate magnitudes. For example, the following breakdown of financial units was provided by official statistical sources in February 1992: shareholding societies, 8,902; associations, 3,076; commercial banks, 1,304; concerns, consortiums, and unions, 539; and stock exchanges, 108. If one takes as a definition of elite status the headship (say) of these undertakings, the financial elite totals about 14,000. But this is a very narrow concept. In October 1991 the 110 stock exchanges alone had a membership of 5,100. The growth of the number of entities has been impressive: over the last six months of 1991 the number of societies increased by a factor of 7.5, stock exchanges by 3, while the number of associations and unions almost doubled.[14] In addition, official sources listed some 64,000 partnerships and 200,000 small private enterprises. In 1991 approximately 80,000 new businesses were registered.[15] Obviously, even the upper parts of this pyramid must comprise tens of thousands of successful individuals. The definition and description of a "business elite" should become easier if the establishment of a national tax inspectorate allows personal financial data to be collected and a wealth distribution to be published, as in the United States.

It must be remembered that though the Russian business community may already be wealthy relative to other parts of the society, it is

---

[12]Goskomstat RSFSR, *Sotsial'no-ekonomicheskoe polozhenie Rossiiskoi Federatsii v 1991* (booklet), 25 January 1992, 7.

[13]John Tedstron, "Russia: Progress Report on Industrial Privatization," *RFE/RL Research Report*, 24 April 1992, 46.

[14]Goskomstat RSFSR, *Press-vypusk*, 7 February 1992.

[15]Ibid.; *Statisticheskii press-byulleten'*, no. 1 (1992): 5; see also *Moscow Business Week*, no. 8 (30 April 1992).

poor by Western standards. In about 1991, the average capital of the shareholding societies averaged only 2 million rubles. Also, it is unlikely that the agricultural sector will contribute many elite figures, since the average plot owned by the country's fifty-eight thousand private farmers was only forty-three hectares, and agricultural development was greatly retarded.[16]

Moreover, much of the private sector is less "private" than would appear at first sight. Many of the new businesses have been generated by local organs of the state as protective mechanisms for their staff, or as money-making enterprises for the administrators who ran them. The ownership of funds is indicative in this respect. The statistical source used for the data on financial units previously cited gave the following distribution of ownership of the shareholding societies: state enterprises, 82 percent; state administrative organs, 3 percent; social organizations, 1 percent; private citizens, 5 percent; others, 9 percent. Another specific example: in 1991 all five Moscow building trusts were formally privatized, but continued to operate as exclusive bureaucratic entities, much as before. The genuinely private businesses tend to be small.[17]

What can be said about the social provenance of the new business elite? As far as we are aware, no comprehensive study of it is as yet available, but two reports on a small investigation conducted in Moscow deserve mention. One of these was organized by the Institute of Sociology of the USSR Academy of Sciences, backed by the newspaper *Moskovskie novosti*. Some fifty "millionaire" businessmen were questioned.[18] The writers found that the first post-1987 entrepreneurs came primarily from two groups—nomenklatura personnel who were involved in privatizing party and/or state property, and parvenus who had often been employed in the so-called second economy. Some 87 percent of the whole group came from the intelligentsia, 70 percent had higher education, 15 percent were of worker origin, and 2.5 percent were born in the village.

[16]Goskomstat RSFSR, *Press-vypusk*, 6 February 1992.
[17]Ibid., 7 February 1992.
[18]As yet we have no proper account of this work. The data was collected apparently from one or two samples of fifty and eighty by the group for the study of the Soviet elite at the Institute of Sociology of the USSR Academy of Sciences and *Moskovskie novosti*. The relationship between the studies was not made clear, but various results collected by O. Kryshtanovskaia, A. Pavlyukov, and E. Chekalova were made available in *Moskovskie novosti*, 21 July 1991, and in an unpublished paper presented by O. Kryshtanovskaia, "The Emerging Business Elite." (The paper was cyclostyled and not, I believe, in its final form.)

The *Moskovskie novosti* survey showed that the outlook of these entrepreneurs was quite conservative—all claimed to observe Christian morals, while 62 percent were believers or respectful of religious belief. Their average working day was thirteen hours; two-thirds of their wives worked; a third of them drank no alcohol, a remarkably high proportion for Russian conditions; and only 15 percent dressed like rich persons.

The so-called nomenklatura managers are an especially interesting group, in that they represent the transformation of a party elite into a commercially based one. Their characteristic function was to privatize (for their personal benefit) property that belonged to the state, the CPSU, the army, and so on.

A typical procedure was for CPSU and state officials responsible for property, capital equipment, transport facilities, and military installations to establish them as separate legal entities, on a profit-making basis. The officials would then take financial control as directors or associates. Another procedure involved setting artificially low values for property so that shares in it could be acquired by people "in the know" at highly advantageous rates.[19] There is evidence that local politicians obtained positions on management boards as a reward for promoting their establishment. Some element of state verification was attempted by the establishment of local privatization commissions, but given the dubious character of Russian local government, these commissions may have connived in dishonest practice and exacerbated, rather than eased, the problem.

The development of a stable and respectable business elite obviously depends much on economic progress, and the hindrances to this have been discussed ad nauseam. In an article published in October 1991, Oleg Ozherel'ev, Gorbachev's assistant on economic questions, stated the three principal obstacles as: ideological prejudice against the market; the opposition of ministerial officials; and the opposition of local soviets, all of which are included in the impediments I listed.[20] No less than 90 percent of the respondents in the *Moskovskie novosti* report on private enterprise declared bribery and the corruption of local officials to be essential, and some even bribed the KGB. Fear of the mafia was such that a majority would give only anonymous interviews.

[19]For some particularly interesting cases see: *Rossiiskie vesti*, no. 3 (1992) (privatization of a medical complex near Moscow); *Kuranty*, 25 April 1992 (cases in Moscow); *Komsomol'skaia pravda*, 1 and 21 April 1992 (illegal privatization of military facilities); *Moskovskaia pravda*, 15 October 1991 (on the scandalous sale of government dachas).
[20]*Rabochaia tribuna*, 3 October 1991, 1, 2.

OLD PRIVILEGES AND NEW

The system of privileges that developed soon after the Revolution and remained characteristic of the Soviet Union throughout its history has already been investigated in depth, and the attempts to limit it under perestroika have been described elsewhere.[21] The privileges, it will be recalled, comprised mainly special salaries and supplements; closed distribution systems for food and consumer goods; canteens with restricted access; better-quality housing; personal transport, holiday, dacha, and foreign travel facilities; superior educational and medical services; and the use of otherwise restricted information channels. The party-state-military nomenklatura was the prime beneficiary, but other elite groups were also admitted. The question arises as to what is now happening in this sphere: with the advent of glasnost, old-style privileges attracted much opprobrium, and the dissolution of the CPSU gave the question a particular urgency.

It was adjudged important enough for consideration at the highest level, and in July 1989 a Deputies' Commission on the Review of Privileges was established in the USSR Supreme Soviet under the chairmanship of E. M. Primakov, a political heavyweight who went on to head Russian foreign intelligence. The commission's declared aim was not to abolish privilege, but to make it accord with the "principles of social justice" and the law; the commission could make recommendations to the Supreme Soviet itself. The only privileges subject to legalization were those destined for "an extremely limited circle of persons" so as to ensure "that they work effectively in the interests of the whole of society, without which society would lose more than the privileges cost." The commission reported at the end of the year and again in July 1991, but was destined to disappear, together with all of the USSR apparatus, shortly afterward.[22]

Yeltsin was anxious to have his own cutting edge, partly, no doubt, because he was genuinely concerned about abuses, but also on account of his suspicion of the all-union apparatus. On 9 August 1990, the

[21]M. Voslensky, *Nomenklatura* (London: Overseas Publications Interchange, 1984); Matthews, *Privilege in the Soviet Union*; see also M. Matthews, "The End of Privilege?" in J. Riordan, ed., *Soviet Social Reality in the Mirror of Glasnost* (New York: St. Martin's Press, 1992): written early in 1991, it has now been partly overtaken by events.
[22]*Vedomosti Verkhovnogo Soveta SSR*, no. 8 (1989), Articles 191, 192; also no. 29 (1989), Article 580; the second report may be found in *Byulleten' Verkhovnogo Soveta SSR, 5-aya sessiya*, no. 102 (6 July 1991).

Russian republic acquired the Commission for the Ordering of Benefits and Privileges, lodged under the aegis of the Presidium of the Supreme Soviet. Its aims were more trenchant than those of the USSR commission and were defined by a decree signed earlier, on 17 July. This decree proclaimed "the intolerability of any privileges for individual officials or groups of officials, regardless of their posts, or for any organizations or their staffs, and the rejection of all kinds of privilege relating to political power, unearned rewards, undeserved benefits, undeservedly comfortable working and living conditions for managers of organizations, enterprises and institutions, and the staff of state offices."[23]

From 1 August 1990, all the RSFSR legislation on which such privileges were based was to be invalidated. Working conditions for staff were to be properly defined and published by local soviets in the course of ten days; verification was to be the responsibility of the cumbersomely named RSFSR Supreme Soviet Committee for the Media, Information, Social Organizations, Mass Movements, and Public Opinion Studies.

The most detailed information we have to date on the drive against privilege concerns the work of the USSR Commission on the Review of Privileges. The data were provided by the deputy chairman, K. N. Kozyrev, in July 1991, and they revealed that the commission did indeed make genuine efforts to analyze the system and disclose abuses. The main areas of investigation were the misuse of air transport; the construction, use, and privatization of state dachas; and the financial activities of the USSR Ministry of Defense. The extent of abuse led the commission to conclude that the "higher executive power in the country was traditionally above the law" in this respect. Most of the regulations on privilege (purportedly comprising no less than 1,561 documents) had been devised by the CPSU Central Committee and the USSR Council of Ministers, and were secret.[24]

Attempts to dismantle privilege met with fierce opposition. According to the journalist Yuri Feofanov, the commission was much more successful in revealing abuses than in correcting them. It was opposed by

ministers, heads of the Cabinet of Ministers apparatus, and the People's Control, who either refused to give information or falsified it. They often refused to react, regardless of press comment and public indignation. ... All of these parliamentary commissions, investigations, the revelations of journalists, "Down

---

[23] *Vedomosti Verkhovnogo Soveta RSFSR*, no. 8 (1990), Articles 115–16; no. 10 (1990), Article 130.
[24] *Byulleten' Verkhovnogo Soveta SSR, 5-aya sessiya*, no. 102 (6 July 1991): 6, 10.

with Privilege" slogans and other splashes of emotion do not disturb the nomenklatura bog. It will gurgle if a stone is thrown in, and will settle again. The holders of the privilege fear the market, with its honest competition, payment for talent, labor and success, equality for all, not just those chosen. . . . Market relationships and democracy are fatal to it.[25]

In October 1991 E. Pamfilova, a former secretary of the commission, gave a revealing radio interview on the investigation of privilege.[26] She maintained that the whole system, which was created in the time of Lenin and perfected under Stalin, existed up to the present. One might have hoped that in the two months that had elapsed since the August 1991 coup the system ran on merely by inertia. The commission came to the conclusion, however, that the system was retained because it satisfied many people in power. A Supreme Soviet decree on investigating and reversing dacha sales had not been fulfilled. Restricted food distribution centers still functioned, often for former members of the CPSU. Personal pensions and personal transport were still operative. Despite the fact that the activities of the CPSU had been stopped, three-and-a-half thousand former members and their families were still served by the former Council of Ministers health facilities.

Pamfilova's warning was dramatically underscored by the unauthorized publication in *Ekspress khronika* (April 1992) of a presidential instruction marked "Not for the Press."[27] This document (passed on by the Moscow City Council Permanent Commission for Law, Order, and the Defense of Civil Rights) contained a list of objects which in view of their function were not to be privatized or otherwise disposed of, and were to remain "under the economic management of the Russian Federation President's Office." No less than six children's nurseries, fifteen holiday and rest homes, three dacha enclosures, a farm, two hotels, a polyclinic, a pharmacy, a laundry, a design office, and a warehouse were included.

This action was interpreted as a deliberate transfer of old nomenklatura privileges to the President's Office (and, presumably, its appendages). The significance of the incident cannot be adequately assessed at the time of writing: but it clearly reflects a trend toward the reestablishment of old practices under conditions of acute shortage and hyperinfla-

---

[25] *Golos*, no. 30 (1991): 5.
[26] *USSR Today (RFE/RL Digest)*, no. 95513, 22 October 1991; "What Was in Gorbachev's Black Folder," *Komsomol'skaia pravda*, 15 October 1991.
[27] *Ekspress khronika*, no. 15 (7–13 April 1992): 8.

Table 13.2. *Salaries in selected branches, November 1991*

	Salary (rubles)	Multiple of 342 (base salary)
President of the RSFSR	7,182	(21)
Chair of the Supreme Soviet		
Chair of Mossovet	4,788	(14)
Deputy of Mossovet, full-time	2,394	(7)
President's representative in Novgorod	3,420	(10)
Chair of Novgorod soviet	3,420	(10)

tion. If this is so, then we hear a strange echo from the postrevolutionary years.

At the same time, the shift to more openness in certain government practices is real enough, and this, too, must find a place in any assessment of developments. We may take as an example the decree of the RSFSR Supreme Soviet of 14 November 1991 announcing the salaries of responsible personnel in the legislative, executive, and juridical branches of state employment.[28] Table 13.2 shows some of the more significant rates, shown also as multiples of the minimum salary, then 342 rubles. The differentials, it will be noted, are substantial and akin to those in capitalist lands. At the same time the basic income of people in these categories would often be supplemented by sums earned on the side, in the form of directorships and administrative perks.

DIFFERENTIATION IN THE SOCIAL SERVICES

Any discussion of privilege in Russia must take account of different degrees of access to the social services. The three principal spheres into which such services are normally divided are education, health, and social security, of which the pension system is the most important element. One of the characteristics of postcommunism is an increase in the privatization and diversity of such services; the end result seems to be greater opportunity for the elite.

Education. Access to the best schooling is a common benefit of elite status in advanced societies. Official accounts of the Soviet educational system always emphasized its egalitarian character; but in fact it has, for

[28] *Kontrargumenty i fakty,* no. 2 (1992).

most of its history, been quite differentiated. Within the two main sectors—the general school and higher education—the children of well-placed families tended to monopolize the best establishments. Khrushchev made efforts to counter this tendency, but as has been shown elsewhere, he was not very successful.[29]

With perestroika, differentiating tendencies got stronger. Facilities in general schools have on the whole deteriorated, but individual institutions have gained more freedom to change their curricula and provide more choice for their pupils. Against the country's 69,700 general schools, 306 "gymnasiums," 198 "lycées," and 85 private schools have been opened. These new types may have their own entrance requirements and higher standards, but they also require parental subsidy or the payment of fees.[30]

At the higher education level the "quota" admission system, which gave some protection to less prepared candidates of worker and peasant origin, is now to be restricted to orphans, invalids, and reserve military personnel. Higher education institutes are to become self-governing organizations, which means they will have more control over their own intakes. Institutes have acquired the right to claim university status, implying more differentiation in the hierarchy. A private Russian-American University has made its appearance, offering courses in finance, business, and law, and many private courses are now available.[31]

Although liberalization of the educational system affords children from favored family backgrounds greater opportunity, the national decline in living standards must make it harder for poor children to stay on in school. Recent rises in students' grants have not kept pace with inflation, and student poverty has become a public issue.

Medical services. Before perestroika there were at least four well-recognized ways of obtaining superior medical treatment: through the "closed" hospitals and sanatoriums run by the Fourth Directorate of the Ministry of Health, primarily for apparatchiks; through public fee-paying clinics, of which there were seven in Moscow and an unknown

[29]M. Matthews, *Education in the Soviet Union* (London: Allen and Unwin, 1982).

[30]See *Statisticheskii press-byulleten'*, no. 1 (1992): 46; *Narodnoe khozyastvo RSFSR 1991*, Naroduoe Khozyaistvo RSFSR v 1990 (1991), 225; Goskomstat RSFSR, *Sotsial'no-ekonomichskoe polozhenie Rossiiskoi Federatsii v 1991 godu*, 25 January 1992; *Current Digest of the Soviet Press* (hereafter CDSP) 42, no. 47 (1990): 26.

[31]CDSP 42, no. 43 (1990): 32; CDSP 42, no. 42 (1990): 31; *USSR Today (RFE/RL Digest)*, 2 November 1991.

number in other large towns; by using the legal, though little-publicized services of private practitioners; and of course by giving bribes to obtain better service or scarce drugs anywhere. These practices flourished because medical services for the common people, though free or provided at nominal charges, were of very poor quality.

The changes most relevant to the well-being of the elite in this sphere, apart from bribery, which of course continued, may be listed as follows. First, the abolition of the Fourth Directorate in October 1989 did not as originally anticipated mean the transfer of facilities to underprivileged groups in society. According to E. Pamfilova and others, the CPSU hospital complex was passed to the Council of Ministers and continued to serve former members of the Central Committee and their families.[32]

Second, under a decree passed in June 1988, the state hospital system lost some of its rigidities; medical institutions were encouraged to find new sources of finance and commercialize some secondary services. Third, the cooperative movement, despite initial discouragement, developed a sturdy private medical sector. By January 1991, 2,006 medical cooperatives were in existence, with a staff of nearly 40,000 and a turnover of 256.8 million rubles. We may recall, by way of comparison, that there were 12,800 hospitals in the country as a whole.[33]

Although we have no statistics at hand for individual private practice, it apparently flourished: in any case, advertising by practitioners, formerly much restricted, became common. The rates were high and excluded usage by the average citizen. It is also noteworthy that a voluntary medical insurance scheme was included in a draft law on health service reforms in January 1992, giving the better-paid an opportunity, albeit of doubtful value in the current economic climate, of getting above-average medical care if needed. The draft also envisaged a free choice of doctor and health care unit.[34]

Social security. Formerly Soviet pensions were set in a rather egalitarian mold, insofar as they were noncontributory and depended entirely on wage and length of service. The maximum payment was normally 50 percent of the monthly wage up to a maximum of 120 rubles, though

[32]See Riordan, *Soviet Social Reality in the Mirror of Glasnost,* 62.
[33]*Spravochnik partiingo rabotnika,* no. 29 (1989): 435; *Kommercheskaia khronika* (*Fakt* information booklet), 1–15 December 1988. Interestingly enough, of some thirty-two thousand telephone enquiries about cooperative services directed to the *Fakt* information agency in December 1988, no less than 37.1 percent concerned medical attention.
[34]M. Ryan, *British Medical Journal* 304 (11 January 1992): 102.

"special" pensions were available at 300 rubles. Obviously, the highest earners tended to end up with the best pensions, but the ceiling, at least by the values of the late 1980s, was modest. Elite pensioners continued to benefit from access to restricted distribution services, superior housing, and their own accumulated wealth.

The most significant postcommunist change in the pension system, from the elite pensioners' point of view, was the abolition of the old fixed ceilings. The RSFSR law on state pensions of 20 November 1990, however, stipulated a maximum pension of only three times the minimum rate, with certain extras, which worked out, in practice, to less than four hundred rubles. In addition, the new pension scheme was quickly undermined by inflation rates reaching several hundred percent a year: and arrangements for indexation (introduced in December 1991) could help but marginally. Even elite pensioners were likely to suffer a sharp fall in their standard of living. So far as we have been able to ascertain, no arrangements have been made to ensure or protect high pensions as such.[35]

A final aspect of social differentiation is one that Thorstein Veblen termed "conspicuous consumption."[36] The partial discrediting of the old system of confidential administrative privilege has been accompanied by the appearance of new, overt, capitalist-style ones. Thus expensive private restaurants have opened, together with nightclubs and casinos. Some of these establishments function on a ruble, others on a dollar basis. There are auctions at which cars and flats may sell for astronomic prices, though tales of failure are frequent. A few exclusive business clubs have been organized, and new business magazines are on sale for very high prices. All of these services are designed to meet the ever-more sophisticated needs of a rich, outgoing clientele.[37]

CONCLUSION

Given the problems of investigation mentioned at the outset, there is not a great deal to add by way of conclusion. Privileges of the old, communist variety have at least been exposed to public criticism, and postcom-

[35]Yu. P. Orlovski, *Kak poluchit' pensiyu po novomu zakonu* (1991): 5–6, 15, 114. See also discussion in V. I. Nikitinski, *Novoe v zakonodatel'stve o trude i sotsial'nom obespechenii* (1992).
[36]T. Veblen, *The Theory of the Leisure Class* (London: Unwin Books, [1925] 1970).
[37]*Evening Standard*, 26 November 1992; *Sunday Times*, 8 December 1991.

munist elitism is not without positive perspectives; it is regrettable that
the criminal world is engendering so vigorous a mafia to go with it.

Administrative privilege may now be modified and transferred to
another elite—part of which is trying to acquire a more expansive Western life-style. Elitism as such is subject for some positive public comment, and is taken as an indication of economic advance. In addition,
channels exist for the transfer of benign "capitalist" ethics from the
West. If we judge the situation against the outcome in other lands and
epochs, the Russian experience contains few surprises. One cannot deny,
however, that current developments are of enormous interest, and that
further change well deserves carefully monitoring.

14

Labor politics in postcommunist Russia:
a preliminary assessment

WALTER D. CONNOR

Mr. Sumin responds that he is for reform, but not of the variety that Mr. Yeltsin preaches. "I'm against a chaotically accelerated transition to the market," he says. His top aide, Mr. Kosilov, outlines an alternative: "people oriented" reforms, including guaranteed jobs for all, high salaries, plentiful credits to needy factories, help to the elderly.

Wall Street Journal, 4 May 1993, reporting from Cheliabinsk

Pyotr Sumin is the newly elected boss of Cheliabinsk; he has a rival in Vadim Solov'ev, Yeltsin's selected governor, but in early May 1993 Sumin seemed to hold the high cards.

One cannot generalize from Cheliabinsk to the whole of Russia— indeed one cannot generalize from any part of Russia to the whole without trepidation. Hence the question of whether postcommunist Russia's glass of economic transformation is half-full or half-empty is as much a matter of observers' perceptions as of the precise measurement of "real" economic indicators. What to Sumin is a "chaotically acceler-ated transition" still falls far short of many elements necessary to stabi-lize and sustain a market: a currency that inspires confidence, similar commercial and property laws, budget constraints hard enough to put value-subtracting enterprises out of business, among others. Yet the earth has moved since 1 January 1992. Russia has felt the effects of decontrolled retail prices, seen substantial privatization of trade, ser-vices, and some smaller-scale manufacturing, and witnessed early phases of a division of the population into winners and losers, dependent on a

Research for this chapter was partly supported by the National Council for Soviet and Eastern Research through a grant (contract #807-27) to Boston University; conclusions are the author's.

myriad of individual and group characteristics that leave people more or
less able to exploit the opportunities of a painful period of economic
change. A "Schumpeterian whirlwind of creative destruction," as Richard Ericson terms it,[1] is under way—but it has not yet blown its entire
course.

Where that whirlwind blows, ideas of people-oriented reforms, like
those of Sumin's aide Kosilov, are bound to be popular. There is a
conceptual as well as institutional revolution under way in the Russian
economy, but current pains and the "legacy" of communism naturally
dispose many to long for the guaranteed employment, good pay, and
enterprise survival the Kosilovs would offer as "reform."

Tensions—between institutional heritage and institutional needs, between governmental visions of necessary change and governmental fears
of social explosion, and between strong proponents of democratic market reform, centrists who advocate a strong state role in a lengthy
transition, and neocommunist and nationalist reactionaries—have
marked postcommunist Russian politics since the outset. As it is in
politics as a whole, so it is in the arena of labor politics, the focus of
this chapter.

One of the subjects of labor politics is labor itself, the more than 70
million workers of the Russian Federation, still heavily tilted toward the
hypertrophic heavy industry sector. Although there are critical differences within the labor force (and within its factory worker segment) of
a psychological sort over readiness to cope with the disciplines and
uncertainties of a nascent market, and differences in the survivability of
the diversity of plants in which they work, all have been beneficiaries of
the old social contract, however tattered it was by the late Gorbachev
period.[2] The interests of much of labor, short- and medium-term, cannot
but conflict with much of the agenda of a reformist government, however much workers may give general assent to a market economy future.
The difference between the pains of transition, where those short- and
medium-range interests are violated, and the promise of the future is one
exploited by trade unions.

---

[1]See Richard E. Ericson, "Economics," in Timothy J. Colton and Robert Legvold, eds.,
After the Soviet Union: From Empire to Nations (New York: Norton, 1992), 49–83.

[2]As Gorbachev's reformist economic thinking advanced, aspects of the social contract
came more and more under attack as major problems of the old economy. But the
evidence is strong that fear of explicit violation of the contract constrained policy and its
implementation (as opposed to rhetoric); see Linda J. Cook, *The Soviet Social Contract
and Why It Failed* (Cambridge, Mass.: Harvard University Press, 1993).

It is also a difference made the most of by employers. A heterogeneous category, and likely to become more so as "de-etatization" and privatization processes work their way, employers are still largely the directors and managers of what are *state* industrial enterprises. Long accustomed to a world of plan targets and state orders, to allocation of inputs and government subsidizing of all financial operations, to a monopolist's plan—a guaranteed secure place in an economy of shortage—these employers find their practices and interests counterpoised to those of a market-oriented government. To a significant degree, they, like many workers, now acknowledge the inevitability of economic change and the market; the issue is the length, and nature, of the transition. Here, employer-labor interests may line up quite logically, one with another, in the state sector: another complexity of labor politics, Russian-style. (The "private" employers, as an interest group of owners employing significant numbers of the "hired," are still too small to figure as a major force—though at present, on certain taxation and other issues, their interests are not necessarily divergent from their state counterparts.)

Government is inescapably another subject, another "party" in the business of labor politics. But it is a divided, confused player. Shifting the whole mode of rule toward democracy, the Moscow government has also found itself with less power to govern than it needs for some of its objectives (something felt in the autonomy with which many of Russia's provinces operate). Beyond this, government is divided in policy and procedural terms. A prime objective of the Yegor Gaidar–led reformist cabinet through mid-1992 was to end the government's role as the all-proprietor, all-employer, all-paymaster. Developments since then, with exits from the cabinet and entrances by elements of the employers' industrial lobby, have complicated matters: echoes of early-1992 shock therapy mixing with the different sounds of "managed transition" and "preventing the collapse of production." The extrication of the government from the primary role in the economy could not be performed all at once, to be sure: the real issue, with profound implications for government's future status as player or referee (or the balance to be struck between these two roles), is whether and what kind of gradualism can move matters decisively in this direction.

What follows, after a brief review of the general political-economic state of play as of early May 1993, is an attempt to deal with some of the major issues involving labor, employers, and government in the postcommunist period, focusing especially on trade unions and on the government's first attempt to regulate the multiple problems of early-phase transition through a consultative mechanism bringing these three sides together. The chapter concludes with some general thoughts on the relevance of what has become a major governmental weapon—privatization—and on the possible future(s) before an economy seemingly equally pained by the burden of past inheritance and the daunting problem of finding mechanisms to cope with those pains in the context of an unprecedented transition. Under the heading "USSR" was created, with great effort, the world's first nonmarket-based industrial civilization; moving away from that civilization is a process equally arduous.

MOSCOW, MAY 1993

Majorities of those who turned out for Russia's 25 April 1993 referendum voted as liberal reformers had hoped: "da, da, nyet, da," expressing support for Yeltsin as president, for his economic policies, rejecting an early election for the presidency, and backing an election to replace the current parliament. In the muddled Russian political-constitutional situation, no automatic consequences could follow. Voter approval put no big stick in Yeltsin's hand; voter disapproval of the Parliament could not force new elections on any accelerated timetable. The anti-Yeltsin forces and foes of reform who dominated the Congress of People's Deputies refused to treat the vote as meaning anything. On 1 May, violent confrontations between police and protest marchers from various neocommunist and nationalist groups, antidemocratic and antireform, escalated street tensions to levels not seen since August 1991. A politics already strife-ridden threatened to turn uglier.

The background provided by spring economic indicators, too, had its ambiguities. If not so grim as it might have been, the economic picture, when juxtaposed to unruly, venomous presidential-parliamentary politics, had prompted the G-7 group of seven major industrial nations to support the president with a $28.4 billion aid package in mid-April. How much Russia could draw on depended on its fulfillment of a number of conditions requiring toughness and discipline: The lack of such in 1992 had made that year's similar package largely a nonstarter.

Industrial production continued to fall: the specific numbers matter less than they might, excluding unreported production of various sorts, while including the output of value-subtracting factories better closed on strictly economic grounds (one of the areas where the conditions of

Western aid set the bar rather too high for the Yeltsin government to clear). Inflation moved along at a rapid clip, against calendar 1992 price rises of over 2,000 percent. For the four months of December 1992 through March 1993, retail prices had risen 27, 27, 25, and 17.4 percent, respectively. Average wage growth, after hitting a staggering 52 percent in December, trailed off to −2.4, 15, and 17 percent in the three months of the first quarter of 1993.[3] The troubling wage-price spiral continued, with the numbers indicating increasing retail misery for many.

The credit and money-supply situation, so critical an index of discipline, looked confused as well. Through 1992, the Gaidar core of the cabinet never succeeded in getting money and credit under control, lacking as it did control of the Central Bank and its head, Viktor Gerashchenko. The credit flood of 1992—bailing out the enterprises that continued to operate while running up massive networks of "credits" and debts—had in the end not really been resisted by the government. Even the marketeer Aleksandr Shokhin, on his way out of the labor minister post in June 1992, allowed that credits "had" to be allocated to preserve enterprises and prevent "tens of millions" unemployed, when the government lacked resources to accommodate more than three to four million jobless.[4] Government financial discipline continued to war with enterprise hunger (and an indulgent bank) in 1993. On 10 April Finance Minister Boris Fedorov announced an agreement that second-quarter credits would not exceed first-quarter ones by more than 30 percent—but two days later Gerashchenko cited money-supply growth targets April through June at 18 percent monthly.[5]

Given this failure to gain control, unemployment was, by market economy standards, much too low, though rising and emerging as a politically volatile issue. No wave of bankruptcies and closures had come in 1992 to put workers into the street and on to the support of a new and primitive unemployment system. Russia had begun the post-communist era with about 70,000 registered as unemployed, and saw this number grow to 200,000 by mid-1992. By 1 April 1993, the "registered" figure was 730,000 and the state employment service estimated another 1.5 million working short hours or on unpaid furlough. The

[3]See ITAR-TASS, 9 April 1993, in *RFE/RL News Briefs* (hereafter *RFE/RL NB*), 13–16 April 1993, 4.
[4]*RFE/RL Research Report,* 26 June 1992, 53, citing the *Independent,* 14 June 1992.
[5]*RFE/RL NB,* 13–16 April 1993, 1.

Labor Ministry's estimate of total unemployed (registered and unregistered) was in the 4.5 to 5 million range.[6]

The government that confronted these figures was not really the same one that had begun 1992. The Gaidar cabinet, with the minister of finance and later acting prime minister backed by Aleksandr Shokhin as labor minister, Anatoly Chubais in charge of privatization programs, as well as other convinced reformers, had for a time enjoyed Yeltsin's full backing. By mid-1992, falling production and other ripple effects of shock therapy had generated resistance from the industrial lobby sufficient that three of its representatives—Vladimir Shumeiko, Georgi Khizha, and Viktor Chernomyrdin—were added to the cabinet.

Read variously as capitulation to the make-haste-slowly industrialists, or as a compromise dictated by the impossibility of governing without some understanding with the centrists, the new cabinet configuration did not in the end signal any radical change of course: The government was already temporizing on biting bullets in any case. By fall, with the Yeltsin–Ruslan Khasbulatov president-parliament fight heating up, and economic indicators worsening as the government pushed Chubais's voucher-privatization program to make economic change irreversible, issues assumed a sharper outline. At the December Congress of People's Deputies, Gaidar was "sacrificed" and Chernomyrdin was named prime minister.

Chernomyrdin first confirmed fears, signing off on a decree that sought to put a cap on prices indirectly via profit controls. This move, threatening shortages and black marketeering, was greeted with alarm and criticism by many reformers, including new Deputy Prime Minister and Finance Minister Fedorov, a marketeer returned from the World Bank. Chernomyrdin then reversed himself, and for a while spoke the language of financial constraint. But in the run-up to the April referendum, he would cross swords with Chubais, denouncing the privatization program well under way (and being resisted by the local elites in several cities) as a process akin to Stalin's bloody agricultural collectivization campaign of six decades before.

Yeltsin, in the immediate prelude to and aftermath of the referendum, seemed to drift away from the very economic policies for which he was asking approval. The appointments of two more deputy prime ministers, Oleg Lobov and Oleg Soskovets, seemed to augment the industrialist

[6]See ibid., 4; for 1992, see *RFE/RL Research Report*, 8 May 1992, 46, citing ITAR-TASS, 23 April 1992; ibid., 31 July 1992, 58, citing *Izvestiia*, 16 July 1992.

faction. Yeltsin talked approvingly of more support for state enterprises and issued a decree on workers' rights on 21 April, which provided for administrative limits on "permissible" unemployment levels and topping-up—adding something to pay—of reduced wages for those on short time—reduced work hours.[7] Added to Yeltsin's statements on the need to index savings accounts against inflation, and a softening of earlier resistance to raising the minimum wage once again,[8] these were moves not likely to reassure those who would encourage Yeltsin, after his referendum victory, to seize the day and move ahead with measures which, while unpopular, would not be less so if delayed.

But early May saw, as well, other hints and rumors—that Yeltsin was preparing a number of moves to solidify a reform cabinet once again, then pursue policies to match. These involved, among others, dropping Chernomyrdin as prime minister, to be replaced by Shumeiko, who among the industrialist additions of spring 1992 had cleaved closest to Yeltsin and reform policies; then with a new premier in place to provide protection, bringing Gaidar back as finance minister and, as this would release Fedorov from the post, sending the latter to take over the Central Bank, forcing Gerashchenko out.

Was Yeltsin compromising, moving slowly toward the center? Or was the first quarter of 1993 a prelude, buying time for a return to Gaidar-type policies? Whatever the answer, it would be important for the realm of labor politics and the actors in it. We now turn to those players.

TRADE UNIONS: SURVIVORS AND NEWCOMERS

With the time rapidly moving toward the 25 April referendum, Boris Yeltsin had gotten the backing, at a 19 April meeting, of an assembly of independent trade union leaders. About thirty unions, none of them associated with the Federation of Independent Trade Unions of Russia (FNPR), were represented at the meeting, which asserted support for the president and the need for an early legislative election (and thus, by implication, the end of the Congress of People's Deputies).[9] Miners', metallurgists', and aviation and transport workers' unions were all part

---

[7] *RFE/RL Daily Report,* 22 April 1993.

[8] A wage raised to parity with the minimum *pension* level of 4,275 rubles monthly, which became effective 1 February 1993—a year earlier it had been 410 rubles; see Sheila Marnie, "The Social Safety Net in Russia," *RFE/RL Research Report,* 23 April 1993, 19.

[9] ITAR-TASS (Russian), 1428 GMT (Greenwich Mean Time), 19 April 1993; *Foreign Broadcast Information Service* (hereafter *FBIS*), 20 April 1993, 14.

of the meeting, offering programmatic support for privatization and other Yeltsin measures and, according to a not unbiased source, representing more than five million members.[10]

The next day Igor Klochkov, head of the FNPR, mocked the "mythical five million" figure. He reminded Yeltsin that counterposing independent unions (with, as he put it, a "several tens of thousands" membership—also a not unbiased number, this time on the low side) to his 60 million–plus membership underrated FNPR's importance.[11] It was one more instance of the opposition of two poles in the unsettled world of postcommunist labor in Russia, and in the confrontation of a remarkable "survivor" organization and newcomer unions offering a challenge to it.

How labor politics has evolved (and it has not, on the whole, evolved far) in postcommunist Russia points to some important aspects of the legacy of communism. Despite economic changes, the state remains the major employer. Despite political changes of monumental scale, one massive "old" union structure survives in Russia, along with labor organizations of undeniably independent provenance that trace their origins to the late-1980 beginnings of the Soviet Union's terminal crisis. Understanding 1992–93 involves a certain amount of prehistory.

The massive mine strikes of July 1989, paralyzing the coalfields of the Kuzbass, Donbass, Karaganda, and Vorkuta, dramatized on the national stage the bankruptcy of the All-Union Central Council of Trade Unions (VTsSPS, AUCCTU) as a defender of workers' collective interests. Four years into the Gorbachev era, things were changing. The strike wave evoked new rhetoric from the AUCCTU head at the time, Stepan Shalaev, who had earlier in 1989 (in response to frequent, but smaller strikes in the spring) criticized the supine stance of the unions versus management and the state, and defended workers' aspirations, if not their proclivities toward striking.[12] Now, in Kemerovo in the Kuzbass, he avowed AUCCTU support for the miners[13] and later admitted to *Pravda* that "since V. I. Lenin's death"[14] (1924) the unions had been subordinated to the party. This rejection of "transmission belt" status of the unions became a constant refrain of AUCCTU leaders, after a half-century and more of precisely that.

[10]Radio Rossii (Russian), 1600 GMT, 19 April 1993; *FBIS,* 20 April 1993, 14.
[11]ITAR-TASS (English), 1605 GMT, 20 April 1993; *FBIS,* 21 April 1993, 28.
[12]*Wochenpresse* (Vienna), 10 February 1989, 34; *FBIS,* 14 February 1989, 75.
[13]*Trud,* 18 July 1989, 1; *FBIS,* 18 July 1989, 76.
[14]*Pravda,* 31 July 1989, 1–2; *FBIS,* 11 August 1989, 75–78.

Caught flat-footed by the coalfield militancy, however, and seeming too much a late convert to combative unionism, Shalaev gave way in April 1990 to a new AUCCTU head—Gennadi Yanaev (who would, as Soviet vice-president, front the August 1991 coup attempt). The scenario, at the union plenum, involved the resignation of Shalaev; the nomination of four potential replacements; the resignation of three, leading to Yanaev's "unanimous" election—all in thirty-three minutes; and his delivery after a ten-minute break of an hour-long speech to the assembled unionists.[15] It was a less-than-convincing demonstration of union renewal and of democratic procedures.

Although the year 1990 was not one to match 1989 in labor militancy, it was a peculiar one for the AUCCTU. Yanaev departed in July 1990, having been elected a Politburo member (by then an office of much-diminished status) and Central Committee secretary at the Twenty-eighth Communist Party of the Soviet Union (CPSU) Congress. The union's number two man, V. P. Shcherbakov, served as interim chair pending the October-scheduled Eighteenth AUCCTU Congress. At that congress, the AUCCTU dissolved itself and simultaneously voted its rebirth as the General Confederation of Trade Unions of the USSR (VKP), with Shcherbakov as head. To some degree this was simply the inertia of an organization that was the automatic recipient of large sums in members' "dues," the proprietor of sanatoriums and newspapers, and still the government-financed agent for various welfare functions. It also signaled recognition of the progressive weakening of the old USSR central structures in politics. Although various independent unions had been founded in the wake of the 1989 strikes, the new unions, generally small and uncoordinated, showed little tendency to affiliate with the new VKP. The latter's major component was itself a new organization, of prime concern in this chapter: at a fall 1989 AUCCTU plenum, a Russian republic trade union organization had been created, the FNPR, with its base the seventy-six million RSFSR workers hitherto unrepresented by a republic-level union body.[16] It mirrored in its structure the "old" AUCCTU.

In 1990 and 1991, both the VKP and FNPR took increasingly combative stands for the workers and against the tougher projections of reform policies (which saw in any case virtually no implementation in these years), while at the same time drawing toward an acceptance of

[15]*Izvestiia*, 18 April 1990, 1.
[16]TASS (English), 1723 GMT, 6 September 1989; *FBIS*, 7 September 1989, 70.

the market's inevitability. This meant criticism not only of the economic radicals of 1990–91 and their ideas, but also of the stabilization plans fronted by Prime Ministers Ryzhkov and Pavlov. Further criticism was extended toward union demands for maximum efforts to limit unemployment, for maximum compensation for the increased living costs engendered by state price decontrol (whose first phase came in April 1991), and for the recognition of ever-broader trade union rights. The FNPR, simply, wanted "more": the government should pay. So went union politics up to the August coup attempt.

And so, in many ways, have they continued since in Russia. The CPSU is gone; the Soviet Union, with its ministries, state committees, and Supreme Soviet, is gone. But the structures of old, "official" trade unionism remain. The persistence of these institutions, toothless as they or their predecessors were only three to four years ago, is at first glance remarkable. But it is also part of a pattern: these old trade unions have persisted in much of Eastern Europe as well.[17] Thus, in the post-Soviet phase, the FNPR survives in Russia. The VKP, persisting at least as an organizational husk, has been engaged since late 1991 in attempts to turn itself into an international trade union center to coordinate labor issues across the ex-republics. Given the similarity of certain labor problems, this is not completely illogical. But given the divisions among the states, their differing roads, and the ephemeral nature of Commonwealth of Independent States (CIS) political structures, the VKP has not achieved much.[18] The FNPR survives for several reasons. First, it has not been dispossessed of its funds or welfare functions. Second, it has taken a logical and opportunistic line in the current tense situation—to talk and act proworker and prostrike. Third, the various independent unions and federations of such that have grown, since 1989, into a more and more important force, have not yet managed to displace the FNPR unions, however much independent union leaders may distrust the holdovers. Nor, of course, are those holdovers anxious to give up *their* powers, their organizational resources. In a peculiar way, the old, formally independent juridical status of the official unions (as neither state nor party organs)[19] became real in the process of the Soviet collapse, though they hardly played a major role in precipitating it.

[17]"Roundtable: Trade Unions in Post Communist Society: The USSR Learns from Eastern Europe's Experience," *Report on the USSR,* no. 41 (1991): 16–22.
[18]See *Trud,* 4 January 1992, 1, and 17 April 1992, 1.
[19]Jerry Hough, some years ago, ascribed perhaps excessive significance to the AUCCTU's independence from governmental bodies; see his "Policy-Making and the Worker," in

Contemporary Russian labor politics is still to a degree rooted in the last seven to eight months of the Soviet Union's existence, in Russia's emergence as a secessionist republic in 1991, and in the emergence of Yeltsin as its prime political personality. Yeltsin, as Russia's first popularly elected president, evoked both cheers and concerns with his July 1991 "departyization" decree, aimed mainly at getting the CPSU out of factories, enterprises, and so on, but couched in broader language. Earlier, the FNPR had hailed Yeltsin's election, but demanded attention to the social protection of workers and the economically vulnerable. The FNPR presented itself as a cooperative element in the new Russian political picture, but also as a constructive opposition.[20] On the heels of the 1991 decree, banning activity of "political parties and mass public movements" in state enterprises and organizations, Yeltsin and his team made haste, in response to union protests, to assure the VKP and FNPR that trade unions and their activities were not subject to the ban.[21] Yeltsin met with Klochkov of the FNPR on 25 July and with Shcherbakov of the VKP on 30 July[22] to offer further reassurance. Still, they expressed fears that unions might be deprived of their rights against employers in the move toward privatization of the economy—worker rights in managerial elections had already been cut back since the State Enterprise Law of 1987. Yeltsin in response once again affirmed unions' rights, but also suggested they get accustomed to the word "employer" and to dealing with such people[23]—an intimation of hopes that the government could gradually shed the employer role.

The August coup came, and failed. If Yeltsin's call from Moscow for a general strike did not evoke overwhelming support, the VKP and FNPR did protest the coup, though they avoided issuing a strike call.[24] The unions had, at least, passed the test of *not* backing the coup. The VKP organ *Trud* reviewed its own performance during the coup, gave itself high marks, and announced that it had dissolved its own party organization.[25]

With the onset of autumn, the unions' focus returned to matters economic. Wage indexation in the face of rapidly rising prices, minimum

Arcadius Kahan and Blair Ruble, eds., *Industrial Labor in the USSR* (New York: Pergamon, 1979), 383.

[20] *Rossiiskaia gazeta*, 4 July 1991, 1.

[21] *Pravda*, 24 July 1991, 2.

[22] INTERFAX (English), 1000 GMT, 25 July 1991; *FBIS*, 26 July 1991, 61; TASS (English), 1931 GMT, 31 July 1991; *FBIS*, 1 August 1991, 61.

[23] *Izvestiia*, 12 August 1991, 1.

[24] TASS (Russian), 1604 GMT, 20 August 1991; *FBIS*, 21 August 1991, 19–20.

[25] *Trud*, 23 August 1991, 1.

income legislation, collective bargaining rights, and general labor protection were recurrent themes. The FNPR announced "unity of action" days for trade unions for 21–26 October, to press the Russian government toward meeting union demands, and threatened a one-hour strike for 13 November if demands were not met.[26]

In October the VKP appealed to Russian and other republican governments for action establishing a minimum "market basket" for each republic and a keying of wages, pensions, and allowances to the cost of the basket. Admitting that the "sick economy" might find this difficult, it insisted that such measures must be implemented.[27] Yeltsin on 16 October promised consultation with the FNPR and other unions before his government took any major social and/or economic policy action.[28] But he also found reason to accuse the FNPR of being monopolist in the manner of the old AUCCTU.[29]

In the final weeks of the Soviet Union, then, unions were asking for more protection from economic pain and the disciplines of the market mechanism than governments could afford. Nor could those governments afford total denial of such demands. It was the end of an era, the end of a system. Neither government nor unions had yet mastered a language to fit the times. An assembly of leaders of branch trade unions made the quite logical point that forthcoming price liberalization, without demonopolization, would raise prices but hardly guarantee more supplies, and reasserted its by-now standard set of protection demands on 1 November, without offering any concrete notions of how they might be met.[30] At the swan-song meeting on 13 November between Gorbachev and union leaders, VKP leader Shcherbakov spoke of the risk of "masses driven to despair by falling living standards [coming] out into the streets." Gorbachev, looking backward, criticized the union for not supporting with sufficient force the economic treaty that might save something of the old Soviet Union.[31]

Some indication of Yeltsin's developing post-Soviet concepts of union-government dealings came in a Russian government decree on 15 November on "social partnership."[32] Welcomed by Klochkov of the

[26]Moscow, Radio Mayak, 0900 GMT, 9 October 1991; *FBIS,* 9 October 1991, 55.
[27]TASS (English), 2301 GMT, 14 October 1991; *FBIS,* 16 October 1991, 37.
[28]See *Trud,* 30 October 1991; *Rabochaia tribuna,* 30 October 1991.
[29]INTERFAX (English), 1700 GMT, 31 October 1991.
[30]*Trud,* 2 November 1991, 1.
[31]INTERFAX (English), 1930 GMT, 13 November 1991; *FBIS,* 14 November 1991, 18.
[32]Text in *Rossiiskaia gazeta,* 19 November 1991, 2.

FNPR as an important move toward meeting the unions' demands of the October "action days,"[33] the decree envisaged cooperation between government, unions, and "employers" (regardless of the "form of ownership") on setting wages and other conditions. The vehicle for this cooperation would be a trilateral commission, in which the three sides would meet. It was unclear at the time,[34] however, how the "sides"—at least, employers and the unions—would be constituted. Who had a right to a seat at the table? Was the FNPR to represent labor? If so, what of the independent unions, especially the militant Independent Union of Miners (NPG), contemptuous of the FNPR-related unions? Who would represent "employers" versus the state and labor, when the state was still the main employer? These were hard questions, and the answers satisfied no one.

FNPR activity in 1992 can be traced by the reader for the most part through the following section on trilateralism and the corporate approach to labor relations. Looking at it as a major, indeed *the* major, survivor organization of Soviet times, however, some further comments are best made here.

The FNPR remains huge—the 60 million figure Klochkov gave in April 1993 was not a numerical exaggeration. A major defection in late 1992 involved the 2 million–member miners and metallurgists union, in an acrimonious split, with the FNPR accusing the union of playing politics and cozying up to the government,[35] whereas the union criticized the FNPR for a too predictable antigovernment stance that left little room for the interests workers in this branch had in privatization.

Why do workers remain in the FNPR-affiliated unions? A June 1992 report cited 36 percent remaining out of "habit" and another 32 percent seeking the various material benefits that might come to them through the trade unions' old distribution system in a time of "total shortage."[36] Such people would, according to the author of the study, be the first to answer strike calls in defense of the "pseudosocial guarantees" of the old system—but also the first to leave when shortages were over. That 96 percent of FNPR union members in mid-1992 did not plan to leave did not mean strong, affective loyalties. Some belonged as well to other independent unions in the same workplace (though this is less prevalent

---

[33]TASS (Russian), 1502 GMT, 18 November 1991; *FBIS*, 19 November 1991, 61.
[34]See the partnership decree text in *Rossiiskaia gazeta*, 19 November 1991, 1.
[35]See the coverage of this defection in *Rabochaia tribuna*, 6 November, 27 November, 11 December, and 15 December 1992.
[36]*Rossiiskaia gazeta*, 4 June 1992, 2.

in radicalized sectors like coal mining, which gave rise to relatively strong independent unions). Claims that 80 to 90 percent of the pre-1992 membership of FNPR unions still remain (a figure cited in August 1992)[37] were probably not far off the mark.

The times, after all, remain very uncertain. If it is not the time to join new organizations (and despite the proliferation of groups claiming the status of fronts, parties, or movements, all seem vague about their memberships), neither is it necessarily the time to leave old organizations. Union membership came with one's job; the dues, after all, are only 1 percent of wages. The official unions were the traditional channel for pensions, housing lists, and other welfare benefits. Plants that refuse to maintain the dues check-off may precipitate defections from union membership,[38] but there is, overall, an inertia factor in membership.

Furthermore, for many workers who seek an organized defense of their interests, there may be no real choices evident, other than the FNPR. Independent unionism is still relatively weakly developed in many sectors and branches. Political parties are weak, on whatever side of the spectrum they locate themselves. Although various parties have been founded since 1990 that claim the mantle of workers' defense, from Marxist-socialist but anticommunist all the way to neocommunist successors to the CPSU, politics—executive and legislative—has not assumed a shape that allows the stabilization of any party spectrum, or a uniting of particular constituencies with particular party labels. Nor have obviously reactionary movements that are engaged primarily in rhetoric and street politics (like *Trudovaia Rossiia,* linked to the Russian Communist Workers' party) really attracted, it seems, the allegiance of any significant portion of workers.[39] That some 14 percent of FNPR members see the union as the last available defender of workers' interests may be testimony to its familiarity as the only old organization still represented on the factory floor (the Komsomol and CPSU are gone), and to the underdevelopment of civic culture, but it is not the oddest of a set of odd realities.[40]

Weak affiliation with the FNPR means, as well, that despite its millions of members, the union leadership cannot claim a strong hold on

[37]*Trud,* 13 August 1992, 2.

[38]*Rossiiskaia gazeta,* 4 June 1992, 2.

[39]The Russian political party spectrum, even as it relates only to specific issues of labor politics, would require a whole chapter on its own; the picture is so inchoate and confusing that such an essay might provide little by way of enlightenment.

[40]*Rossiiskaia gazeta,* 4 June 1992, 2.

them or the ability to deploy them in strike actions. FNPR Deputy Chair Vasilii Romanov, in an October 1992 interview, claimed that one-third of his membership was ready for an all-Russian strike if demands were not met by the government: a rise from only 6 percent declaring themselves so militant in an earlier (August) FNPR poll. How he had ascertained the implied rise in militancy was unclear, as were any thoughts prompted by the evidence that some two-thirds were still *not* ready to strike.[41]

Still tough in rhetoric, conflictual in its relations with the independent unions, prone to accuse breakaways like the mining and metallurgy union of corrupt political motives while highly politicized itself, the FNPR finished 1992 and moved into 1993. It still defended its old prerogatives, with Klochkov on 25 December asserting that "logic and facts" supported its retention of its "self-managing social security fund" in the transition period.[42] Increasingly though, defection—both organizational and individual—looked like a future trend. A long article by a former worker activist and "assistant to the Chair, FNPR"[43] accused the union of inflating participation figures for the October 1992 protest days from two hundred thousand (his estimate) to the official 2 million. "I was convinced that the FNPR is not a trade union, but some sort of political party of the former nomenklatura." The government and no doubt most independent unions, especially those that traced their roots back to the same 1989 that saw the political and social bankruptcy of the old AUCCTU, would have agreed.

CORPORATIST FORMULA: THE TRILATERAL COMMISSION

The by now standard formulation in discussing post-Soviet affairs—that old institutional structures have been demolished and new institutions, fit to the tasks of establishing stable democracy and a functioning market economy, are yet to be created—fits labor politics as well. In this case, an important part of the story thus far is that of a new institution, a product of the post-Soviet era in Russia, aimed at regulating labor problems but ill-fit to do so. Although not quite an autopsy—for the institution in question was rechartered in early 1993—this examination is surely a lesson in the strength of both structural and psychological

---

[41]*Nezavisimaia gazeta*, 17 October 1992, 2; *FBIS*, 20 October 1992, 17.
[42]*Rabochaia tribuna*, 25 December 1992, 1.
[43]*Trud*, 21 November 1992, 6.

legacies, or as the first chapter in this volume terms them, aftermaths of the old system.

The organizational expression of the November 1992 Yeltsin commitment to social partnership, bearing the stamp of some policy thinking by labor specialists,[44] the Russian Federation's "trilateral commission for the regulation of social-labor problems" began operating in January 1992. The general design was logical: government, "business," and labor meet weekly to manage the conflict potential of a difficult transition to the market under the economic crisis conditions created by the 1991 free-fall of the Soviet economy. This was a corporatist design of benign variety: West European social-democratic precedents argued for it, as against the governmental hands-off style of U.S. labor politics. Given Russia's history of hyperstatism, as well as the crisis situation, it would have been hard to see government out of the matter, in any case. But given the specifics of the situation and how these still, in early 1992, differed from any kind of market economy, it was hard to see how the paradigm might work successfully. The experience with trilateralism can be divided into the early phase—until, roughly, mid-1992 and the entrance into the cabinet of the industrialists—and the period since. Some main elements of the earlier period emerge clearly.

First, the commission presided over a degree of (relative) labor peace, in light of worst-case expectations about public reactions to the new policies of 1992. But this circumstance had little to do with any procedural regularization the commission imposed. Despite the tough talk of the Gaidar team, despite trilateral coordinator and State Secretary Gennadi Burbulis's warnings that the government would resist "unreasonable demands,"[45] the commission became a venue for huge concessions on the wages for militant workers in critical industries, rather than a regulator of their demands.[46]

Actors on the government side were at pains to distance the commission from the government per se. When a massive strike in the Kuzbass coalfields threatened in mid-March, Labor Minister Aleksandr Shokhin advised a commission delegation being sent to the area to show "tough-

---

[44]Labor specialists were aware of the difficulties associated with the connectedness of the three sides; however, see L. A. Gordon, E. V. Klopov, "Trudovye otnosheniia: k trekhstoronnemu sotsial'nomu partnerstvu," *Polis*, nos. 1–2 (1992): 167–77.

[45]Moscow, Radio Mayak, 1880 GMT, 24 January 1992; *FBIS*, 27 January 1992, 35.

[46]For a detailed discussion of early commission activity and the nature of the 1992 social agreement, see Elizabeth Teague, "Russian Government Seeks 'Social Partnership,' " *RFE/RL Research Report*, 19 June 1992, 16–23.

ness" and asserted that the government was not a "fire brigade."[47] When the commission then hosted, in Moscow, a delegation from the Kuzbass area, Burbulis asserted that the commission, not the government, was acting as arbiter.[48] But this was not really the case: the government still, necessarily, sat on the "business/employer" side of the table.

Nor did the new organizational context regularize union politics. There was much posturing, especially from the FNPR, and no evidence that labor had become united (although to consider this as an objective of the commission's[49] architecture may be to miss the point). The FNPR was critical of the first draft of the 1992 "social agreement," refused to sign the final version (reached by the commission on 25 March), delayed with some fanfare until "consultations" were completed, and then signed on 3 April. The FNPR had thus demonstrated its independence by withholding the signatures of nine of the fourteen representatives on the labor side; the *Sotsprof,* a quasi union generally supportive of Yeltsin, then commanded three signatures, and the independent miners' union (NPG) one, as did the union of civil-aviation personnel. Conflict between the latter unions, especially *Sotsprof* and the FNPR elements, was more typical than not. Politically, the independents generally supported the Yeltsin government and dealt with matters of economic policy disagreement in pragmatic terms. The FNPR accused *Sotsprof* of being the Yeltsin government's "tame" union.[50] But earlier, the FNPR had seen no reason *any* other unions should sit on the commission, and tried to maintain its monopoly of facilities, resources, and social welfare functions. Independents, notably the NPG, argued for redistribution of these resources.[51] The FNPR had also tried to retain a monopoly on plant-level negotiations, backing a regulation that the largest union organization in a given enterprise would negotiate and sign agreements on behalf of all the workers. *Sotsprof* fought this and won, depriving the FNPR of its ability to preempt other unions.[52]

The motivation and rationale of labor protest and strike actions also

---

[47]Moscow, Radio Odin (Russian), 1600 GMT, 11 March 1992; *FBIS,* 13 March 1992, 25.
[48]Moscow, Ostankino Television, First Program, 1200 GMT, 18 March 1992; *FBIS,* 20 March 1992, 55–56.
[49]*Rabochaia tribuna,* 7 March 1992, 3.
[50]*Trud,* 14 March 1992, 2.
[51]*Komsomol'skaia pravda,* 7 April 1992, 2; *Izvestiia,* 6 April 1992, 2; *FBIS,* 14 April 1992, 34–37.
[52]Teague, "Russian Government," 20, note 26.

afford a great deal of room for intralabor squabbles. The March strike threats in the Kuzbass region,[53] launched by FNPR affiliates mainly outside the mining sector, got no support from the local (mainly miner) independent unions. These characterized the former official unions as the "last bastion of reactionary communist forces," aiming their strike threat at the Yeltsin government, in an attempt to make Russia ungovernable. (The FNPR had played on the quite real issue of intersectoral wage differences in mining regions: miners' and other coal industry workers' wage increases drove prices beyond the reach of those in other sectors. True, the independent unions, heavily weighted toward the miners in the area, might be accused of some insensitivity to the issue. But FNPR unions in the mining sector had obviously not been reluctant to push for the miners' pay raises, which had contributed to the "spiral.") When the trilateral commission's delegation visited Kuzbass and the strike threat was suspended, sources obviously sympathetic to the independents observed that the strike had been stillborn not because the delegation had been accommodating, but because of lack of worker support for what they regarded as an FNPR political provocation.[54]

Thus no real solidarity emerged on the labor side of the triangle. The FNPR, headed by ex-apparatchik Klochkov, found it difficult to make common cause with unions whose roots went back to the militancy of 1989, or with the politically astute Sotsprof. FNPR affiliates fought over the division of Russian assets with the shell of the transnational VKP.[55] Independents sought a share of the assets of the old official structure, while the FNPR expressed a desire to shed some of its "nonprofit" functions (for example, technical inspection) to the government and get on with the task of defending workers.[56] But throughout 1992 and into 1993, the FNPR did fight attempts to deprive it of the check-off procedure, whereby it automatically collects members' dues, and of its pension and other benefit functions as agent of the government (which still makes subventions to the FNPR budget for this purpose). These matters, at the time of writing, are in the constitutional court.

Central in the (mal)functioning of the trilateral commission has been the geometric illogic of the situation. Ministers sit on the government

[53]See Nezavisimaia gazeta, 4 March 1992, 2, and other coverage in FBIS, 9 March 1992, 31–33.
[54]Nezavisimaia gazeta, 12 March 1992, 2; FBIS, 13 March 1992, 35–36.
[55]Trud, 15 January 1992, 1.
[56]Ibid., 14 March 1992, 2.

side. On the employer side, directors of state enterprises—with the same paymasters as the ministers they face—occupy seats, along with representatives of industrial lobby organizations (discussed later). The side of the government committed to the market thus negotiates with the side of the government committed to preservation of plant, employment, and a continuing large state role in the economy. Nor is the corner of the triangle that separates employers from labor a particularly sharp one: Government-as-reformer came, fairly early, to face concerted pressure from an employer-labor combination.[57]

This was, broadly considered, the essence of the industrial lobby. What had emerged in late 1991 as a confluence of interest, especially in heavy, defense-related industries, between the employers' Scientific-Industrial Union (NPS) and the Interrepublican Council of Labor Collectives (MSTK), continued into 1992. The NPS became, after the Soviet Union ended, Arkadii Vol'skii's Russian Union of Industrialists and Entrepreneurs (RSPP) and occupied a seat on the employers' side of the trilateral, as did the more "private" Congress of Russian Business Circles. The RSPP, along with the Confederation of Unions of Entrepreneurs of Russia (headed earlier in 1992 by Vladimir Shumeiko before his joining the cabinet), represented the complex of interests, managerial and labor, that sought survival as production and/or employment organizations. Then and now, such fears are real. The prospect of a crisis-inflation-deficit–driven deindustrialization of Russia, a collapse of the economy, before any plans could be carried out for conversion of relatively high-tech industry to nondefense uses within any tolerable context of privatization, is a frightening one. Beyond the preservationist concerns of defense industrialists, they and genuine emerging private-sector enterprises shared positions on aspects of tax policy and other matters. It was not as if real private entrepreneurs had no complaints about the procedures and operation of the trilateral commission.[58]

Industrial lobbying has not been confined to the framework of the trilateral, of course. On the broader field of politics, the RSPP's political creation, the Renewal party (*Obnovlenie*), united with Aleksandr Rutskoi's People's Party of Free Russia, Nikolai Travkin's Democratic party, and some others to form the Civic Union bloc, the so-called centrist

---

[57]See Philip Hanson and Elizabeth Teague, "The Industrialists and Russian Economic Reform," *RFE/RL Research Report*, 8 May 1992, 1–7.
[58]See the interview with Gennadi Semigin, an official of the Russian Congress of Business Circles, in *Trud*, 22 April 1992, 2.

opposition to Yeltsin. Within the trilateral, a formal alliance of a sort was declared in July between employer RSPP and labor FNPR, as the Russian Assembly of Social Partnership (RASP),[59] although—as with so many other founding meetings, congresses, and so on, in post-Soviet Russia—few concrete organizational consequences followed.

By late summer 1992, it was clear that the trilateral was not functioning to any of the social partners' satisfactions. The FNPR was disaffected, seeing the trilateral as a government body,[60] and refused to assume the "transmission belt" function under a government pushing toward capitalism.[61] Nor could the commission channel new or more extravagant demands from the industrialists' side. In mid-August, a raucous All-Russian Conference of Commodity Producers met in Moscow, bringing together about two thousand directors, union affiliates, local government officials, and others to attack the government and Gaidar's second-phase reform plans. Nearly every conceivable antimarket idea was broached during the meeting, organized mainly by the Industrial Union parliamentary faction headed by Yuri Gekht—an industrialist even less oriented toward a market transition than Vol'skii.[62] The FNPR, represented at the conference, showed signs of aligning itself with Gekht's harder line, only a month after its RASP agreement with the RSPP.[63]

Later 1992 saw trilateralism marginalized in favor of bilateral dealings by the government and its not quite "sociable" partners. With the FNPR announcing its second annual Day of Protest for 24 October, government and FNPR representatives gathered on 20 October and scheduled further meetings in a conciliation (soglasitel'naia) commission to deal with differences over minimum wage levels and other economic demands.[64] On 25 October, an industrial policy council was announced after a meeting of government and industrial management representatives,[65] again with no mention of the older trilateral context.

[59]The employer RSPP and labor FNPR copublished the newspaper Rabochaia tribuna as well.

[60]See, e.g., Rabochaia tribuna, 16 June 1992, 1; Trud, 20 June 1992, 1.

[61]This, of course, is to distinguish itself from the old AUCCTU and its role of "transmission belt" for the CPSU and Soviet government. The Yeltsin government has been accused of being a "traditional autocrat, enriched by Bolshevik experience"; see Rabochaia tribuna, 10 July 1992, 1.

[62]See Elizabeth Teague, "Splits in the Ranks of Russia's 'Red Directors,' " RFE/RL Report, 4 September 1992, 6–10.

[63]Ibid.

[64]INTERFAX (English), 1944 GMT, 23 October 1992; FBIS, 26 October 1992, 34; INTERFAX (English), 1909 GMT, 27 October 1992; FBIS, 28 October 1992, 38.

[65]ITAR-TASS (English), 1100 GMT, 2 November 1992; FBIS, 2 November 1992, 44–45.

By year's end, it was clear that trilateral corporatism had failed. The commission received briefings from Labor Minister Gennadi Melikian (Shokhin's successor) and Klochkov on the results of a month of government-FNPR conciliation commission talks in early December.[66] Few had any good words for the trilateral—some hopes were expressed that it might still work, but generally these aspirations were accompanied by complaints about the negotiating partners. That in the end the body was rechartered for 1993[67] gave little reason to assume, given the fundamental problems of economic reality and group identity still unsolved, that it would have better going in its second year.

PRIVATIZATION, CONTROL, AND SOCIAL JUSTICE

A new and controversial element, playing its own potentially important role in labor politics, was privatization. Too complicated and incomplete to be treated at length here, the original 1992 privatization program provided three variants of privatization for the state firms scheduled for such. All three variants granted advantages to the sitting work collectives and management, in a commitment of blocks of free shares (typically nonvoting) and discounts on the purchase of yet more shares. None, however, at least in principle, were giveaways to the workforce. Advocated early on by some of a syndicalist orientation, as well as by others who saw this as the cleanest, quickest break the state might make with ownership, giveaway privatization was a point on which the government drew the line, or attempted to.

Resistance had at least two sources. First, the logical notion that giveaway privatizations would in no way alter plant behavior, or make for entrepreneurial operation, militated against the idea. Second was the social justice issue—sole receivership by the workers and managements of enterprises in material production would cut out massive numbers of the population who worked outside the productive sector, doctors, teachers, soldiers, and so on, who had made their own contributions and sacrifices in assembling the national capital due for privatization. Hence, the giant voucher scheme was born: approximately 150 million vouchers issued to every man, woman, and child, their ten thousand–ruble face values adding up roughly to 35 percent of the 1991 valuation of the total plant scheduled for privatization under the scheme.

Vouchers could be bid as offerings on shares in enterprises or sold.

[66]*Rabochaia tribuna,* 8 December 1992, 2.
[67]See INTERFAX (English), 1732 GMT, 8 February 1993; *FBIS,* 8 February 1993, 15.

Some people sold them, some placed them with newly established funds, which would bid blocks of vouchers in privatization auctions. Some funds absconded, leaving hapless would-be investors victimized. How well the honest funds could work—to become major shareholders in enterprises, providing external discipline and "owners" to whom management would be partially responsible—remained unclear.[68] It was guaranteed that patterns would remain far from the Western mode of share capitalism by the lack of all sorts of critical auxiliary institutions and institutionalized behavior patterns. But it was a start—and under the circumstances, the government could not be too choosy in its search for a way out of the ownership business.

Still, the challenge of a fourth variant of privatization rose in Parliament in winter 1993—a new giveaway program[69] against which privatization boss Chubais railed. It would allow bargain-price purchases by workers and managers of their plants, paid in installments over a five-year period from factory profits, shutting out external investors. Who stood behind it? Among its backers were the sorts of local government power brokers and political eminences who, basically, oppose privatization in general and see any diffusion of ownership (especially via vouchers) as a threat to their own exercise of power and extraction of advantage. In Cheliabinsk and in Novosibirsk, local bosses simply suspended voucher auctions,[70] citing in both cases the threat that outsiders might acquire the region's wealth, that local citizens' vouchers would lose value.

Such moves are not atypical. In Nizhnyi Novgorod, where privatization is well advanced, cash auctions are the rule, vouchers largely cut out. Large blocks of shares, generally priced at one million rubles or more, are put up for sale—beyond the reach of individuals, but not the enterprises that are effectively buying themselves. Cash-starved local governments go along, since they receive most of the proceeds. Among the three original variants of privatization, most enterprises have opted for the one that seems more expensive, but allows the combination of management and employees to acquire up to 51 percent of equity at a negotiated price.[71] All this tends to reduce the management potential of voucher funds.

[68]See *Wall Street Journal*, 23 April 1993, A18.
[69]See *Nezavisimaia gazeta*, 18 February 1993, 1; *Current Digest of the Soviet Press*, 24 March 1993, 25–26.
[70]*Wall Street Journal*, 27 April 1993, A16; *Commersant*, 7 April 1993, 6–9.
[71]*Commersant*, 2 March 1993, 16–21.

All in all, then, privatization leaves many questions open. It is far too early to tell whether a broad population of owners will be able to exercise any control over management. It is unlikely to happen soon. If it does, it will affect workers and the management-labor relationship. How, meanwhile, will self-privatizing plants, wherein the management and workers have acquired the majority, controlling interest, operate? Work collectives and managers went into the secondary market in early 1993 to buy vouchers to use in privatization buy-outs,[72] further distorting the original intent. Will management be the major partner, with workers relegated to minority status? In this case, shedding excess labor becomes a possibility—but unions still have rights over authorizing lay-offs and are unlikely to take such moves with equanimity; here, the FNPR and independents may share the same position.

Manager-owners will still have incentives to behave in "old" ways— especially the many monopolists. They will raise prices; they will still lean on the state for credits to keep "their" enterprises going. Absent the sort of tough measures the Yeltsin government did not seem ready to take in the postreferendum days, much may go on as before for workers and managers, against a background of continuing decline in the heavy industrial sector where so many still work.

The legacy of the old Soviet economy is a heavy one. In large-scale industry, realism indicates that government's role will remain large. Even the sectors scheduled for privatization are proving difficult to "de-etatize." Privatization minister Chubais, typically managing to put a brave face on the process, noted in April 1993 that only 4 percent of the population had sold their vouchers, and 17 to 20 percent of the vouchers issued had already been invested, directly or via funds. He expected that 50 percent of Russia's small enterprises would be privatized by the end of the year, and noted a growing number of auctions for larger enterprises.[73] But while all this to some degree showed progress, Prime Minister Chernomyrdin, reverting to his industrialist background, was comparing the privatization process with Stalin's agricultural collectivization.[74] How privatization would proceed—with Chernomyrdin tilting back toward Soviet-style ideas he had earlier seemed to abandon, with Chubais himself under pressure from Parliament (and denounced by Khasbulatov at the Eighth Congress of People's Deputies, which had

[72]Ibid., 19.
[73]*RFE/RL NB*, 5–8 April 1993, 3.
[74]Ibid., 2.

preceded the referendum),[75] with Yeltsin showing signs of waffling in the Lobov and Soskovets appointments—was difficult to predict.

CONCLUDING THOUGHTS

We are too close to events to develop much perspective on them. To a significant degree, 1992 was a year of moves and countermoves, none of them clearly decisive, in labor politics. Gaidar was no Leszak Balcerowicz. Even at its most "Gaidarite" phase, the government shied away from the Polish finance minister's approach of shock therapy: Prices were freed (though not on all items), but wages were not controlled. Though the government could denounce the Central Bank's soft credit policies, it did not move to stop them as it might have (it, too, needed credits). On the business of credits to industry, the government jawboned the bank, but the credits kept flowing. The workers received raises, delayed by the cash shortage of mid-1992, and the factories stayed open. The FNPR was loud in its complaints, sniping continually at "reforms that hurt," but—after March 1992 at least—did not really seem to have attempted to create governmental crisis via a massive, multisector strike. Given members' weak sense of affiliation, it is not clear that the FNPR would have succeeded had it tried. Given the governmental moderation that meant no large-scale plant closing or consequent unemployment, the FNPR lacked the ultimate crisis issue.

What did not happen in 1992 and early 1993 meant as well that employers, in the sense of a category of "capital" versus labor, did not emerge as a distinct group. To expect that this would happen quickly would have been unrealistic. Entrepreneurs continue to grow in numbers and weight, but the industrial lobby, however diverse a group it is, rooted in state industry, made the running. The RSPP and others' Civic Union represented as much an alternative vision of political economy as distinct group interests; the game it played was thus a broad one, in Parliament, in the media, in cabinet politics. Coy and confusing about its status—alternative government or constructive opposition—the Civic Union did not win, nor did it decisively lose.

Of course, it is not all that easy to define what the various parties felt to be at stake in this first seventeen months of postcommunist Russian history. Russia still largely lacks accepted rules of contestation and

[75]*Rossiiskaia gazeta,* 12 March 1993, 1; *Current Digest of the Post-Soviet Press,* 7 April 1993, 7–8.

institutions with some history of operation, which play a major role in defining the stakes of political games. The big political dramas—president versus Parliament, Yeltsin versus Khasbulatov (and Rutskoi)—are about the type of rule Russia will have, the shape of a constitution and political institutions. It is not yet over, and on its outcome depends the shape of labor politics in the future. Given the speed and nature of the Soviet Union's collapse, the deals cut to facilitate new arrangements were not outcomes of government negotiations or pacting with independent groups and parties, but they were deals between governmental actors.[76] Politics, labor politics included, still thus has elements of bureaucratic politics of a pronounced sort, though without the authoritative central arbitration of the past. The FNPR opposes the government, but depends on government funds; the government reformers denounce FNPR populist demagogy, but go on paying the union to perform functions elsewhere in the sphere of government. The industrialists fight the government, to keep it *in* the economy on the industrial lobby's terms. The government seeks extrication through privatization, but is as yet far from its goal. All remain linked together, on the one hand lacking distinct, stable bases, on the other hand without internal cohesion: neither government, nor labor, nor employers speak with one voice.

It is extremely unlikely that this situation will last much longer in quite the manner of spring 1993. But it is also difficult to see any scenario of breakthrough, wherein a once again reorganized Yeltsin government pushes simultaneously on the labor and employer fronts to alter it drastically. The president is a politician, not an economist. Crisis seems to loom, whether created by a hard line forcing plant closings and unemployment, or by an economic collapse as a result of government inaction, which will bring similar results. The avoidance of such a crisis thus far is an uncertain guide even to the near future, as the government's room to maneuver lessens. Although government, labor, and employers may all understand that there is no going back to the old system, each in its own way finds important elements of the legacy of communism difficult to discard. The business of deconstruction is not yet completed, the building of new institutions still in progress. Both processes will shape politics for some time to come.

[76]On this point, see Timothy J. Colton, "Politics," in Colton and Legvold, *After the Soviet Union*, 21. On the difficulty of "fitting" the 1991 USSR into the scenarios of democratic transition—and for that matter, Russia today, once the linkage of politics and economics is taken into account—see also W. Connor, *The Accidental Proletariat: Workers, Politics and Crisis in Gorbachev's Russia* (Princeton: Princeton University Press, 1991), 320–21.

15

Unemployment in the former Soviet Union

WILLIAM MOSKOFF

Full employment was a promise honored for more than half a century by successive leaderships in the Soviet Union. But even before the union withered away at the end of 1991, unemployment had become a stark reality. Where but a few years ago the question was whether there was a sufficient labor supply in the country, today the preoccupation both within and without the country is about how much unemployment there is and what it might be in the future.

I argue here that unemployment is not nearly as high as would be expected, given the dismal performance of the economy, and that this is because of the tenacity of the old Soviet system. That is, part of the legacy of communism is a set of institutions and ways of thinking about the economic world that have shaped the unemployment issue. I also argue that in spite of potential constraints on the future acceleration of unemployment, the situation will get a great deal worse.

HOW MANY UNEMPLOYED?

Trying to secure dependable estimates of the number of unemployed has been futile. The basic reason for this is that for almost sixty years full employment was the ideologically established norm; there was no need to count what did not exist. But once unemployment began to become a reality, and it was readily apparent that there would be even more unemployment, a mechanism should have been established to count the unemployed for all the reasons that this is done in capitalist economies.

The author thanks Richard Dye and Jeffrey Sundberg for their suggestions on an earlier draft and especially Carol Gayle for her many helpful comments. The work leading to this chapter was supported from funds provided by the National Council for Soviet and East European Research, which, however, is not responsible for the contents or findings herein.

In fact, through 1988 and 1989 and into 1990, as unemployment increased, no official measure of the number of unemployed was available, a fact that hampered the country's ability to define the extent of the problem, its sources, and how much and what kind of assistance were necessary for those without jobs.

One of the problematics in this endeavor is that there is a difference between the standard definition of the unemployed—that is, those who are without work but seek work—and the old Soviet definition that labeled as unemployed all those not working who were able-bodied and not in school, even if they did not want to work. The underlying ideological principle in the Soviet Union was that every potentially productive member of society should be involved in what used to be called "social production." Using the Soviet definition of unemployment, it was not possible to distinguish between the truly unemployed (someone who was out of work and seeking paid employment) and someone who was not working and did not care to work, such as a woman choosing to stay at home to take care of young children: they were both among the "unemployed."

It was not until the fall of 1990 that the State Committee for Statistics (Goskomstat) reported an official unemployment figure of 2 million. Goskomstat used the International Labor Organization's definition of unemployment, namely, that a person must be without remunerative employment, must be looking for work, and must be willing to start working at once.[1] The official nature of this figure notwithstanding, the Soviet Union was still without a method of counting the unemployed. Where it mattered most, in the halls of government, they were really still in the dark as to how to count the unemployed.

TYPES OF UNEMPLOYMENT

There are three general categories of unemployment: cyclical unemployment, when there is an inadequate level of total demand for goods and services in the economy to support full employment; structural unemployment, which occurs when the vacancies that exist in the economy do not match the skills that are available; and frictional unemployment, due to regular turnover in the labor market, such as when people voluntarily decide to change jobs. In the Soviet case, cyclical unemploy-

[1] *Ekonomika i zhizn'*, no. 43 (1990).

ment has not been an issue since the five-year plans began. Frictional unemployment occurred for two reasons: first, because of the extraordinarily high labor turnover that was voluntarily engaged in by as many as 25 million persons a year and, second (although of much less importance), because there were short-term variations in the demand for labor in a number of industries, as in the case of seasonal employment, a commonplace in the Soviet Union throughout its history.[2]

Under perestroika we can discern two new phenomena related to unemployment. The first was the emergence of structural unemployment, that is, the growth of unemployment with the simultaneous presence of an allegedly large number of job vacancies. The myriad changes that took place in the functioning of the economy, intended and unintended alike, gave rise to structural unemployment, the first sizable amount of involuntary unemployment since central planning was introduced. But a second type of unemployment also emerged, which I call involuntary frictional unemployment. It resulted from the breakdown in central planning and the frequent interruptions in the flow of capital inputs into production.

Structural unemployment. There were a variety of sources of structural unemployment. One was the impact of self-financing of Soviet enterprises. The Law on the Enterprise went into effect on 1 January 1988 and, among other things, required Soviet enterprises to fund investment from their profits. This was a new responsibility for Soviet enterprises, which had previously relied on the state budget for funding. The new law had an impact on employment in unprofitable enterprises. During 1987–89, 1.6 million people lost their jobs because of the closing of failing enterprises.[3] For example, a fall in profitability led to a decline in the ability of Leningrad enterprises to buy more machine tools, which in turn led to the loss of eight thousand industrial jobs in the city.[4]

After Gorbachev announced the first substantial cuts in defense spending in his United Nations speech of December 1988, the Soviets began in 1989 to convert defense-related production facilities to the production of civilian goods. By mid-1991, civilian goods comprised about half of the output of the enterprises in the military-industrial

---

[2]*Pravda*, 6 April 1990, 2.
[3]*Rabochaia tribuna*, 30 April 1991, 2.
[4]TASS, 31 March 1988, from *Foreign Broadcast Information Service, Soviet Union* (hereafter *FBIS-SOV*) 88-063, 1 April 1988, 53.

sector.[5] The shift had an appreciable effect on employment. About three hundred thousand workers lost their jobs in defense plants in 1990, only 76 percent of whom found jobs in civilian production.[6] That is, about seventy-five thousand people lost their jobs in the process of implementing the shift away from defense spending.

The Russian Federation was disproportionately affected by the conversion process because 82 percent of the former Soviet military-industrial complex was located there.[7] About 8 million people were employed in Russia's defense sector—and when families are included, some 30 million persons were dependent on the Russian military-industrial sector.[8]

The very vocal and articulate environmental movement that emerged under the protection of glasnost also had an impact on unemployment. There was an unrelenting antinuclear drive in many places in the wake of the April 1986 Chernobyl disaster. Some functioning nuclear power plants were simply closed down, the construction of others was put on hold, and still others were converted to nonnuclear purposes. By the spring of 1991, four years of activity had resulted in the halting of construction and design work for sixty nuclear power plants with a capacity of about 100 million kilowatts.[9] Whatever the merits of the antinuclear cause, there is no doubt that the movement's efforts had an adverse effect on employment.

Nuclear power plants were not the only ones to close down. About twenty-six thousand major construction projects, representing 500 billion rubles in spending, were closed down during the Gorbachev era, with a resulting loss of a sizable but unknown number of construction jobs.[10] As part of the restructuring of investment policies, a large number of construction workers lost their jobs, for example, those building pipelines and power stations in Siberia.[11]

---

[5]*Pravda,* 25 July 1991, 2.

[6]TASS, 16 August 1991, 39, from *Report on the USSR,* 16 August 1991, 39. About 70,000 of the 380,000 persons who were to be taken out of military-related production were expected to become unemployed.

[7]Moscow World Service (Russian), 5 April 1991, in *FBIS-SOV-91-069,* 10 April 1991, 45.

[8]Moscow Television Service (Russian), 18 January 1992, from *FBIS-SOV-92-015,* 23 January 1992, 56.

[9]*Izvestiia,* 23 March 1991, 1.

[10]*Trud,* 25 September 1990, 2. Not all of these abandoned projects meant the loss of jobs, because so many of them had been lying fallow for a long time.

[11]*Izvestiia,* 16 October 1989, 2.

Involuntary frictional unemployment. A second major cause of unemployment was fostered by the breakdown in the discipline of central planning at the end of the 1980s. While the nation floundered in a state of limbo because of Gorbachev's ambivalent approach to economic reform, the republics and their constituent enterprises lost faith in the central planning system. The resulting shortfalls in supplies led to unemployment in a number of areas of the economy, including both light and heavy industry. At the end of 1990, the weaving and textile divisions in about forty clothing factories shut down because of a shortfall in inputs. In the Russian Light Industry Association, Roslegprom, alone, 77,000 workers were laid off. And almost 33,000 home workers, mostly mothers with young children, were also laid off, in all cases because suppliers had not sent supplies to the producing enterprises.[12] By early 1991, it was reported that due to the absence of raw material inputs, 340,000 out of 770,000 Russian republic textile workers were out of work and another 100,000 leather, shoe, and sewing industry workers had lost their jobs. Factory closings kept mounting and by spring, more than 400 light industry plants were reported shut down because of a lack of raw materials.[13]

Workers in heavy industry were also affected. In the city of Donetsk, eight hundred workers at a plant producing large-diameter piping were let go at the end of 1990 because their factory had been unable to acquire crucial inputs from either domestic or foreign sources during the last six months of the year.[14]

WHO ARE THE UNEMPLOYED?

We can get some sense of who has been affected by unemployment by looking at the 1991 figures for officially registered unemployed in the Russian republic. The social composition of the twenty-five thousand persons who signed up during the first month of registration may be broken down as follows: 43 percent blue-collar workers, 33 percent white-collar workers, 8 percent young people, and an unspecified number of women made up a "significant" portion of those registered.[15] However, the social composition was quite different in Moscow. Of the

[12]*Rabochaia tribuna,* 23 December 1990, 2.
[13]*Argumenty i fakty,* no. 14 (April 1991): 6.
[14]*Rabochaia tribuna,* 25 December 1990, 2.
[15]Moscow TASS International Service (Russian), from *FBIS-SOV-91-134,* 12 July 1991, 92.

first 37,600 unemployed who registered at the city's labor exchange, 90 percent were either office workers or specialists with a secondary or higher education. Perversely, 85 percent of the 96,000 job openings in the city were for blue-collar workers.[16]

The Soviet economic bureaucracy, a major target of those carrying the banner of economic reform, employed nearly 14 million persons by early 1988, in more than eight hundred all-union and republican ministries and departments. Early expectations were that the personnel in these ministries and departments would be reduced by about one-third, or about 5 million persons.[17] At least in the early stages of the shakeout process, however, the evidence is that those in the bureaucracy seemed to emerge relatively unscathed, even after the initial loss of a job.

On the other hand, certain groups have been more at risk than others of becoming casualties of unemployment. One of the groups to be hard hit is women. Although there are no systematic national data regarding the gender of the unemployed, the Moscow unemployment figures showed that of the sixty thousand who registered as unemployed in the first six months after the unemployment offices opened, 70 percent were women.[18] Data from the first two months showed that women were disproportionately the targets of job loss whether they were blue-collar or white-collar workers. Women constituted 80 percent of the white-collar workers laid off, explained perhaps by the fact that they predominate in low-level jobs. But this does not explain why 75 percent of the blue-collar workers laid off in the city were women.[19] It does not seem imprudent to suggest that sex discrimination is a cause of this pattern.

In addition, young people constitute a disproportionate share of the unemployed in the country. The employment situation of young people changed because of two broad reasons. First, the higher education system was taking a smaller percentage of secondary school graduates, and, second, the demand for secondary school graduates in the labor market was declining.[20] Unemployment is especially high among the young, especially young men, in Central Asia.

Central Asia suffers from great impoverishment and higher levels of unemployment than the rest of the country. It is worth exploring the

[16]*Argumenty i fakty*, no. 44 (1991): 3.
[17]TASS, 13 March 1988, from *FBIS-SOV-88-049*, 14 March 1988, 72.
[18]Moscow TASS (English), 24 January 1992, from *FBIS-SOV-92-018*, 50.
[19]Elizabeth Teague, "Tackling the Problem of Unemployment," *Report on the USSR*, 8 November 1991, 6.
[20]*Sovetskaia kul'tura*, 10 November 1990, 5.

dimensions of unemployment in this region for several reasons. It is a hotbed of tension. There is a great deal of uncertainty about whether the indigenous ethnic groups are willing to tolerate the presence of "outsiders" as unemployment increases. Furthermore, there are national implications to all regional economic problems, including unemployment. Although labor mobility in Central Asia has not been as high as in other parts of the country, massive unemployment could force a shift in behavior, and workers could spill into other areas of the country as they seek scarce jobs.

What follows is an examination of the unemployment situation in Uzbekistan, Tajikistan, and Kirghizia. In Uzbekistan, with a population just under 20 million, perhaps 9 million lived below the poverty line in 1990.[21] By one estimate, unemployment was between eight hundred thousand and 1 million in mid-1990.[22] A large number of these people, such as nonworking mothers of large families and seasonal agricultural workers, however, were probably not unemployed in the Western sense of the term. As elsewhere, the republican government really did not know the true number of unemployed.[23] The causes of unemployment are not difficult to identify. In the Fergana Valley the primary reason was the predominance of a single crop, cotton, in the republic's economy, accompanied by large families and high population density. The narrowness of Uzbekistan's economic base was compounded by the fact that only 8 percent of the cotton was processed within the republic—the spinning, weaving, and sewing of cotton goods took place overwhelmingly in other republics.[24] There is a second set of reasons for high unemployment in the region of Karakalpakia. Ecological disasters became a serious problem in this area because the waters from the Aral Sea that used to irrigate this land have dissipated and the waters from the Syr-Darya and the Amu-Darya rivers were wasted. The land is now semidesert.[25]

The unemployment situation in Tajikistan has been described as a crisis.[26] The Tajik population of 5.3 million is about 70 percent rural and only about one-fifth have been employed in industry. There are several problems that face the population. On the one hand, there is a

[21]*Trud*, 12 May 1990, 2.
[22]Ibid.
[23]Ibid.
[24]*Pravda*, 13 May 1988, 2.
[25]Ibid.
[26]*Trud*, 30 April 1991, 2.

mismatch between the skills demanded and the capacities of the labor force.[27] On the other hand, there have been job shortages for the educated so that the economy has not been able to absorb the graduates of higher education institutions, technical schools, and secondary schools.[28] As elsewhere, estimates of unemployment are not totally reliable. At the beginning of 1990, it was estimated that about 117,000 young persons were only partially employed, doing seasonal work. In the capital city of Dushanbe, about 70,000 were without work.[29] A little more than a year later unemployment estimates were quite a bit higher: It was thought that between 230,000 and 600,000 were unemployed, with the forecast of another 47,000 soon to become unemployed.[30] The effect of this dire situation in the republic was to create a class of severely underemployed people, most of whom are quite young. Toward the end of 1989, it was believed that more than 130,000 young persons, about 10 percent of the group, were neither employed nor in school.[31] The consequences have been socially calamitous—the one common characteristic of people involved in recent vandalism and rioting in the republic is that they were unemployed.[32]

The threat to civil order that resulted from high unemployment in Tajikistan was also present in Kirghizia, where there is a population of 4.5 million, more than 60 percent of whom are rural. In the capital city of Frunze, the main participants in spontaneous demonstrations held in early 1990 were young and unemployed. There were an estimated one hundred thousand unemployed in the republic at the time and large numbers of unemployed young people had come to the city from the countryside in search of jobs. They were living in what were described as horrible conditions—semibasements, barracks, and crowded dormitories. Then a rumor spread that thousands of refugees were coming from Azerbaijan to the city and that they would receive apartments.[33] The subsequent demonstrations not only displayed the xenophobic mentality of ethnic groups in the country, they also showed the volatile feelings over the issues of employment and housing.

There has been substantial agreement among observers that unem-

---

[27]Ibid.
[28]*Krasnaia zvezda*, 10 September 1989, 1–2.
[29]*Pravda*, 18 February 1990, 3.
[30]*Trud*, 30 April 1991, 2.
[31]*Izvestiia*, 26 September 1989, 2.
[32]*Trud*, 30 April 1991, 2.
[33]*Komsomol'skaia pravda*, 13 February 1990, 1.

ployment has contributed to the rise in crime in the country. When the crime rate rose by 37 percent in Turkmenia in the first four months of 1989, the authorities claimed that one explanation was the increase in unemployment. At the time there were two hundred thousand unemployed workers, including fifty thousand adult men who were not working because of a "lack of jobs in the republic."[34]

THE PROBLEM OF REFUGEES

There is a special variant of the unemployment problem that is caused by the interethnic tensions in a number of republics, especially in Central Asia and the Baltics. The targets of the indigenous group's anger were typically ethnic Russians, who subsequently left these areas in large numbers because of the discomfort and, sometimes, danger they felt living in a hostile environment. By the spring of 1990, there were about 600,000 refugees of all ethnic groups in the country: In Armenia there were 230,000, in Azerbaijan 210,000, and in the RSFSR more than 150,000.[35]

There were a variety of reasons why Russians were the victims of campaigns in non-Russian republics. Principally, they were handy scapegoats for the imperial policies pursued by the central government over decades of rule at a time when nationalism became a great force within many republics. We may use as an example Uzbekistan, where the nationalist Erk (Will) party adopted a nativist stance. "The Erk Democratic Party is the first party in Uzbekistan and in Central Asia that gives pride of place to the interest of the indigenous nationality."[36] After riots in Fergana in June 1989, about 177,000 Russians, many of whom were highly skilled specialists, left Uzbekistan "under duress." The migration continued in 1990,[37] as tensions mounted in the aftermath of conflicts in neighboring Tajikistan, where there were riots after rumors spread that Armenians fleeing Baku were going to receive preferential treatment in the allocation of scarce apartments.[38] The Tashkent newspaper was filled with the advertisements of Russians trying to exchange their apartment for one in *any* Russian city, so desperate were people to leave the republic.[39]

[34]*Izvestiia*, 12 May 1989, 8.
[35]*Trud*, 4 May 1990, 2.
[36]*Soiuz*, no. 40 (October 1990): 6, from *FBIS-SOV-90-203*, 19 October 1990, 103–4.
[37]*Report on the USSR*, 14 September 1990, 39.
[38]*Izvestiia*, 13 February 1990, 8.
[39]*Soiuz*, no. 40 (October 1990): 6. Although Russians strongly dominated the group leaving Uzbekistan, there were also Armenians, Jews, and Greeks; and although the

In Tajikistan itself, anti-Russian sentiments had a significant impact. In the first seven months of 1990, some twenty-three thousand Russians left the republic. These included not only workers in the construction industry and the Ministry of Light Industry, but personnel seen as absolutely vital to running the local economy.[40] In Estonia, Russians were regarded as the "least welcome"—they were literally regarded as a fifth column in the republic.[41]

A couple of republics put up barriers to entry of anyone, including refugees. Fearful of refugees coming into their republics, both Estonia and Moldavia instituted immigration quotas. Moldavia allowed immigration equal to 0.05 percent of the population in 1991, which meant a quota equal to about 2,000 people.[42] The Estonian Parliament imposed an immigration quota of 2,290 persons at the beginning of the same year.[43]

Unemployment was an obvious result of the refugee phenomenon. Regrettably, there does not seem to have been any follow-up on the problem, and consequently it is not known how many of the refugees experienced only short-term unemployment, how many were victims of long unemployment, or how many may never have found a job.

UNEMPLOYMENT LEGISLATION

There were two important pieces of legislation on the unemployment question during the Gorbachev era. The first came in January 1988 when unemployment was first emerging as an issue. The second was signed into law three years later, in January 1991, when there were many more unemployed and a recognition that the problem was growing. The 1988 legislation was a joint resolution originating with the old party and government hierarchy structure; the second was a law that came out of the Supreme Soviet, the Parliament.

The text of the joint resolution reflected the ambivalence of Gorbachev's political and economic leadership. On the one hand, there was the long-standing socialist commitment to everyone's right to have a job. On the other hand, there was recognition of the burden of an inefficient

---

RSFSR was the principal point of destination, there were those who went to Belorussia and Ukraine, and even some who left the country. *Izvestiia,* 12 September 1990, 2.

[40]*Izvestiia,* 5 August 1990, 2.

[41]*Pravda,* 11 September 1990, 2.

[42]*Report on the USSR,* 19 April 1991, 33.

[43]Moscow World Service (English), 5 January 1991, from *FBIS-SOV-91-004,* 7 January 1991, 50.

economy. Thus the resolution said: "All working people . . . should be confident that their right to work is truly guaranteed. At the same time, every worker, specialist, and office employee must work properly, at peak efficiency."[44] The issue of efficiency versus equity, which every market economy has struggled with in the twentieth century, had now become part of the Soviet agenda. Perestroika was walking a high tightrope above a net with many holes. The resolution considered the retraining, job placement, and the dismissal of workers. Regarding the first two issues, the resolution was merely a statement of desiderata without the commitment of additional resources to deal with unemployment. For the time being, the leadership had sidestepped some of the tough issues.

The failure to confront emerging joblessness was reflected in the resolution's statement that the first line of defense against unemployment was to find released workers jobs within the enterprise that had just fired them. The substantive heart of the resolution was its effort to protect worker rights. There was a dismissal procedure that required management to give workers two months' notice if they were going to lose their jobs. A person losing his or her job was also entitled to a severance allowance equal to one month's pay, instead of the two weeks that they had previously been allowed. In addition, if the person did not find a new job, the former employer was required to give the worker another two weeks' wages.[45] At the level of official policy making, there was simply no real understanding of what it meant to fight unemployment.

Three years of experience with unemployment proved a great teacher. The January 1991 legislation was a serious document that took great pains to define the problem and to establish a framework for ameliorating unemployment.[46] There was also a second important dimension that distinguished this legislation from the 1988 document. The changed political landscape had accorded the republics new status, and the new division of power and responsibility between the center and the republics was explicitly recognized in the new law.

There were two key changes in the right of citizens to work. The first was to be found in Article 5, the State Guarantees of the Right to Work. In the new order, the state guaranteed a free education and retraining, freedom to choose one's job, free assistance in finding a job, and protec-

[44]*Pravda*, 19 January 1988, 1–2.
[45]Ibid.
[46]The January 1991 employment legislation was published in *Sovetskaia Rossiia*, 25 January 1991, 1, and was translated in *Joint Publications Research Service, JPRS-UEA-91-009*, 26 February 1991, 49–61.

tion against job discrimination. There was the promise of a job for at least three years to specialists graduating from state schools. But no longer was there the guarantee of a job. Section IV detailed the benefits for someone who loses a job.

The second crucial change was that work was now defined as a voluntary act. No longer could able-bodied people who did not work automatically be placed in the pejorative category of "parasite" or "vagrant" (Article 4). Article 2 defined the unemployed as "able-bodied citizens of working age who for reasons that do not depend on themselves do not have work and earnings (income from work), who are registered with the state employment service as persons seeking work, who are able and ready to work, and to whom that service has not made offers of a suitable job." Suitable work meant jobs that matched people's education and considered their age, length of job experience, and the distance they would have to travel to work (Article 3).

UNEMPLOYMENT BENEFITS

For the first time since 1930, unemployment benefits became part of the government's responsibility after the new legislation went into effect. There were both philosophical and practical considerations. Not only were such benefits ideologically alien, but the state was now faced with another large social assistance program at the very time that its capacity to finance such programs was shrinking. Confusion reigned as well because the nation was faced with questions that never had to be asked before: How much money would the state need for the program? Who was to pick up the tab, the center or the republics? Who would be eligible for these benefits? How could eligibility be determined, and who would be the final arbitrator of who was unemployed?

The January 1991 employment legislation went into effect immediately, except for payment of unemployment benefits, which were to begin six months later on 1 July. The basic terms were that if people lost their jobs they were entitled to receive their average wages for a period of three months, provided that they registered with the employment service within days after they are laid off. If at the end of this three-month period they did not have "suitable work," they then became classified as unemployed and eligible for unemployment benefits. Although the actual length of time one could receive benefits was determined at the republic level, the minimum period was specified as twenty-six calendar weeks during a twelve-month period for people who lost their jobs and thirteen calendar weeks for people trying to find a job for the first time.

Funding for the new unemployment benefits has been a problem at both the central and the republican levels. First of all, the six-month delay in beginning the payment of unemployment benefits was caused by insufficient money.[47] Because of funding problems, only eleven of the republics agreed to start paying unemployment benefits on 1 July.[48]

The RSFSR had set aside one billion rubles for unemployment benefits, and Ukraine had allocated 200 million rubles, with the intention of increasing this amount to two billion before the end of 1991. But the Central Asian republics, beset by great poverty, had not allocated a single ruble for unemployment benefits.[49]

EMPLOYMENT SERVICES

The labor market under central planning had consisted of two main segments. One segment was a labor market that worked much like that of a market economy. In this market, workers were free to find their own jobs with the state, and enterprises were free to hire whomever they wished. The high level of voluntary turnover in the labor market is evidence of how much freedom there was in this part of the labor market. On the other hand, the labor market under the dominant central planning also had a strong component of administrative direction. Workers who graduated from higher education institutions were assigned their first jobs. Outside of their state jobs, with certain rare exceptions, individuals were not really free to sell their labor on the market as they chose, although many did so anyway on the black market as doctors, carpenters, tailors, and so on.

Employment bureaus (*byoro trudoustroistva*) had been established in 1967 to help alleviate the labor shortages that were being felt in the country at that time.[50] They were intended neither to cast a wide net nor to register the unemployed and they were opened only in selected Soviet cities. In the major oblasts of the country there were fifty-three career guidance centers (*proforientatsionny*). These were augmented by about 2,000 autonomous bureaus for helping people find jobs operating on the

[47]*Rabochaia tribuna*, 29 January 1991, 1.
[48]Moscow All-Union Radio Mayak Network, 6 May 1991, from *FBIS-SOV-91-091*, 10 May 1991, 22.
[49]Moscow INTERFAX (English), 27 June 1991, from *FBIS-SOV-91-126*, 1 July 1991, 28.
[50]Teague, "Tackling the Problem of Unemployment," 4.

basis of contracts with individual enterprises, and by another 903 job points (*profpunkty*) which were exclusively to help young workers find jobs.[51] There were several major criticisms levied against these organizations. The first was that the largest enterprises tended to monopolize them and dictate how many employees they wanted. Most of the jobs found through these organizations were also low-paying, menial jobs.[52] Moreover, as the numbers cited earlier suggest, they were located in too few places. In Ukraine, there were employment services in only half of the cities and districts of the republic. They tended to be located well away from city centers. Only 14 of the 750 bureaus were computerized.[53] There was, therefore, no system that covered everyone in all places.

The new involuntary unemployment created a new role for the state, in particular for job placement and the retraining of the structurally unemployed. When the Supreme Soviet passed the new legislation on unemployment in January 1991, it did so with the expectation that employment services would play a major part in the new conditions. Nikolai Gritsenko, chair of the parliamentary Commission on Labor, Prices, and Social Policy, said that they expected 23 million persons to enter the labor market in 1991, an estimated 12.7 million of whom would find jobs on their own, but almost 10 million of whom were expected to be helped by the unemployment service after retraining.[54] Even allowing for a certain amount of error in the estimate of how many positions state placement centers would and could find for job seekers, there is no mistaking the major role they were expected to play as the nature of the labor market changed.

A nationwide job placement system was supposed to have been set up by the end of 1988.[55] Such a system had not been completed by the time the Gorbachev era ended. It fell to individual republics to pick up the slack that developed when the national placement system failed to materialize. The Ukrainian Council of Ministers decided in January 1991 to set up such a service in order to help the unemployed when the republic was going through its transition to the market.[56] Few of the

[51]*Trud*, 29 March 1990, 2.
[52]Ibid.
[53]*Radianska Ukraina*, 6 November 1990, 1, 2.
[54]Moscow TASS (English), 15 January 1991, from *FBIS-SOV-91-011*, 16 January 1991, 35–36.
[55]*Izvestiia*, 21 January 1988, 3.
[56]Moscow TASS International Service (Russian), 4 January 1991, from *FBIS-SOV-91-005*, 8 January 1991, 52.

republics set up a well-functioning employment service, although along with Ukraine, the RSFSR, Belorussia, and Kirghizia claimed to have good success in placing people in new jobs. In the first ten days after the employment law went into effect, twenty-four thousand persons used the Russian state employment service, and 90 percent of them were said to have found new jobs.[57] The state employment system did not develop in much of the rest of the country, however, because the 1991 law shifted the financing away from the center to the republics. This was part of the general drive to decentralize control over major areas of the economy and give the republics more autonomy. But this move was counterproductive because the poorest republics (Central Asia and Azerbaijan) were the ones with the worst unemployment problems, and their financial base was also insufficient to support a state employment service. The inadequacy of resources for social services was demonstrated in these republics by the closing of even the small job placement services that had existed.[58]

THE MOSCOW LABOR EXCHANGE

The Moscow Labor Exchange, bearing the same name as the old exchange that existed until the end of 1930, was reborn in October 1990, although it did not begin formal operations until 1991. It was placed under the command of Igor Zaslavsky, who was named director general.[59] The exchange was organized around a central office, but the plan was to decentralize quickly so that each of the ten prefectures of Moscow (about one million residents in each) would have its own exchange. In turn, each of the 124 municipal districts would have its own social protection service, where people could file for unemployment benefits. This was in contrast to the thirty-district employment bureaus that existed under the old system, which were regarded as far too few in number to do much good.[60] The exchange was to be funded from three sources. The first source was to be a state employment assistance fund, as called for by the 1991 national employment legislation, and to which the city of Moscow would also contribute. The second source was money that the exchange would make by charging fees to enterprises for finding workers for them. Finally, they expected contributions from the

[57]*Sovetskaia Rossiia,* 7 August 1991, 1.
[58]*Izvestiia,* 6 February 1991, 3.
[59]*Moscow News,* no. 50 (1990): 10.
[60]*Sovetskaia Rossiia,* 7 August 1991, 1.

public.[61] The exchange also made the decision about who was eligible for unemployment benefits, and it was only through the exchange that a Muscovite could receive such benefits.[62] The exchange registered as unemployed and provided retraining only for people with Moscow residence permits (*propiski*), although there were some early assertions that nonresidents of the city would be allowed to take the most undesired jobs in the city, such as loading and unloading tasks.[63]

Quite early in 1991, all over Moscow, the exchange was holding job fairs, which Zaslavsky unabashedly described as "auctions" of workers. The fairs involved both state enterprises and the new cooperatives that were looking for workers. People looking for jobs would come to the fairs, and the enterprises and cooperatives would literally bid for the workers on a competitive basis.[64]

On 1 July 1991, the Moscow exchange opened its doors to the unemployed of the city under the terms of the new employment legislation. During the first twenty-five days of July, slightly more than 12,000 persons showed up at the exchange looking for jobs; only 1,649 of them were officially designated as unemployed and eligible for unemployment benefits.[65] For the first two months, more than 23,000 Muscovites came to look for jobs, their numbers evenly divided between those with a higher education and those who were unskilled.[66] The 23,000 unemployed were far fewer than the predicted 125,000 unemployed in Moscow by the end of 1991.[67] On 1 July, Zaslavsky expected some 35,000 officials in the state bureaucracy alone to make use of the exchange.[68] In fact, by the end of the year, of the 6,000 party people who had lost their jobs in the city, only 466 had looked to the exchange for employment.[69]

In the earliest days of the state's new approach to unemployment, the Moscow Labor Exchange became a prototype. Whether it would succeed would not be known until the issues of purpose, financing, and organization were fully resolved.

[61]*Pravda*, 1 February 1991, 2.

[62]*Izvestiia*, 5 July 1991, 3.

[63]Teague, "Tackling the Problem of Unemployment," 5; *Pravda*, 1 February 1991, 2.

[64]*Pravda*, 1 February 1991, 2.

[65]*Sovetskaia Rossiia*, 7 August 1991, 1.

[66]Moscow Radio Moscow World Service (English), from *FBIS-SOV-91-172*, 5 September 1991, 48.

[67]Moscow Television (Russian), 4 January 1992, from *FBIS-SOV-92-005*, 8 January 1992, 57.

[68]Moscow Television (Russian), 30 May 1991, from *FBIS-SOV-91-106*, 3 June 1991, 41.

[69]Moscow Television (Russian), 4 January 1992, from *FBIS-SOV-92-005*, 8 January 1992, 57.

OKUN'S LAW, JOB RIGHTS, AND HIDDEN UNEMPLOYMENT

Was the level of unemployment high at the end of the Gorbachev era? Should we be shocked by the official Goskomstat figure of two million jobless? It is arguable that given the collapse of the Soviet economy in 1991, unemployment should have been much higher than it actually was at the end of that year.

Let us apply Okun's Law to the Soviet economy. The late American economist Arthur Okun demonstrated with U.S. data that there is a quantitative relationship between the deviation of actual from potential gross national product (GNP) and changes in the unemployment rate. In the United States, Okun initially found that a 3 percent decline in GNP was associated with a 1 percent increase in unemployment. Later empirical work modified this measure, with the most recent version showing that a 2.5 percent decrease in GNP is associated with a 1 percent increase in unemployment.[70] If we accept this ratio, the numerical relationship has to be modified in order to apply it to the Soviet Union because labor productivity is so much lower there than in the United States. Labor productivity in the former Soviet Union was estimated to be about 40 percent that of the United States;[71] that is, labor productivity in the United States is about 2.5 times higher than it is in the former Soviet Union. If a decline in U.S. GNP of 2.5 percent is associated with a 1 percent rise in unemployment, then in the former Soviet Union, a 1 percent decline in actual from potential GNP should be associated with a rise in unemployment of about 1 percent.[72] In 1991, from January through September, Soviet GNP fell 12 percent. That means unemployment should have risen by approximately 12 percent as well. Given a labor force of 115 million in the state sector in 1990,[73]

---

[70]Paul A. Samuelson and William D. Nordhaus, *Economics*, 12th ed. (New York: McGraw-Hill, 1985), 187.

[71]John S. Pizer and Andrew P. Baukol, "Recent GNP and Productivity Trends," *Soviet Economy* 7 (January–March 1991): 71.

[72]This assumes, of course, that the ratio of the marginal productivity of labor of Soviet workers to the marginal productivity of U.S. workers is 0.4. The truth is that this is not measurable. The problem is complicated by the fact that there are huge numbers of workers in the former Soviet Union who are regarded as superfluous workers, perhaps as much as 20 percent of the labor force. These workers either have a zero productivity or a low productivity and therefore their unemployment does not alter GNP. But, at bottom, it is more reasonable to speak of the ratio of the average productivity of laid-off labor in the two countries as being the same as everyone else in the respective labor forces.

[73]*Rabochaia tribuna*, 14 December 1990, 1.

this means that, according to Okun's Law, Soviet unemployment should have risen by roughly 13.8 million in 1991, a far cry from the official figure of 2 million total unemployed at the end of the year.

How can we account for the fact that through the end of 1991 the Soviet system was so impervious to unemployment? The answer lies in two directions. The primary reason can be found in the job-rights argument David Granick proposed, namely, that employees in Soviet state enterprises have a right to keep their jobs.[74] There is anecdotal evidence that in spite of the well-known inefficiencies and unprofitability of Soviet enterprises, workers who were fired from their positions managed to find other jobs within their enterprises with relative ease. A 1988 poll of enterprise managers revealed that 82 percent of them "believe that workers should be reassigned within the enterprise."[75] Director Zaslavsky of the Moscow Labor Exchange said he could name "dozens of enterprises" that operated well below capacity but maintained their labor forces and still found the money to pay them.[76] In early 1988, when unemployment admittedly had not risen as much as it did later, it was found that more than 60 percent of the workers who lost their primary jobs stayed at the same enterprise.[77] For others, particularly managers and members of the economic and planning bureaucracy, there was also a soft landing. Many in these positions seem to have been able to emerge from the effort to streamline the operation of the economy with another job without serious difficulty. For example, when the USSR Ministry of Machine Building for Light and Food Industry and Household Appliances was completely eliminated in 1988, of the 500 people who lost their jobs in the first round of firings in November 1987, jobs were found for 460 of them.[78]

Second, in the wake of supply breakdowns, enterprises probably substituted labor for capital in the production process. Although there is no direct evidence for this, it is plausible given the fact that Soviet managers frequently did so in order to keep production flowing.

The fact that unemployment was actually considerably below what it "should" have been demonstrates the capacity of the economy to hide the unemployed. Some of it resulted from the efforts by enterprise man-

[74]David Granick, *Job Rights in the Soviet Union: Their Consequences* (Cambridge: Cambridge University Press, 1987).
[75]Moscow Television (Russian), 12 February 1988, in *FBIS-SOV-88-033*, 19 February 1988, 78–79.
[76]*Sovetskaia Rossiia*, 7 August 1991, 1.
[77]*Trud*, 28 January 1988, 1.
[78]*Pravda*, 2 March 1988, 1.

agers to insulate themselves from the vagaries of supply deliveries by maintaining a sufficiently large roster of workers to carry out the feverish production activity at the end of the month known as "storming." Part was related to the promise to provide jobs for everyone. One of the costs of maintaining full employment was the great inefficiency in the operation of Soviet enterprises, many of which were grossly overstaffed. There was a long tradition in the Soviet period of hidden unemployment (*skrytaia bezrabotitsa*). Estimates of superfluous employment were staggering: One estimate was that 8 million to 10 million persons fell into this category.[79] A Soviet sociologist suggested that 10 million to 16 million persons were working at "lucrative but unnecessary jobs" (*izbytochnye*), what one would call cushy bureaucratic jobs in the West.[80] Vice-Chair of the USSR Council of Ministers I. Postiakov said at the beginning of 1988 that there were 17,718,000 employees in the country's administrative apparatus. He thought that about half of the employees in the republic ministries and departments and 30 to 35 percent of those at the provincial level would have to be let go.[81] A year later, a high-level Gosplan official said that by any conservative estimate, "overemployment" in the economy was at least 10 million persons.[82]

The entire population is, of course, aware of hidden unemployment. What is feared now is that in the transition the right to a job will be jettisoned and that enterprises, instead of hiding unemployment, will start firing workers under the pressure of market forces. Several polls revealed the great fear that marked the country over the possibility of unemployment. In the summer of 1991 a nationwide survey of five thousand persons asked the question: Do you believe that you may lose your job in the transition to the market? Forty-six percent said yes, and only 40 percent said no.[83] Another survey conducted in Russia only, at about the same time, asked the question: Do you personally consider it probable that you may become unemployed during the next one or two years? Overall, 27 percent of the Russians thought they would be future victims of unemployment—28 percent in urban areas and 21 percent in rural areas.[84]

---

[79]*Ekonomika i zhizn'*, no. 15 (April 1990): 12.
[80]*Rabochaia tribuna*, 7 December 1990, 2.
[81]*Pravda*, 21 January 1988, 2.
[82]*Izvestiia*, 11 January 1989, 5.
[83]*Moscow News*, no. 31 (1991): 10.
[84]Moscow Television (Russian), 29 June 1991, from *FBIS-SOV-91-127*, 2 July 1991, 79.

UNEMPLOYMENT AND EMIGRATION

The danger of unemployment seems to be leading many people to consider emigration. Emigration in the late 1970s and through most of the 1980s was defined in terms of political or religious repression, as in the cases of the Soviet Jews and the ethnic Germans, although there is little doubt that economic considerations affected the decisions of many to leave. One of the by-products of perestroika was an acknowledged desire by many individuals to emigrate because of the visible crumbling of the economy. In a 1991 poll, 24 percent said they were prepared to leave the country because of their fears of even more disintegration of the Soviet economy.[85] Emigration became an escape from a deteriorating standard of living and the growing prospect of unemployment.

Short-term emigration—that is, going abroad temporarily to work—also presented itself as an alternative for solving the country's growing unemployment problems. The evidence from public opinion polls is that as many as 3 million Soviet citizens want to go abroad to work on a temporary basis.[86] When asked their "attitude toward someone who decides to emigrate to a capitalist country to work on a temporary basis," 33 percent of poll respondents said they approve and would themselves like to leave.[87] Most of the people who want to work abroad are young; only 3 percent of those who expressed a desire for foreign employment were over the age of forty.[88] The government also understood the payoff from temporary migration. Labor Minister Vladimir Shcherbakov was frank in stating that temporary employment abroad of Soviet workers could diminish the impact of the shift to a market economy.[89]

There was great concern in the West that economic refugees would flood the developed European countries. Sweden, Norway, and Finland decided not to allow Soviet citizens to work in their countries, and Germany set a quota of fifteen thousand persons who could work there in 1991.[90] The restrictions reflect the consensus position of a December

[85]INTERFAX, 23 May 1991, from *FBIS-SOV*-91-101, 24 May 1991, 36.
[86]Moscow World Service (Russian), 8 August 1990, from *FBIS-SOV*-90-154, 9 August 1990, 36; *Dialog*, no. 5 (March 1990).
[87]*Moscow News*, no. 34 (1990): 9.
[88]*Izvestiia*, 11 August 1990, 7.
[89]*Report on the USSR*, 22 June 1990, 35.
[90]*Izvestiia*, 13 October 1990, 2; Paris AFP (English), 13 June 1991, from *FBIS-SOV*-91-115, 14 June 1991, 31.

1990 seminar jointly hosted by the Institute for East-West Security Studies and the Refugee Policy Group. Fourteen countries, East and West, including the Soviet Union, met to discuss emigration possibilities, and it was clear that the thirteen other nations did not desire emigration from the Soviet Union.[91]

CONCLUSION: THE FUTURE PICTURE OF UNEMPLOYMENT

There are dire predictions within and without the former Soviet Union of high levels of unemployment to come. Some are predicting as many as 30 million unemployed, or about 25 percent of the labor force in the state sector. The International Labor Organization predicted in March 1992 that unemployment would rise to 15 million by the end of the year in the twelve former Soviet republics (excluding the Baltic countries).[92] As what I have discussed here suggests, I think there will be a substantial increase in unemployment in the next several years. However, I would like to suggest that there are pressures and constraints that have the potential for mitigating the numerical increase of the unemployed, that is, for preventing the bottom from falling out. Let me start with two general scenarios.

The first possibility is the "they won't let it happen" scenario. In this script, the past—when employment was assured—becomes prologue to the future under the market. The pressure from below not to allow many millions to be out of work will be enormous. And the more people who become unemployed, the more pressure will build. I do not believe that any politician in the former Soviet Union can convince his or her constituents that unemployment is only a temporary phenomenon, a mere adjustment while the ineptitude of the past is undone, and that, if they will only wait, it will (mostly) go away. That is what people were told for decades about the arrival of the messianic era under the old regime. They became cynical then, and I do not believe they will buy that idea now.

I believe that we will also see enormous pressure placed on the

---

[91]See Meeting Report, "Ramifications of the USSR Emigration Law," Institute for East-West Security Studies (New York, 1991). The fourteen countries attending the seminar were the Soviet Union, the Czech and Slovak Federal Republic, Finland, Hungary, and Poland (the latter four being border states), Australia, Austria, Canada, France, Germany, Sweden, Switzerland, the United Kingdom, and the United States.

[92]*New York Times*, 31 March 1992, A7.

political leadership by the new independent and often militant trade unions to put a floor under the fall in employment. In seeming anticipation of diffusing the bomb from below, the resolution On the Organization of Paid Public Service Jobs was adopted in July 1991. Expectations were that by mid-1992 it would be necessary to organize public service employment for 1.4 million persons. The jobs were to involve "improving public areas, providing municipal services, building and doing repair work on institutions in the social sphere, and improving care for the sick and elderly."[93] It is tempting for history's largest and longest-running Works Progress Administration project to turn to old-fashioned Keynesian pump-priming to achieve a short-term rescue of the unemployed.

Second is the "We won't let it happen" scenario. By "we" I mean the advanced industrialized nations. We are shipping emergency food supplies to the former Soviet Union not only for humanitarian reasons, but also because it is in our national interests that this area not become embroiled in a civil war. I believe the dangers of civil war are great if unemployment rises to substantial levels—and the unemployment rate will not even have to get close to mind-boggling levels such as 30 million unemployed before there is social disorder. After all, people may be able to grow carrots on a private plot, but they cannot grow jobs, and they cannot hoard a job the way they can hoard laundry detergent in the closet or potatoes in the bathtub. Thus the twenty-four billion dollar package proposed by the Western nations in March 1992 addressed this issue.

There are some other possible developments that could moderate unemployment:

1. Capital shortages in a poorer, leaner country will lead to a partial shift to more labor-intensive production processes.

2. I suspect there will be pressure on many workers to take early retirement and on pensioners who are currently working to resign their jobs. Of course, given the state of poverty in which pensioners live, this would doom as many as 8 million persons to an abysmal standard of living.

3. Governments could engage in a massive retraining program that provides the skills that are required in the economy. This would have to

[93]*Izvestiia*, 31 July 1991, 2.

be combined with a job placement structure that would be able to deal with easing the path of people to be absorbed into the labor market. Such a capability and the funding for such a program do not currently exist. Overall, of the 4.1 million persons who used job placement centers in 1990, 2.7 million (65.9 percent) of the applicants found jobs. More than a third could not be placed in jobs.[94] But of those who lost their jobs because of the liquidation or reorganization of the enterprise or organization, more than 60 percent could not find a job through a job placement center.[95]

4. If institutions were created to allow the private sector to flourish, it might absorb large numbers of unemployed. The cooperative movement, which absorbed several million people who chose this alternative to state employment, could be allowed to blossom. But so far the story is one of many obstacles being placed in its path. If unemployment really does have a tendency to gravitate to the levels predicted under the worst-case scenarios, however, it will take an astonishing increase in the private sector in a very short period of time to make a serious dent in unemployment. I am not optimistic that this will happen. Even a doubling of the private sector in, say, two years would only remove 5 million from the rolls of the unemployed.

After putting all scenarios and possible moderating factors on the table, it is still difficult to be optimistic. And the worst has yet to come. When and if the market economy finally comes to pass, the imposition of real discipline on enterprises will not save those who have managed to hide successfully somewhere in a failing enterprise. Okun's Law will take hold, and Granick's Law will erode.

The government will probably seek to limit foreign workers, now numbering one hundred thousand. Indeed, the government seems to have anticipated this possibility. In 1990, only four thousand Vietnamese workers were admitted to the country, in contrast to previous years when about twenty thousand came to work in the country.[96] But there is potential here for racist and xenophobic violence, which has already shown its ugly head in actions against the Vietnamese who live and work in the former Soviet Union. So far much of this behavior has had to do with Soviet citizens feeling aggrieved that the Vietnamese were buying scarce consumer goods. But it does not take a great deal of

[94]*Ekonomika i zhizn'*, no. 19 (May 1991): 12.
[95]Ibid.
[96]*Argumenty i fakty,* no. 12 (1990).

imagination to picture the hostility against foreigners that will exist when they begin to be seen as holding scarce jobs.

As competition for jobs grows more intense, there is the potential for serious civil strife as people fight over limited jobs. One can easily imagine the following scenario.[97] Individuals living in relatively high unemployment areas of the country will flow to the relatively low unemployment areas. Moreover, given the different budgetary capacities of the various republics, there are likely to be higher unemployment benefits in some places than in others. Rationally, the unemployed will move to where higher unemployment benefits are issued. And in the receiving areas there will be real anger over outsiders using precious resources as the pie shrinks.

In addition, without a real housing market and with the likely impoverishment of those seeking work, there is also the potential for the development of poverty-stricken ghettos in cities where the unemployed think they have their best chance of finding jobs. In the worst-case scenario there will be a breakdown of social order and even the return of authoritarian rule, and it could have an ugly nationalist tone, with minorities becoming scapegoats.

How can this situation be summed up? Unemployment has risen, but old habits and institutions have thus far kept unemployment at levels lower than might be predicted. There will be a great confrontation between the frightening consequence of market economics and the unwillingness of Soviet citizens to accept unemployment. This is inevitable. Part of the legacy of the old order was the guarantee of employment, and for all intents and purposes this was a reality in the lives of Soviet citizens.

The transition to an unknown future has already produced economic depression and inflation. From the population's perspective, can the frightening prospect of mass unemployment be far behind? Ordinary people will not blithely accept unemployment as an inevitable price to pay for getting to the vaunted market and its promise of plenty. They are much more likely to fight for all the protection they can get from unemployment and its accompanying loss of income. In the past, the right to a job existed in spite of the fact that the economy was so inefficient. Employment was part of the social contract; indeed, the security it provided was a crucial means by which the governed conceded

[97]*Pravda*, 23 December 1991, 1.

that the party could rule their lives in every imaginable way. Reasonable citizens are not going to shift suddenly from an understanding of what their "rights" were to a new mind-set in which they consent to unemployment. Hence we know where the battle will be joined. What we do not know is what the outcome will be.

16

Conclusion:
Reflections on the social legacy of communism

JOSEPH S. BERLINER

In the normal course of scholarship the social fabric is examined one strand at a time: politics, the family, ethnicity, and so on. This volume of essays, however, invites the reader to contemplate the fabric on a grand scale. The entire social legacy of Soviet-type communism is spread out for examination.

If the past is truly prologue, this broad review forebodes a rough road ahead for the peoples of the formerly communist lands. In one respect after another, the legacy takes the form of an obstacle to be overcome rather than an endowment on which to build.

It is not that the Soviets[1] have invented new social pathologies that were unknown in other civilizations. The social ills detailed in this volume are all too familiar: pollution, drug abuse, prostitution, pornography, organized crime, the sale of babies, and all manner of mayhem and perversion. The Soviets appear to have been no more innovative in the social sphere than in the economic sphere. In the seventy years of Soviet power they have not created one really imaginative new form of social pathology.

Except one. The Soviet official list includes a set of "system-specific" forms of deviance that are not found on the corresponding lists of other countries: speculation, parasitism, and such (Shelley, Chapter 6). This is surely important in understanding the social legacy of communism, but it should not count as a genuinely new social pathology, for those activities are found in all market-based societies. The Soviet innovation was merely to have criminalized them.

---

[1] I refer primarily to the former Soviet Union, but most of the comments are also of general application to the formerly communist European countries.

If the catalog of social ills is similar to those of other countries, why the sense of alarm generated by these essays? One possibility is that these ills may be of more serious proportions than elsewhere. The authors were not asked to provide comparative data, but some general impressions may be gleaned from their chapters. There appear to be three different levels of intensity, relative to other countries. The worst part of the legacy is the state of health and of the environment (Field, Chapter 8, and Eberstadt, Chapter 9). Nationalist and ethnic tensions are in the middle range; they are more intense than in the stabler countries of the world, but no more furious than in parts of Europe or other continents (Balzer, Chapter 3, and Todorova, Chapter 4). Most of the run-of-the-mill social ills, however, seem to be no more serious at present than in most other countries and perhaps less so, for example, crime rates, drug abuse, and the distribution of poverty (Shelley, Chapter 6; Kramer, Chapter 7; and Kligman, Chapter 11). All in all, the intensity of social problems may be somewhat more serious than elsewhere but not so much more as to warrant great alarm.

A second possibility is that the sense of alarm springs not from the intensity levels but from the rates of change of those levels. A society can get used to living with a high but stable crime rate, for example, but a crime rate that is rising, from whatever level, is a source of great anxiety. It may betoken some new and unknown force of evil that has been let loose, and one can never be sure whether it can be contained. If it cannot, the crime rate may keep rising to ever more threatening levels.

Again, one would need a fuller set of statistical data to assess that possibility. The general impression conveyed by these essays, however, is that Soviet society was relatively stable before 1985. Health and environment were deteriorating gradually, there was perhaps some gradual rise in rates of crime and deviance, and ethnic tensions were slowly intensifying. It may well have been that if Gorbachev had not come to power, the communist society could have survived for a long time, perhaps even indefinitely, although the social cement was gradually cracking. That, I think, should be regarded as the legacy of communism, if the notion of a "legacy" is to convey the social world of Soviet communism at the time of its demise.

I am sure that some of the authors would disagree with this assessment, but I believe it is a plausible interpretation of the evidence in the chapters. None would disagree, however, that there has been sharp deterioration in many spheres of social life since 1985. It is, therefore, important to be clear that most of the social malaise in the region today is not the legacy of *communism* but the legacy of that legacy. In evaluating the communist social regime, it is important not to tar it with the brush of the unhappy postcommunist years of transition.

The experience since 1985, however, should not be regarded as entirely irrelevant in the assessment of the legacy of the preceding system. If one were to assess the lifetime social costs of building a large new dam or a nuclear power plant, it would be wise to consider the costs of dismantling it at some future date and turning the land back to some other use. In the same way, in assessing a large prospective change in a social system, it would be prudent to consider the costs that would have to be borne if it is unsuccessful and has to be undone. When the experience of communism is evaluated by scholars in the distant future, they will no doubt include an assessment of the costs borne in the process of abandoning it for a different system.

Why have societal conditions deteriorated so dramatically since the end of communism? Part of the explanation may be quite general; crime rates, for example, generally rise during periods of political and social transition (Shelley, Chapter 6). A number of the authors, however, converge on a system-specific explanation that may be called the "societal-void theory." The idea is that communism suppressed or destroyed the traditional institutions of social authority and control, such as the family, the church, the ethnos, and the other constituents of a civil society. Those institutions were replaced, however, by a system of party-state social controls based on a social contract between the party and the people. The terms of that contract are familiar: The people surrendered their rights to individual freedom, but they received in return such benefits as job security, free medical care and education for their children, and a spare but adequate level of consumption. It made for a drab way of life, but the streets were free of crime.

In many areas of public life the system worked—in military attainment, in science, in the containment of ethnic hostility, even in education and health if one judged by the results of public opinion polls. But there were several areas in which it did not work, even in the eyes of leadership—notably, the cluster of activities involving economic growth and technological advance. In the end it was the eroding performance in these activities that motivated the fateful decisions to introduce perestroika and glasnost, culminating in the eventual collapse of the system of party-state controls. With the traditional institutions of civil society long gone and central party-state power largely eroded, the postcommunist countries faced an unprecedented void in the kinds of controls that make social life possible.

Two consequences followed from that void: One is the dramatic rise in crime, violence, and other forms of social deviance. The other is the clash among the objectives pursued by different groups. Freedom of the press has been used to promote ethnic tensions. Freedom of religion has led to "retraditionalization" and the backlash against the freedoms women had acquired under communism (Kligman, Chapter 11, and Powell, Chapter 12). The weakening of internal police controls fanned long-smoldering ethnic grievances (Balzer, Chapter 3). These manifestations differ in the various countries of the postcommunist world, but the pattern seems to be present in all.

I find this theory of the societal void a convincing explanation of the rapidity and extent of the postcommunist deterioration. There is only one feature I would add to the picture. The social contract served as an adequate substitute for a civil society in maintaining social controls, but it suffered from one defect, even from the perspective of the party's own interest. The suppression of organized opposition enabled the party to pursue its objectives unrestrained by the protests of interest groups, but that very fact led to certain outcomes that in the long run aggravated the conditions that precipitated the end of the system. The chapters herein provide abundant examples of that effect. The health system (Field, Chapter 8, and Eberstadt, Chapter 9), women's interests and procreation (Kligman, Chapter 11), the environment, the trade unions (Connor, Chapter 14) were all pressed into the service of economic development rather than the pursuit of the professional goals of those activities. Ethnic identity was suppressed in favor of party objectives (Todorova, Chapter 4). Had independent groups been permitted to give political expression to their views by forming organized interest groups in the manner of normal societies, the party might have been persuaded or compelled to modify its drive for economic growth at the expense of other social objectives.

In that case the social legacy of communism might have been more benign, with better conditions of environment, health, the family, and ethnic relations. Much of that social legacy, therefore, derives from the suppression of all political forces that might have served as a "feedback mechanism," compelling some recognition of the social costs of forced economic development well before they reached the point they did.

Could the sharp postcommunist unraveling have been avoided? Some observers contend that it could have, and that the fault lies with Mikhail Gorbachev. It was irresponsible for him to have led the way to so sudden a collapse of the party-state power first in Central and Eastern Europe, then in the Soviet Union. It would have been better to have sustained that power for a period of time long enough to promote and guide the changeover to a new economy and society. In this view the transition to a decentralized society should have been managed in a manner similar to that of China and the Pacific Rim countries, or like that of Augusto Pinochet's Chile to some degree.

I share the view that such a path would have made for a smoother transition, had it been feasible. There were many steps Gorbachev's government might have taken to help prepare the way for a market-based economy so that the shock would not have been as great when the planning mechanism was finally abandoned. For example, the government might have begun the process of closing down some of the enterprises that were most inefficient or most responsible for pollution, and of transferring and retraining the released labor. It could have raised the prices of heavily subsidized consumer goods, which would have put the black market out of business and taken much of the pressure off the state budget. Instead, for lack of such prior preparation, these processes are now occurring at the same time as markets are in the process of formation. As a result, the fragile market and the present weak government are taking the heat for the social costs that had been inflicted on the society by the former party-state power. If a reactionary backlash should occur, the fault will lie in part with the premature collapse of that power under Gorbachev's leadership.

There are two reasons, in my opinion, that Gorbachev did not take this path. One is that he never did feel as comfortable with the idea of markets and private property as the present Chinese leadership does, to say nothing of the Pacific Rim and Pinochet Chile. The second is that even if Gorbachev had been so disposed, political conditions were such that he would probably not have been able to pull it off. A Soviet government seeking radical economic reform was in a much weaker position than a corresponding government in communist China. On the one hand, the Russian masses were not as desperate and as insistent on reform as the Chinese peasants who spontaneously abandoned the communes after Chairman Mao's death. On the other hand, the Soviet nomenklatura had not suffered the harsh fate of their Chinese counterparts under Mao, and were therefore not as supportive of radical transformation of government and economy. I think it was this awareness of the weakness of the support for perestroika that caused Gorbachev to promote the policy of glasnost. The people, he felt, had to be told the harsh facts of Soviet life and history before they could understand and then support his program. In the telling, however, masses of Soviet citizens were provided with their first opportunity to express their long-suppressed sentiments—notably, on ethnic and environmental matters—which launched the chain of events culminating in the end of party and state.

I, therefore, share the view that the precipitous collapse of party-state power contributed to the unfortunate postcommunist legacy of the communist legacy. One could write a scenario under which that collapse might have been avoided, but I doubt that Gorbachev or any other Soviet leader could have played the lead in that drama. There is some support for this view in the experience of the Central and Eastern European countries, whose legacies have been similar to that of the post-Soviet, if not as extreme in all respects.

The social legacy of communism will, no doubt, leave its traces on the society of the future, whatever form it may take. It may be fitting to ask in conclusion what the chapters in this volume suggest about the forms that influence might take.

First, some of the elements of the old social contract will, no doubt, endure. Government policy is likely to be dominated by an effort to minimize unemployment (Moskoff, Chapter 15), much as Germany's policy has been dominated by an obsession with price stability that originated in the trauma of the hyperinflation following World War I. The continued wide acceptance of the legitimacy of state ownership (Dobson, Chapter 10) suggests that the role of the state will be larger in the future of Russia than in that of other countries, especially compared with those that have not had the communist legacy. The social safety net that constituted the party's side of the social contract is likely to prevail in the future to a greater extent than elsewhere.

Second, once public order is restored, the legal sanctions against deviance are likely to be harsher than elsewhere. The principal reason is the relative weakness of the tradition of civil liberties, but it will also reflect the absence for so many decades of interest groups that might have contributed to raising the public consciousness on such issues as the status of women, homosexuals, and ethnic minorities.

Third, the political system is likely to be based on an electoral process, but with a strong populist and majoritarian cast. The protection of individual rights against the majority will be weaker than in Western democracies, and political diversity will be constrained by public hostility. The populist element will also find reflection in more curbs on the development of capitalist institutions, on income inequality, on wealth accumulation, and on those commercial activities that are lumped together in the popular mind as "speculation."

One might hazard other guesses about the postcommunist societies of the future, but it is a game with which social scientists should not feel entirely comfortable. Judging from the forecasts of the Soviet future that were common before 1985, there is little one can be confident about in such an exercise, other than that these new societies will bear some unmistakable traces of the social legacy of their communist past.

About the authors

EDITORS

JAMES R. MILLAR is director of the Institute for European, Russian, and Eurasian Studies and professor of economics and international affairs at George Washington University. A leading expert on the economies and economic history of Russia and the Soviet Union, he is the author of *The Soviet Economic Experiment* and *The ABCs of Soviet Socialism*. He serves as chair of the Executive Committee of Delegates, American Council of Learned Societies, and is a member of the International Council of the Russian journal *Voprosy Ekonomiki*. Millar was a fellow of the Woodrow Wilson Center in 1988–89.

SHARON L. WOLCHIK is director of Russian and East European studies and professor of political science and international affairs at George Washington University. Her writings cover a variety of social and political issues, including elite policies toward women and gender issues, ethnicity in communist and postcommunist states, and various aspects of the political transition in Central and Eastern Europe. Her most recent book is *Czechoslovakia in Transition: Politics, Economics, and Society*. She is a member of the board of directors of the Council for International Exchanges of Scholars and of the program committee of the International Research and Exchanges Board.

CONTRIBUTORS

MARJORIE MANDELSTAM BALZER, editor of *Anthropology and Archeology of Eurasia,* is adjunct associate professor of sociology at Georgetown University.

JOSEPH S. BERLINER, a fellow of the Russian Research Center of Harvard University, is professor of economics emeritus at Brandeis University.

386

WALTER D. CONNOR is a professor in the Departments of Political Science, Sociology, and International Relations at Boston University.

RICHARD B. DOBSON is a social science analyst in the Office of Research of the United States Information Agency.

NICHOLAS EBERSTADT is a researcher with the American Enterprise Institute and the Harvard Center for Population and Development Studies.

MARK G. FIELD, a fellow of the Russian Research Center of Harvard University, is professor of sociology emeritus, Boston University.

PETER JUVILER is a professor in the Department of Political Science at Barnard College, Columbia University.

GAIL KLIGMAN is Ion Ratiu Visiting Associate Professor in the Department of Government at Georgetown University.

JOHN M. KRAMER is a professor in the Department of Political Science at Mary Washington College.

MERVYN MATTHEWS is a reader in the Department of Linguistic and International Studies at the University of Surrey, England.

WILLIAM MOSKOFF is a professor in the Department of Economics and Business at Lake Forest College.

DAVID E. POWELL is a fellow of the Russian Research Center of Harvard University and Shelby Collum Davis Professor of Russian Studies at Wheaton College.

ANDREA STEVENSON SANJIAN is a professor in the Department of Political Science at Bucknell University.

LOUISE SHELLEY is a professor in the Department of Justice, Law and Society at the American University.

MARIA N. TODOROVA is a professor in the Department of History at the University of Florida.

Index

389

Brence, Anita, 45
Brezhnev, Leonid, 173, 286
Bromlei, Iulian, 85
Buddhism, 70–71, 74–77, 79–80
Bulgar-al-jadid, 68
Bulgaria: democracy in, 15–16; drug
abuse and, 149, 151–52, 155–56, 167;
drug trade in, 173–74; ethnic conflict
in, 100–101; mortality levels in, 203,
206, 211, 223; nationalist communism
in, 100–102; Yugoslavian breakup and,
105–6
Bulgarian Socialist Party, 100
Burbulis, Gennadi, 344–45
bureaucracy: anti-Semitism and, 291; communist, 253; crime and, 124–25; economic reform and, 359; elitism and,
312; gender and, 253; health care and,
186–89, 192; post-Soviet, 124–25, 192,
312; Soviet, 186–89, 291, 359
Buryat-Mongol Autonomous Republic,
74–75
Buryatia, 51, 57, 74–79
Buryats, ethnic, 75–76, 78–79
Bushnell, John, 231
business interests, elite, 317–20

cancer, 211, 221–22
capitalism: drug abuse and, 163; state,
349–50
Caribbean, 200, 206, 223–24
Catholic church: abortion and, 268–69;
drug abuse and, 164, 170; Polish, 164,
170, 262, 268–69; pornography and,
262; Russian Orthodox church and,
300, 305; Soviet propaganda and, 298;
in Ukraine, 297–303
Ceausescu, Nikolae, 265–66, 268
censorship: of crime statistics, 131; of Soviet mortality levels, 198
census data, 60, 65; *see also* population
center-periphery relations: collapse of,
31–32; nationalism and, 58, 87–88; in
post-Soviet Russia, 51–52; Tyva and,
72, 74
Central Asia: ethnic conflict in, 46–49,
360–63; health care in, 189; Islamic religion and, 282, 284, 286–89; unemployment in, 359–63
Central Bank, 333, 335, 352
Central Europe: communist values and attitudes in, 7–8, 11–13; concept of democracy in, 14–15; drug abuse in,
149–77; ethnic relations in, 24–25;
health levels in, 196–225; illegal eco-

nomic activity in, 22–23; mortality levels in, 208–15; political alienation in,
20–21; social change in, 3–4; social
contract in, 7–8; women in, 253–70;
see also names of specific countries
Central Intelligence Agency (CIA), 174,
281; *Handbook of Economic Performance* by, 217–18
central planning: labor market and, 366–
68; labor politics and, 337; unemployment and, 358
centralization: crime and, 131, 138, 147–
48; police system and, 138; Soviet
health care and, 186–90
charitable organizations: CPSU officials in,
317; religious organizations and, 277–
78
Charter 77, 162
Chazov, E. I., 178–80, 188–89
Chechen-Ingush Autonomous Soviet Socialist Republic, 60–61
Chechen-Ingushetia, 51
Chechen republic, 60–64
Chechens, 127
Chechnia, 51, 57, 62–64, 287
Chernobyl disaster, 238, 357
Chernomyrdin, Viktor, 334–35, 351
child support, 260–61
childbearing, 253–55
children: adoption trade and, 256, 263–
64; crime and, 134–35; drug abuse
and, 156–57, 159, 171–72; health care
and, 191–92; socialism and, 254–56;
suicide and, 238; transition and, 258–
61, 263–69
China, 49, 383–84
Chisinau, 38–41
Chubais, Anatoly, 334, 350–52
churches: return of, 278–79; Russian Orthodox, 279–82; Soviet communism
and, 230, 280, 299, 301; Uniate, 299
Churmit-Dazy, 71
CIA, *see* Central Intelligence Agency
Cilinckis, Einars, 45
CIS, *see* Commonwealth of Independent
States
citizenship, 41, 43–46, 65
civic action groups, Russian attitudes and,
238–39
civic socialization, 229–30
Civic Union bloc, 347–48, 352
civil rights, post-Soviet, 123
civil society, 28, 33, 235
class differentiation, communist transition
and, 257–58
Colby, William, 174